SPELT HEALTHY!™

Quality Whole Food Cooking and Baking with Spelt

Grain Harvest with the goddess Ceres (in circle) rising from the field, 15th century French manuscript illustration.

SPELT HEALTHY!™

Quality Whole Food Cooking and Baking with Spelt

MARSHA COSENTINO, M.A.

First Edition

Autumn Rose Press
Payson, Arizona

SPELT HEALTHY!
QUALITY WHOLE FOOD COOKING AND BAKING WITH SPELT
by Marsha Cosentino

Published by Autumn Rose Press
Payson, Arizona, U.S.A.
www.spelthealthy.com

Autumn Rose™ and colophon are registered trademarks of Autumn Rose Corporation.

ISBN, print ed. 0-9774635-5-9
Printed in the United States of America

Page 116 Spelt Sproutcakes is from sproutpeople.com. © 1993–2005 by The Sprout People. Reprinted as amended by permission of The Sprout People. Page 118 Ebleskivers is from NordicWare. © 1994 by Northland Aluminum Products/NordicWare. Reprinted as amended to Spelt by permission of Northland Aluminum Products/NordicWare. Page 216 Dove's Farm Soda Bread is from dovesfarm.co.uk and provided as amended courtesy of Dove's Farm Foods, Ltd. Page 304 Pizza D'Adamo and pages 305–307 Topping and Filling Many Small Things: Garlic Shallot Mixture, Artichoke Hearts and Onions, California Pizza, Zucchini and Basil, Spinach and Ricotta; page 267 Sweet Potato Fritters are from *Cook Right for Your Type* by Dr. Peter J. D'Adamo with Catherine Whitney. © 1998 by Peter J. D'Adamo. Reprinted by permission of Dr. Peter J. D'Adamo. Page 356 Black Forest Cookies recipe courtesy Ocean Spray Cranberries Inc. Page 393 Auld Lang Syne (Remembrance) Bread is from *Body, Mind & Spirit: Native Cooking of the Americas* by Beverly Cox and Martin Jacobs © 2004. Reprinted as amended to Spelt by permission of *Native Peoples* magazine.

Publisher's Cataloging-in-Publication Data

Cosentino, Marsha.
    Spelt healthy! : quality whole food cooking and baking with spelt / Marsha Cosentino.
    p. cm.
    Includes bibliographical references and index.
    ISBN 0-9774635-5-9

1. Cookery (Spelt). 2. Spelt. 3. Cookery (Natural foods). 4. Natural foods. 5. Food crops -- Heirloom varieties. I. Title.

TX809.S64 C66 2006
641.6311--dc22   Library of Congress Control Number: 2005937667

Dedicated to the memory of

Dr. Alejandro Duran,
physician, healer, friend

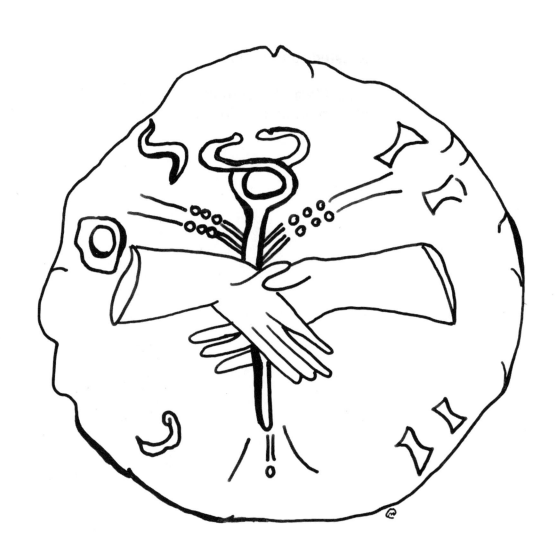

FOREWORD

I would recommend this book to anyone seeking to improve his or her health without the strictures of a diet. This groundbreaking book presents a nutritional lifestyle that I heartily recommend for all who want to eat healthfully and at the same time enjoy fine food.

The high protein, high fiber and complex carbohydrate structure of Spelt grain makes it a natural for Whole Food Cooking. Spelt is the best all around replacement for common wheat, the use of which is fraught with allergies, potential for weight gain and slowed metabolism. Spelt in concert with natural foods as presented in this book is a first-rate way to manage weight, high blood pressure, high LDL cholesterol, some types of arthritis and low energy levels that can contribute to depression and anxiety. It is extremely beneficial to those with Type II Diabetes in managing portion control and the quality of intake. As Ms. Cosentino rightly points out, all carbohydrates are not the same, especially when it comes to grains. *Spelt Healthy!* gives both the athlete and exercise-minded individual the nutritional elements for maximum efficiency in exertion.

Spelt Healthy! is not a diet or a magical cure for any of the conditions described above. The author is clear about that. *Spelt Healthy!* is a *lifestyle change* beginning with the *change of a grain* and the *consistent use of natural foods* in one's cooking.

Ms. Cosentino provides a good variety of palate-pleasing recipes. Just as importantly, she offers ingredient options within the recipes, most notably in the consistent alternative of vegetable oil to replace butter in many recipes.

Where Dr. D'Adamo's Blood Type Diet has not been widely embraced by the traditional medical community, one can see its usefulness is evident in encouraging people to consider the choices they make—choices in something as basic as pizza dough and selection of cheeses that Ms. Cosentino writes about. The recipes in the book tilt toward the Mediterranean eating style, which I applaud because of the use of olive oil, fresh vegetables, fruits and the traditional Spelt and other Farro whole grains.

Lively, enjoyable and loaded with useful information, I highly recommend *Spelt Healthy!* This book makes cooking with Spelt a pleasure. Ms. Cosentino has answered many questions about Spelt, cleared away a good many misconceptions and made Spelt accessible to all. With the publication of *Spelt Healthy!,* I predict we will see Spelt products in all the mainstream supermarkets and more people turning to the *Spelt Healthy!* lifestyle because Spelt really is "nutritious and delicious" and poses fewer health risks than common wheat flour. I have tasted many of the recipes in this book and look forward to more *Spelt Healthy!* food.

—Dr. Suzanne Bentz
Red Mountain Family Medicine

Dr. Suzanne Bentz, Red Mountain Family Medicine, Mesa, Arizona, is a Board Certified Family Physician and Diplomate of the American Board of Geriatric Medicine.

Visit us at www.spelthealthy.com

AUTHOR'S FOREWORD

Hello and welcome to *Spelt Healthy!* The idea is to turn your kitchen into an international food bazaar called Spelta's Place with all your favorite places to eat rolled into one. It is a place you, your family, friends and guests gather to enjoy good life and good health.

Spelt Healthy! is two books in one and both are firsts. Both have been years in the making.

It is the first time such a comprehensive review of Spelt has appeared in one place. The first part of the book is devoted to the qualities, nutrition, agri-science, archaeology and history of Spelt. This is a reference book designed to help you answer questions such as: What is Spelt? How does Spelt differ from the modern wheats? Why consider making Spelt the basic grain in your life? How does Spelt fit into quality whole food cooking? What is Farro? How do I cook and bake with Spelt?

This is also the first time so many Spelt and *only* Spelt recipes have appeared in one place and include the entire available range of Spelt products from Whole Grain and White Spelt flours to Spelt berries, sprouts, pasta and more. The book contains over 200 delectable whole food recipes that contain from a teaspoonful to eight cups of Spelt flour or contain other forms of Spelt.

The recipes are annotated for those following Blood Type Eating plans. You will find those notations on the recipe pages. Complete nutritional information (per serving) is provided in Appendix 1 for those people with Type 2 Diabetes and other conditions being managed through nutrition and exercise.

In designing the recipes, my intent was not to re-create the past, but to draw on recipes and ingredients from the past that have stood the tests of taste and time. It is noteworthy how many intertwine with the popular foods of today when you start using Spelt. It is a natural with Whole Food Cooking. At Spelta's Place there is a variety of delicious, nutritious quality foods with different tastes, textures and nutritional elements that will hopefully keep you interested in cooking with Spelt and by doing so give you the energy and health to accomplish all you want to do in life.

May the wealth of health be yours,

> Marsha Cosentino
> Payson, Arizona

ACKNOWLEDGMENTS

There is a kindly magic in the making of a cookery book; it comes from many sources because food and cooking touch us all. A stone thrown in still water, an idea, ripples wide from the source.

✳

The source was home. This book was years in the making. There is no person to whom more credit is due than my most excellent friend, partner and husband, Joey. He inspired *Spelt Healthy!* and has seen it through with me while wearing many hats: food mine canary, crash chef dummy, wrangler, tech man—so many hats, so many responsibilities, all cheerfully worn and borne.

Right next to him stands Pete Huie, *son* in deed; his vision is clear, his belief never wavers.

✳

Jacqueline Justman, treasured eloquent friend, took on the task of editing *Spelt Healthy!* Her knowledge, her grace, her abiding love of words helped make this book bloom. I thank you, Bob, for your encouragement over the years to write, write, write.

✳

Z, from a distance, gave us something from the heart when we needed it most. Thank you Vern, Gary and Greg.

✳

To my late father, Frank Cosentino, and my mother, Catherine, I offer thanks for giving me life, so many cookbooks and encouraging me to create in the kitchen.

✳

Cooking is community; it is a cultural legacy. *Spelt Healthy!* has been a community endeavor from the start.

Cali Cole, proprietor of Back to Basics Natural Foods Store, Payson, I cannot thank you enough for the many things you did and do for me. Cali shared her knowledge and her store. She is always there, always a friend. Back to Basics is the epitome of what a local natural foods store should be.

To all of you at Back to Basics who tasted yet another recipe for me, I thank you: Christine Bollier, Bobbi Vermuelen, Cheryl Waldron. Thank you also Gary Cole of Back to Basics Natural Foods in Globe, Arizona. Their critiques and commentaries were vital to making finer recipes.

Quality whole food cooking depends upon the freshness of the ingredients. In particular, I wish to thank our greengrocer, Armando Flores Jr. for his help and expertise. Nan Lawler, Natural Foods manager, thank you for your smile that beams across the store and for locating and stocking many fine things like the nuts.

✳

I owe the testers and tasters of *Spelt Healthy!* recipes across the country and in Canada a debt of gratitude. In particular, I wish to thank Ann Faulds and all the members of the Sun City Ceramic Club for your testing time, effort and expertise. Angela Goudey of Nova Scotia I thank you for taking up with Spelt and your information. Rich and Judy Reddinger and kids, Shyanne and Lewis, you make writing cookbooks fun. Enthusiasm is always a spur to creation. Thank you, Jerry and Ellaina Semifero for being among the first to volunteer.

A hearty thank you to Heather Slater, Chet Kitchell, Tom Cunningham, Michelle Broski, Donny Brenner, James Turco, Jason Knoell, Chet Rugel, Doreen and Jim Mandel and Amanda Korth. All of you made a difference. Rebecca Christenson, I thank you for your unflagging enthusiasm and making recipes, like Spelta's Cinnamon Rolls, better. Thanks to your kids, too.

Special thanks and recognition to Don Ray, Certified Physical Trainer and Nutrition Counselor, for all the tasting—from A to Z—and for shepherding the four-inch pile of *Spelt Healthy!* evaluation forms from the many people at the Athletic Club. Your straightforward comments and suggestions were invaluable in the making of this book.

✻

Nowhere in the community was a whole foods cooking book more readily encouraged than by the doctors and staff at the offices of Red Mountain Medicine. I would especially like to thank Drs. Suzanne Bentz and Diana Easton for their assistance and encouragement and allowing themselves to be test subjects. Manager Barbara Maksymowski did yeoman's work in organizing and seeing those many invaluable evaluation forms got back to me. Thank you from the bottom of my heart, Barb, for all your help! Thank you Linda Bonnewell for your fine critiques and Susan Edwardson for the good cheer.

✻

I communicated with many people in the Spelt production, milling and natural foods business during the writing of this book and I thank all of you for your help and invaluable information. In particular:

Some people know Spelt from below the ground up, from the inside out, perhaps no one more than Dr. G. F. Stallknecht, one of the world's experts on Spelt and the other ancient grains. He answered many a question and directed me to places where I could learn more. I am especially grateful to him for his patience and for asking questions that in return made *Spelt Healthy!* a better book. Dr. Stallknecht, known kindly in the business as "Dr. Spelt," is one of those people I refer to in the book who has actively worked to preserve Spelt and the ancient grains and continues to do so through the Spelt Institute.

Mr. Joe Lindley of Lindley Mills, a most gracious gentleman, took the time with a stranger to paint a picture of Spelt agriculture and milling that remains in my mind still.

LEGAL NOTICES AND DISCLAIMER

AN IMPORTANT NOTE: This book is not a substitute for the professional medical advice of medical doctors or other health care professionals. Always seek the advice of your doctor in reference to medical conditions and when considering changes in diet and exercise.

The publisher and author are not responsible for any products and/or services offered or referred to in this book and expressly disclaim all liability in connection with the fulfillment of orders for any such goods and/or services and for any damage, loss, or expense to person or property arising out of or relating to them.

The author and publisher disclaim any warranties (express or implied), including but not limited to accuracy, completeness or fitness for any particular purpose. The information contained in *Spelt Healthy!* is produced for educational and entertainment purposes. The author, Autumn Rose Press and Autumn Rose Corporation shall in no event be held liable to any party for any direct, indirect, punitive, special, incidental or other consequential damages arising directly or indirectly for any use of this material, which is provided, as is, and without warranties.

Autumn Rose and Colophon and *Spelt Healthy!*™ are trademarks of the Autumn Rose Corporation.

Spelt Healthy!
Quality Whole Food Cooking and Baking with Spelt

Contents

WELCOME TO

MORNING MENU/BRUNCH

Here you will find everything from Spelt breakfast cereals to egg dishes from Quiche and Frittata to Chiles Rellenos. Morning favorites from crepes, pancakes, waffles, bagels and English muffins to mouth-watering Danish, beignes, biscuits and cinnamon rolls.

SANDWICH SUGGESTIONS

Patty melts, burgers, subs, deli sandwiches, tea sandwiches. It's amazing what Spelt can offer.

THE BAKERY

The most extensive selection of Spelt breads in print. Beginning Loaf and Speltessence Bread, Challah, Feast Rolls and Fun Forms, French Bread/Rolls, Breadsticks, Dark and Light Rye, Brioche and Pao Doce. Rustic free-form breads such as Brundisi Pesto and Campocosenza Rustic Wheel, Roasted Garlic and Mozzarella Baguettes, Medi Crostini and many more.

THE MIGHTY MEATBALL

Classic to New Swedish Meatballs, Albondigas Soups.

HOMEMADE HERITAGE SOUPS OF THE DAY (OR NIGHT)

Ancient soups for modern times.

SAUCES

The classics are here…Aioli (garlic mayo), Aglio e Olio (garlic and oil) for dipping, spreading and pasta and more.

THE BREAD BASKET

Quick/batter breads from Soda Bread and Blueberry Coffeecake to Cherried Plum Bread, Carrot Nut to Chocolate Variety Bread and more.

BREAD MACHINE

Moist, delicious Speltessence, Rosemary Cheese and the terrific Seattle Supreme Sandwich Loaf.

ON THE RUN AND WORKING OUT

Try an ancient traveler's food or the new Evil Don's Energy Bar for a boost.

THE VEGETABLE STAND

Salads like Caesar, Panzanella, Rotini with Tumeric, Singla to Waldorf, Phytos, Sprouts, Grünkern, luscious veggie dishes from Asparagus to Stuffed Mushrooms to Zucchini Fries

AFTERNOON TEA OR COFFEE BREAK

Wait until you try the Lemon Shorties, Cherry Almond Biscotti or the four tempting types of Spelt Scones!

Spelta's Place

MANY SMALL THINGS— THE APPETIZING WORLD OF SPELT©

Foods for any time of the day or night. These are the foods you may often eat out or take-out and bring home.

Small Beginnings includes Cheese Spuffs, Yogurt Cheese Spread and Broiled Cheese (the original Mozzarella stick). Find Roasted Garlic and Spinach Pesto here.

Pastas—try Gnocci or the New Spelt Pastas.

A World of Spelt Flatbreads— Pizzas, Focaccia, Calzones.

Here you will find a delicious, nutritious array of toppings for your Spelt Medi Crostini or Roman Bread Bruschetta along with fillings for your favorite Many Small Things like subs.

Flour Tortillas and foods to make with them: Baked Meat Turnovers (Empanadas), Sonoran Style Enchiladas, Pita Bread with Pita Wedges, Gyros and Falafal with Tsatski Sauce and Hummus.

Tod Mun Pia (Thai-style Fish Cakes) and Chinese Steamed Barbecue Buns (Char Shiu Bao) made with Cherried Beef, Eggs Foo Young with Spelt Sprouts and more in Many Small Things.

MAIN DISH (ENTREES)

Among the choices: Macao Pepper Steak, Stuffed Gourmet Pasilla Peppers, Lamb Tangine and Oven Baked Fish Filets with Crunchy Lemon Herb Topping.

PASTRIES, PIES AND OTHER SWEET DELIGHTS

Here you will find the helpful Pastry and Pie Crust Chart along with sumptuous pies like Pinyon or Pineapple Cheese, pastries such as Cannoli and Crostate di Fichi (Fig Tarts) and the bright, light Raspberry Valentine Cake.

THE COOKIE TRAY

An unusually delicious selection from Chocolate Chip Florentines, Lemon Blossoms, Flash Brownies, Ginger Medley and Ice Cream Sandwiches to the Good Day Basic—a cookie designed by you.

SWEET TOPPINGS

From Crumble (Streusel) to Honey Butter Nut to Batangas Bananas and fruit purees and sauces.

ANCIENT OFFERINGS

Delicious remembrance of the past.

AND AN AFTERWORD... A TOAST TO TODAY

PART 1:
INTRODUCTION
TO SPELT

Chapter 1: The Qualities of Spelt

 Spelt has strength of character. She is stalwart when treated with gentle strength; she is sensual and sure. Spelt flits about in history's shadows and comes into the light at human turning points and crossroads from Black Sea shores to Neolithic Northern Europe to Ancient Greece and all the way to modern America in the twenty-first century A.D.

Her mother was the grain of Sumer and of Egypt; her wild, nomadic steppe father grass is still not clearly known. Spelt is one of the three most ancient grains upon which humans survived. She is Demeter, she is Ceres; she is Spelta; she is many things. Long ago Spelta bore seeds that may have contributed to some of the modern wheats, yet Spelt remains the same. An ancient grain, the heritage form, is full of nutrients Spelt lifts from soil under the harshest of conditions—yet inside she remains much unchanged in a world where genetically modified wheats are given traits that change from year to year. Their faces blur they change so fast; Spelta remains much the same. Hers is a trustworthy, recognizable face, a fine food friend.

Spelta will appear to you in many forms: sprout, berry, farro, bulgar, cracked grain, creamed for cereal. You will often see her robed as whole grain flour of excellent taste and range due to the millers' art; she dresses elegantly as cream-colored light or white Spelt flour that is the pastry and sauce-making boon. Ah, there she is, gracefully changed into sprouted Spelt flour. She comes to you as pancake mix and many pastas, garlic bread and grünkern and even more. What you can make of her—well, it would take a lifetime to explore her complex being. She tantalizes. It is likely once you try her you will keep coming back for more.

I recommend my friend, *Spelta L.,* to you. Her impressive resume ("Why Choose Spelt?") is further on but let me say these things to you so you know something of the story. Please come in, gather 'round the fire for a few minutes before you go to meet her.

The Siren's Call

Spelt was born and left progeny in the rough Transcaucasus, that Eurasian land bridge between the Black and Caspian Seas. Like the mist, one ancient eon, she went on her way, settling in places like the Carpathians, that hoary place where legends of Dracula and vampires were born and some of the modern wheats as well. From that place, there is the medieval legend of the Rusalka, a siren who perches languorously on the river mill wheel, turning round and round, droplets of water gleam like jewels in her long hair. She calls to the preoccupied passerby, "Come hither, come to me, I can be all things to you." Is it not curious that the new siren of the wheel that grinds the modern wheat berries into flour should sing so prettily?

In some ways, we are not far from our ancient ancestors, hunters and gatherers new to grain, who went about searching for foods that would sustain life in a wilderness of things that could make them sick or kill them. What could they digest? That question looms large again.

Making Choices

It is difficult to resist the siren's call of quick or attractive food and the lure of packaging promises. Whether going through a menu while eating out or walking down the aisle in a food market, you become wedded to your choices. Either activity—restaurant or market—can be risky because there are so many alluring foods that claim to be what they are not. Look up, observe. The shelves are packed; the menus stacked. We are caught in an avalanche of choices.

"Ah, it is so good!" We eat the food quickly; it is gone. Then the lethargy comes, or the crankiness. Torpor invades the body; it fogs the mind. It becomes hard to see clearly. We sing the blues. It is hard to move through the cloying, sticky mud; we become submerged in swampy waters. Because the siren did not kill outright, she slips away, without reproach. We blame self or others for the storms that rage inside. It is hard to get clear of the fight, to get to the high ground long enough to see, to think, to breathe freely, to consider all that we eat and the fact that common wheat flour cuts through most everything. It is the binder, the envelope that contains some very disturbing news.

Why Spelt Healthy?

My wheat intolerant husband described the above symptoms. I enjoy quality food and have a passion for cooking and baking. How were we to reconcile the two so that we could enjoy food that is both healthful and delicious when wheat flour is in so many recipes eating out or eating in?

One day we sat down and examined just *what* we were eating. Flour cut across all things. We read available scientific literature; soon we searched out more. A friend suggested Dr. Peter J. D'Adamo's *Eat Right for Your Type* because Dr. D'Adamo suggests Spelt over wheat. Some of the information in that book was strikingly interesting especially from a cultural point of view. My graduate academic training is in Archaeology, a field subsumed under Anthropology, which studies humankind, especially its origins and changes throughout time. I view food as a cultural heritage that reflects past environments.

Blood Types, Food Intolerances and the New Gastronomic Ideal

If you receive the wrong blood in a transfusion, you can die. On that basis alone, blood typing related to eating merits a closer look. There is wisdom in the genes.

A plausible reason for there to be major and minor blood types is through time humans came to depend upon different foods for sustenance as they spread to different environments. Perhaps this helps explain why the most ancient of foods such as Spelt, olive oil, dates and chard generally cause the fewest modern food reactions. Our ancestors' bodies adapted to these foods a very long time ago during the first great diet revolution, the change from hunting and gathering to domesticated livestock, dairy products and grains. From one blood type perhaps came the many that exist today, each responding to foods in different ways based on blood type, genetic heritage, and cultural preferences honed by time and circumstance. It is not as simplistic as many of Dr. D'Adamo's critics would have us believe.

Examine the literature. Take a close, hard look at what is going on around you.

Many people, maybe you, are growing increasingly intolerant of modern foods. These new foods constitute the second great diet revolution, the one we are going through today, that being the extreme processing of foodstuffs, food additives, and genetic modification of basic foodstuffs such as wheat and corn to feed an ever-growing world population and satisfy consumer demand for perfect looking food.

My husband is an example of food adaptation. Spelt harms him not at all, in fact, Spelt gives him zip and energy. He digests it very well. He is my food mine canary when it comes to wheat—if it is in a product, he will start to wheeze and have a variety of reactions, none of which could be termed healthy. I do not know if Dr. D'Adamo's research is right or wrong— or for that matter any of the many other researchers' work I have read is either. What I *am* is healthier and immensely grateful to Dr. D'Adamo and others who are bringing such things to light for us to consider and determine for ourselves. What I do know is that in the case of "us" the change to Spelt and then other whole foods worked remarkably well and quickly. We changed to Spelt. Within two weeks things changed; our bodies were happily responding. Two months went by, and we changed for the much better. We then eliminated corn. Thus, in 1999, began the recipes for *Spelt Healthy!*

There Is No Corn in Spelt

I practiced Field Archaeology. I have seen for myself that diet makes a difference.

In the Southwest and Mesoamerica, there was no native wheat. The Spaniards brought it. Prior to 1500, New World people changed culturally and physically when they shifted to a diet based on New World corn. When hunting diminished, they were hard pressed for protein—they combined corn with squash and beans and spiced it with Vitamin C loaded chili. Corn was their staple. After 800 A.D. in the Southwest, when corn became king, the skeletons become different. Osteoporosis, weakness of the skeletal structure—it is there. Diet is in the bones. If it was in their bones, what might be happening today as a result of eating so much of it?

As I saw the change in my husband just by eating Spelt instead of wheat, I saw the change in both of us when we eliminated corn as a basic ingredient in cooking and snacking. When we started to examine it more closely we found corn is now in almost every processed food we buy in the form of corn solids, cornstarch, corn syrup and high fructose corn syrup. Consider also that GMO-corn is a major ingredient in livestock feed given to everything from chickens to cattle and critters in between. What happened to moderation? Like modern wheats, corn has been extensively modified.

Diets Don't Work and the Food Pyramid Isn't

No matter what system you follow or if you follow none at all, you are the arbiter of what is good for you. Start small. Make a change in one basic but major component of your diet, a thing like substituting Spelt for wheat, and see what happens. Give it time to work. Run your own experiment. Do not take my word for it. Do not take anybody else's word or research for it. Try it for yourself.

I am not a gastronomic purist nor do I believe in diets. A line hewed too tight will snap; looseness allows more life. I have plenty of bad habits. Each of us is different. Only you know how *you* feel and what makes you feel good over the long run: no doctor, no guru, just you. I advocate no particular diet; I have no dog in the food fight. What I have learned is health is not a pyramid. It is a table: consistency in exercise, drinking pure plain water, sleeping soundly, and fueling the metabolism with the best foods possible, these are four legs of the table upon which all else in life rests.

The Blaze of Being Alive

Shake the table once in awhile. Why else would there be Pistachio Sticky Buns or Beignes in a Whole Food cookbook? People enjoy them. Food ought not be boring if it can be made otherwise. The flavors of Spelt are as remarkable as its healthful properties. Fine food, flavor and pleasure in the partaking are all parts of basking in the blaze of being alive.

Chapter 2: Why Choose Spelt?

Non est vivere, sed valere vita est.
Life is not just living, it is living in health.
~ MARTIAL, 1ST CENTURY A.D.

Staying alive and staying healthy are different things.

Modern free-threshing hull-less wheat of the type that comprises the majority of our grain foods has been designed by scientists for high yield so that as many people everywhere can eat to live. High yields became critical as a direct result of urbanization and greatly increased population. Inexpensive plentiful wheat was, and is, considered a necessity to feed a large part of the world's population.

The modern wheats are designed to be as free of pests, insect and microbial, as possible to sustain that higher yield. They are designed to fit the specific requirements of a multitude of baking needs especially for packaged and processed foods such as pizza dough. The flour is de-natured. It undergoes multiple steps in processing and then the minimal nutritional requirements are added back in because the government requires them to be there. Enriched flour contains less than one fifth of the original vitamins and minerals the grain possessed prior to processing. The phytochemicals are gone.

The hulled *Triticums*—einkorn, emmer, Spelt—survived the first transition to the unhulled wheats (free-threshing wheats), a transition that began about 4000 years ago. They survived in different parts of the world, including the United States, until the first decade of the 20th century. They became obsolete and were left, cast aside, to languish in the backcountry and by-ways because of population pressure, the new machinery and scientific methods of crop production including engineering wheat for the specific purposes above. The result in the long run was in the hulled grains' and our favor. These grains were not genetically modified so there is valuable genetic variation among them. Their hull remains intact until milling and so does the nutrient composition. Spelt, emmer and einkorn are as close to nature as domesticated plants can be.

✳ Spelt is a food that is full of life, food with character, flavor and freshness.

❋ Spelt is a *quality, complex carbohydrate.* Complex carbohydrates take longer to break down in the digestive system as well as providing nutrients such as vitamins and minerals. The glucose (sugar) releases slowly into the system obviating sharp spikes in blood sugar that come with simple carbohydrates.

❋ Spelt cultivars in the U.S. are higher than common wheat flours in *water-soluble vitamins* especially the *B complex* such as B1/thiamine, riboflavin/B2, niacin/ B3 and iron. Iron is critical to the transportation of oxygen throughout the body via hemoglobin. Spelt is much *higher in fat-soluble Vitamin A* (beta-carotene) critical to vision and resistance to infection as well as being an antioxidant. The B vitamins as a group are critical in maintaining a healthy immune system, lubricating nerve sheaths, proper metabolism and optimal brain functioning.

❋ *Spelt has greater mineral uptake and comes naturally higher than common wheat in vital trace elements* (minerals) such as Lithium, Selenium and Zinc, which is necessary for growth and sexual maturation, immune system activity and DNA translation. It is higher in the minerals Potassium, Sulfur and Magnesium.

❋ *Spelt has high fiber content both insoluble and soluble.* It is higher than wheat in soluble water fiber.

This characteristic makes gluten more digestible. Water soluble fiber slows down the rate at which glucose (sugar) is absorbed. The insoluble fiber allows foods to move more rapidly through the intestinal tract. Spelt makes you feel fuller thus reducing consumption. It attaches to cholesterol and other potentially harmful products for more rapid elimination from the body. Fiber lowers the risk of coronary heart disease and Type 2 diabetes. High fiber foods require you take more liquid into your system which is a further benefit for overall metabolism and general health.

❋ U.S. Spelt cultivars contain *more proteins* than does common wheat.

❋ *Spelt contains all the essential amino acids necessary to make proteins and contains all the non-essential amino acids* as well (Alanine, Arginine, Aspartic Acid, Cystine, Glutamic Acid, Glycine, Histidine, Isoleucine, Leucine, Lysine, Methionine, Phenylalanine, Proline, Serine, Threonine, Tryptophan, Tyrosine and Valine). Spelt is higher than wheat in all but Lysine. (Note: The higher the protein, the lower the Lysine.) It is much higher than wheat in Phenylalaine and Leucine. Among the non-essential amino acids it contains is Cystine. Here is a short list of what these powerful amino acids in Spelt do for you:

Phenylalanine sparks production of the neurotransmitters dopamine and norepinephrine. It is a natural antidepressant and increases energy. It assists in improving memory. It is one of the chemicals that naturally manages chronic pain.

Leucine, Isoleucine, Valine are real chemical powerhouses. A third of our muscle tissue is composed of these chemicals, which is why people who engage in high levels of physical activity often take them as supplements to build muscle mass. It is the same reason farmers used to feed Spelt to draft horses and trainers now feed it to pedigreed competitive livestock. That is not all. Leucine and Isoleucine increase energy levels and alertness. Valine increases brain functioning and at the same time is a calmative.

Threonine (precursor of Isoleucine) is necessary for proper growth of the thymus for thymus activity and for liver function. The balance of proteins in the body is one of Threonine's duties along with creating elastin and collagen and creating antibodies.

Methionine. Reduces cholesterol by boosting production of lecithin in the liver and lowers liver fat. It helps get rid of toxic elements such as mercury and is necessary for healthy hair growth.

Tryptophane. Natural way of lowering anxiety levels and keeping depression away. It is used to treat migraines. It boosts the immune system. From tryptophane comes serotonin, the neurotransmitter so important for that feeling of well being. It is a natural pain reliever and sedative, helps us relax.

Cystine. It protects the body by neutralizing toxins and is an antioxidant. It is required for cell growth and assists in slowing the aging process. About 12 percent of the body's skin and hair are made of cystine.

✳ *Spelt contains no cholesterol but does contain plant sterols* known to lower blood cholesterol.

✳ *Spelt is high in potassium, low in sodium*—both important in managing hypertension.

✳ Spelt at the genetic level differs distinctly from wheat in both gliadin structure and fat composition. *Spelt has more monounsaturated fats* (oleic acid) than modern wheat yet contains polyunsaturated fats/essential fatty acids (linoleic acid) necessary for cellular activity.

✳ Spelt is an ancient grain that has come down to us with its genetic structure intact. There are many genotypes of Spelt (*genetic diversity*). Heritage forms still exist that have not been genetically modified (*non-GMO*) as have the modern designer wheats. Variations among genotypes and environments produce plants that vary in characteristics such as the amount of protein. The variation in genotypes allows Spelt to adapt to a wider range of environments such as arid Eastern Washington and Arizona, wet and cool maritime environments in the British Isles to the Alps to the Transcaucasus.

❋ *Spelt is an eco-friendly crop that can adapt itself to highly variable conditions* just as it was doing when humans found it and domesticated it. It has higher mineral uptake than modern wheat, yet requires much less fertilization (nitrogen additions).

❋ *Nothing has to be added back in to Spelt* to make it nutritious—it is self-enriched. It is a hulled grain; the kernel does not thresh freely. The valuable grain is protected by the hull all the way to the milling process. The strong coating keeps it fresh and less subject to insect and microbial infestation. It is alive and healthful including containing valuable phytochemicals such as antioxidant phenolic acids and lignans that are anticarcinogenics. Spelt sprouts even contain Vitamin C.

❋ The taste of Spelt is superior. The flavors have height, depth and variety not found in modern wheat. *Spelt gives a symphony not a sound bite of taste sensations.*

Chapter 3: Food Intolerances and Allergies

Much confusion reigns on the subject of food intolerances and allergies because there are so many and they can be hard to diagnose. They are also hard to define. Each person is different. As no two sets of fingerprints are the same, no two people have exactly the same nutrition or intolerance profile.

As an example of the confusion, consider just one product: milk. Milk can be the source of a food allergy, which is a form of food intolerance. Or milk can be the cause of a specific metabolic food intolerance.

Confused? So is much of the indeterminate food research upon which we base laws and regulations, medical guidance and personal nutrition plans. Nutritional Science is very new; it is evolving and it is complex. There is what the National Institute of Allergy and Infectious Diseases (NIAID) terms a "lack of consensus" on what to do. Following are a few examples of the problems involved in Food and Nutrition that may be of interest to some of you.

Food Intolerance—Non-Immune Response

The symptoms of food intolerance are not caused by the immune system although the symptoms can and often do resemble a food allergy. Food intolerance is more common than food allergies.

Food Allergies—Immune Response

In one sense, food allergies are a form of the category "Food Intolerance" meaning they arise from foods you eat. The National Institute of Health/National Library of Medicine defines a genuine food allergy as "an exaggerated immune response triggered by eggs, peanuts, milk or some other specific food." In its third National Health and Nutrition Survey completed in 1994 (August, 2005), the NIH (testing for 10 allergens) estimates more than 50% of Americans have an allergic reaction to something—from mold and dust to cats and various foods.

A food allergy is an abnormal response or hypersensitivity to a food. The allergens are proteins "within the food that enter your bloodstream after the food is digested. From there, they go to target organs, such as skin and nose, and cause allergic reactions" (NIAID, 2004, Overview). The reason for calling it an abnormal response is the body acts against a food protein as it would a genuinely harmful substance such as a microbe. The body thinks a food is harmful so it creates an antibody, i.e. histamine, to protect itself. There is research to suggest that allergies may be genetically linked, that is, allergies seem to run in families where members have other non-food allergies such as asthma (which may or may not arise as a food allergy), or eczema, or react strongly to cat fur or dog dander. The symptoms can range from mild to life threatening.

According to current research, eight foods are the cause of the majority (90%) of allergic responses, at least in children: milk, egg, peanut, tree nut, fish, shellfish, soy and wheat. The wheat category is lumped (the constituents of gluten being the criteria), irrespective of the differences between the cereal grains, such that Spelt is considered by the Food and Drug Administration as a *wheat* even though its protein structure (amino acid composition) diverges significantly from the modern wheats— and other distinct genetic differences exist as well. Spelt also differs in chemical composition from other members of the *Poaceae* family (the grasses) such as rye, barley and oats. The USDA classifies Spelt as non-wheat and places it in the "Other Grain" category along with rye and others. In short, here are two important government entities that define wheat two different ways.

There are people who cannot tolerate the modern wheats who do tolerate Spelt. My husband is one of them. Why is this so? Allergy testing is not to the stage where there is testing of different wheat varieties. Testing does not take into account whether the grain

is grown organically or in conventional (chemically treated) fields. Similarly, the tests do not rule out such factors as cross contamination such as whether the grain undergoing testing was contaminated with other grains or foreign food residues such as those that can reside in multi-use farm equipment or bins. The tests do not discriminate whether the grain being tested was genetically crossed with another wheat at some time in its past. All of these factors and more affect how an individual will respond to eating "wheat" especially in processed and refined foods. This is one of the strongest reasons for eating whole foods and using their natural flavors to enhance the taste.

Enzyme Deficiency

Other kinds of food intolerance include the inability to digest certain foods because the body does not produce the necessary enzymes. Milk is the most frequently cited culprit. My mother is the perfect example. She grew up on a diary farm yet for her to survive childhood, Grandfather had to buy her a goat for her milk. She not only survived, she thrived. There are people with genuine food allergies to some or all milk products. The allergenic response is not the same as a food intolerance based on enzyme deficiency.

Gluten Intolerance and Celiac (Coeliac) Diseases

Spelt is a cereal grain. It contains gluten. Gluten is the elastic protein that allows bread to expand. The gluten in turn is comprised of protein molecules that fall into two groups: gliadens and glutenins, the chemical properties of which vary from grain to grain as mentioned above. Spelt differs significantly from wheat, rye, barley, oats and other grains in the chemical make-up of these molecules. Spelt especially has a distinctly different genetic gliaden pattern than is found in modern wheats. Spelt also has higher soluble fiber content than wheat, which can reduce problems of the digestive tract. Nevertheless, for some people, ingesting gluten can cause mild to severe health problems.

On the severe end of the scale are those who suffer from the genetically transmitted disease variously diagnosed as Celiac Disease, Nontropical Sprue, Gluten Intolerant Enteropathy and Celiac Sprue. For such people, ingesting gluten triggers a negative autoimmune (non-allergenic) response that ranges from irritating the small intestine to damaging the digestive tract such that it cannot absorb nutrients. For some with this medical condition, eating such things as soy sauce or canned broth, licking an envelope, chewing gum or using laxatives can set off an autoimmune response. The severity of response depends upon the individual's unique body chemistry. Some with this medical condition tolerate the gluten in Spelt and others do not. Currently researchers do not know why this is so, nor do they know why gluten is harmful to the digestive tract in the case of Celiac disease. Many Celiac organizations, e.g. Celiac.com, advise against eating or ingesting any wheat (gluten) products and have Food Avoidance lists to follow.

Immune Response and Blood Type

Food allergies are responses by the body's immune system. The "food allergy is an immunologic disease" (NIAID 2004). Food allergy "is an antigen-specific reaction" (NIAID 2003).

The immune response described by Dr. D'Adamo as the basis for Blood Type Eating outlines the nature of some of these responses. Simply put, all people carry antigens on their red blood cells. They are proteins that chemically identify "self" from "non-self", friend or foe. The basic job description for the antigen is to be on the alert for foe. When it finds foe it emits a signal. The signal creates antibodies. They seek out and destroy foe. This is the body's immune system. Carried out to eating, the body recognizes some foods as friendly to its blood type and others that are not. Some get under the radar and cause problems, especially in the digestive tract. The body's immune response to food developed over a long period and became part of each person's genetic inheritance. This inheritance, in turn, is based on the foods our ancestors ate and how they responded to the dietary changes (ability to digest) such as the shift from eating meat to grain or milk products. What is good for you may be bad for another person based on the difference of your blood type and how, when and where your ancestors lived, among other factors.

Eat Right for Your Type is not a theory generally accepted by the medical establishment and science community for a variety of reasons—yet in practice it has cut a wide swathe through popular dietary practices and continues to do so quietly. This is because of its accent on whole food cooking and eating and the connection between how humans evolved, with which foods, to explain some harmful food reactions in the present day. For example, Dr. D'Adamo's research suggests the modern common wheats are anathema to the O blood type, probably the original type, which still constitutes the majority of people in the world. He was among the first to advocate the change to Spelt. Because of its antiquity, many humans had time to adjust to Spelt. The modern wheats keep changing which makes it difficult for the body to adjust.

Food and the Healthiest You

Humans are going through the second great diet revolution. We are inundated with chemical compositions in refined, processed and genetically modified foods the like of which our bodies have not heretofore seen. Note that the NIAID states, "The single effective strategy to prevent food allergic reactions is strict food avoidance; however, increased use of prepackaged and processed foods limits the utility of this approach" (2003:3). Even the vegetables we use in our cooking have been greatly changed by researchers through genetic modification, hence their physical perfection. Every

gardener who has ever worked with heirloom varieties of vegetables knows this supposed perfection is not attainable in nature.

What to do?

Educate yourself. Read the abundant literature in circulation. Start reading package labels carefully and hone in on things like the Whole Grains Stamp on the wrappers of real whole grain breads and other products. These stamps are not marketing ploys (see Appendix 2 for Whole Grains Council website). The Whole Grains Stamp alerts you whether or not you are eating a product containing authentic whole grains and gives a rating for quality. Eat foods you can identify. Be aware of when you react to foods. Reaction does not mean just the serious life-threatening reactions such as occur with Celiac diseases. Reactions include slowed metabolism, fuzzy thinking, lethargy, depression, wheezing and erratic moods. In other words, pay attention to what is happening with your body.

You are not a victim. Become active in maintaining your health by paying close attention to how you feel before, during and after you eat. Separate the *pleasure*—that siren's call—of eating particular foods from the *results* of eating all foods. Notice what works for you and what does not. Only you know how you feel. If you are preparing your own meals from quality whole foods, there is less likelihood of reactions from unknown ingredients. The choice is yours. When you have done all you can, go on and enjoy your life. Worrying can be as harmful to health as bad food.

Chapter 4: Coming Home

Lost and Found

Spelt came close to extinction in the late 20th century. Intrepid people revived her. Still, she is elusive.

You will not find Spelt as an ingredient in foods on most restaurant menus nor will Spelt be among the selections in most bread baskets served at restaurants. You will find Spelt in whole food markets, increasingly in the health food/whole foods section of large supermarket chains and in health food stores like Back to Basics in my town. Spelt is sold as gourmet or health food flour, grain and other products on the Internet.

Spelt in many forms can be found at the wonderful open-air markets such as Pike's in Seattle or Hillsdale in Portland—must-go places on the American Gastronomic Tour as are the excellent artisan bakeries spreading across America.

If you are east of the Mississippi, you will often encounter Spelt as one of the grains in a multi-wholegrain bread. On the West Coast, many artisan bakers make fine breads from Spelt alone. Some of those breads are now in stores.

All of this means that for Spelt to become *a* or *the* basic grain in your life—or even if you just want to experiment—you must cook and bake with Spelt at home. The ingredients are all out there and *Spelt Healthy!* is here to help you go from eating out to eating in, to turning your kitchen into your favorite restaurants, delicatessen and bakery all in one. See Appendix 2 Shopping for Spelt—Resources and Information or visit www.spelthealthy.com.

Investing in Yourself

*The cost of a thing is the amount of what
I call life which is required to be exchanged
for it, immediately or in the long run.*
~ Henry David Thoreau

You have invested in all manner of things: clothes, cars, education, real estate. Now perhaps it is time to invest in your *state of being.*

During the course of this project, I questioned many people about cooking—or not. About *not* cooking, I am most frequently told, "I don't have the time."

An artist friend of mine was fond of saying to people, "Everything's a matter of choice." There were times I would respond, "Yes, but—" and then wanted to clunk him up beside the head 'cause it really got my goat. Instead, the conversation would end right there because his comment always resulted in me thinking about my choices, choices like "I don't have time." When you value something, you make the time, and when you do, you discover some unexpected and full of wonder benefits. That can be particularly true with cooking in your kitchen. Here are some things you might consider.

✳ You create more choices for yourself, not fewer. Creation feeds on itself and cooking is creation. It is not a chore; it is not a bore. It is what you make it.

✳ Cooking at home gives you direct control over what you eat, how much you eat, and leads to less impulse and more mindful eating.

✳ Junk in, not out. New idea: you make the junk at home, "junk" meaning the foods that taste terrific but offer no nutritional advantage over other foods. They are for satisfying the sweet tooth or for comfort or it's just flat giggly fun like being a kid again. When made with Spelt, you eat less junk because Spelt is more filling and deeply satisfying. Very few of the sumptuous recipes in *Spelt Healthy!* use only Light or White Spelt flour. Even if they do, most White Spelt contains bran and is still more nutritious than almost any flour, especially white wheat. You can change them to all Whole Grain and measures in between and they are still mouth-watering. Spelt keeps far better than ordinary wheat flour. Spelta's Cinnamon Rolls stay fresh for days because the recipe uses some or all Whole Grain Spelt depending on your preference. You do not have to feel you need to eat them all right away or worry about throwing them out. The Chocolate Transgression Brownies in this book are more delicious *after* being frozen *and* they keep for months. That way you spread them out over time and the taste is still terrific. I designed them with that in mind. That's the junk food angle. It makes sense for you and, if you have kids, it makes even better sense.

✳ Good nutrition gives you more energy and a brighter outlook on life so you do not have so much "down" time or spinning of the wheels and getting nowhere feeling. When you feel better, you make different choices. You also start making time for things you decide are important to you.

✳ There are benefits that go far beyond the mundane—things having to do with sustenance of the spirit, that illusive but critical spark called being truly alive. You need to tend the flame. When you work with the Spelt dough and feel it growing with life beneath your fingers, that life energy passes into you. Spelt is ancient; she has much to teach and give. It may sound strange, but rolling meatballs, or falafel or breadsticks, is a calming, tranquil act. The heartbeat slows down. The whirring that is the background noise of modern American life goes away. You can hear yourself think. You begin to focus and then you are living in the here and now. And isn't that what it's all about?

✳ Cooking in pleasure and eating in peace are worthy goals. In cooking with Spelt, you enjoy the fruits of your labor. There is satisfaction that goes beyond your stomach saying it is full. Making a simple Paradell and enjoying it in quietude is a gift you give yourself. Making a dozen pizzas on Friday night with family or friends and music and laughter is life. When you take the time to prepare quality foods, you are not just enjoying the taste of fine food, you are *putting life into yourself instead of draining it away.* As in Mr. Thoreau's quotation above, "The cost of a thing is the amount of what I call life which is required to be exchanged for it, immediately or in the long run." You exchange a little of your time, invest a little of yourself and watch the big returns. Spelt returns your investment manifold.

Our Culinary Heritage

Our foods and our recipes are legacies of the past bequeathed to us by trial and error from our ancestors. Life has always revolved around food. *Food is the sun of social life,* the family bond, that which seals the deal.

Recipe books are repositories of food fact and lore that until recently was passed down by word of mouth from one generation to the next. The Empanada Valenciana recipe in this book is one of those recipes. It was written down for me by a Spanish friend who learned it by doing it with her grandmother who never wrote down a thing. The ink is runny from sangria and the paper is curling with age. The same goes for my late Aunt Annie's Italian recipes that appear, amended to Spelt, in this book. These are but a few of the many such treasures that fill a large recipe box of mine, a box full of recipes written on gift-wrapping paper or cocktail napkins or the backs of postcards from other places. They are tucked into the pages of old recipe books my mother gave to me, as do hers and others in the Kachina Women's Club cookbooks that go back fifty years. My *memories* are part of my cooking—like seeing my great-Uncle mix up bread dough in the big wash basin or picking blackberries for pies or making Ceviche in Mexico with freshly-caught shrimp and whitefish and luscious chiles.

My Grandmother's cookbook is filled with her writing and commentary. Old newspaper articles from the Depression era talk of putting foods by and how to make whole grain bread using a sponge to make it higher and lighter. I amended her Buckwheat pancake recipe for this book and now it lives again (Spukwheat Pancakes). My mother's awesome Chocolate Variety Bread and Zucchini cookies (Back to Basics Zucchini Spice Cookie) are in *Spelt Healthy!* too. So are a multitude of recipes from the far more distant past that are still with us and still popular. Foods, recipes and kitchen tools are all part of our culinary heritage.

Recipes and remembrance of active kitchen life are gifts to the next generation. I have been in the kitchen since I was nose high to a countertop. My parents encouraged it. When I go out and eat something intriguing or unforgettable, I try to reproduce it in my kitchen. The effort may not result in the same thing but it turns into a new and often delicious thing and always rewards me for trying. Pan Andrea was a wedding gift. It merges into their cookbook of life that will, in turn, be passed on to their children, amended by them, a part of culinary history.

Our ancestors used decorative molds to bake the breads they offered to divinities. Instead of sacrificing animals, they baked their shapes and offered them instead—the cookie cutter of holiday times. The much

admired épi loaf, made as a sheaf of wheat, is with us from those times.

The Auld Lang Syne (Remembrance) Bread in *Spelt Healthy!* is likewise a rendition of ancient offerings to divinities and human ancestors. As once these offerings were coiled from clay, people coiled dough into forms such as the crossed arms of praying children, which became the familiar pretzel of today. The Pao Doce recipe is the specialty sweet bread of medieval holy-days and weddings and other great feasts and celebrations. The Sproutcakes recipe was the first cake—a paste made of wet, smashed grain and baked by the side of the fire. Pitas are thousands of years old, as are the Zuppa de Farro and the Minestrone soups you will also find in this book.

This book is not an attempt to re-create the past. Rather, whole food cooking and ancient recipes go hand in hand. Some foods then and now create a suite of savory, sumptuous, simple yet complex tastes and textures that stand the test of time. Like broiled Kasseri cheese. Like Roman Bread and crusted fish and salads with croutons. Like pancakes made with Spelt flour. Such recipes endure because they have solid underpinnings. They have stood the nutritional and taste test of time. They give us nourishment; they give us delight; they connect us to the past.

When we eat meals made in our kitchen or prepare special foods for marked calendar days, our histories and our traditions, old and new, come alive

and help us understand we are a part not apart or outside the circle of all things. You touch the past deeply, that circle is joined, in cooking and baking—in your kitchen—with that ancient, life-giving grain, Spelt.

Every Day Fine Food

To Go Gourmet Is the Question

Cooking is the oldest of the Fine Arts; gourmet cooking is one of the highest expressions of that art. Spelt is in the unusual dual food category of being both a health food and a gourmet food. That is nice, but what does it mean? Who or what is a gourmet?

"Gourmet" is a much bandied about word. For purposes here, it refers to refinement of taste based on expertise in food and/or wine, and, as a result of this learning, that knowledgeable person is able to keenly discriminate in matters of taste. Hence, a gourmet product is one that has special qualities related to good taste. "Gastronomy" refers to the application of knowledge to the selection and enjoyment of fine foods.

Do you have to be a gourmet cook or a chef to make use of Spelt?

No, it does not take a chef nor do you have to be a gourmet cook to produce quality food, fine food. It takes heart, intention and knowledge gained by *doing*. We are all beginners at something. Begin. Creativity comes in the wake of doing.

"Doing" is a confidence builder; it engenders creativity. The more you cook and bake with Spelt, the more creative and audacious you may become because of the qualities of Spelt and the generous range of flavors and foods you can coax from her.

The *Fine* in Fine Food

The "fine" in fine food really comes from two things. Fine ingredients and the refined skill and artistry of the person who combines, tweaks, coaxes, plies, multiplies flavor to create sensory delights. Fine dining is fine food and theatre. It is learning and delight. It is conviviality.

The reason for whole foods in gourmet cooking is that whole foods are alive. Because of that quality of aliveness, they burst with or exude flavor and they offer great contrast in form and texture. They are beautiful to behold and each has individual integrity and character, qualities that translate into a variety of flavors and sensations. Taste and eye appeal are fundamentals of gourmet cooking. Using whole foods in gourmet cooking is nothing more or nothing less than the freshest of foods cooked or brought together by the chef or gourmet cook in a way that brings out the best of each ingredient to complement or accent the whole. Again, it is food prepared with care to sensations and presentation.

Gourmet cooking has often been associated with the use of whole foods because of their taste, color and form, not their inherent nutritional qualities. Gourmet cooking is wildly experimental and has been since people first had the wherewithal to seek out finer more flavorful foods, condiments and spices and took knowledgeable slaves or hired people to prepare these expensive foods. Famous gourmands such as the Roman, M. Gavius Apicius of the 1st Century A.D. and the Late Middle Ages French chef, Tailevent, were concerned with novelty and rarity to the end of gustatory delight. The nutritional aspect of whole foods has not been, until relatively recently, a primary consideration for using whole foods in gourmet cooking. Or rather, I should say, people thought of nutrition differently in past centuries and the combining of foods was more philosophy than science. When it comes to Authentic Cuisine or Slow Food, philosophy and science, nutrition and fine taste are combined.

Slow Food, Authentic Food—The Gastronomic Turn Around

One of the significant "food" changes in the last few decades is the Slow Food movement, the appreciation of whole, non-genetically modified foods and their use in Authentic Cuisine. Spelt is authentic and inextricably linked to world history (and prehistory) and to regional cuisines. This is why you will see Spelt increasingly on the menus of fine food restaurants, not just in the United States but in Europe and elsewhere,

and one of the reasons, aside from taste, that it is considered a gourmet food. For example, one of the gastronomic draws of Asturias in Northern Spain is its authentic foods. One of these foods is the delicacy, *escanda,* a bread made from Spelt.

Quality Whole Food Cooking with Spelt is the combining of sensory appeal with good nutrition. It is uncomplicated and authentic cooking that produces complex taste sensations. The life of the food is transmitted to you. You learn by experience, you become more discriminating and the effort amply rewards you.

One of the skills you accrue from cooking is that it makes you far more discriminating when you do go out for a fine dining experience or when you travel. Most chefs will be pleased that you notice the effort and ingredients that have gone into making your fine food for you. If you only read this book and never pick up a kitchen utensil, you have still extended your learning. You will be able to apply it when you travel and knowledge is part of the definition of "gourmet."

Your Kitchen Palette and Sculptural Tools

View your kitchen as a studio, the setting for creation. You are the artist. Consider that you are working with a palette of the most beautiful natural colors on earth—that deep glossy purple of the eggplant and pasilla, the vermilion tomato, the white and deep green stripe of zucchini, the shiny dimpled yellow lemon, the pearly translucence of onions. See the glory that is the range of color and flavors in the spices—from the gamboge yellow of the mustards, grain golds, the fiery red of cayenne, the oranges of turmeric and saffron, the sienna of Spelt. What contrast of color, shade and texture exists between the lettuces, the rough texture of pesto and the smoothness of vanilla-colored béchamel, the glassy palomino finish of Pao Doce, the rough thatching of intertwined leek greens. You are creating, combining anew, with materials that are among nature's finest works of art. Is it any wonder that cooking is the first Fine Art?

Spelt: The Fine Wine of Flours

When you are cooking and baking with Spelt, you are using the fine wine of flours. No two millers produce the exact same grind of flour. No two Spelt crops are identical. Like grapes, grains are the result of the "seed" stock, their natural surroundings, and the farmer's skill and dedication, just as gourmet cooking is imbued with natural flavors heightened by the chef. These factors in turn affect the taste and baking properties of the Spelt flour. The flours of Italy and those of France are different than the ones grown in Australia or Canada; the Spelt flours of the Midwest or Northwest of the United States differ from one another. An organic field differs from a conventional stand in the same area. It is one of the singular beauties of a genetically unmodified grain, the seed stock, the range of farming methods and the current system of milling specialty grains like Spelt.

Because Spelt retains its hull until just prior to milling, it has a freshness that translates to flavor. This property cannot be underestimated in baking nor can Spelt's water-absorbing characteristics, because water develops flavor. There are many varieties of flours, increasingly more, from which to choose: a range of Whole Grain, Light and White. All produce differences in texture, flavor and baking properties. There is a fine palette of Whole Grain Spelt flours from which to create your own unique artisan and specialty breads.

The flavors and textures of Spelt baked products are delightfully varied. Spelt can produce, especially through ferments, a range of flavors just like wines.

PART II
SPELTOIDS: FACTS AND OTHER CURIOUS THINGS ABOUT SPELT AND HER CLOSEST RELATIVES

Chapter 1: What, Exactly, Is Spelt?

Language of Science and Hulled Grains

Spelt is a flowering grass (Family *Poaceae*). Its fruit is a grain (Tribe *Triticeae*). The scientific nomenclature for the Spelt we use in food today is *Triticum aestivum* subspecies *spelta* L. Spelt belongs to the same family of plants that include bamboo, rice, sorghum, sugarcane and the modern bread wheats.

Spelt is classified as a *Triticum;* it is an ancient relative of wheat, but not wheat. The United States Department of Agriculture (U.S. Standards for Wheat effective May 1993, Section 810.2201, Definition of Wheat), defines "Wheat" as common wheat (*Triticum aestivum* L.), club wheat (*T. compactum* Host.), and durum wheat (*T. durum* Desf.). The USDA places Spelt in the "Other Grains" category along with such other grains as barley, einkorn, emmer, corn, safflower, soybeans and sunflower seeds.

Spelt is a hulled grain ("covered wheat") along with emmer and einkorn. These are the first *Triticums* documented in association with human gathering and, later, agricultural activities. Scientists located the wild ancestors of emmer and einkorn, but not for mysterious Spelt.

Image, actual size, of Spelt spike, spikelet, and the two kernels contained in the spikelet that sticks to anything it touches.

All *Triticums* have a basic genomic structure, that is, there are seven chromosomes on each genome. Einkorn is diploid meaning 2n=2x=14 (AA). Emmer is tetraploid: 2n=4x=28 (AABB). Spelt is hexaploid: 2n=6x=42 (AABBDD). The numbers represent sets of chromosomes; the letters are expressions of characteristics.

The prevailing theory is that emmer is one of Spelt's "parents". Emmer originated in the Fertile Crescent especially in the Levant, Jordan, Iraq and Iran. It was abundant even before agriculture began. Dr. Gil Stallknecht, one of the foremost experts on Spelt, says (pers. comm.), "Emmer expanded because of a BB genome which meant it could be grown in a wider range of environments including regions having high growing season temperatures." Because of its adaptability, emmer spread widely. As it moved north, emmer crossed with a wild grass species to create a new form, one that was hexaploid in nature. Spelt was born. It was a fertile hybrid very much like cultivated Spelt. Because of the genomic structure of the wild grass, Spelt could now move into an even wider range of environments than emmer. Spelt could grow in extremes including colder and colder/wetter environments such as areas of retreating glacial activity in Europe. It grows in such extremes today, for example, the eastern part of Washington State which is classified, agriculturally, as one of the most arid places on earth, to the Austrian and Italian Alps and cold, wet Asturias in Spain.

The other "parent" of Spelt was likely *Aegilops tauschii*, a wild grass growing in a band across the northern part of the Fertile Crescent, especially the Transcaucasus region, along the Black Sea and coastal region and points south of the Caspian Sea. Spelt as a species probably began at least 8000 years ago about the time humans began domesticating animals. Again, no one is quite certain because the wild ancestor of Spelt remains elusive. Archaeologists have identified Spelt seed remains dating back to 5000–6000 B.C. where *A. tauschii* originated.

Spelt appears to be one of the ancient genetic bridges to the modern domesticated wheats, which have a hexaploid genomic

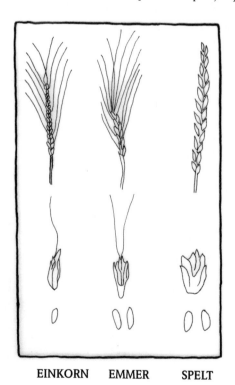

EINKORN   EMMER   SPELT

Comparative illustration of the Ancient Hulled Grains: (top row) spikes, (middle row) spikelets, (bottom row) the grain kernels from each spikelet.

make-up. Durum wheat is an example. The DD genes (the additional chromosomes) gave the excellent bread-making quality to the hexaploid wheats as opposed to einkorn and emmer. They have traditionally been used in whole grain versus flour form. Spelt has traditionally been used in a variety of forms that express the range of grain from whole grain to fine flour such as semolina (*alica* in Roman times). After Spelt, a variety of wheats came into being that led to the over 200,000 varieties of bread-making wheats that exist today. Some species, like durum, a free-threshing wheat, may have developed as species soon after Spelt but were not selected by humans for widespread use until conditions arose such as increased population and demand for higher yields that suddenly made them more desirable.

What Is A Hulled Grain?

It is necessary to free the grain from its husk to make the grain digestible for humans. Modern wheats are free-threshing. This means that when threshed in the field the kernel is released; the chaff is then winnowed. The grain is stored "naked" until being milled and processed. The free-threshing grains do not require the additional step of removing the tough hull like Spelt, emmer and einkorn do.

The seed head of the primitive hulled grains, like Spelt, thresh into individual spikelets not grains (see spikelet, center, of Spelt picture). This spikelet is an armored coating. The hulled grains stay in this casing until the process of de-hulling prior to other steps in milling. This additional de-hulling step is one of the reasons Spelt is more expensive to buy than regular wheat and one of the big reasons why it is better.

Chapter 2: Spelt Time

Spelt's Origins and Spread

Most of human life has been lived prior to the keeping of records, in other words, prehistory. It has also been lived with the ancient grains—einkorn, emmer and Spelt. What we know about the origins and spread of Spelt and the other hulled grains comes from Archaeology and related fields such as Archaeobotany and Palaeobotany. Modern analytic tools such as genetic identification markers (the AA/BB/DD from the previous chapter) on ancient grains found in sites are redefining and expanding our knowledge of how our ancestors survived. However, we have to dig to know. Tracking Spelt through time is doing detective work because Spelt is so elusive. We have a thimbleful of knowledge and a storage bin as big as a barn that is empty and waiting to receive information. There is, in particular, a paucity of information from the Transcaucasus region, Iran, Iraq, Moldavia, Bulgaria and the Stan countries to make a clear picture of Spelt. The following section is a compressed timeline based on Archaeological and Palaeobotanical evidence (prehistory). Written sources of information (historical records), i.e. Greek and Roman, follow in the section "Writing Things Down."

Material Evidence (from Plants)

Human beings were experimenting with grains as a food source long before the last ice sheets retreated, especially in S.W. Asia. Archaeologists (Weiss, 2005) recently reported what may be the first evidence of grains being processed into seed along with baking ovens at a site in Israel dated circa 21,000 B.C.

Perhaps the first grain that humans embraced was wild einkorn. Wild einkorn probably crossed with a wild grass *(Aegilops speltoides)* to produce wild emmer *(T. dicoccoides)*. At another Israeli site, Ohalo II, people were threshing wild emmer *(T. dicoccoides)* about 17,000 B.C. Further hybrids with grasses occurred. Around 8,000 B.C. people began settling down and making use of wild grains at places like Abu Hureyra and Mureybit in modern-day Syria. Through the centuries, they started domesticating animals like goats and sheep. As people spread, so did the hulled grains. Hybridization occurred between emmer and a wild grass circa 6500 B.C. to bring about the hexaploid species, Spelt.

The earliest archaeological evidence (as wild species and associated with humans) for Spelt comes from Transcaucasia (Bulgaria), Moldavia (north of the Black Sea) and areas around the Caspian Sea.

From the contemporary site of Yarym-Tepe II in northern Iraq circa 5000 B.C. comes evidence of domesticated Spelt. There is a terrific gap in our knowledge of Spelt from these regions and a long period of time that remains to be documented. The hulled grains were staples in agriculture for thousands of years in a wide variety of environments—from scorching Egypt to the Alps—before the free-threshing bread wheats came to be widely used following introduction of leavening from Egypt in the Hellenistic period.

What is known is that 8000–7000 years ago Spelt started to spread from its place of origin. The Vavilov Institute of Plant Industry in Russia has been collecting Spelt cultivars since 1910 from many places including Spain, Morocco, Iran, Azerbaijan, Tajikstan, Germany, Poland, Latvia, Ukraine, Switzerland, Austria, Denmark, France and the United States. Among the cultivars, they have identified two subspecies of Spelt: one is distinct for

Western Europe *(spelta)* and the other isolated to Iran, Transcaucasia and Central Asia *(Kuckuckianum)*. This in turn has given rise to the occasional suggestion that Spelt originated in more than one place: Europe and Asia.

Neolithic/Copper and Bronze Ages and Otzi the Iceman

"Otzi the Iceman" was discovered in the Alps near the Austrian-Italian border in 1991. He lived more than 5000 years ago (Copper Age) and is the oldest human mummy yet discovered. Scientific analysis of Otzi's intestines showed that eight hours prior to his possibly violent death on that lonely mountaintop he ate unleavened einkorn bread. Einkorn and barley seeds were found in his clothing.

From the regions mentioned above, emmer is archaeologically documented circa 3900 B.C. at Swifterbant on the North European Plain. By 2500–1700 B.C. Spelt appears in northern Europe, i.e. Poland, Jutland (Danish mainland and northern Germany) and other parts of Germany including the southwestern portion where it is still grown today.

The Grain of the Trojan War (Late Bronze Age/Iron Age)

From 1800–1200 B.C. Spelt is abundant in Bronze Age sites in Greece, for example, at Assiros Toumba circa 1300 B.C. There archaeologists found it as a mixed grain (maslin) crop with emmer and einkorn. Spelt is also well documented archaeologically in the extreme north of

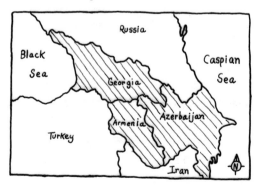

TRANSCAUCASUS REGION

Italy at the site of Fiave. Spelt and emmer were cultivated in Spain during this period as they were in parts of France. In Greece, Spelt replaced emmer as the principal hulled grain species well into the Iron Age (circa 550 B.C.)

There is a similar pattern with Spelt at the end of the second millennium B.C. where it was cultivated then replaced emmer at sites in southern Britain and Scotland by 500 B.C. For example, archaeologists found Spelt at Loch Tay in the Scottish highlands at a farming site they dated to circa 400 B.C.

In mainland Europe, emmer continued to be important in northern Germany and the lowlands of western continental Europe while Spelt appears in the uplands in regions such as the northern border of the Alps, southern Sweden and in portions of Jutland. Again, the archaeological evidence is spotty.

Roman Times

Both emmer and Spelt were cultivated in Britain and Germany during Roman times. In excavations at the Roman Fort at Beardon, Scotland (dated to 142–165 A.D.) both emmer and Spelt were staple grains made into bread and gruel and eaten with figs, raspberries, coriander and dill.

In Shropshire County, England, excavations at two towns, Viroconium Cornoviorum and Mediolanum, both established by the Romans beginning 52 A.D., indicated that Spelt and emmer were the dominant grains. As for Rome and other areas of the empire, there are many references to "Spelt" from Roman literary sources; however, it remains unclear because of lack of archaeological evidence whether the sources refer to Spelt, emmer or einkorn or all three as you will see in Chapter 3.

Medieval Europe

Spelt continued to be a staple in regions of Germany where it has existed ever since. It appears in portions of the Alps and France. The archaeological documentation of material remains for other regions is far less clear. The free-threshing wheats came to dominate almost everywhere in Europe beginning 1000 A.D. yet people persisted in old ways, especially those people off the

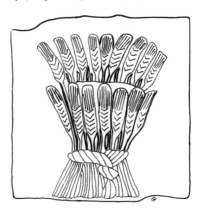

Drawing of a bundle of wheat carved on lintel (circa 800 B.C.) at shrine of Demeter at Eleusis, near Athens. Demeter was goddess of agriculture, grain and the harvest to the Greeks and is immortalized in the myth of Demeter and her daughter Persephone to account for cycles of nature. In Greek, Demeter's name means **SPELT MOTHER**. During the season of sowing (September) she was worshipped at a festival, the Eleusian Mysteries. The festival originated far earlier (1500 B.C. or before) when Spelt and Demeter were one.

major river trade routes or the later interior oxen trails. This urban/rural pattern may account for the surviving stands of Spelt and emmer in isolated pockets of central and Eastern Europe and the Balkan region and Eastern Turkey (Anatolia) to this day.

Modern Period

Spelt reached the United States in the early 19th century where it was first grown by Pennsylvania Dutch farmers of Swiss, Alsatian and German origins. Spelt moved along the immigrant trail into the heartlands of America and Canada by the late 1800s. In the United States there were still five cultivars, yet between 1910 and the 1960s Spelt came close to dying out in many areas where once it thrived. Purity Foods revived commercial Spelt in 1987, a story in itself (see Purity Foods—Appendix 2).

Acreage in Spelt is increasing in the United States and countries of the European Union, Canada and Australia. Of the cereal crops (grasses) ranked in greatest annual production, wheat is first, followed by rice then maize, the millets, sorghum, rye and triticale, oats, barley, teff, wild rice and then Spelt. Thirty years ago Spelt would not have appeared on the list at all.

A Glimpse Through the Veil of Time: Asturias, Spain and Spelt

Megalithic stone monuments dot the landscape of Asturias, funeral tombs from the Neolithic and Bronze Age of northern, rocky Spain. They are testaments to times when early farmers grew einkorn and emmer in that isolated region. As elsewhere in Europe, Spelt came to the Iberian Peninsula late in the Bronze Age and early in the Iron (1500–1200 B.C.). It has been there ever since.

In 883 A.D. the Arabic *Cronicon Albendense*, a tabulation of all the products of Spain, showed the *escandu* of Asturias. At that time, *escandu* meant either emmer or Spelt and dates from the age when peasants paid taxes with grain. Emmer has almost died out in the region or it is found in mixtures (maslin crops) of 25% or less emmer. *Pan de escanda* (emmer/Spelt) is described by people of the region as "a variety of wheat that belongs to the cold and poor lands" (belmontedemiranda.com/ Cosentino translation). The reason emmer is now rare in Asturias and other regions is possibly because it was largely used as animal fodder and, because of its bulkiness, to pay the taxes while farmers kept Spelt for their own consumption (Oliveira, 1996:16).

Landraces (native species) of Spelt still exist in Asturias along with customs and recipes that center around the grain, which is grown at a variety of altitudes. For example, at Brana de Aristebano there was the tradition of an annual Fiesta de Vaqueros, an equestrian fair for the nobility. During the 1950s, *empanadas* and *escanda* were served. *Escanda* of Spelt was once associated with tables of the well-to-do or feast days, just as it was in other places in Europe.

Farmers plant the Spelt spikelets. There is a tradition among the farmers of the region of growing peas or broad beans with the Spelt to keep the Spelt from lodging (falling down) and to provide a border for the field (Peña-Chocarro, 1996:133). This custom of growing peas or beans is an ancient one, reflected also in Italy's Tuscan Farro Soup (recipe in *Spelt Healthy!*). Joining the beans or peas with the grain gave a person sufficient protein without eating meat, a rarity, or dairy foods.

Escanda bread is a bread made for special occasions such as the Fiesta above or marriages and religious feasts such as Easter or the village saint's day. Traditionally, people ground their *escanda* flour in a water-powered mill. Using meshes of ever-smaller size, the flour was sifted finer and finer. This is reminiscent of the Romans who sifted theirs through silk, gauze or other cloth, a tradition that continued through the Middle Ages as did using light Spelt flour for fine breads and pastries.

The bran or coarser flour of Spelt or emmer was used for chicken feed and then *fogaza* (Italian *focaccia*), which was a coarse bread. The fine-sifted flour, much like the white or light Spelt flour sold in markets today, was used for the special *escanda* bread. The *escanda* flour was also made into a delicacy called *panchon* that was wrapped in husks and baked in the fireplace. *Pao Doce* in this cookbook is a continuation of that long tradition of making delicate, sweet breads for religious and special occasions. Peña-Chocarro (1996:142) observed, "There seems to be a preference for spelt bread over emmer bread, and spelt has traditionally been considered as the richest and most valuable for use in bread." He says (1996:142) that according to farmers, "Spelt is more easily kneaded because it mixes better," and is not so flat and dark as emmer.

Incidentally, the northern part of Spain, including Asturias, has now become part of the Gastronomic Grand Tour of Europe because of its cheeses, sausages, seafood and Spelt *escanda* bread that is sold as a delicacy in many Asturian towns.

Chapter 3: The Tangled Web of Words: Spelt, Emmer, Einkorn and Farro

The Big Three, the brethren of ancient *Triticums*, are inextricably bound. They are subjects of some of civilizations' first pictures, myths and picture-writings. Then there came the words that were created to make pictures in the mind so we could talk about them with one another. I hope you will read about these convolutions of history and how these ancient grains and ancient words are with us still. Very few things have such continuity in time; the words are expressions of their value to humankind.

Writing Things Down

People started writing things down in a systematic way about 5000 years ago in Mesopotamia, smack dab in the center of that place called the Fertile Crescent, the place where humans and the hulled wheats first got married. It began by someone using a stick or a stamp to impress an image into clay—the original hard copy. People needed a record that would keep for purposes of taxes, trade and loans. In some ways, things do not change.

Mesopotamia and the Sumerians

(Circa 4000 B.C.) The first coin known to history comes from the site of Sippar (in present day Iraq). It is bronze and upon it is pictured a wheat sheaf, not barley their other grain, but wheat. That "wheat" was mostly likely emmer. On the other side of the coin is Ishtar, the goddess responsible for fertility—the difference between life and death. From the beginning grain—a hulled grain—and life are pictured as a unity.

Map of Mesopotamia, the land between the two rivers—Tigris and Euphrates. Dotted area is the Fertile Crescent. To the north between the Black and Caspian Seas is where Spelt probably came into existence.

Jansdat Nasr (circa 3000–2900 B.C.) The Sumerians learned to write on clay using pictograms, a simplified drawing that symbolizes a word or group of words. They and their successors left an abundance of these tablets, large and small. One at Jansdat Nasr is a proto-cuneiform, meaning one of the first. They were trying to work out the system. This one documents the distribution of grain from a large temple devoted to Ishtar. Religion was a major organizing force of societies in those times. These temples were the original grain warehouses. Whoever controlled the grain controlled the state. The cone probably represents a bag of emmer.

Egypt (circa 2500 B.C.) Through the long history of Egypt until Greco-Roman times, the wheat of Egypt was emmer. With

Jansdat Nasr proto-cunieform; cones indicate emmer. Grain appears at upper left and upper center. Ishtar's Temple appears as the upright cone with "house" on top in lower register. Two spikes of grain appear on the upper register.

emmer, they made the first leavened bread and they made a lot of beer. Their only other grain was barley from which they made a lot of beer (useful for yeast) too. If there is a reference to wheat in the same breath as Egypt prior to about 0 in history, that meant emmer or "mummy wheat" as the Romans called it.

Drawing based on bas relief from Thebes, Egypt, showing men dehusking emmer by driving cattle over the ground where the grain is being threshed. It shows that extra step of dehulling mentioned earlier.

Records from Biblical Times

The Seventh Plague. Variously set circa 1500 or 1300 B.C. From Exodus: 9:31 referring to the Seventh Plague (Hail): "The flax and barley have been destroyed, since the barley was ripe, and the flax had formed stalks." Exodus 9:32 "But the wheat and spelt were not smitten for they were not grown up." That the *grain* of Egypt was emmer, not Spelt, is well documented. The error is in the translation(s). This may be one of the original cases of lumping the hulled wheats under the collective *Spelt.* Spelt was familiar to Europeans originally translating the Bible, but then again so was emmer.

Detail drawn from Egyptian painting depicting bread-baking. Dough is placed in terracotta forms that resemble the cones engraved earlier on the ancient Mesopotamian proto-cunieform above.

Passover/Matzah. The Israelites fled from Egypt (circa 1500 or 1300 B.C.) in such a hurry they had no time to leaven their bread. The flight and the bread are central to Jewish theology and dietary proscriptions have evolved concerning bread. On the Passover holiday, the commandments require the eating of *matzah*, an unleavened bread. The *matzah* must be made from one of the five principal grains: emmer/lesser spelt/also known as rice wheat *(Triticum dicoccum)*, Spelt *(Triticum spelta L.)*, wheat *(Triticum durum* or *vulgare)*, 6- or 4- or 2-rowed barley, oats or rye. *Rie* in translation may not mean the rye of today but *Kussemeth*, originally meaning 'spelt' depending on translation so that the original "other grain" to make the five was 2-rowed barley.

The original five grains were excluded from being eaten on Passover, or even in the house, except in the form of matzah, because they could be leavened.

Oats and rye do not leaven. They are added to grains in baking that do rise.

Challah. In later times, a piece of the matzah dough was taken separately and burned in remembrance of the Temple sacrifice, the burnt offering, from which the phrase "Challah is Taken." The braided bread, the familiar Challah of today, is a bread made to be taken apart or torn, hence the braided form. (See Challah recipe.)

Writing on the Sky

The Constellation Virgo and the Weight of Grain (1200–800 B.C.) From Sumerian times into ancient Greek culture passed the lore of stars and their forms as constellations. The Mul Apin cuneiform tablet of Babylon (Mesopotamia) describes constellations and stars and uses them to help forecast events.

They saw stars and galaxies and created lore around them. They brought them from the sky. They made them

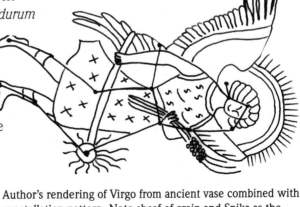

Author's rendering of Virgo from ancient vase combined with constellation pattern. Note sheaf of grain and Spika as the head of Virgo's torch. The torch and sheaf are also symbols of goddesses of agriculture Demeter and the later Ceres.

personal and gave them names such as Ishtar, the goddess in whose temple the grain was stored in early Sumer. In their time, our Virgo was likely part of Scorpio. Egyptians came to call the constellation Isis, who like, Ishtar, was the goddess of fertility. She was Khoshu (Ear of Wheat) to the Persians and to the Hebrews she was Bethulah (Good Harvest). The position of the stars changed but the tradition of writing in the sky passed to the Greeks.

The Greeks looked up and saw Demeter, the goddess who brings the growing season. They marked the constellation by the very bright star that they called *Spika*. It means *spike* as in spike of wheat and is another way of saying ear of wheat. Virgo carries the wheat in her hand. They also saw Themis, the goddess of justice in the constellation. Where there had been one large constellation in ancient times, by late Greek and Roman times now they were distinct. The Romans saw Libra (their goddess of justice) and Virgo who held the scales marked by Spika. Those scales referred to equinoxes but also to justice in the sense of measurement.

There was nothing so measured in ancient times as the weight of grain. The smallest unit of value or measure beginning with the Egyptians and then the Greeks was the individual grain of wheat. At the time the measure was adapted in Greece that grain was likely Spelt.

The Earliest Greek Coins (circa 700–400 B.C.) Grain is on one side of some of the earliest Greek coins. Also horse and grain are pictured together. At the time the first coin was stamped, that grain was likely Spelt or emmer. The hulled grains were replaced during this period with the free-threshing wheats. It was also during this long period that bread baking "bloomed" as it is believed the Egyptian knowledge of leavening was passed by the Israelites to other cultures through long distance trade. For Egyptians, emmer was *alura*. The Greeks called Spelt *zeia* and emmer *alura*. Einkorn was called *tiphe*.

Drawing of one of the oldest Greek coins (5th century, Archaic period) of a grain sprout. Grain was called "corn"; some of Western Civilization's first laws are corn laws regulating import/export. In the late 5th century, a corn measure was worth 3 drachmas a year. Allotments of Spelt and other grains to people of different standing are the source of our term "measuring up."

Drawing based on one of the earliest coins of Western Civilization. Hemidrachm (Thessaly, Greece). Grain is probably Spelt.

When the food we eat on the Fourth of July and in movie theatres was discovered in the New World it was called *teosinte* by the Mexica. Europeans called it *corn* and its name in scientific classification became *zea mays* (mais) after *spelt* meaning *zeia* as above. Corn in the Old World referred to the flowering grains and included barley, Spelt and others. So the confusion of corn was born. Corn in the time of the Romans did not mean New World corn on the cob it meant grain as in "barleycorn." "Corn" laws refer to restrictions on grain imports or exports.

Other Biblical References

Ezekiel 4:9 (circa 592–585 B.C.) "Take thou also unto thee wheat, and barley, and beans, and lentils, and millet and spelt, and put them in one vessel, and make thee bread thereof; according to the number of the days that thou shalt lie upon thy side, even three hundred and ninety days, shalt thou eat thereof" (ASV).

Isaiah 28:25 (circa 500 B.C.) "When he hath leveled the face thereof, doth he not cast abroad the fitches, and scatter the cumin, and put in the wheat in rows, and the barley in the appointed place, and the spelt in the border thereof" (ASV).

Depending upon the translation, other words are used for Spelt. In Spanish it can be *el centeno*, in Norwegian and Swedish it is *spelt*, in Italian it is *spelta*, in Romanian it is *alacul*. Yet in almost all translations the word for "wheat" is a distinctly different word, e.g. usually *trigo* (as in *Triticum*).

Roman Times

Beginning with Classical Greece and then Roman times there is textual information about the grains and reported customs. Their meanings are lost to us today because the cultural context is no longer the same. We get back to the question: What was Spelt to them?

One of the greatest sources of historical information is *Pliny the Elder* (*Gaius Plinius Secundas,* A.D. 23–79) who died in the explosion of Vesuvius where fresh-baked loaves of bread were found, preserved, in the ashes. (See recipe for *Roman Bread* in *Spelt Healthy!*) He was a widely traveled man of his times. We know him by his encyclopedia of more than 150 volumes, *Naturalis historia,* which is a compendium of the knowledge of the natural world. He had much to say about **Wheat.** No, not all was accurate. How could it have been? Science was new and much of his information was

Greek Stater, coin from the late Classical period. Work horses could not thrive on the sparse grass and had to be fed grain.

second-hand or historical. It is especially difficult given we must read his work in translation which presents other problems, especially with Spelt. Spelt was a familiar wheat to the Europeans who did many of the translations. As you will see, it may have meant emmer, einkorn or Spelt or a mixture of all three. Here are several examples from Pliny. The editors of the translation are noted { }; author comments are [ ].

Chapter 2: When the First Wreaths of Corn Were Used at Rome

"Numa first established the custom of offering corn [grain] to the gods, and of propitiating them with the salted cake {eds. salt plus meal plus flour of *spelt*}; he was the first, took, as we learn from Hemina, to parch *spelt,* the fact that when in this state, it is more wholesome as an aliment [digestible]. This method, however, he could only

Drawing of *corona spicea,* the most ancient of wreaths. Worn by priests and high public figures when making the enactments (offerings) referred to by Pliny and others. In Roman times the offerings were to Ceres, goddess of agriculture and grain. The wreath was hung on her temple. The Grain Corona is still to be seen on everything from the facades of public buildings to flour sacks.

establish one way: by making an enactment, to the effect the *spelt* is not in a pure state of offering, except when parched." Chapter 2:2: "He it was, too, who instituted **fornicalia** [Feast of the Furnace or Oven], festivals appropriated for the parching of corn, and others observed with equal solemnity."

Chapter 3: The Jugerum of Land

"That portion of land used to be known as the *jugerum* which was capable of being ploughed by a single *jugum* or yoke of oxen, in one day; an *actus* being as much as the oxen could plow in a single spell ... the most considerable recompense that could be bestowed upon generals and valiant citizens was the utmost extent of land around which a person could trace a furrow with the plow in a single day. The whole population, too, used to contribute a quarter of a sextarious of *spelt* ... Even to glory itself, in compliment to conquest the name was given of *adorea* as the chief reward given to the conqueror, and his temples were graced with a wreath of corn."

Chapter 10: The History of the Various Kinds of Grain

"The cereals are divided again into the same number of varieties, according to the time of year at which they are sown. The winter grains are those which are put into the ground about the setting of the *Virgiliae* [Roman name for the Greeks' *Pleiades*, the daughters of Atlas], and there receive their nutriment throughout the winter, for instance, *wheat {triticum hibernum}, spelt,* and barley. ... Some authors give the name of spring grain to millet ... chick-peas, and *alica* {A variety of *spelt* was grown by this name; but it was more generally applied to a kind of flummery pottage or gruel.}

[The translators are referring to emmer.]

There is a translator's note at *spelt* in the above paragraph. "The word in original is *far.* This name is often used in the classics, to signify corn [grain] in general; but in the restricted sense in which it is employed here, it is *Triticum dicoccum,* the *Zea* of the Greeks. It consists of two varieties, the single grained, the *Triticum monococcum* of Linnaeus, which is still called *farra* in Friuli."

Chapter 11: Spelt

"Of all these grains barley is the lightest, its weight rarely exceeding fifteen pounds a modius, while that of the bean is twenty-two. *Spelt* is much heavier than barley, and *wheat* heavier than *spelt.* In Egypt they make a meal of olyra [*alura* is {meal meaning flour in this context}]. The Translator also goes on to say *olyra* is identified as *Triticum monococcum.*

The above passage gives you a good idea of the confusion of language and the tangled web of words. The translators mean "alura" which means "emmer". In the translator's notes it is identified as einkorn. Spelt is used here as the collective word meaning *Far,* which can mean emmer or Spelt, and sometimes einkorn.

Chapter 12: Wheat

"In Italy beyond the Padus [the Po River], the *spelt* to my knowledge, weighs twenty-five pounds to the modius ..."

The area he speaks of is the homeland of landraces of emmer today and further north are archaeological remains of Bronze Age Spelt. To which was he referring? The general view is Spelt disappeared in Italy circa 400 B.C. Pliny is reporting from the first century A.D. at a time when emmer was thought to have been widespread in Italy. Later in this passage, he talks about other regions to the north and different kinds of wheat. Thrace and the Balkans is where Neolithic occurrences of Spelt have been archaeologically recorded (2900 B.C. onward). Einkorn was also traditionally grown in the Balkan region of Transylvania and the Carpathian Mountains, near Sault in France, and in Switzerland and Germany.

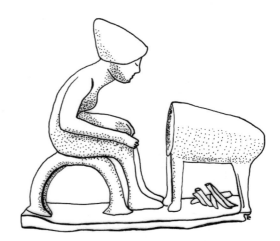

Illustration of 5th century B.C. terracotta from Boetia. Depicts woman baking in oven which is a large clay storage jar. Boetia was a breadbasket of ancient Greece.

Greek and Roman Cooking and References

It is through artifacts like cookbooks, especially one that had five printings during the late 15th and early 16th centuries that survived antiquity, that we have learned about Greek and Roman cooking. The most famous is *de re coquinaria* which is a compendium attributed to several authors named Apicius. The Apicius of Pliny's time (1st century A.D.) was Gavius Apicius, a gourmand, an epicurean in the original sense of the word as tales of him have been passed down to modern times and his recipes still appear in books.

Herbals and Medicine

Recipes are often found in Herbals, those wonderful compendiums of plant life and lore written through the ages, works such as *Materia Medica* written in the 1st century by the Roman, Dioscorides. His work influenced medical practitioners

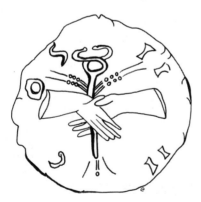

Drawing of Roman denarius from Latium depicting two ears of grain and a caduceus being clasped by two hands. Not just a symbol of medicine, the caduceus in ancient times also represented peace and well-being.

and cooks through the Renaissance. His information and that of others was incorporated in later Herbals such as Gerard's Herbal of 1597 who mentions Spelt. He was not the first to mention Spelt in connection with healing and herbal medicine.

Germany

Spelt has been grown in the southern part of Germany and adjoining areas for thousands of years. It was gradually replaced beginning about 1000 A.D. in favor of the free-threshing wheats. However, Spelt held on in particular places and it is evident in the names.

In Germany, *Spelt* is known generally as *Dinkel.* Other terms for Spelt include *Swabian Grain* or *Aleman Grain.* It was the main "wheat" in the southern part of Germany until the mid-19th century. It almost disappeared in the 1950s as a crop except for small fields kept for special purposes such as making Grünkern (roasted green Spelt) and beer.

Its history in the region is reflected by surnames and place names that include the words *dinkel* or *Spelt. Dinkel* is a last name from southern Germany and means a grain (Spelt) farmer. The surname *Spelz* is also derived from Spelt.

Dinkelsbuhl, a city since the 13th century, bears a coat of arms that has been in use since 1446 that bears three Spelt ears. The mounds on the coat of arms may be an allusion to mountains or the way Spelt was planted or its bundled root system but there is a remarkable similarity between this shield and a Greek coin of 42/43 A.D. as in the drawing on this page.

The last name of noted Carl Dinkelacker, who started the Dinkelacker Brewery (Brauerei Dinkelacker) in 1888, means "spelt field".

Hildegard of Bingen—Patron Saint of Spelt

Of all the gods and goddesses who were *adored* and people who wrote about Spelt in history, St. Hildegard of Bingen (b. 1098, d. 1179) deserves credit as being the Keeper of the Spelt tradition. She was canonized for many remarkable qualities. You can read about her on the multiple websites and books about this woman's remarkable life and the struggle of her order to remain alive. That communal struggle in some ways resembles the history of Spelt itself, which almost died out in the last century.

She was a woman ahead of her time and she lived in the one place where Spelt has been preserved through thousands of years of alternating plenty with war and famine and changing food fashions. Following is a quotation, taken from the German from her *Causa Medica*. You may find an analysis and deconstruction of the quotation on the purityfoods.com website.

"Spelt is the best grain, warming, lubricating and of high nutritional value. It is better tolerated by the body than any other grain. Spelt provides the consumer with good flesh and good blood and cofers a cheerful disposition. It provides a happy mind and a joyful spirit. No matter how you eat spelt, either as a bread or in other foods, it is good and easy to digest."

The Abbey produces the Spelt products from fields surrounding the Abtei at Rudesheim am Rhein. There are tours of the region, you can go to the Abbey and buy Spelt products from liquors to flour. This tradition of Spelt and monasteries and the production of spirits is a history in itself.

Grain Has Many Uses—Spelt and the Spirits

The liquors and bitters produced and sold at the Abbey of St. Hildegard are the continuation of long tradition. So is the

Comparison of 1st century A.D. Greek coin and the Dinkelsbuhl (14th century A.D.) coat of arms depicting Spelt that is still in use today.

wine and beer, especially in regional consumption and trade.

Wines in Antiquity

Vitus vinifera grew wild in the same place that Spelt was born—the Transcaucasus region. Enterprising ancient people took it and spread it so that by 3000 B.C. it was in the Fertile Crescent and in Egypt. By 1000 B.C. it was in the hands of the Greeks who later were the first to corner the fine wine market and then came the Romans.

Wines of antiquity were hot items in trade. Just as today, there were highly prized wines especially Greek varieties from regions such as Thrace and islands like Chios and Cos. In one such wine, Spelt would be formed into a dough using honey as a sweetener and binder. The bit of dough would be placed in a special cup, the *prytaneion,* and the wine poured over the dough. The dough would imbue the wine with the natural mild sweetness of the Spelt as well as the honey. Alternately, they worked wine into a delicate dough such as the Cannoli shells in *Spelt Healthy!*

Beer

It is difficult to say which came first: bread or beer. Beer is a food, a thin fermented high vitamin broth—or would have been in antiquity. The idea stayed around a long time. Drinking beer for health was a practice encouraged into the 1950s in the United States when doctors prescribed a bottle of beer, especially "Dutch" beer, a day for pregnant women as a way of supplying additional Vitamin B and others nutrients. Beer is still considered a food in some places. In antiquity, drinking beer was a way of slaking thirst and taking food and preserving food, not just a means of kicking back from the day's labor and watching the original Olympic Games.

A high percentage of grain grown through time was specifically grown for the purpose of making beer the same way grapes and berries have been used to make wine. In Sumer, almost half the barley crop went to beer. Of that beer, less than half was made with mixed grains. Beer made the right way keeps for months. Inside the jars or containers are yeasts that help ferment dough for bread. The foam or barm was the original yeast for leavening bread. The brewers were women and they, incidentally, became the dough makers, the men were the bakers.

Drawn from a bas relief of beer-drinking in Mesopotamia where the custom was to drink beer from a jar through long straws made of reeds.

A bison drinking horn from a Bronze Age bog in Northern Germany contained remnants of emmer beer. At Roman forts in the British Isles they were brewing beer from Spelt and emmer. The brew has been around probably since humans encountered grain.

Whole grain foods constituted the basic diet of most people in the Near East and Europe and required drinking much liquid to digest the grains. Beer and wine were perfect complements to whole grains. They also made it safe to drink some very bad water from canals, rivers or wells. It was also a highly digestible form of grain.

Beer continued to be ale until the time of St. Hildegard of Bingen, who was the inventor of the idea of adding hops to beer for flavor and preservation. She was also a person who believed highly in the benefits of Spelt in the diet for in her view it was the best of grains.

The connection between Spelt and beer is strong in Germany as indicated elsewhere in town names and the name of one of Germany's most famous breweries and its founder Carl Dinkelacker. Germany passed a Beer Purity law, the *Reinheitsgebot*, in 1516, for the purpose of insuring beers contain only barley, hops and water (and yeast). The only exception to that law was an amendment to it, which allowed Southern Germany to brew their wheat beers. That law is in effect today and some of the "wheat" is Spelt.

Dinkel Acker Dunkel is a Spelt beer. Benediktinerabtei Plankstetten is another Spelt beer, one grown at the Abbey for which the beer is named. 5-Korn Ur Bier

is beer made from Spelt, emmer, einkorn, modern wheat and barley. Riedenburger Edel is made with einkorn. Johaness Limbrunner has made a beer from emmer (grown in Italy) and barley malt. It is called Keltisches Emmerbier.

Making specialty German beer now extends to Japan. Christian Mitterbauer manages the Kowedo Brewery. He is a fourth generation Bavarian brew-master. He creates his own specialties such as apple beer for the Japanese but also oversees brewing of the venerable German beers including Weizen, Pilsner and Dinkel (Spelt) beers.

In France at the micro-brewery of Brasserie de Silenrieux, a Spelt beer is being brewed by Eric Bedoret. Called Joseph Spelt Ale, it is certified organic. It is interesting to note it won a prize in Belgium, where beer

Illustration of ancient terracotta from Boetia, Greece. It shows women mixing/kneading dough while a man forms it. This artifact is in keeping with the custom of men being the professional bakers in Ancient Greece/Rome continuing into later times (see Middle Ages roundel in Introduction). Drawing of Egyptian bread-baking scene (see Records from Biblical Times section) also depicts men as bakers.

is considered food, thus when he won a prize for Joseph Spelt Ale it was in the *Other Food Products* competition.

Hulled Grains as Livestock Feed

Modern consumers have little to do with farming nowadays so it may be hard to imagine that the hulls in particular of the Big Three grains have been used through time as a source of quality food for ruminants and poultry. (See coin with horse and wheat earlier.) The stalks are used for fodder and bedding. In the United States farmers fed Spelt to draft horses—the animals that pulled the plow and did the heavy lifting. You still see these horses on particular beer commercials. There is a relationship. If you go to the Berlin Bakery website (Appendix 2) you will see draft horses in use on Spelt farms.

One of the major reasons the hulled grains survived into the present day is because of their continued use as animal feed, a principal use through time especially of emmer and einkorn. Feeding alternative grains to livestock is increasingly the subject of research (e.g. Stallknecht, Kling) because these grains are eco-friendly (wide range of environments plus little need for additional fertilizers) and provide excellent nourishment during the growth period. This type of research is not the kind that filters down to the average consumer—except in the quality of food you eat. It matters because we are what *they* eat, even with cheese. For example, Parmigiana Reggiano is the treasured product it is because these rare-breed cattle eat a particular kind of grass.

The word *farrago* mentioned by Pliny (above) was exactly in the context of animal feed: fodder. One researcher found an ancient stand of einkorn in Castelfranco, situated in the Appenine Mountains of Italy. It was still being grown because it was considered quality pig food "as on einkorn they were supposed to be healthy, grow fast and have shiny bristle hide" (Darzau, nd). In the Asturian example earlier, it is clear the hulls were fed to animals, the finer flour kept for human consumption and even then the flours had different uses—from coarse emmer *focaccia* to fine Spelt *escanda*.

Dante's Inferno—Hard Times

Famine and grain are linked to survival throughout human history. The first civilizations (Mesopotamia, Egypt) combined temples with warehouses to store and allot grain. Securing grain has always been a driving force of governments.

The Middle Ages in Europe was a hard time for peasants and urban dwellers alike, a time of political turmoil and food shortages, especially grain. A man involved in those politics, a man from the region where Farro is still grown, wrote (1306–1321) one of literature's most exemplary works, *Dante's Divine Comedy*. Dante Alighieri (b. 1265, d. 1321) of Tuscany did not write in Latin. He wrote his book using courtly language and regional dialects of his time. It was a time when population was growing so rapidly it outstripped the food supply and exactly while he was writing nothing mattered more than an assured supply of grain.

Drawing from an illustration of a medieval view of provisioning Rome with grain during a famine in the 5th century B.C. It is a "fanciful" view of Rome with castles but people drew what they knew—the subject was serious as people from ancient times and through the Middle Ages in Europe suffered repeated famines.

In Tuscany, agriculture was pushed up the slopes of the Appenines where native stands of hulled grains are being grown today. Spelt's important qualities were well-known. Spelt is immortalized by Dante in Canto XIII (Inferno) (Alighieri, 1950:73).

> "When the fierce spirit quits the body, from which it has torn itself, Minos sends it to the seventh gulf. It falls into the wood, and no place is chosen for it but wherever fortune flings it, there it sprouts; like grain of spelt."

One of the qualities of Spelt that has made it a favored cultivar is its hardiness, that ability to withstand the rigors of a variety of environments especially the extremes. Here is a literary testament to its remarkable quality. Alighieri likely observed the plant, the grain in 14th century

Tuscany, in the hills, the marketplace. He would no doubt have heard of its merits from the many people involved in the trade of grain to the north of Italy. That trade in grain was the European economic engine of his age and grain has many uses.

The relationship between wheat, food, famine, death is seen in the Holkham illuminated manuscript (Oxford) of the *Divine Comedy*. In the Canto XIII illuminated picture, the same where Spelt is mentioned, there are harpies, demons that punish by snatching food away as they did to Phineus in the Argonauts, in the wood.

The Language of Celebration: I ADORE THEE, OH, COME LET US ADORE HIM and Celebration Always Means Feasting

From 500 B.C. through the present, writers have referred to *Spelt* in a variety of ways: *ador, adora, alica, alura, far, farris, farrago* to the *spelta* and *farro* of the early Middle Ages to the Linnaean classification system, *Triticum spelta L.,* in use today. The word, *Spelt,* today is a reflection of changing times. Where once people grew these grains out of necessity and had a multitude of uses for them, who knew them intimately, through time the free-threshing wheats replaced them, certainly in the popular vocabulary, with the collective "Spelt" or German "Dinkel". For example, each of the words cited at the outset has specific meanings based on category of use such as an offering *(ador)* to *farrago* (animal fodder) to *alica* (finely sifted Spelt for delicacies, semolina) or *far* as porridge or *alura* the Egyptian wheat, emmer, for bread or beer.

Emmer and Spelt have always been associated with religion and mythology. Witness Isis of the Egyptians and the Mesopotamians (above in Writing Things Down). The first coins, first Sumer, then Greece, had the image of emmer and Spelt stamped on them. The hulled grains meant life. It is no wonder they were used in offerings.

One of the first and important uses of the hulled grains was in offerings, as in the quotations from Pliny. The word "adore" means the hulled grains. The wreath that still adorns (from *ador*) our public buildings was emmer or Spelt. The victor was given a field (the *jugerum* above in Pliny) and portions of Spelt. It is interesting that *ador* as an offering comes into romantic/chivalric poetry and songs during the Middle Ages in phrases such as "I adore thee" and into the language

of the Church in carols, such as "Oh, come all ye Faithful ... Let us adore him." *Far* is also cause for celebration for in the earliest English/Italian dictionary (1611) *farnatale* means to keep "Christmasse" and "Farneticanza," meaning adoring. It is associated with feasting and abundance. But what is what? Or which is which, emmer, Spelt or einkorn or farro? They are all adored. The story continues.

Farro: That Marvelous Medley of Meanings

Three centuries passed between Dante's reference to Spelt in the book that helped create the Italian language that we know today and the first Italian/English dictionary. The language is an artifact of culture like the Spelt that survived the

Illustration of Corinthian Greek coin circa 5th century B.C. with the goddess Demeter as Athena. On coin is a horn of plenty (cornucopia) containing grain, over which Demeter ruled. Grain was *the* staple; obtaining it was cause for trade, war and territorial expansion as populations grew.

Illustration of Roman coin minted after 27 B.C. by Augustus Caesar. "Augustus" means exalted one, someone adored, as was the goddess of agriculture and grain, Ceres. Grain was exalted; it was life. Both the horn of plenty and grain bundles are associated with feasting, abundance and celebration as in the familiar Thanksgiving horn of plenty in the United States.

Middle Ages grown in places such as Belgium, Germany, Switzerland and adjacent Alpine regions. Spelt is in the first dictionary of Italian/English languages and so is *far* and *farro* (Florio's 1611 *Dictionarie of the Italian and English Tongue*). The world was changing quickly in the 16th century—wars, plagues, discovery of a new world—yet words relating to Spelt, emmer and einkorn remained:

Adoreo, a red bearded wheat, so called in old times

Adorea, the glory and honor belonging to corn [grain] in general

Alica, as Alga

Alga, sea-grass, reete, rites. Also Ducke-weede. Also *Spelt-corne*

Alicastro, the wheat called *Far*

Farina, all manner of meale or flower

Farinaccia, any course meal

Farinaccio, made of meal

Farinaio, Farinaro, a meale-man. Also a hutch or bin to keep meale in

Farinaiuolo, a Miller or Meale-man

Farinare, to be -meale or be -flowre

Farinolo, mealy, flowry, that hath meale in it

Farraina, a mash made of divers sortes of graines together for a sick horse

Farro, Spelt-corne or Beere-barly. Also a kind of wheat or furmenty to make pottage of

Farro adoreo, a kind of red wheat

You will find no semolina (fine flour *alica* made of Spelt of Roman times, now made with Durum not *spelta L. or emmer finely sifted*) but you will find:

Semola, bran or grets of corne

Semolato, course, unbolted [unsifted] or brannie bread

Semolalla, fine bran. Also a kind of pudding made from coarse meal

Semolofo, brannie, course, full of bran

I said at the outset this is a tangled web of words. Let us go to some age old practices of mixing things in the field and in the kitchen for a better understanding.

At the very well documented site of Assiros Toumba in Greece, archaeologists found Spelt, emmer and einkorn. Spelt was the dominant crop followed by emmer and to a much smaller extent einkorn. Einkorn is a smaller grain. People at Assiros Toumba seem to have been growing the Big Three as a maslin crop. Maslin means mixed. In this context it was probably purposeful, meaning they were not in there as weeds but intentionally planted. Each of those grains likely had different uses, for example, livestock, whole grain and porridge, and flour. Here archaeology, material examples of past practices and languages, are directly connected.

Take a close look at Pliny more than a thousand years later in Rome (Chapter 10: The History of the Various Kinds of Grains) who also speaks of this practice of mixing grains:

"Certain species of wheat are only sown to make fodder for cattle, and are known by the name of farrago, or mixed grain. ..."

Farrago continues into the English and other Romantic languages today. Only recently, I saw the word used in a French newspaper article in reference to a mystery.

In English, *farrago* means mixed fodder for cattle or a mixture or medley. The roots of the word are from *far, farris, spelt.*

In Medieval times, *maslin* was the category for the all-round coarse breads, made from mixed grains such as Spelt and rye. These breads were also turned into very hard trenchers. Trenchers were both bowl and plate, because people ate things, like salted or decomposing meat, with much gravy. This is the non-porcelain, non-metal dinnerware you see in early illuminated manuscripts depicting feasting or meals at the "high table".

Trenchers were likewise the first cereal "doggie bones" since they were thrown on the floor with the table scraps. (See Appendix 2—Spelt products for Spelt Doggie treats.) The finer breads were made from "semolina" or finely sifted bread flour, the creamier colored or whiter the better like the Pao Doce in this book or the delicacy *escanda* breads of Asturias where maslin crops of mostly Spelt and a lesser amount of emmer are occasionally grown. *Escanda* traditionally means either emmer or Spelt. It is a category like *farro,* and like *farro,* it may represent the different uses of each grain.

Well, haven't I just clarified *farro* for you! It gets better. There is great debate among scholars today whether *far, farro* originally referred to emmer or Spelt (and maybe einkorn too) or if it could refer to either one or all three depending on its use as with the maslin crops and maslin bread mentioned above.

In 2005, no less a source than the official website of the Italian Trade Commission, the Italian government's agency for trade, uses *Spelt* for *farro* on its site. On a link from their site, you will find information for the Comunita Montana della Garfagnana, Tuscany, which is the *epicenter* in Italy for the revival of the Big Three hulled grains. Garfagnana's information can be viewed by going italianmade.com. Enter the key word "Garfagnana" and go to the Region of Tuscany. Under Garfagnana, you will see these words: Farro della Garfagnana (IGP).

Then you will read that in Garfagnana Spelt has been grown since antiquity. The Spelt is listed as *Triticum dicoccum.*

The Spelt mentioned, however, is emmer. (Cultivated emmer is *Triticum dicoccum.*)

So if you are touring Italy, you visit Tuscany, the likelihood is high you will be eating emmer *farro* soup. Then again, you may be eating Spelt *(Spelta L.)* farro soup or bread or other foods a few miles down the road. A little further on, your soup, bread or snack may be a mixture of all three—Spelt, emmer, einkorn with a little modern wheat thrown into the mixture.

Mixture.

Farrago.

Farro.

Farro is a collective word that can mean one or all: Spelt, emmer, einkorn. It usually refers to Spelt or emmer.

Farro In Modern Times and You, the Consumer

The nutritional profiles of each of these grains are similar but not the same. Which one is just right? It depends on the use to which you want to put it.

Einkorn is the smallest and the oldest of these grains, which is why einkorn is sometimes called *Farro Piccolo.* (See einkorn, emmer, Spelt illustration in Chapter 1.) Emmer is larger than einkorn and is sometimes called *lesser spelt* as in the case of matzah reference. Emmer is also referred to as the rice grain as in Orzo, the wheat that resembles a grain of rice, made with semolina. (Modern semolina is made from Durum wheat, a hexaploid relative of the Big Three, one of the first bread flours to come into cultivation and closest of all to Spelt.) Spelt is larger still. Of the three, Spelt is considered to have the best bread making properties with respect to extensibility and fineness and lightness of flour. Taste is in the eye of the beholder.

The fact that I am able to write about these magnificent ancient grains is because of the effort that people have made to see them resurrected. They were almost gone, extinct, foooof, like the dodo bird and the Neanderthals who roamed the lands where Spelt first came to be grown. I am grateful to farmers who fed einkorn to their pigs in a hidden valley in the Appenines and to the myriad others in the recent past who said, "Let's preserve these grains that are the collective heritage of Western Civilization."

The reason for this section on the Tangled Web of Words is to convey to you how intertwined Spelt, emmer and einkorn are with life and how it is expressed through language and custom.

It is also to tell you that many types of *farro* are now being planted each year and sold to consumers worldwide. It comes in a variety of forms but its uses are what they were in the past: human consumption, animal feed and beer. Many new human uses are being created each year like Pop Farro and Farro Nuts.

The types of *farro* range from pure and ancient landraces to modern crosses or mixtures with modern wheats. There is much research being done on Spelt and the other hulled grains in order to assure baking and nutritional quality and purity (non-mixture with other grains such as modern wheat) because the two—quality and purity—are related. There is also the conservation effort of ensuring that the genomics of ancient strains remain intact so the qualities that made these grains the basis of Western Civilization are not lost.

This effort of assuring baking quality is reflected in the choice of seed. Some farmers use foundation stock for their seed. This is seed farmers buy from a certified source and plant anew each year to assure the grain has the desired characteristics. It goes through a certification process that proves the purity of the grain. For example, of all the types of hulled wheats now raised in Europe and exported, only a few are

currently registered and they are all *spelta
L.* Another example closer to home, Lentz
Farms, producer of all three of the ancient
grains, prints right on their bags of Emmer-
Farro that it is grown from foundation seed
so you know it is only emmer.

I have based the recipes in this book
on *Spelta L.* with some exceptions, all of
which I have noted in the recipe section of
Spelt Healthy! The purpose of explaining
about farro is to help you become more
discriminating as a consumer. It is a different
thing to eat *farro* soup in Tuscany than to
cook and bake with Spelt consistently at
home. Know when you are eating Spelt,
emmer, or einkorn or a mixture of all three.
Each has different qualities, which will affect
cooking and baking properties and taste.

PART III
SPELTA'S PLACE FOR
EVERY DAY FINE FOOD

Chapter 1
Whole Food Cooking and Baking with Spelt—
It's a Natural

Some Basic Ingredients in *Spelt Healthy!*
Quality Foods

Chapter 2: What's On the Menu at Spelta's
Place? The Recipes at a Glance

Chapter 1: Whole Food Cooking and Baking with Spelt—It's a Natural

> **WHOLE FOOD IS AUTHENTIC FOOD.**
> **IT IS WHAT IT IS PURPORTED TO BE.**
> **THAT IS ITS LINK TO HISTORY AND**
> **THAT IS ITS INESTIMABLE VALUE**
> **TO US IN THE 21ST CENTURY.**

Whole food comes in its natural wrapper. You can tell by looking what it is, from a grain of Spelt to a watermelon. It is identifiable even if minimally processed. For example, White Spelt Flour is unbleached, unbromated and unenriched. When one cooks with whole foods like spinach, goat's milk, yogurt, onions, honey, blueberries and Spelt, there are no additives or preservatives to confuse the flavor. These are nutrient rich foods whose natural pure flavors—not artificial additives—imbue the food with goodness and life.

Spelt Healthy! is an uncomplicated way to cook; the goal is preservation of nutrients; fine, fresh taste; a variety of textures; and a wide menu of nutritious, delicious choices. Many herbs go into *Spelt Healthy!* fare as do fresh vegetables and fruits in season. You will find olive oil throughout *Spelt Healthy!* because of its complementary taste and varieties, its freshness and methods of production.

There are two other threads also woven into the book, a design for the millions of people following blood type eating and managing Type 2 diabetes or other impediments to health through nutrition and exercise. This is what accounts for the prevalence of Mozzarella and the sheep and goat cheeses and yogurt throughout *Spelt Healthy!*

It is not that I am unaware of the many fine cheeses available. They are among my favorite foods. It is because there are many types of cheese that are not recommended, or encouraged, for people who follow the aforementioned (or other) eating plans. You can substitute your favorite cheese in most any *Spelt Healthy!* recipe.

As with cheese, there are some popular vegetables and meats, which do not appear as major ingredients in the recipes of this book. Among them are the "white" potato, corn and pork. Instead, I encouraged other foods such as substituting zucchini fries in place of French fries; sweet potatoes instead of white potatoes or shredded Dried Sweet Potato in place of coconut. The idea of *Spelt Healthy!* is to offer delicious, healthful alternatives to common foods as you are cooking and baking with Spelt.

Blood Type Notations and Nutrition Information

For those people following Blood Type Eating (BTE) plans, you will find BTE notations on the recipe pages. Some recipes are not rated for BTE because of conflicts inherent in the recipe and substitutions are not feasible.

To help you plan your menus, Nutrition Information for the recipes is all contained in *Appendix 1*. The information includes Calories, Calories from Fat, Total Fat, Saturated Fat, Cholesterol, Sodium, Total Carbohydrate, Dietary Fiber and Protein and percentages of calories from Fat, Carbohydrates and Protein. Flavorings like Vanilla and Almond are not factored into the Nutrition Information.

Some Basic Ingredients in *Spelt Healthy!* Quality Foods

Oils

All fat is not bad; in fact, it is critical to the functioning of the body. The first choice of oil in almost all of the recipes in the book is olive oil. Of all the oils, it is the highest in monounsaturated fat and contains essential Omega-3 fatty acids. It is excellent for the digestive system.

Like Spelt, olive oil comes in different "flavors" and uses from Extra Virgin for marinating and dressing to Extra Light for frying. At this Light end of the flavor spectrum, olive oil is mild and slightly sweet in taste in the range of Canola but far less flat. Spanish olive oil, for example, is slightly nutty and sweet like Spelt so it is complementary. The olive oils are like wine, they vary from region to region which is one of its benefits to a fresh, whole food cuisine.

Honey

In ancient times, honey was called the dew distilled from rainbows. You will see honey in a variety of recipes, for example, Hais, and as a spread on waffles, pancakes, bread or mixed with yogurt. Like domestic livestock, humans ultimately domesticated honeybees. They came to the New World after 1492 with things like wheat. Bees pollinate our domestic crops from almonds and apples to tomatoes, our flowers and many other plants, too.

Honey is a preservative, and it is a binder along with being the original sweetener. Honey comes in many colors and flavors from deep dark tones to spicy to the light, delicate honeys bees make from the pollen of so many things—orange blossoms to raspberries to thyme.

Goat's Milk and Goat's Milk Yogurt

Goats and sheep were the first animals domesticated by humans as livestock. This occurred about the time Spelt was born. In the United States, we tend to think of milk as coming from cows because that is our agricultural tradition. Goats have often been given a bad rap, like "Oh, goat milk is too

strong." It is a story from the past. Modern dairy goat practices have given us sweet, reliable products from milk to yogurt to cheese and ice cream.

I have raised goats (Saanen, Nubian and Alpine) and admit my cooking and baking bias. In an earlier section, I mentioned my mother survived her early years on a cow dairy farm by being fed goat's milk because she lacked a lactodigesting enzyme. Beyond personal preference, I am partial to goat's milk products and these are some of the reasons why:

* No additional treatment is required to homogenize goat's milk. It comes naturally homogenized meaning the fat particles do not have to be heated and broken up.

* The structure of the fat is different than cow's milk which makes the fat particles in goat's milk easier to disperse in the body. They do not clump or agglutinate like milk, hence goat's milk does not cream well—it also does not block your arteries well.

* Goat's milk has chemical qualities (for example, Capric, Caprylic, Caproic acids all named from Capra or goat) that diminish fatty liver syndrome, a real problem in diabetes and other diseases. These same acids are all being used in treating diseases from Cystic Fibrosis to coronary disease.

* The protein in goat's milk is more easily digestible meaning it is less work for the body.

* It is higher in Vitamins A and B— especially riboflavin, B6 and B12—and is higher in niacin than cow's milk. It is also higher in magnesium, manganese, calcium, potassium and phosphorus.

* It has greater buffering (pH) ability which makes it a better choice for people with gastric ulcers.

* It reduces infant colic and possibly dairy allergies as well.

It makes high quality unadulterated yogurt that is great for marinating, eating fresh or cooking because goat's milk yogurt does not clabber at temperature the way that cow's milk yogurt does.

In *Spelt Healthy!* recipes goat's milk is the first choice of yogurts because of its taste and purity. You will find it in recipes from Soft Cheese Spread to Pound Cake. There are many good, plain goat's milk yogurts available in stores along side other goat's milk products such as creamy Chevres cheese. Plain goat's milk yogurt does not contain additives or sugars for preservation.

Nuts

Again, fat is necessary for the body to function. Humankind evolved eating a variety of nuts, a nutrient dense class of foods that are high in protein, fiber, manganese, magnesium, phosphorus and zinc. Nuts are integral to many recipes in *Spelt Healthy!* particularly walnuts, almonds, pistachios and pine nuts—all part of diets in antiquity. Such nuts are high in Vitamin E, they contain no cholesterol but do contain essential Omega-3 fatty acids.

Nuts provide the *crunch* factor, something modern snack foods were designed to satisfy. Nuts have long been used in whole form but also as oil and flour so you will find them as a portion of the flour or grain in recipes such as Choco Spiced Dainties (cookie) and ground in Coated Pan Fried Fish Fillets. In the new Diet Pyramid, they are a replacement for meat in small quantities at a ratio of ⅓ cup of nuts equals 1 ounce of meat.

Fruit

Many recipes in this book make use of fresh fruit in season such as raspberries, blueberries, cranberries and cherries. Their season is now year round because of freezing and drying. Just a few years ago, cranberries were only available during the holiday season, now they are available fresh-frozen or in snack bags year round. The whole range of dried fruits is expanding rapidly. They are the original sweet dessert yet are "good" sweets full of fiber and nutrients such as Vitamin C and potassium. Many recipes in *Spelt Healthy!* use fruits, for example, Cherry Almond Biscotti and Cherried Plum Bread.

Blue Eyes? Researchers are looking into the blueberry's store of anthocyanins as a means of improving vision. Blueberries are high in iron, potassium, Vitamin C and antioxidants and are a boon to any cook because of their baking properties from sprinkling on Athena Crepes to adding to Blueberry Coffeecake.

Cranberries lower the risk of kidney and bladder infections because of their tannins; they are bacteria fighters that may prove valuable against periodontal disease and ulcers.

Cherries. We often take medicine to counter inflammation and pain. As with Spelt, almonds and turkey products, cherries, especially tart cherries, contain higher amounts of the essential amino acid, Tryptophane (see *Why Choose Spelt?*) which produces the neurotransmitter serotonin. It induces level moods and quality sleep, one of the most important factors in good health along with good nutrition, exercise and water.

Soy

Soy is an alternative liquid in some recipes for those who believe in its efficacy and do not take dairy. It is a highly genetically modified and refined food product. Soy has come to replace some of the older traditional and more nutritious sweet liquids such as almond milk.

Notes on Some of the Spices and Seasonings and Their Healthful Properties

The science of Phytochemicals and Micronutrients is in its infancy (see "Phytochemicals" in *The Vegetable Stand* section). This is the study of what researchers currently consider "non-nutritive" plant chemicals. As with fruit and other whole foods, these chemical compounds are medicinal along with tasting good. Here are some examples:

Turmeric. You will find it featured, for example, in the Spelt Rotini Salad. This is a "feel good" herb that is a strong antioxidant, it aids digestion, and is a natural anti-inflammatory like tart cherries. It has a slightly zingy taste that can substitute for cayenne for those of you who cannot eat the capsicum peppers.

Cayenne and the Capsicums. These are the New World peppers, the familiar red chile rastras of Santa Fe, the Enchilada Sauce Sabrosa in this book. The hot capsicums are loaded with Vitamin C and antioxidants such as beta-carotene. Researchers are beginning to find what chili-heads have known all along; they relieve congestion often brought on by allergies and they may help prevent heart problems. Capsaicin, the chemical that makes chiles hot, is an anticoagulant and an anti-inflammatory. Chiles contain bioflavinoids that may be responsible for reducing risks of various types of cancer.

Ginger. The list is long about ginger's known benefits including its ability to neutralize stomach acid and relieve nausea. It is used in the non-drowsy formulas for motion sickness. It reduces inflammation especially associated with rheumatoid arthritis. It is a natural antihistamine and decongestant.

Some of the Vegetables and Herbs—No Longer in the Realm of Folk Medicine

Spinach. Throughout the book, *spinach* is featured in recipes from Spinach Pesto to Florentine Topping for Bagels to a bedding for Turkey or Chicken Toscano. It is a staple in *Spelt Healthy!* cooking for its wide and fresh availability, its high folic acid (B9) and beta-carotene content and other cancer-reducing properties.

Rosemary is related to Marjoram, another frequent herb in this book. Rosemary is replete with antioxidants and antimicrobials that make it effective against bronchial asthma, afflictions of the elimination system, ulcers and inflammation. It is one of the great herbs of antiquity, valued for its flavor, its natural preservative (antimicrobial) properties and health benefits. In Roman times, it was used in the treatment of wounds.

Garlic. It is used frequently in recipes not just for its taste. Garlic controls blood sugar and protects against coronary diseases. It lowers bad cholesterol and is an anti-inflammatory.

Onions and Shallots. Garlic and onions were paired in antiquity for more than reasons of flavor. Like garlic, onions fight bacteria, reduce cancer risks and diabetes because of both increasing HDL and lowering LDL cholesterol.

Instead of White Potatoes

The Sweet Potato is not just a substitute; it is a wonderful food in itself. It is naturally sweet and does not require the heavy syrup and marshmallows of many T-Day feasts. It is an anti-diabetic food because it stabilizes blood sugar. It is also high in antioxidants (Vitamins B6 and C) and combats Emphysema through its Vitamin A properties. You will find a recipe for Shredded Dried Sweet Potatoes. Try it instead of coconut for a delightful fresh taste and fiber in muffins, cookies such as the Back to Basics Cookie and in quick breads.

Chapter 2: What's On the Menu at Spelta's Place? The Recipes at a Glance

Hello and Welcome to Spelta's Place

I designed the recipes in *Spelt Healthy! Quality Whole Food Cooking and Baking with Spelt* to help you turn your kitchen into an international food bazaar, a place where you will find a delicatessen, a bakery, your favorite restaurants or cafés. It is a place where you make foods for eating in or taking out; for a picnic, a little box lunch for the office or a lunchbox for your kids; foods for a hike, a bike ride or a journey. This is a fine, great place where you create what you will. I call it Spelta's Place. It is open for business all hours with a menu to match.

American cuisine is global because of increasing travel and work abroad. Even more, America is a land of immigrants. We brought, and bring, our customs and food preferences with us, and continue to make America the most exciting, vibrant and eclectic place to eat in the world. That is why Tod Mun Pla and Char Shiu Bao and Pita and Minestrone de Farro appear in the same cookbook.

Despite the travel, we still retain traditional and regional foods. That is

why you will find centuries-old American standards such as real old-fashioned Pumpkin Pie, a rich, dense, deep and spicy pie not a frothy confection. American Apple Pie is a reflection of our agrarian past. There are regional favorites like Beignes and Stuffed Portabella Mushrooms from New Orleans, Chiles Rellenos and Enchiladas from the Southwest, Collard Greens and Turkey Ham Soup with Dumplings from the southern hinterland, the Water Bagels of the eastern U.S. and Ebelskivers from the snowy north. All these mingle with varied and far older traditions from the Baked Empanadas (meat pies) of Spain and the Mediterranean to Hais, the ancient travelers' food from the deserts of Southwest Asia. The recipes encompass the world of the ancient grain *Spelt*.

Spelt Healthy! is arranged in the following way, more like a delicatessen menu than a traditional cook book. A "map" of Spelta's Place follows the Table of Contents to help you visualize where things are in the book.

The Morning Menu: Breakfast/Brunch

Americans are "morning food" eaters. It is just that we eat these foods at different times of the day and night. At Spelta's Place, you will find the Morning Menu arranged this way:

What we call breakfast cereal may be the oldest form of cooking; they still come first. Each year our Spelt choices are expanding. In *Hot and Cold Cereals* section are some of the basics.

Athena Crepes, Spelt Sproutcakes, Pancakes, Ebleskivers with suggestions for fresh fruit toppings and Waffles from Whole Grain to Chocolate.

Baking Powder Biscuits for breakfast or Breakfast Biscuits to Go; Rosemary and Cheese Biscuits for dinner, easy shortcake for fresh fruit in season desserts.

Eggs in a Tart Shell and Eggs from Quiche and Frittata to Mexican favorites like Chiles Rellenos and Huevos Rancheros made with your own Spelt tortillas.

Fruit Empanadas. These baked fruit turnovers enjoyed a long tradition in the Mediterranean before they reached Mexico where the pineapple of the Philippines joined in Mexico with wheat flour that came from Europe. Try the Apple or the Raspberry with soft goat cheese.

New Braunfels, Texas Custard Toast, French-toast American style.

Cheese and Pineapple Danish Modern, is a whole new Cheese Danish pastry delight.

Beignes, those wonderful New Orleans style doughnuts. In the Southwest they are sopaipillas.

Bagels. Water Bagels from plain to topped with Feta, Spinach and Pine Nuts to Sprouted Wheat Bagels.

Carns English Muffins that peel apart and freeze exceptionally well so you can take them out for the morning rush hour or a leisurely brunch, or Sweet Muffins with Crunchy Topping, mouthwatering and tender delights.

Spelta's Cinnamon Rolls ... that are so very succulent along with the sweet crunchy Pistachio Sticky Buns.

Scones. From Cranberry to Maple to Blueberry Lemon, you will find scones and Lemon Shorties in the Afternoon Tea or Coffee Break section of Spelta's Place

Toast of the Day? There are so many from which to choose. Visit the *Bakery*. A Beginning Loaf is small and slightly sweet, Auld Lang Syne Bread makes excellent raisin toast. Try the Speltessence or Spelt Wheat Berry and Honey breads as well. Why not Zucchini or Carrot Nut from the *Bread Basket* section?

The Bakery

In *The Bakery* expect to find an assortment of breads to suit many tastes and traditions. The breads are arranged according to the method used to make them. The flatbreads such as pizza, calzones, and pita are in the *Many Small Things* section.

Direct Method of Making Breads. All of the ingredients are mixed at one time and go through the traditional rising and baking steps and many are baked in pans to give them form unless making rolls or loaves such as baguettes. Here you will find

A Beginning Loaf, Speltessence, No-Knead Molasses & Spelt, Cardamom Gold Pumpkin Bread, Classic White Spelt, Traditional Feast Rolls and forms, Brundisi Pesto Bread and Rolls, French Bread, Breadsticks and Rolls, Dark Rye and Challah. The Sweet Doughs are here too: Brioche and Pao Doce (Massa Sovada or Portuguese Sweet Bread). The goodies from the Morning Menu— Cinnamon Rolls, Pistachio Sticky Buns and the Danish (made with the Auld Lang Syne Bread recipe) are Direct Method doughs as well. You may be surprised at how little time these breads take because you are working with Spelt.

Indirect Method (Sponge/Biga).

These are the "ferments" where a portion of the liquid and flour are combined and chemical reactions begun prior to inclusion in the dough to give the bread taste, texture and keeping properties. It is an ancient method of working with heavier flours. The bread is made in stages not all at once which is why it is called "indirect". The dough is developed through fermentation as opposed to kneading and you do little work. This way of making bread is intermediate between direct method and sourdough. Here you will find Spelt Wheat Berry & Honey Bread and Light Rye. This is also the Rustic Bread place to go for making "free-form" breads—the boules, rounds, torpedo shapes, and wheels. Here you will find Roman Bread/Focaccia Rounds, Compocosenza Country Wheel, All-Purpose Italian Biga/Dough, Roasted Garlic and Mozzarella Cheese Baguettes, Medi Crostini and Pan Andrea Festival and Wedding Bread/Wheel.

Bread Machine Recipes. You will

find several moist and tasty recipes in the book for bread machine recipes like the outstanding Seattle Supreme Sandwich Loaf, Speltessence and a terrific Rosemary Cheese Bread. However, the cycles of current home bread-makers are not designed for Spelt, which mixes differently and has a far shorter rising/proofing time than do breads made from common wheat. I know there are many good recipes out there that combine Spelt with other flours in Bread Machine recipes to make satisfactory loaves. *Spelt Healthy!* uses only Spelt combined with itself in different flour forms or by adding Spelt berries or sprouts. There are only a few exceptions such as rye breads or products made from emmer/farro. You pay a premium for Spelt and buy it for nutritional or gourmet properties, neither of which is fully realized in current bread machines. It seems only natural to bring Spelt breads to their full potentials outside the breadmaker.

What to Do With Bits of Bread...

Croutons and Crumbs is a section in *The Bakery*. There are so many ways to cook and bake with Spelt and these are some of the staple ingredients in everything from Oven Baked Fish Fillets with Crunch Lemon Herb Topping to croutons for Caesar Salad. Right behind it you will find savory Spelt Dressing/Stuffing and Stuffing Sticks that are easy to make, delicious with many dishes and a great means of portion control.

The Bread Basket

These are the traditional Quick or Batter breads, leavened with baking powder or soda. These are excellent breads for serving with fruit or a turkey/chicken salad, for taking with you for lunch or for tea in the afternoon. These are the classic Bridge Party and Luncheon breads and simple, lovely, late evening treats.

The Cherried Plum Bread is one of the most fragrant of breads imaginable—while it is baking and on the tongue. The Blueberry and Whole Grain Spelt Coffeecake with Crumble Topping is one of the easiest and best ways to start with Spelt. It can be made with Whole Grain or in mixtures of the other Spelt flours, each providing a slightly different taste and texture. It is always a hit. Dove's Farm Soda Bread is also a good place to start. It is not the dry, extraordinarily crumbly, hard bread you get so often. It is a shiny boule with that slightly salty taste you expect and goes just right with stews and soup—and it can be on your table in an hour from start to finish. The Carrot Nut Bread is sweet sunshine and the Spelt Gingerbread is "the kind" and no longer a memory of times gone by. The Chocolate Variety Bread is velvet, rich and fine with zucchini or bananas. When you bite into the Zucchini Bread you have the sensation of sweet crunch in the thin crust with complex flavor and texture inside.

Sandwiches, Subs, Panini and Other Grilled Sandwiches

Imagine the things you can make from the breads from your Spelt Bakery!

Patty Melt on Rye made from Dark or Light Spelt Rye.

Hamburger, Hot Dog or Sausage Buns made from a variety of Spelt breads from the Classic White Spelt, Speltessence, French Bread, and All-Purpose Italian breads or some that may be new to you.

Hoagies and Subs from the French or All-Purpose Italian Biga Recipe. The basic "torpedo" form or French roll form is perfect for the Classic Meatball sandwich (see the Mighty Meatball below for a Classic Meatball).

Deli Sandwiches, Open-Faced Panini or Other Grilled Sandwiches. Try making them with Roasted Garlic and Mozarella Baguettes or Bâtards. The Pesto Bread is perfect.

Rolls, Bowls, Brioches, Wraps.

Try the Brundisi Pesto Rolls and use as you would a Kaiser bun for that terrific deli taste. Spread the bread with your own homemade Aioli (Garlic Mayonaise). For other small sandwiches, try the Traditional Feast Rolls or the Seattle Supreme Sandwich Loaf or Rosemary Cheese. They all go well with sliced turkey, chicken or milder cheeses.

Bread Bowls can be made from many different breads in this book. Match the taste and texture with the filling. Make four to six boules or rounds instead of the basic two loaves. Campocosenza, the Calabrese or Brundisi Pesto Breads, the French Bread are all excellent choices. There are illustrations in *Knead to Know* Chapter 3 to help you form them.

Baby Brioches with Hint of Lemon for filling with fruits or berries in season.

Wraps. Make your own wraps from the Spelt Tortilla recipe. You will be astonished how versatile the recipe is from making world-class enchiladas to a wrap for fillings such as grilled squash, roasted peppers and sweet onions.

Have You Considered the Mighty Meatball?

The meatball is the ultimate in portion control. It is a wonderful and versatile food that can be made from beef, turkey or lamb. It is a perfect food to enhance with herbs and spices. The Classic Meatball for pasta, calzones, pizzas and subs is here along with the New Swedish Meatballs that will melt in your mouth. You will find Sopa de Albondigas (Meatball Soup) and delicate Sopa de Albondigas con Camarones (with shrimp).

And Speaking of Soup ... Try the Homemade Heritage Soup of the Day (or Night)

Spelt Healthy! features three soups for the soul in addition to the ones above. Collard Greens (or Chard) and Turkey Ham Soup with Spelt Dumplings is a classic. From the northern Italian heartland of Spelt come Tuscan Farro Soup made with the traditional cannellini beans and basil. The

Minestrone di Farro … I don't want to describe it; I want you to make it and savor it. There is a reason it survived from antiquity. It is bliss in a bowl; it is the fragrance of the soul.

Sauces

Simple, basic sauces are in this section. They include Aioli, the remarkable sauce of Provence that is a garlic-flavored mayonnaise, Aglio e Olio, a garlic and oil sauce for pasta, over vegetables, for dipping crudités or for making garlic toast. Add herbs for a Green Spaghetti Sauce alternative to tomato. There is basic White Sauce (Béchamel) for vegetables and soups. See also Enchilada Sauce Sabrosa for Mexican dishes and Tsatsiki Sauce for gyros, pita, crudités and fresh salads under *Many Small Things.*

The Vegetable Stand

The "Harmonies of Nature: Phytochemicals" extols the virtues of eating fresh foods and why they may be better for us than we know, like "Spelt Sprouts: Sweet Burst of Power". Want an alternative to rice or Orzo? Take a look at the page on Grünkern.

This is the place to go for an array of Salads for lunch or dinner from Turkey Waldorf to Caesar to Singla with Steak. There is Panzanella and Spelt Rotini and Turmeric Salad to tempt you.

Here you will find Side Dishes such as Crusty Creamy Baked Artichokes and Asparagus al Limon. The Portabella Mushrooms New Orleans make a perfect side with a tender beefsteak or salmon—

and are perfect for the person who prefers vegetarian fare. Sweet Potato Puffs, Sweet Potato Fritters and Zucchini Fritters or Fries are great tasting in themselves and excellent alternatives to the white potato. See also *Many Small Things* for Roasted Garlic, Fried Rice with Spelt Sprouts and Yusef's Hummus.

On the Run and Working Out

These are foods for energy and quick snacking, like Evil Don's Delicious Energy Bars or Applesauce Muffins so good it's worth working for, and Hais, the ancient traveler's food which is the original candy bar made from figs and dates, honey and nuts. Speaking of nuts, there are snack foods out there as well, like Emmer Nuts you can order, granola and Spelt Pretzels now in your stores (see *Appendix 2* for sources).

Afternoon Tea and Quiet Time

Biscotti, a twice-baked bread, is one of the original traveler's foods just like Hais only it often traveled aboard ship not across land. You will find Lemon Shorties and Cherry Almond Biscotti here along with luscious, tender, fresh Scones—Honey, Maple, Blueberry Lemon or Fresh Cranberry. There is a small and delectable recipe you might miss in the passing called the Paradell (Sweet Crepe). It is a simple, slightly sweet and true delight. Look for even more biscotti and scones in the upcoming *Spelt Healthy! Many Small Things—The Appetizing World of Spelt©.*

Many Small Things

Start small! These anytime foods are a good way of getting into cooking and baking with Spelt. Call these foods dim sum, tapas, appetizers, finger foods, or small plates … so many names and faces but they are all small things of the heart. These are the foods we so often go out to eat. But have you ever considered they are the ultimate in portion control along with being of great variety and delight?

Many Small Things are fresh foods from the around the world that can be tailored to individual tastes and times. Take an Empanada (baked turnover) for lunch instead of eating a fast food meal. Make individual Pizzas by the dozen and have people sprinkle them with their favorite things from the many choices under *Topping and Filling Many Small Things.* Take Spelt Char Shiu Bao on a trip—the buns will keep and keep on pleasing. Another thing about this category—you will enjoy the taste but just as much enjoy knowing you can freeze so many of these foods and they retain their character and freshness. Freshness equals flavor.

Look for Small Beginnings such as Broiled Kasseri Cheese with Breadcrumbs, the original mozzarella stick. There are delicate Cheese Spuffs. Dip your Spelt Tortilla chips, pita wedges, croutons, or chunks of bread in Aioli or top with Roasted Garlic or spread with Spinach Pesto.

Pasta, Pizza and Flatbreads. The Spelt Pastas now available will certainly make spaghetti and other pasta meals simple and more nutritious. Or make your own Gnocci, a truly ancient and delicious food. There are recipes aplenty for making your own Focaccia, Calzones and Pizzas.

Have you ever thought of the Tortilla as a flatbread? It is. Try making pizzas with tortillas for an extremely thin crust and fine taste. Enjoy Quesadillas, Cheese Crisps, Tortilla Chips and Nachos or Empanadas Fritas de Chile y Queso.

There are Baked Empanadas filled with beef or lamb and vegetables.

Rich dark Enchilada Sauce Sabrosa over Epic of Enchi-Mesh Sonoran-Style Enchiladas of turkey or chicken.

Falafel, Gyros *(Doner Kebab),* Pita and Pita Wedges to dip into Yusef's Hummus or spread with Tsatsiki Sauce.

Thai Fish Cakes (Tod Mun Pla with Spicy Sauce) that are not rubbery, Char Shiu Bao made with cherried beef instead of syrup and pork. Eggs Foo Young with Spelt Sprouts or Fried Rice with crunchy, sweet Spelt sprouts.

Main Dish (Entrée)

Throw away your cornstarch or other thickeners. Spelt excels in making very fine and delicate sauces featured in the Macao Pepper Steak and Lemon Chicken recipes, in self-gravy as with Classic Meatloaf or with Lamb Tagine Magrib.

Breadcrumbs enliven Coated Pan Fried Fish Fillets and the Turkey or Chicken Toscano, the Moussaka with crumbs and Stuffed Pasilla Peppers with crunchy sprouts.

There is a spiced and flavorful Asian Sunrise Chicken or Rabbit recipe as well and a luscious dish with great eye appeal, the Oven Baked Fish Fillets with Crunchy Lemon Herb Topping.

Cookie Tray

When you are done with your day, cooking for special occasions or with kids, wander over to the Cookie Tray. You will find Spelta's own Flash Brownies and *bon amie* in the Gingerfella Ice Cream Sandwiches. Speaking of ginger, there is a medley of ginger cookies. Every day there seems to be more good news about the benefits of ginger. Try the Ginger Daddies! The Black Forest Cookies are an excellent way to begin with Spelt. The Choco Spiced Dainties is a recipe for a haystack cookie that merits a paragraph on its divine taste. There are many others like Cacao Cashews, Date Layer Bars, and the Back to Basics Zucchini Spice Variety Cookie with Shredded Dried Sweet Potato from the Vegetable Stand. The Good Day Cookie can be chocolate chip and rolled Spelt, it can be oatmeal and raisin, it can be dates and nuts, or a variety of fruits— the basic recipe is there.

Pastries and Pies and Other Sweet Delights

Spelt excels in the sweet category. Because of its naturally sweet, slightly nutty taste it brings its own wonderful character and moistness to what are often dry, over-sugared treats.

Spelt Pastry Crust Chart. Spelt makes excellent butter crusts; but the Pastry Crusts here are all made with vegetable oil. I encourage use of Light Olive Oil for its complementary taste and its nutritional properties. Spelt oil-based crusts are flaky, immensely tasty and stay fresh much longer than other pastry you may be accustomed to eating. It does not get soggy nor does it fall apart. Spelt pastry is easy and quick to make; you can freeze the unbaked pastry and still it will be as fresh as when you made it.

Among the Sweet Delights, you will find a Pineapple Cheese Pie that will awaken your taste buds, but then again, so does the Crostate di Fichi (Fig Tarts) and my father's Cannoli with Cream Filling. The Old Times Pumpkin or Sweet Potato Pie is dense and rich and made without milk, just the sweet taste of squash, Spelt, brown sugar and a hint of cardamom. It has likely been years since you have tasted such an old-fashioned and natural dessert. The Raspberry Valentine Cake is small and fine, delicate and light and accented in and out with fresh raspberries to make it bright. There are more—like American Apple Pie, Pinyon or Pecan Pie. Pound Cake (made with yogurt) that is perfect with fresh fruit toppings.

Sweet Toppings. As you thumb through *Spelt Healthy!* you will see so many recipes made with fresh or dried fruit—blueberry, raspberry, cranberry, figs, dates, raisins and more. This section features Sweet Toppings made from fresh fruits in the form of purees and sauces. These are excellent not just for cakes but especially for crepes, pancakes and waffles in place of heavy syrups.

Ancient Offerings, Many Forms

The book ends where it begins—with an ancient grain and an ancient way of paying tribute to the powers-that-be by making a special bread.

Auld Lang Syne (Remembrance) Bread is wonderful bread that has many uses, like simple raisin toast in the morning. It makes lovely plump rolls and good loaves. The full sweet taste and character of Spelt that I spoke to you about in the Introduction and just above are in it. It is also the bread of the New Year, a time of looking back and looking forward, and being present in the right here and right now.

In the **Afterword,** please find a toast to celebrate and accompany the quality foods you have cooked and baked with Spelt.

PART IV
KNEAD TO KNOW ABOUT COOKING AND BAKING WITH SPELT: GOING BEYOND THE BASICS

Chapter 1: Spelt Flour

Every day I learn something new about Spelt, and I am confident I will be learning from you. Spelt has her own personality and behavior patterns; she has her idiosyncrasies. There are some very important things you "Knead to Know" about cooking and baking with Spelt if you wish to go beyond the basics. It begins with the flour.

Flour is What Makes Bread: Good Bread Requires Good Flour

If you buy a bag of just plain "Farro" and grind it at home for flour, do not expect the same results as buying flour from a reliable source that is packaged in a bag clearly labeled "Spelt" meaning *Triticum spelta L.* Reliable to me means the grower is using foundation seed, certified for purity. Purity means it is *T. spelta L.* and only *T. Spelta L.* in that package. Secondly, it means the foundation seed is seed that has certified proven qualities related to baking. It has been tested by the miller and/or purveyor for those important qualities.

All of the bread recipes in *Spelt Healthy!* are based on *Triticum spelta L.*

Each bread-making grain, Spelt or otherwise, has its own baking and cooking properties. It is fun to experiment with them all. "Farro," meaning the berry or flour of Spelt, emmer or einkorn and sometimes something else, is wonderful for soup or enrichments, but when you want to make a quality bread, be certain you know what flour you are using. Know something of its pedigree because not all grains are the same (see Part II—Chapter 3, especially on Farro).

Many factors affect the quality of the flour. Spelt flours vary and these variances will affect your recipe results, especially breads. That is why I hope you will choose well. Spelt is alive when you get it. That life goes into you. You want the best. The quality of the flour's protein is affected not just by the farmer's skill in growing the grain to fruition but also by the climate, soil, and weather conditions in the region where it was grown. Farmers grow Spelt in many places. There is a variety of cultivars. For example, your flour may come from Canada or Texas, east of the Mississippi or Washington State, Australia or Germany. Flour from one place might be combined with the flour of another place for balancing protein content. It matters how old the flour is, and how it was stored, how it is *stored by you* (more on that in Chapter 5).

All of these factors and others affect Spelt's *water absorption capacity,* which is the single greatest distinction I have found in cooking and baking with Spelt as opposed to the modern wheats. In my opinion, the most significant differences in procedures, cooking and baking qualities between Spelt and modern wheat flow from the striking genetic differences in the gliaden and glutenin (precursors of gluten) structure that become apparent when you *just add water.*

Whole Grain and White Spelt Flour

Several variations of Spelt flour appear in this volume of *Spelt Healthy!* They are Whole Grain (also known as Whole Meal) and White. There are varieties of White according to sift and a Light that is an intermediate between whole and white. The white is not the stark white bleached flour you may be accustomed to using. In fact, it is unbleached, unbromated and unenriched. The Whites and the Light are a lovely cream color with warm vanilla hues. The reason they are not white is due to the high beta-carotene (Vitamin A) you read about in the Introduction ("Why Choose Spelt?"). It gives color, flavor and aroma, and is one of the reasons Spelt, emmer and einkorn are all three being researched as possible diabetic foods (regulation of blood sugar). The beta-carotene is responsible for those warm sienna, deep reddish gold crust colors you get with many of the Spelt breads, Whole Grain or White. With White

or Light Spelt, the contrast between that warm-colored, inviting crust and creamy crumb is positively sensuous.

Many of the recipes in this book call for a combination of the two flours because the combination gives greater volume to breads and provides a finer texture in some recipes. You can adjust the ratios to suit your tastes, nutrition requirements and experimental urges. There are many Spelt flours on the market from which to choose.

Combining for Creation—The Fine Wine of Flours

When you are contemplating making a recipe that uses Spelt flour, consider how you want it to taste and which form you want it to take to bring out the qualities you desire. For example, braided bread is for tearing apart; a loaf is for slicing. Torpedo freeform loaves like the classic bâtard or rustic breads are designed for maximum crust. A simple recipe like Speltessence or Classic White can be changed dramatically by adding high-quality enrichments like reconstituted dried fruits, green olives, cheese or by different kinds of sugar such as maple or molasses, with fruit juice as liquid or wine. The possibilities are many and exciting.

A truly good thing about the Spelt flours on the market today is the range of opportunities they provide us to make different choices. You can vary a recipe according to the type of flour grind and how much whole bran is in it, by the amounts of each used, by the variety put into a ferment, by how much time the flour is given to open and develop. You will see a number of recipes where Whole Grain Spelt is the flour that makes the "sponge" or ferment. This brings out the flavor, it allows time for the particles to release nutrients, and the process softens the husk for greater digestibility. Similarly, Whole Grain Spelt adds naturally sweet tastes and textures to recipes often considered "White Bread" territory like cinnamon rolls, brioche, biscuits and American French or Italian Bread. It really is exciting, this world of Spelt Flours. So often now the flour is nothing more than a wrapper, something filling but not tasty except for the *added* ingredients. The flour itself is something humdrum, tasteless and inert, lifeless. Those flours made of common wheat are not at all like the products of the Spelt growers and millers who are the vintners of Spelt, the fine wine of flours.

We would love to hear from you about your
experiences in cooking and baking with Spelt.
Go to www.spelthealthy.com and follow the links
to Contact Us. You will get a reply.

Chapter 2: Cooking and Baking Processes

Cooking in *Spelt Healthy!* extends from sprouting Spelt seed and using it fresh or as an ingredient in something else to baking breads at high temperature. That is quite a range. What do *cooking* and *baking* really mean? Why are they separated in the title of this book? What does it mean to you?

❋ Cooking is preparing food for consumption. It comprises many methods, tools and ways of combining ingredients to make food digestible and give it flavors and other desirable attributes such as tenderness of crumb.

❋ Baking is one means of cooking, a large subcategory. It refers to heating food in a dry environment such as an oven, until the food reaches a minimum of about 190° F inside. For bread, that is about the minimum temperature required for the starches in the dough to *gelatinize* which is critical for bread to be digestible as well as meeting the criterion of flavor.

❋ The Baking Process—It takes water to make it happen. Gasses in the dough expand, the cells become bigger, the particles of starch swell, the matrix becomes more rigid, yeast begin to die and release sugars that sweeten the bread and turn it brown. The crust reaches oven temperature and the middle stops heating at points below 212°. Most importantly, the dough thickens (gelatinizes) which makes it possible for us to cut it, to eat and to digest what was, in dough form, indigestible. That is why mom always said, "Never eat the dough. It will make you sick."

Water Absorption and Spelt

❋ *Absorption.* The ability of a flour to take up and hold water. Liquid is necessary for yeast activation and gluten formation.

Spelt is a water lover. You will see numerous references to this characteristic in the *Spelt Healthy!* recipes. This water absorption capacity keeps Spelt products fresh long after ordinary flour products turn crumbly or dry out and is what keeps the taste alive where other flours taste like sawdust.

The water absorption capacity of flour relates to the amount of protein it contains and how that protein is constituted. It's in the genes. Earlier in *Why Choose Spelt?* I mentioned Spelt is *not* modern wheat. If it was wheat, you could grab any old cookbook off the shelf, set to making and baking according to the standard steps and take a long time doing it. It does not work that way with Spelt.

The protein in Spelt is different from the protein in modern wheats. The category "Wheat" is based on the fact they all have gluten precursor proteins, *glutenin* and *gliadin*. You may have read about this in the sections *Why Choose Spelt?* and *Food Intolerances and Allergies.* This difference comes to the fore in baking with Spelt. When water is added to flour, it begins the process of bonding *glutenin* and *gliadin* to form gluten. Gluten forms the three-dimensional matrix that allows the making of leavened bread. The gluten development determines the quality of the bread. Too much water or too little affects the end result as do the processes that follow. In making bread from any flour, there is always a tug-of-war between the following factors.

Extensibility refers to the *pliability* of dough, its ability to stretch and hold its form. Can you pull the dough without its breaking?

Elasticity. This quality gives the dough its ability to *spring* back after handling which is why you see the references to rubber bands in relation to dough. Too elastic and it won't hold its shape. The dough will tighten up which you also see

in many bread recipes "Cover and let rest for 10 minutes." Is it strong enough to hold the shape you give it?

Tolerance refers to the dough's ability to be handled without breaking down. Wheat flours were selected for baking because they have a high tolerance for handling. The standard cookbook bread recipes reflect this: punch down, beat, throw, knead ten minutes, rest, then knead ten minutes more. Modern wheats are bred to have high tolerance.

✳ Spelt does not have these same high tolerances. If beaten too much, it will go slack. *Treat Spelt with gentle strength and do not over-mix.* Spelt absorbs water differently. It has a shorter development time (generally half that of modern wheat). It does not require the mixing and kneading time that modern wheat flours do!

There are two, opposite, things that happen with over-mixing and over-handling:

Slackness. The processes that are set in motion starting with mixing/kneading and fermentation to build the wonderful gluten matrix *reverse* themselves. The dough becomes too extensible and slumps.

Too elastic. The gluten net may not form and the bread remains dense and low; it does not increase sufficiently in volume. It is like having a tight rubber band around your loaf. This can happen if the dough becomes dry, the surface dries out, or too much flour is worked into the dough.

Basic Steps in Making Bread and How Working with Spelt Differs

In *Spelt Healthy!* you will encounter a variety of breads. They fall into two categories based on the methods described below.

Direct Method

All of the ingredients are added to the bowl during the mixing and kneading stage. Typically the flavor of these breads or rolls come from the addition of enrichments such as butter, milk, sugar, herbs or spices to make tender, tasty products. Sandwich breads or rolls such as the Classic White Bread, Brioche and Traditional Feast Rolls recipes are examples. These are often fast breads in the sense there are no long ferment periods. These breads are often tender with a fine crumb. Some lean breads such as the French Bread recipe fall in this category. Lean breads are those made only with the traditional four ingredients—flour, water, salt, yeast. (Most lean breads in the book are made by the sponge method.)

✳ Direct Method recipes generally take half as long to make as modern wheat bread recipes. This is one of the great advantages of using Spelt.

The Life of A Sponge—Huh? The Indirect or Sponge Method

This was the first method of leavened bread making. It developed in the time of only whole grain flours and no machinery to do the mixing and kneading. The word "Sponge" developed from the ferment, which is full of holes from bubbling action and can look like the sea creature or the shower accoutrement. These breads are made in more than one stage. They use fermented dough. There are many names for ferments and ways to make them. In *Spelt Healthy,* the ferments fall into the category of "Sponge" or "Biga" because they are made from commercial yeast versus wild yeast as in sourdough and ferment over a shorter time than does a sourdough.

What makes this method *indirect* is that water, a small amount of yeast and a part of the flour that is going to be used in the recipe are mixed in advance and allowed to ferment. It is the *first* rise for this type of bread. In *fermentation,* sugars in the flour interact with yeast, to produce bread with greater volume, better flavor and more moisture, which in turn adds to the flavor and helps it keep much longer. These doughs require gentle strength to handle so that the carefully developed gases are not released causing the dough to slump or become non-elastic. When using the sponge method, mixing/kneading time is kept to a minimum. The fermentation process develops the gluten structure instead of the machine or you. This is the basic method for making many of the free-form rustic breads that require minimal shaping, because the fermentation process has done the work for you.

✳ Sponge method: the dough develops while you do other things.

Fermentation

Fermentation refers to the interaction of yeast with liquid and with flour to produce chemical reactions and by-products useful in baking. Activating the yeast is the initial step in the bread-making recipes whether using the Direct or Indirect Methods. In this book, standard commercial yeast is used. The yeast is most often activated or *proofed* by sprinkling it over warm water (110°–115° F) and stirring. The process is usually done outside the mixing bowl. The purpose of this is to assure the yeast is active, let it begin fermenting, and to bring down the temperature of the water before it goes into the bowl. Occasionally you will see an exception to this in a recipe like Auld Lang Syne Bread or Pita. The fermentation process in Spelt dough occurs more rapidly with Spelt than common wheat flours.

✳ The fermentation process occurs much more rapidly with Spelt.

Mixing/Kneading

The purpose of mixing is to start the development of the gluten and thoroughly distribute all the ingredients through the rough dough. Kneading strengthens the gluten network. With the Indirect Method, both of these processes begin in the sponge and the links referred to earlier are already being made so even less time is required during the mixing/kneading process. Irrespective of the method, it takes less than half the time to mix and knead Spelt dough than it does for recipes using common wheat flours.

✳ Spelt mixes/kneads in less than half the time than dough made from modern wheat flours.

✳ It is not the chore of days of yore and modern kitchen lore.

It is easy to over-mix Spelt if you are accustomed to the traditional modern wheat ways of making bread. That is why all of the recipes in *Spelt Healthy!* refer to either the hand method or stand mixer and there are times recommended. (A hand mixer is not powerful enough for this heavy bread dough.) It takes little time to mix and knead Spelt by hand in comparison to dough with common wheat and is not the chore you may think. With a stand mixer the time is even less.

✳ In home baking, it is best not to use the bread-maker or food processor for the purpose of mixing/kneading Spelt dough.

Machines create heat. Excess heat from friction during this all-important gluten-formation process can break down the Spelt gluten. The activity of fermentation itself creates heat so additional heat can stop or reverse the gluten forming process. It is very difficult to get that kind of heat from good hand mixing and kneading or from using the stand mixer in the way recommended here.

✳ Excess heat during mixing can contribute to the break down of Spelt gluten. Keep mixing/kneading times in the stand mixer to about or under $3\frac{1}{2}$ minutes total and most of that on low speed. Many recipes require even less mixing time. Mixing by hand does not take much longer than the stand mixer method because of Spelt's water absorption capacity.

Whether using the Direct or Indirect methods of making bread please follow the recipe. You will see the rule of thumb approximates this order: add the yeast, half the flour and *most, not all,* of the water and/or other enrichments such as oil or egg, and use the paddle on the next to lowest speed to mix for 1 to $1\frac{1}{2}$ minutes to form a rough dough. Reduce the speed and add flour by the half cup, adjust the water if necessary. As the dough begins to consolidate, change to the dough hook at about the $2\frac{1}{2}$ minute mark. Keep it on the lowest speed going no longer than $3\frac{1}{2}$ minutes except in the case of dough like the one for Rye bread. I seldom use the dough hook for long because it can pull the dough too much. It works better all the way around to finish kneading by hand and that is what I recommend for most Spelt dough.

✳ Mix and knead only as long as it takes not what you think it should take based on prior experiences with modern wheat flours. The water absorption capacity of Spelt is different; it is faster.

If you are working the dough with your fingers, you can feel the gentle pressure start to form.

A third reason for reducing the mixing/kneading time is due to the flour itself and the bran content. Whole Grain bread dough is rougher in texture. The bran can abrade the dough. This is another reason why I suggest you let the dough rest if it needs to between the time you take the dough from the bowl and knead it. It gives it time to absorb water, softening the bran. That is also one of the beauties of the sponge method. It does this for you.

✳ Let the dough rest if it needs to rest.

Direct dough forms very quickly with Spelt; indirect dough may take a little longer. In either case, take the ball or scrape the dough out of the bowl and onto a lightly floured surface. If the dough needs to rest, let it. Cover the dough with the bowl and let the dough rest for 5–10 minutes, let it take a breath, and then finish kneading the dough by sprinkling small amounts of flour over and under the dough, and all the time use a pastry (bench) scraper to keep the dough from sticking. Spelt is loaded with protein and that makes sticky dough. The pastry scraper (bench scraper) is your friend; in fact, it is often your right hand.

✳ Become accustomed to working with wetter, rougher, stickier dough.

Become accustomed to working with wetter, rougher dough in the initial mixing/kneading stages. These are especially common with the Indirect (Sponge) method used in making superlative rustic or freeform breads. Scrape the bowl out and onto a floured surface, cover with the bowl, let the dough rest if necessary, and finish kneading it with sprinklings of flour under and over the dough. Knead lightly; feel for that springiness in the dough, which tells you it is ready for the next stage. If the dough is tacky, and sometimes it is, put a very light coating of flour on your hands or spray your hands lightly with water to form the dough into a smooth ball for rising.

✳ Resist the temptation to work in too much flour.

Because Spelt dough is often wetter and stickier, there is the tendency to work in too much flour because of the common phrase "until smooth and elastic." Resist the tendency. If you are perplexed about going on or not, if you are trying to decide whether or not to work more flour into the dough to get that smooth, elastic, non-sticky dough you have heard about, always opt for moist over dry, slightly sticky or tacky over dry powdery smooth. You want the gluten net to form. In the absence of sufficient moisture it has a hard time so that the dough may end up firm but not springy.

✳ Always opt for wet over dry, a surface that is moist and slightly tacky over smooth but powdery dry.

Direct Dough like D'Adamo Pizza or Auld Lang Syne Bread or Cinnamon Rolls form quickly in the stand mixer or by hand. They will start to smooth ball in the bowl. Let the dough rest on a lightly floured surface, and knead with gentle strength for a short time, four to six turns of the dough and sometimes not that much, and they are ready for the next stage, rising.

Rising (Fermentation)

The initial rising times for breads made from modern wheat flours vary according to recipe. A standard Whole Wheat loaf may take 90 minutes to two hours. For Spelt, the time is half that or less, 45 minutes to an hour. As altitude increases, rising time decreases. At 4000–5000 feet expect rising times to be 25–30 minutes for the example given here.

✳ Spelt rises in half the time.

The time will depend upon the temperature of the room as well as the recipe. Many recipes are based on an average of 80°. Because Spelt rises so rapidly, there is generally no reason to force it to a faster rise like putting it in the oven with the light on or in the laundry room or on top of a refrigerator, all those methods you may have learned. It rises plenty fast on its own. One of the tricks with Spelt is to get it to slow down at times.

How do I tell if it is ripe and ready for the next step? Common recipes usually ask you to look for "doubled in volume." Looks may be deceiving so use the age-old *Fingertip Test.* It is a good indicator of maximum expansion.

❋ Use the Fingertip test. It is a good indicator of maximum expansion whether the dough is doubled in volume or not (usually not).

Fingertip Test. To test if the dough is ripe, press, do not poke, the tip of one or two fingers, quickly and lightly, about half an inch, slightly off center, into the crown of the dough (area of maximum expansion). If the indentation(s) remain, the dough is ripe and ready for the next step. If the dents fill in quickly, give the dough another five to ten minutes. For stickier dough, moisten or flour your fingertip(s). There are other signs of ripeness, especially with Indirect Method (Sponge) dough and occasionally with the quicker Direct Method dough. For example, there may be bubbling under the skin, which is a characteristic you may be looking for depending upon the recipe, which will let you know.

Degassing (Deflating) the Dough

❋ Do not "punch down" or bang Spelt, instead use gentle strength in degassing and in handling.

Detach the dough from the edges of the bowl with a spatula. Place the edges on top of the dough and gently deflate the dough by curving your fingers and pressing down with the heel and palm of your hand (loose fist) and work your hand around the bowl. You will hear soft hissing sounds not the great whoosh that comes from punching or banging. This process is particularly important in the sponge dough recipes where an uneven texture is desirable (those large holes that give lean bread its flavor and distinct texture). So as a rule of thumb, gently tip the bowl, and turn the dough out onto on a lightly floured surface (White Spelt where possible) and follow the recipe.

Dividing and Shaping

Simply dividing the dough expels some of its gasses and begins the redistribution of the gluten so the dough can begin its last rise. Most recipes call for the division of bread in some way—into two or more loaves or rolls or coils.

❋ Use a pastry (bench) scraper or very sharp knife to cut the dough without tearing or stretching it.

Again, the pastry scraper is an excellent tool for dividing the dough, as is a very sharp knife. If the dough is sticky, and some of them like Roasted Garlic and Mozzarella Baguettes are, dip the scraper or knife in cold water and then make the cuts. The important thing is to cut the dough cleanly and quickly without stretching or tearing.

Tears allow gas to escape during baking and can cause problems with the crust.

✳ Again, let the dough rest if it needs to rest and catch its breath.

The dough may need to rest even if you are eager to get on to the next stage. I think one of the most important things in working with Spelt is learning to let it rest when it needs to between processes, for example, between kneading in the bowl and the final kneading on the work surface or between dividing and shaping. Resting time varies according to the recipe. Some doughs do not require it at all where others may need to rest several times. There is a variety of reasons for this including temperature, weather, the age of the flour, your mood and, who knows, the movement of the spheres. The resting period allows Spelt to catch its breath and relax enough to take a shape and hold it. This is the opposite problem from slackness and you will encounter this. Let it rest, covered, 5 to 10 minutes. Shape it. If it is still acting like a rubber band instead of that malleable perfect dough you desire, let it rest, covered, again if it needs to rest.

✳ The forms are many, the techniques few.

The forms Spelt can take are many just like other breads but most start with the basic shapes: the ball (boule), the torpedo (long loaves like baguettes), the braid. (See drawings and instructions for the basic forms.) Spend as little time as possible in shaping Spelt breads so excessive flour is not worked into them at this stage or lest they become overworked and fizz out. Again, moist is better than dry. The bread is too dry if it is hard to seal the seams.

✳ The bread is too dry if it is hard to seal the seams.

Many of the rustic breads, for example those made from the All-Italian Biga/Dough Recipe may need some assistance while rising to set them up for baking if you want them to form boules (spherical shape) as opposed to large rounds or wheels.

✳ Some dough will slump during the last rise because that is its nature. Give it a little help if you want to by providing a form.

Dough that slumps the most is often the one made from ferments. The rigid paper forms now on the market work very well and come in many traditional shapes and forms and others like the heart, the pandoro or bells. Use traditional canvas that bakers use. Use pie plates, wicker baskets, bannetons, baguette and bâtard forms. There are many things you can use for forms as has been done since humans first figured out how to raise bread. I will occasionally use my great uncle's ancient high-sided iron skillet (half a

Dutch oven) in making a particular large country loaf and it works magnificently. I am always on the lookout for new forms. They are not only fun they help you to learn new things about baking.

✳   Parchment paper is your friend in baking with Spelt.

Parchment paper limits the handling. The breads do not stick as much, which matters when you are dealing with sticky dough. Parchment takes care of both of those problems along with providing a dull finish if you are baking on shiny pans, which reflect the heat and can cause uneven baking. It also makes for easy cleanup whether you are baking cookies or wedding bread.

I often use the back of large rimmed baking pans for both rising and baking especially in several small boules or baguettes at a time without using forms at all. Lightly spray the parchment with oil and sprinkle it with White Spelt Flour, which works like semolina (the alica of Roman times). The cooking surface of insulated cookie sheets with that curved end make excellent peels for rising and shifting risen dough onto the stone if you do not have a professional peel.

The Final Rise (Proofing)

The first rise develops flavor and gluten; the second rise develops the volume to its greatest extent before baking. That first fermentation may be from the Indirect Method (making a sponge) or may be the Direct Method where this is accomplished in the first and longest rise and possibly a second. Irrespective of the method, the last rise is generally much faster with Spelt, half or less time than the first rise. This is the case with almost all breads, but it is especially so with Spelt.

✳   The final rise is generally much faster than the first. Watch it closely.

If a regular bread recipe made from modern wheats calls for a 40-minute Second Rise, expect it to be 15 to 20 or so with Spelt. There are some exceptions such as Light Rye where both rise times are almost the same. The point here is that rising in Spelt will still be faster than recipes using common wheat flours. You really must watch it, especially when making rolls or buns or brioche. If you are baking one part of the recipe at a time, as with Char Shiu Bao or Brioches, retard the dough rising by covering it securely and placing it in the refrigerator. Get it out in sufficient time to let it come to room temperature.

I have learned that spraying the dough lightly with oil and covering it loosely with plastic wrap or placing the dough inside big plastic bags that can be puffed up (tented) but closed work very well for the last rise. It helps the home baker create a more humid environment. Another alternative is spraying the dough lightly with oil to keep the wrap or cloth from sticking to the dough and causing a potential tear or disturbance to the dough, neither of which is desirable at this stage.

A Comment on the Final Product

If you expect high light spongy marshmallow-like bread that looks like that balloon loaf of commercial Italian bread at your local supermarket, do not use Spelt. *Real bread* does not look like that.

✳ If you expect high light spongy mass-produced bread like that balloon loaf of Italian bread at your local supermarket, do not use Spelt. If you are going to compare your homemade bread to any product, visit your artisan bakeries or invest in the increasing number of very good books on artisan breads.

Even professional bakers have bad days. Remember, too, that you are not privy to many baking secrets. You do not use the same kind of yeast. You are not using conditioners that make the fabric of breads more rigid for super expansion. You do not have the humid environment optimal for second fermentation. You may or may not have an oven that has steam jets. What you do have is natural beauty, taste and nutritional properties far superior to what you can buy in many stores or eat in restaurants and the desire to each time make the bread better or the experience more creative. Stick with it. Be patient especially with the rustic breads. They will delight you in the end.

✳ Be proud of your bread. Expectations can be destructive. Do not expect commercial results unless you are in commerce and using the secrets of the trade.

Be proud of your bread. It is a one of a kind when it comes from you and your very own kitchen. Smile big. Hold it high! Look at this miracle! That is how the ancients used to "see" yeast—as a miracle of creation because they could not see it happening under a microscope. It was a wonder to them. Let it be a wonderful thing for you.

✳ Start small. Give yourself time to learn. Most importantly, enjoy your acts of creation for that is what bread-making is … creation.

Chapter 3: Giving Form to Spelt

Spelt Healthy! **Volume 1** is a basic book for home cooks and bakers about working with Spelt across the spectrum of cooking. In "Giving Form to Spelt," you will find guidelines for making the basic forms of baked goods from rounds to ropes. Please remember, dough is alive. By touching it and giving it form, it gives life to you. Do not worry about making mistakes. Simply treat Spelt with gentle strength and learn by doing. Spelt will reward you in unexpected ways.

Mixing/Kneading

The initial mixing/kneading process begins in the bowl. It is the most important step in making quality, baked goods. Most *Spelt Healthy!* recipes suggest you finish kneading by hand. With Spelt, unlike modern wheats, the process takes little time and physical labor because of its amazing water absorption capacity. There are many ways to knead dough. The following one is a basic.

Turn dough out of the bowl. On a lightly floured surface, knead briefly, just enough to form a loose ball. Cover and let the dough rest if the recipe calls for it as many recipes in this book do.

Throughout the kneading process, keep the dough in a ball shape or thick round as much as possible so all the dough receives the benefits of kneading. Using the heels of your hands, push the dough forward (away from you). Push firmly yet lightly and use your whole body not just your arms and shoulders. The dough will lengthen and spread. With your fingertips, fold the far edge of the dough toward you, using the indispensable pastry (bench) scraper to keep dough from sticking. Give the dough a quarter turn. Repeat the process, knead and turn, until dough coheres and develops that springiness and elasticity that indicates it is ready for rising.

Please see individual recipe for desired characteristics because some dough you knead until smooth and springy while others retain a surface stickiness and are less elastic. When working with the latter, dust your hands with flour or mist hands with water instead of continually adding flour to the dough to keep your hands from sticking. Spelt can be over-kneaded. In many instances, the dough will be ready with just a few good turns of the dough. The traditional bread-making maxim, *"You cannot knead too much"* does not apply to Spelt.

The half-moon (below) shows what the dough looks like after folding and a quarter turn. Keep your kneading action towards the center. Keep the dough thick and round. When the dough edge extends beyond your fingertips and becomes much thinner, turn. Begin again. When dough is ready, fold edges over one another to form a ball. This spherical shape allows for maximum gluten development.

Place dough round in a bowl. The recipe will mention whether the bowl should be oiled and/or whether the dough ball should be turned to cover all surfaces with oil. Let dough rise according to instructions. Remember, Spelt rises about twice as fast as modern wheat flours. Also many Spelt breads do not call for doubling in volume. Do the Fingertip Test described in the preceding chapter. Insert finger slightly off the top of dough but on the crown (area of maximum expansion). Detach the edges of the dough with a spatula, laying edges over top of the dough. Degas (deflate) the dough *gently. Do not punch down.* Some recipes, for example, All-Purpose Italian Biga, call for minimal degassing and require little additional work. Follow directions for turning out of bowl. Follow directions for dividing/resting according to recipe.

Shaping

The purpose of shaping is to create a loaf or other baked product with desired characteristics such as size or crustiness. For example, a fairly dense but tender crumb, soft crust, good slicing properties are things you might want in the standard American sandwich bread baked in a bread pan. Free form breads with maximum attention on balance of crunchy chewy crust with tasty open crumb such as the rustic or French breads are another example. Just as there are many ways to knead, so are there many ways to shape dough. Following are basic methods.

Loaf Pan—Method 1

This is a simple method particularly successful with Indirect Method (sponge, biga) breads because it calls for the least handling. Pat, press the round into a plump and symmetrical oval that fits the pan. (The ends of the dough should touch the ends of the pan for support during rising.) There are many pan sizes from the large 10" x 5" to the standard 9" x 5" and 8" by 4". For variety, consider using different pan sizes such as the small individual size loaf forms or "cocktail" bread forms.

Loaf Pan—Method 2

This is an excellent method for shaping Direct Method dough and some Sponge dough. Pat, press the dough into a flat and fairly thick oval that is about 1 inch smaller than the pan size. Or *gently* roll the dough lightly pressing out air bubbles including at the edges. Roll into a cylinder, sealing edges along roll as you go. Tuck the ends under and seal. Place in pan so dough touches ends of pan.

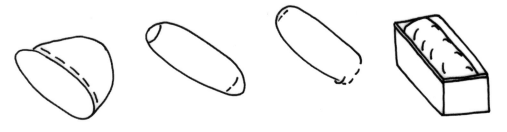

Free-Form Shapes: Basic Ball and Oval

Ball (Boule, Sphere, "Round")

The ball is one of the two, basic forms. It is the optimal shape for allowing gasses to expand upward instead of outward. It makes everything from dainty rolls to the large country round or wheel such as the Campocosenza Wheel or Roman Bread. The key to a firm round that allows for maximum expansion is the use of cupped hands to simultaneously turn the dough and stretch the skin to create a tight strong yet expandable gluten net.

Form dough into a rough ball. Using cupped hands, draw opposite sides of dough down with hands. Take care not to expel too much of the gas. This initial action will form a plump cylinder. Now cup your hands, turn, while pulling down now on the opposite sides. The friction between dough and work surface during turning will help create the ball. When it is well rounded, delicately close the seam on the bottom to tighten the net so you have a ball that is taut but expandable. Take care not to expel too much of the gas from the dough as you work it into a ball. Some Spelt doughs do not require sealing and can be cupped, turned gently to form a beautiful round.

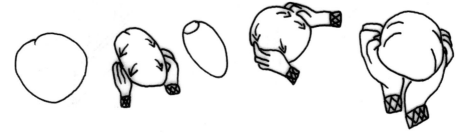

Small Rounds ("Baby Boules") for Breads, Bread Bowls

A standard bread recipe from *Spelt Healthy!* will make 4–8 small rounds. Form the same way as the Ball (Boule) above. Again, some recipes do not require sealing and can be patted, pressed and gently cupped to form excellent rounds.

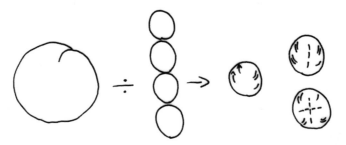

Slashing some dough allows maximum oven spring and also creates a decorative effect. The illustration above shows the two basic methods of slashing: line and the crossed line. Slash in a single resolute motion. Slashing too deep or slashing straight down can tear the skin. Cut at an angle to the bread. You will find slashing tools (curved blade) on the market. Or use a double-edged razor blade or sharp knife. On these small rounds, slash along the crown (area of maximum expansion). Because you are often working with moist dough, the slit may have to be re-accomplished immediately prior to baking. Follow the recipe instructions. Many Spelt breads may not call for slashing. Long loaves like the Bâtard and Baguette are slashed at an angle (not straight down) and on the diagonal for best effect.

Free Form Torpedo (Basic Oval)

This is the second basic free-form shape. It is a basic oval elongated to various degrees and often given tapered ends.

Basic Torpedo Shape (Bâtard 1)

This is the basic torpedo loaf that is generally between 6–12 inches long, often called the bâtard. The bâtard is shorter, wider, and higher than a baguette. Its varieties include the sub/po-boy/hoagie often 6–8 inches long; French rolls (bolillos) that are often 4–6 inches long.

The first method is excellent for many of the Indirect (sponge) method breads. Gently pat and press rough ball of dough into an oval that tapers to the dimensions you want. Many of the sponge dough recipes do not require to be sealed. Take care not to expel too much of the gas while forming. Tip: Dimple the bread with your fingertips to keep it from rising too fast but still keep maximum gas in the loaf for final rise and initial baking (oven spring).

Basic Torpedo Shape (Bâtard 2)

Good method for Straight Dough recipes such as French Bread and some Indirect Method breads. Form dough into a thick rectangle by patting and pressing or gently rolling. Fold one third over to the center. Fold other edge over to center as show below. Very gently pat again into a rectangle. Fold long edge of dough over to opposite edge. Seal edge with the flat of your hand. Turn so seam is on bottom and as straight as possible. Gently rock and roll to desired taper and length. Do not overwork the dough. If it resists, let it rest (covered). Allow to rise and slash on an angle and at a diagonal to the loaf and across the crown stopping where bread begins downward slope. The number of slashes varies with the length of the bread.

Baguette—Another Basic Torpedo Form

From one bâtard, come 2–3 baguettes that are from 12 to 18 inches long with excellent crisp, chewy crust and open crumb (large holes). Begin by dividing dough into 4–6 portions and let dough rest per recipe. Shape each into basic torpedo as explained under Bâtard 1 or 2 above. With fermented (sponge) breads, the first method is recommended. (See also the complete process for Method 1 for Biga/Sponge doughs under Roasted Garlic and Mozzarella Baguettes.)

Gently, briefly roll the torpedo under your palms. With the back of your hand, make a crease down the middle. Fold half the dough over as with the Bâtard (Method 2). Turn the seam side down, as straight as possible, and gently roll dough on work surface to seal the seam and tighten the skin of the dough. Roll, pat, press to desired length. During any of these stages let the dough rest if necessary and take care not to overwork the dough.

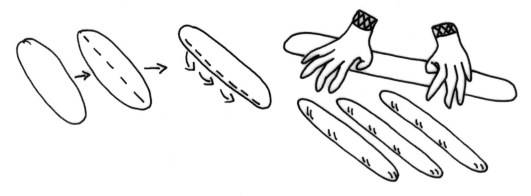

Subs, Hoagie, Po-Boys

These all follow the basic torpedo form. The number per recipe varies according to desired result but 8–10 is a good rule of thumb from standard recipes such as French Bread, All-Purpose Italian Biga, Brundisi, Calabrese, Classic White and others that make 2½ to 3 pounds of wet dough (see Yield under each recipe for guidelines).

Divide the dough per instructions. Round each piece. Pat, press into torpedo form. Slash each prior to baking. Cut an angle down the crown of each roll. Bâtard Method 2 also produces exceptional rolls. For softer, fermented Spelt dough the rounding, patting pressing method is recommended.

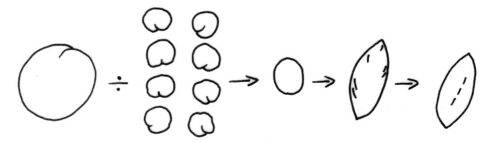

French Rolls, Bolillos, Hot Dog Buns

Basic torpedo form that is 4–6 inches long. The method to shape is same as above. Recipes such as French Bread and Classic White will make from 12–16 rolls. Do not slash the hot dog buns.

Deli Rolls, Hamburger Buns

A variety of recipes in *Spelt Healthy!* make excellent rolls. (See also the Brundisi Pesto Rolls recipe for a modified Kaiser bun.) Classic White and other such recipes will make a dozen or so rolls.

Divide into number of pieces desired according to recipe instructions. Form into rough balls. Let rest, covered, 10 minutes. Form into firm balls as in Ball/Boule above. Flatten each slightly without expelling too much air. In determining size, allow for additional expansion during rising and also in oven. Do not slash.

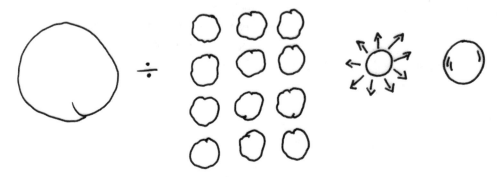

Simple Braid (Challah and Other Breads and Rolls)

A braid is the most elemental form of weaving. It is an over/under process. Almost any recipe for bread or rolls in *Spelt Healthy!* can be braided. They can be placed free-form on a baking pan or doubled over and contained in a loaf pan or wound around and baked in a variety of cake pans. The *Spelt Healthy!* recipe for Challah makes two large beautiful free-form braids.

Sprinkle whole grain Spelt flour on the dough ropes to keep them from excessively melding into one another during rising and baking. Roll gently under your fingertips taking care not to pull or stretch the ropes too much.

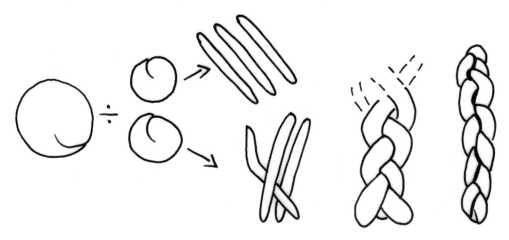

Additional Forms

Check out the many fun roll forms under Traditional Feast Rolls. See also instructions for breadsticks under French Breadsticks. See Roasted Garlic and Mozzarella Baguettes. See Brundisi Pesto Rolls. See Spelta's Cinnamon Rolls and Pistachio Sticky Buns. See also Brioches with Hint of Lemon for the traditional top-knot form. See Auld Lang Syne Bread under Ancient Offerings for Celtic Knot (closed braid) and free-forms.

Watch for Autumn Rose Press' Volume III in the Spelt Healthy Series: *Knead to Know.* It contains simple to elaborate bread forms and types of baked goods from around the world of Spelt baking including the sourdoughs.

Chapter 4: Common Problems and Suggestions for Remedies

Checklist

First and always, read the recipe completely. For longer and more detailed recipes, read the recipe again. Have the right ingredients on hand. For example, if the recipe calls for plain yogurt only do not substitute flavored yogurt or yogurt with additives. Have your utensils out and everything ready including having ingredients at room temperature if that is what is called for in the recipe. Measure the flour and other ingredients carefully. Please read also Chapter 5 that follows called *All Measures Are Not the Same.*

Dense bread with low volume. Too much flour is usually the reason. Work with a wetter dough for maximum expansion. Too much handling in the mixing/kneading stage or over-handling during shaping and the incorporation of too much flour. Spelt needs sufficient moisture to expand. Also it may be the result of too short a rising time; the dough is under-proofed and turns crumbly.

Slackness and slumping. Over-mixing is generally the problem. Again, if using the stand mixer take care to use it at the lowest speed most of the time and limit the time especially with the hook. Spelt doughs come up fast; there are few instances I can think of that require it be mixed beyond 3½ minutes, 4 max. Some come up faster. Also, try using a form for the final rising.

Next, check your *fermentation time.* Yeast can burn through Spelt like wildfire, especially at higher altitudes which is why you occasionally see the heresy of adding flour and water to a ferment a couple of hours after it was started. Spelt ferments are much faster than modern wheat ferments and require fuel to sustain them. Catch it before it burns out, and the fermentation process starts reversing itself and the linkages between *glutenin* and *gliadin* start to slip as mentioned above.

The loaf never changed form; it stayed squat. That may be a problem of over-elasticity resulting from too much flour working in during mixing/kneading. It may result because of fermentation. To start with, give the dough time to breathe meaning give it rest before working with it. Spelt does not like being forced. The dough will sometimes lie down and refuse to work at all. It may slump or stay tight and not expand. Give her a rest for starters. Check your fermentation time. This is also a reason for proofing your yeast outside the bowl. It can go flat just like old flour or flour that has been exposed to too much light.

Fly-Away Crust. This is one of the main reasons professional bakers use dough conditioners. The crust breaks and flies open on the sides. Remember with Spelt, there is a fine line between moist and dry. Always go for the moist because, first, you do not have the humid fermentation conditions that exist in professional bakeries, and, secondly, because of the tolerance problems mentioned in Chapter 1. Improper forming and especially tearing during the shaping process can cause damage to the crust and make it weak. Under-proofing is another cause; the gluten net is not strong enough (sufficiently developed) to hold the expansion during oven rise. Make slits in the crust in the recipes that tell you to do so. They help steam escape in good ways and make for maximum oven bloom, that last magnificent spring when it starts baking. A good crisp crust requires humidity, which is why you see suggestions for spritzing the oven prior to baking baguettes or other free form loaves or using a pan of boiling water. Over-proofing during the final rise can cause splitting higher up in the loaf (especially along the shred line) because the bonds (gluten) have begun to break down. Bread will likely have an uneven crumb and be grainier than usual and crust may be more brittle.

Improper Baking. Check your oven temperature with a separate oven thermometer. Even the best of stoves vary in temperature. Give the oven plenty of time to warm up, especially to the high temperatures of bread baking. That is why you often see preheats to 475° or 450° then backing down to 425° or less. Every time you open the oven door, remember it releases heat.

Remember that recipes are guidelines and not absolutes because of factors that affect the baking properties of our ingredients, weather and temperature conditions and other things. Take time to measure your flours accurately. Move oven racks to the correct position and check the oven temperature for starters.

Storing Spelt Flour

Spelt is alive. Take a look at the package label. For example, Whole Grain Spelt and most of the Whites I have encountered contain the germ, the living part of the plant. Keep Spelt flours in a cool, dark place even when using them often. Do not store them near the refrigerator or stove and not in a transparent or even translucent container. If you do not use the flour often—meaning two to three times a week—store the flour in the freezer in convenient packages. Let it come to room temperature before using it for best results. The same holds true of Spelt flour products like Pancake mixes: freeze what you do not use, and the product will stay fresh and lively for months.

Chapter 5: All Measures Are Not the Same

Some of the most common problems in cooking stem from measuring ingredients. This is a result of technique but it is also because measurements are not the same. This imprecision can be confusing especially if you are trying to convert old recipes or recipes from other countries or substituting Spelt for other flours in a recipe.

Ancient peoples frequently based their units of weight on a kernel of grain. Egypt and Greece are examples (see *Writing Things Down* in Part II, Chapter 3). Units of measurement varied greatly until the last two centuries. Many countries have adopted the metric system but the U.S., Great Britain and other English-speaking nations retain different systems so that for cooking purposes, *a cup is not a cup*. It depends on whether it is a dry measure like flour or a liquid measure like water or a solid measure like butter. All of these factors and others cause problems in converting one unit to another, especially for liquid and dry measures. For example, even though the U.S. system(s) was originally based on the British system, there is a 20% difference between what a U.S. gallon is and the larger English gallon.

Another example is the weight measure. Within this category are several systems. Ounces/pounds for measuring mass is one system; the Troy system for precious metals and related Apothecary measures is another. The Avoirdupois system based on number of grains (7000 grains to the pound) is another. Dry measurement is another system, one based on the bushel and barrel (dry quarts, pints, etc.).

With all these things in mind, the following information and tables are presented to you as approximate guidelines for dry and liquid measurements to help you cook and bake with Spelt. Measurement is not an absolute.

Measuring Spelt Flour and Guidelines for Substitutions

The recipes in *Spelt Healthy!* that call for Whole Grain flour are all based on the U.S. ounce. In my experience, Whole Grain Spelt flour from a variety of U.S. venders generally weighs five ounces per cup or 140 grams. The flour will come in a variety of sifts as mentioned elsewhere. Some contain more whole bran; other millers will grind the bran more completely so the particles are very small. It still measures about 5 ounces per cup.

I have found more variance in White Spelt Flour. For example, I have recorded White Spelt from 4.35 ounces per cup to 4.50 ounces per cup to 5 ounces which seems to hold for many of the Whites. This is the result of different companies and types of White Flour. In many cookbooks and places, All-Purpose White Flour weighs 4.5 ounces per cup. You will see these variances reflected in the recipes and especially in the Pastry/Pie Crust Chart because the water absorption of White Spelt flour is somewhat different from the Whole grain. Remember *all* flour, Spelt or other, varies in weight for a number of reasons such as humidity. That is why you must frequently adjust liquid in recipes. It also varies because of the way you measure the ingredient. These and other factors are why recipes are guidelines; they are not absolutes.

✳ Aerate (fluff) your Spelt flour before measuring it. This lightens it up and unpacks it for more accurate measuring. (More below under Measurements and Conversions.)

✳ Do not sift Spelt flour. If you have a recipe that says, "sift the flour," do not. The husk contains both nutrients and fiber. Do not sift White Spelt either. There are White Spelt flours on the market that work beautifully for cakes and other finer pastry uses such as the *Crostate di Fichi* recipe in this book.

Don't Throw Away Your Favorite Recipes

Please do not throw away your favorite recipes! You can successfully convert many of them to Spelt based on the ratio below as a starting point.

✳ Add ¼ cup (56 grams) more Whole Grain Spelt or use ¼ cup less liquid (59 ml). Remember that ingredients like eggs and oil are liquids, too.

Measurements and Conversions

How you measure can affect the outcome of your recipe. It is important to use the proper tools and a few basic methods.

For such dry ingredients as flours, baking powder, baking soda, cocoa, sugar and fine breadcrumbs—use a dry measure tool starting with the ⅛ cup or ¼ cup dry measure. Before you measure, fluff (aerate) the flour or other ingredient by stirring, whisking or tossing. This keeps it from compacting and eliminates any lumps. Spoon or pour the ingredients *into* the measuring cup; do not scoop the measuring tool into the flour. As you spoon or pour, let the dry ingredient mound in the measuring cup. Do not tap or shake the measuring cup to make it even. Instead, take the flat edge of a table knife and level the dry ingredient that way. Tip: Work over a clean piece of waxed paper so you can pour the excess back into the container.

Weighing Ingredients. Kitchen scales, either manual or digital, are an invaluable kitchen tool from measuring flour to weighing dough or cooled loaves to making uniform cookies and other items. They are excellent for portion control and provide even baking because each unit is the same.

Dry Measures. For Spelt flour, always use a dry measure. These are cups and partial, separate cups designed for dry versus liquid measure. These are metal or plastic, non-transparent, and often come in

gradations so they nest one inside the other in sizes ranging from the full cup to ¼ cup and a variety of measures in-between. The rule of thumb is to use measuring spoons for measurements below ¼ cup and dry measure cups starting at, at least, ¼ cup. Many sets now come with the ⅛ cup measure for greater accuracy.

Whole Grain Spelt generally measures:

2 Tbsp =	.50 oz	14 gr
4 Tbsp =	1.00 oz	28 gr
5 Tbsp =	1.25 oz = ¼ cup	35 gr
8 Tbsp =	2.00 oz	57 gr
10 Tbsp =	2.50 oz = ½ cup	71 gr
12 Tbsp =	3.00 oz	85 gr
15 Tbsp =	3.75 oz = ¾ cup	106 gr
16 Tbsp =	4.00 oz	113 gr
18 Tbsp =	5.00 oz = 1 cup	142 gr

Dry/Solid Measure Approximation   **Metric (1 gram = .035 oz)**
Use measuring spoons for small measurements.

1 pinch	less than ⅛ tsp	
1 dash	less than ¼ tsp	
1 tsp =	⅙ oz	5 gr
1 Tbsp =	½ (.5) oz	14 gr
2 Tbsp =	**1 oz** = ¹⁄₁₆ pound	28 gr

Use measuring cups labeled ¼ cup, ⅓ cup, ½ cup, 1 cup, etc. for dry measurements starting with ¼ cup and, if you can, with the ⅛ cup.

4 Tbsp = 2 oz = ¼ cup	56	gr	
3 oz	85	gr	
4 oz = ¼ pound	113	gr	
5 oz	140	gr	
6 oz	180	gr	
8 oz = ½ pound	225	gr	
9 oz	250	gr =	¼ kg
10 oz	285	gr	
12 oz = ¾ pound	349	gr	
13 oz	369	gr	
14 oz	400	gr	
15 oz	425	gr	
16 oz = **1 pound**	454	gr (453.6)	
18 oz = 1⅛ pounds	500	gr =	½ kg
20 oz = 1¼ pounds	560	gr	
24 oz = 1½ pounds	675	gr	
28 oz = 1¾ pounds	800	gr	
32 oz = 2 pounds	900	gr	
36 oz = 2¼ pounds	1000	gr =	1 kg
40 oz = 2½ pounds	1125	gr =	1¼ kg
48 oz = 3 pounds	1350	gr =	1⅓ kg
56 oz = 3½ pounds	1500	gr =	1½ kg
64 oz = 4 pounds	1800	gr =	1¾ kg
72 oz = 4½ pounds	2000	gr =	2kg

Standard U.S. Dry Measures: 1 dry ounce = 1/16 pound; 16 dry ounces = 1 pound; 2 dry pints = 1 dry quart; 32 dry ounces = 1 quart/2 pounds; 8 dry quarts = 1 peck; 4 pecks = 1 bushel ; 1 U.S. sack = 3 bushels.

Some Useful Measures for Shopping: 2.25 pounds/1 kg; 10 pounds/4.5 kg; 20 pounds/9kg; 25 pounds/11.25 kg; 50 pounds/22.5 kg.

Weight Conversions: Convert ounces to grams by multiplying number of ounces by 28.35. Convert grams to ounces by multiplying grams by .035. For example, 56 grams by .035 = 1.96 ounces, rounded up = 2 ounces or ¼ cup. Pounds to grams: multiply pounds by 453.59. Pounds to kilograms, multiply pounds by .45.

Liquid Measures (Fluid Ounce/Ml Conversions) given in U.S., Metric and Imperial.

Use measuring spoons and standard fluid transparent measuring cups that have markings from ¼, ⅓, ½, ¾, 1 cup, etc. on the container that has a pouring lip.

U.S.	U.S./Metric	Imperial
1 drop = ¹⁄₇₆ tsp		
Pinch = less than ⅛ tsp		As is
Dash = less than ¼ tsp (6 drops)		As is
1 teaspoon (76 drops) = ⅓ Tbsp/⅙ oz	5 ml (4.92 ml)	1 tsp
¼ fl oz = 2 tsp	10 ml	1 dessert spoon
½ fl oz = **1 Tablespoon (Tbsp)**	15 ml (14.79 ml)	1 Tbsp
1 fl oz = 2 Tbsp (¹⁄₁₆ pint) (1 shot)	30 ml (29.57 ml)	1 fl oz (28.41 ml)
1.5 fl oz = 1 jigger	44 ml	

Change to fluid-measuring cups.

2 fl oz = **¼ cup**	59 ml	
3 fl oz = 5⅓ Tbsp = **⅓ cup**	87 ml	
4 fl oz = 8 Tbsp = **½ cup** (24 tsp)	118 ml = 1 U.S. gill	
5 fl oz	148 ml	¼ pint or gill (142 ml)
5.5 fl oz = **⅔ cup**	163 ml	
6 fl oz = 12 Tbsp = **¾ cup**	177 ml	
8 fl oz = 16 Tbsp = **1 cup** (¹⁄₁₆ gal)	237 ml (236.58)	
Metric cup	250 ml = **¼ liter**	1 cup
10 fl oz = 1¼ cups	296 ml	½ pint (284 ml)
12 fl oz = 1½ cups	355 ml	
15 fl oz	443 ml (443.5)	¾ pint (420 fl oz)
2 cups = 1 pint metric	450 ml	
16 fl oz = **2 cups = 1 pint U.S.**	473 ml	
18 fl oz = 2¼ cups	532 ml	
½ liter metric	500 ml = **½ liter**	
20 fl oz = 2½ cups	591 ml	1 pint (568 ml)
24 fl oz = **3 cups**	709 ml (709.6)	
25 fl oz	739 ml (739.25)	1¼ pints (710 ml)
25.6 fl oz = **1 Fifth**	757 ml	
26 fl oz = 3¼ cups	768 ml (768.8)	
27 fl oz = 3½ cups	798 ml	

30 fl oz = 3¾ cups	887 ml	1½ pints (852 ml)
32 fl oz = 4 cups = 2 pints = 1 quart	946 ml	1¾ pints (994 ml)
1 liter metric	1000 ml = **1 liter**	
36 fl oz = 4½ cups	1065 ml	
40 fl oz = **5 cups**	1183 ml	2 pt = 1 quart (1136 ml)
2 liters Metric	2000 ml = **2 liters**	
3 liters Metric	3000 ml = **3 liters**	
128 fl oz = **16 cups = 4 qt = 1 gal**	3785 ml = **3.79 liters**	
1 wine gallon	3785 ml	
1 beer gallon	4621 ml = 4.6 liters	4.54 liters = Imp gallon
1 firkin / 9 U.S. gallons	34,065 ml = 34 liters	
1 barrel = 31½ gal	119,240 ml = 119 liters	

Fluid Conversions: Convert ounces to milliliters by multiplying ounces by 30 (29.57). To convert milliliters to ounces, divide milliliters by number of ounces.

Equivalents and Substitutions

Oven Temperature Information and Conversions

Electric		*Gas Mark*	**Relative Description**
Fahrenheit	*Centigrade*		
175°–200° F	80°–95° C		Keeping cooked foods warm
Baking:			
225° F	105° C	¼	Very cool oven
250° F	120° C	½	
275° F	130° C	1	Cool (very slow oven)
300° F	150° C	2	
325° F	165° C	3	Very moderate oven (slow)
350° F	180° C	4	Moderate
375° F	190° C	5	
400° F	200° C	6	Moderately hot
425° F	220° C	7	
450° F	230° C	8	Hot
475° F	245° C	9	Very hot
500° F	250° C		Extremely hot; broiling

Boiling point at sea level: 212° F / 100° C

High altitude baking: Increase oven temperature by 25° F above 5000 feet; adjust baking time (longer) by 5–10 minutes.

Inches to Centimeters: Multiply to inch by 2.54.
Centimeters to inches: Multiply centimeter(s) by .39

¹⁄₁₆ inch = ¼ cm	¼ inch = ¾ cm	½ inch = 1½ cm	
1 inch = 2½ cm	4 inches = 10 cm	8 inches= 20 cm	10 inches = 25 cm

Some useful dry measurements and equivalents (U.S.):
1 cup Whole Grain flour = 5 oz (140 gr)
1 cup White All Purpose flour = 4½ oz (183 gr)
1 cup granulated sugar = 8 oz (225 gr)
1 cup brown sugar = 6 oz (180 gr)
1 cup Confectioners' sugar = 4½ oz (183 gr)

Useful liquid measurements:
1 large egg = 2 oz = ¼ cup = 4 Tbsp (60 ml)
1 egg yolk = 1 Tbsp + 1 tsp (20 ml)
1 egg white = 2 Tbsp + 2 tsp (40 ml)
12–14 egg yolks = 1 cup (237 ml)
8–10 egg whites = 1 cup (237 ml)

Useful solid measurements:
1 Tbsp butter = .5 oz (14 gr)
4 Tbsp butter = ¼ cup (2 oz) = ½ stick (56.7 gr)
8 Tbsp butter = ½ cup (4 oz) = 1 stick (113.4 gr)
32 Tbsp butter = 2 cups (16 oz) = 4 sticks or 1 package (453.6 gr)

Substitutions:

Oil	*Butter*
¾ tsp	1 tsp
3 Tbsp	¼ cup
¼ cup + 2 Tbsp	½ cup
¾ cup	1 cup

Yeast: Package and Bulk
1 package active dry yeast = 2¼ tsp
¼ oz (.225 oz), 1 oz (7.675 gr)
1 Tbsp bulk yeast = 1 package active dry yeast + ¾ tsp of a second package

Lemons/Limes
1 large lime = about 1½ Tbsp juice; 2–3 limes = about 1 teaspoon zest (rind)
1 large lemon = 3 to 4 Tbsp juice; about 2 tsp zest (rind)

Vegetable/Fruit Equivalents
1 medium apple, chopped = 1 cup
1 medium onion, chopped = ½ cup
2 stalks celery (¼ lb), chopped = 1 cup

Salt
¾ tsp sea salt = 1 tsp table salt

PART V
THE RECIPES

THE MORNING MENU: BREAKFAST/BRUNCH

Cerealia

Toast of the Day

Athena Crepes

Spelt Sproutcakes

Spukwheat Pancakes

Ebleskivers

Spelt and Emmer-Farro Pancake Mixes

Basic Tasty Waffles

Whole Grain Waffles With Spelt Sprouts and Fruit Bits

Chocolate Walnut Waffles

Basic Baking Powder Biscuits

Breakfast Biscuits To Go

Lively Vegetable and Goat Cheese Scramble in Spelt Tart Shell

Quiche

Frittata with Ricotta and Herbed Spelt Crumbs

Breakfast Burrito

Chiles Rellenos

Huevos Rancheros (Mexican Ranch-Style Eggs)

Empanadas de Fruta (Baked Fruit Turnovers)

New Braunfels, Texas Custard Toast (French Toast)

Cheese And Pineapple Danish Modern (Cheese Danish)

Beignes (New Orleans Style French Doughnuts)

Bagels (Water Bagels)

Carns English Muffins

Sweet Muffins With Crumble Topping

Spelta's Cinnamon Rolls

Pistachio Sticky Buns

Cerealia

Cereals are any edible grains and are usually from the *Poeceae* (grass) family like Spelt. They are so important to the history of humankind that in mythology a multitude of gods and goddesses presided over each step of the farming process, phases of the moon and type of cereal, from Ishtar and Isis and Demeter ("Spelt Mother") to the Roman Seia who protected the seed in the ground to Ceres over all. She was the supreme goddess of agriculture and made the lands fertile and gifted humans with the harvest. More than a thousand years later and the Roman Empire long gone, she was still pictured as overseeing fields as in the drawing below.

Redrawn from a Middle Ages woodcut, scene shows Roman Goddess Ceres overseeing plowing of fields, reaping of grain and taking it to a water powered mill (middle right) to be ground into flour. In Roman times, to say that an act or thing was "Fit for Ceres" referred to something that was splendid. Today the saying is "Fit for a King."

Cereal for Breakfast— An Ancient Tradition

In Western cultures, we often eat "cereal" (edible grain) for breakfast. It is synonymous with the morning meal. To make grain edible to humans it requires to be sprouted (as in the Sproutcakes recipe) or it must be cooked. The most elemental form of cooking is to cook the grain in liquid, usually water. *Porridge* is by definition a soft cereal food boiled in a liquid until thick. It is one of the two most ancient forms of cooking grains. Spelt berries do not generally reduce to *mush* like oatmeal does. (An exception is Sprouted Cream of Spelt; it is "mushy" like oatmeal.) Instead, Spelt softens and holds its form until pureed or by some other method. That is why it can be used in place of rice or in other recipes like Spelt Wheat Berry and Honey Bread.

Porridge is made from either the Spelt berry or from cracked grain in pieces. To "crack" the grain is to remove the tough outer hull that protects the Spelt grain. (The process results in the whole berry or sometimes a broken or "cracked" berry which is turned into cracked grain for cereal.) Cracking is accomplished by milling, hand or mechanical. The berry is then cooked in liquid until it splits and exposes the inner portion of the seed so all of the nutrition is released. This is what creates the characteristic *mushiness* or softness of porridge made from cereals like oats. Throughout prehistory and up until a couple of centuries ago, porridge was the staple food for the majority of people, who ate it morning and/or evening (frumenty for example). In some places, porridge introduced a meal.

 Porridge with milk has long been a staple. It simply wasn't only cow's milk that was used. In Europe, the "milk" was frequently made from nuts especially almonds. The nut milk was added or the nuts were broken up and cooked with the porridge creating its own milk while cooking.

Bingen Porridge
Cooked Spelt Berries

Read about St. Hildegard of Bingen, the Patron Saint of Spelt, in Part II, Chapter 3.

1   cup Spelt berries (makes about 2⅓ cups cooked)

Best if soaked overnight in water to cover by 3–4 inches. (Berries can be put on to boil without the soaking—it will just take longer.) Drain and rinse. Add the berries and 4–5 cups water and a dash of salt (optional) to a saucepan and bring to a boil (10 minutes). Reduce heat, simmer for 20–40 minutes or longer until the berries are softened. Stir occasionally to keep from sticking and add water if necessary. Stir in milk, honey, maple chunks, raisins or other dried fruit.

Note: This recipe can be made with Emmer-Farro.

Cracked Spelt Cereal and Granola are on the market
See Appendix 2—Shopping for Spelt

Lentz Farms produces a quick-cooking Cracked Spelt cereal that requires only 8–15 minutes cooking time. It's not just for breakfast—use Cracked Spelt in place of Bulgar Wheat in salads and your favorite Middle Eastern recipes.

Sprouted Cream of Spelt Cereal is now available, too!

Rolled Spelt (Spelt Flakes) Hot Breakfast Cereal

Use Rolled Spelt in place of rolled oats for a simple, nutritious hot morning cereal.

Prep time/Cook time: 10–15 min stovetop; 3–5 minutes microwave • Yield: about 1 cup hot cereal

Ingredients

½ cup Whole Grain Rolled Spelt
1   cup water
dash of salt

1. Stovetop: In saucepan bring 1 cup water to boil. Add Rolled Spelt. Reduce heat and simmer, stirring occasionally, for 10–15 minutes (depending on desired consistency). Serve hot with honey and raisins, milk, turbinado sugar or maple syrup or fresh fruit like fresh sliced peaches.

Microwave: In microwave safe bowl, add ¾ cup water and ½ cup Rolled Spelt. Cover bowl; cook on high 2½ minutes; stir. Replace cover and cook additional 2 to 2½ minutes.

TOAST OF THE DAY— SOME RECOMMENDATIONS FROM SPELTA'S PLACE BAKERY

Speltessence Bread (Regular or
Bread Machine)

Molasses and Spelt No-Knead Bread

Classic White for Cinnamon Toast

Auld Lang Syne (Remembrance)
Bread with Raisins

Challah

Spelt Wheat Berry and Honey Bread

Pan Andrea Festival Bread

Athena Crepes

Athena Crepes are light and moist with a hint of Spelt's natural sweetness.

Blood Type Eating: A, B, AB (O unknown profile for goat's milk yogurt).
Prep time: 5 min • Cook time: 40–50 min • Yield: 16 4" crepes

Ingredients

⅔ cup Whole Grain Spelt flour
1 Tbsp brown sugar
½ tsp salt
1 tsp baking powder
½ tsp baking soda
2 cups plain goat's milk yogurt or other plain yogurt without additives*
1 egg
2 Tbsp vegetable oil

*Additives such as sugar in commercial yogurt change the texture and cause crepes to stick.

1. Combine dry ingredients in large mixing bowl; whisk.

2. In separate bowl mix the yogurt, egg and oil until combined. Add to the dry mixture and blend briefly until all ingredients are thoroughly incorporated. Lumps are okay.

3. Place a large nonstick skillet over medium heat. Lightly spray pan with cooking oil or coat bottom with sheen of vegetable oil.

Using ¼ cup measure, pour rounds of batter into the pan and cook until bubbles form on top and bottom is golden brown (6–8 minutes). Turn crepe and brown other side (4–5 minutes). Continue with rest of batter adding oil as necessary and stirring batter once between batches. Serve warm with honey or maple syrup or top with fresh fruit.

Not only are crepes a wonderful breakfast/brunch food, they are excellent for wrapping chicken or turkey in as a late night snack or quick meal. Good warm or at room temperature; they will keep well in the refrigerator for a couple of days.

Variations:

Turkey in the Spelt: Roll turkey breakfast links inside crepes.

Apollo Cakes: Add ¼ to ½ cup additional Whole Grain Spelt flour to recipe for a hearty pancake.

Spelt Sproutcakes

An alternative to pancakes, these are a terrific complement to omelets. They are also a refreshingly different alternative to potatoes for dinner. Serve Sproutcakes as a side with turkey, lamb or baked fish. Adapted from recipe at sproutpeople.com and printed here courtesy The Sprout People.

Spelt sprouts 3 days into their germination cycle work very well for this recipe. Sprouts are loaded with Phytochemicals. Besides being nutritious, they provide a delicious slightly sweet crunch to food. (See *The Vegetable Stand* section for more information on Spelt Sprouts.)

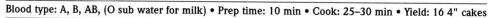

Blood type: A, B, AB, (O sub water for milk) • Prep time: 10 min • Cook: 25–30 min • Yield: 16 4" cakes

 A mash of sprouts placed on a hot rock is one of the two most ancient forms of cooking.

Ingredients

4   egg whites, beaten to stiff peaks
1   cup sprouted Spelt
¾   cup milk
4   egg yolks
1   Tbsp fluid honey
¼   cup vegetable oil
1¼ cups Whole Grain Spelt flour
2   tsp baking powder
½   tsp salt
Additional oil for cooking (2–4 Tbsp)

1. Place a large nonstick skillet or griddle over medium heat. Preheat oven to 200° F and warm a platter. Separate the egg yolks from whites. Beat eggs whites to stiff peaks. Set aside.

2. Add Spelt Sprouts and ¼ cup of the milk to blender or food processor. Blend, gradually adding remaining milk until mixture is smooth. Add the egg yolks, honey and oil and blend until combined but not frothy.

3. In a large bowl, combine the Spelt flour, baking powder and salt. Whisk together. Gradually stir in the Sprout mixture until all ingredients are moist. Fold in the stiff egg whites.

4. Ladle ⅓ cup batter per cake onto griddle. Cook for 2½ to 3 minutes until bottom is brown and edges are slightly dry. Carefully turn and cook other side until brown (about 1½ minutes). The cakes will be somewhat puffy and have a sponge-like appearance when done. Place in stacks on warmed platter and keep Sproutcakes warm until all are cooked. Stir batter once or twice between batches. Serve warm with honey, preserves, and fresh fruit in season or as a side dish for dinner.

Spukwheat Pancakes

Adapted from my Grandmother's recipe for Buttermilk Buckwheat pancakes, these are slightly sweet and tangy with the heartiness of Spelt and, oh, so delicious.

Blood Type: A, B, AB (O sub plain soy milk) • Prep time: 5 min • Cook time: 25–30 min
Yield: 10 6" cakes (about 3 oz) or 20–24 "silver dollar" cakes (about 1 oz each)

Another ancient food, these are OVA SFONGIA EX LACTE from Roman times as mentioned in Apicius.

Ingredients

1   cup Whole Grain Spelt flour
1   cup + 2 Tbsp White Spelt flour
1   tsp salt
4   tsp baking powder
1   Tbsp granulated sugar
1   egg, room temp, beaten
1½ cups milk (or plain soy milk), room temp
4   Tbsp vegetable oil
Additional oil for cooking (2–3 tsp)

1. Place a nonstick griddle or large skillet over medium heat. Griddle is hot enough when a drop of water flicked on it sizzles and jumps. Add 1 tsp oil to the pan or spray lightly. Heat oven to 200° F and place a platter in it to warm if you are not going to be serving pancakes as they are cooked.

2. Combine the dry ingredients in a large mixing bowl; whisk. Add the beaten egg, milk and oil and stir just enough to moisten all ingredients. The batter should be a bit lumpy. Adjust amount of milk or flour, if necessary, to achieve desired texture.

3. Pour ¼ cup batter per pancake onto the griddle leaving a couple of inches between cakes so they cook better and are easier to turn. When edges are dry and bottom lightly browned (about 3 minutes), flip and cook other side (2–3 minutes). Stack on platter and keep warm in oven until all are cooked. Stir batter once or twice between batches. Serve warm with honey, maple syrup, fruit preserves or fresh fruit in season.

Ebleskivers

Simple basic recipe for Danish Pancakes, golden brown spheres cooked on the stovetop in a special pan. Great way to interest kids in cooking and a fine way to make a sampler tray of appetizers for family and friends especially on short notice. Recipe courtesy Northland Aluminum/Nordic Ware, the company that makes this special pan. (See Appendix 2—Spelt Products.)

Blood Type: B, AB (use goat's milk or skim milk), A (sub goat's milk or soy milk), O (use soy milk)
Prep time: 10 min • Cook time: 4½ min (batch of 7) • Yield: 36 (1 Tbsp batter each)

Kitchen Note: Ebleskivers do not shake the Kitchen Richter Scale. Each one weighs less than an ounce. This version eliminates the traditional buttermilk in the batter and replaces oil for butter in cooking. The variety is limited to your imagination because you can amend the recipe in so many ways by changing the ratio of flours and the spices, seasonings. *Example:* Pour half the batter into the cup and drop a morsel of fruit onto the batter. Cover with remaining ½ tablespoon batter and cook. Or incorporate the morsel into the batter such as the spice and fruit version offered here. They cook quickly—a batch of 7 cooks in about 4 minutes with the added bonus the oven isn't tied up while you're cooking a meal.

Ingredients

3   egg yolks, lightly beaten
2   Tbsp sugar
¼   cup vegetable oil
½   cup milk (or soy milk which will slightly alter taste, texture and cooking properties)
¾   cup Whole Grain Spelt flour
¾   cup White Spelt flour
½   tsp salt
½   tsp mace or nutmeg or cardamom (optional)
3   egg whites, stiffly beaten
1   cup raisins or chopped dates (optional)

1. Place Ebleskiver pan on medium heat. Flick a drop of water on pan; if it sizzles, pan is ready for cooking. If using raisins or other dried fruit, soak in hot water to cover (10 min) and drain before mixing into batter.

2. Combine the beaten egg yolk, sugar and oil in a large mixing bowl and stir to incorporate. Stir in half of the milk.

In separate bowl, combine the Spelt flours, salt and spice. Whisk. Add to the wet mixture alternately with the remaining milk.

3. Fold stiffly beaten egg whites into batter. Gently stir in the raisins or dates. Add ½ tsp oil to each of the Ebleskiver cups. Add 1 Tbsp batter to each cup and bake until the edges brown and surface starts to bubble. Turn with wooden skewer (a plastic picnic fork works well also). If they brown too quickly, turn them several times as they are cooking. Pop out the Ebleskivers. Drop oil in cups and repeat procedure. Serve them plain, roll in sugar or cover with sweet syrup or fruit sauce. As savories, incorporate chile/cheese, make with curry, tandoori or other spice seasonings. Add dried fruit such as apricots, sultanas. Vary the ratio of Spelt flours to achieve a different taste and texture such as making with all Whole Grain or more White for treats.

Spelt And Emmer-Farro Pancake Mixes

Spelt pancake and waffle mixes are available on your grocer's shelves or by way of the Internet (see Appendix 2—Shopping for Spelt). In less than 15 minutes, you can have eight four-inch pancakes hot and steaming on your breakfast table. A new entry on the market is Lentz Farms Emmer-Farro Pancake. (Read more about emmer in *Part II: Speltoids.*)

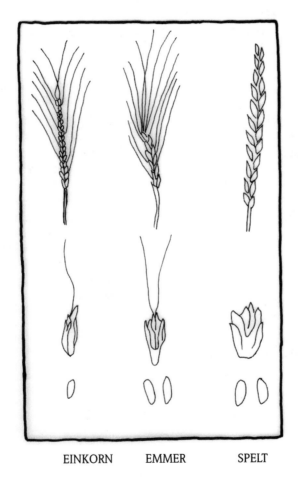

EINKORN   EMMER   SPELT

The Ancient Hulled Grain Family (See Part II, Speltoids)

Basic Tasty Waffles

Waffles have always been a treat but with the variety of waffle makers now available, they have also become festive and fun. In thirty minutes, you can have nutritious tasty waffles. Start with the Basic Tasty Waffle and experiment with ingredients. As an alternative to the traditional whipped cream or syrup, try fresh fruit in season or berry and other easy fruit sauces (see *Sweet Toppings*). They add color and variety and suit all tastes and blood types.

Blood Type: A, B, AB (O use water instead of milk)
Prep time: 5 min • Cook time: 25 • Yield: 16 (1 oz) Size varies w/waffler

Ingredients

1   cup + 2 Tbsp White Spelt flour
½   cup Whole Grain Spelt flour
3   tsp baking powder
2   tsp granulated sugar
½   tsp salt
2   eggs, beaten
¾   cup milk
3   Tbsp vegetable oil

1. Heat waffle maker; oil grids (or not) according to individual waffler instructions. Suggested initial Browning level is 3 to 4 for first batch.

2. Combine flours, baking powder, sugar and salt in mixing bowl. Whisk. Add beaten eggs, milk and oil and mix just enough to moisten all ingredients. Lumps are okay; this is not a smooth batter.

3. Pour into grids according to amount specified for your waffle maker. Cook.

4. Remove from waffler and place on wire rack to keep waffles crisp. If making a whole recipe prior to serving, place wire rack on baking sheet and set in slow 200° F oven. In many of the new machines, the waffles can be put back into the waffler to warm and re-crisp by lining them up with the grids and closing lid and letting them cook a minute. Waffles freeze well. Let them cool completely on a wire rack then place them in a plastic freezer bag. Pull one out and reheat in toaster.

Whole Grain Waffles with Spelt Sprouts and Fruit Bits

These are moist, tender waffles, which you can make with a variety of ingredients such as chopped dates, apricots, apples and blueberries. The sprouts add sweet crunch and nutrients. Reconstitute dried fruit by immersing in hot water for 10 minutes and draining thoroughly prior to adding to the waffles. Some packaged fruits now on the market contain enough moisture they no longer require the soaking.

Blood Type: A, B, AB (O make with water) • Prep time: 5 min
Cook time: 25 min • Yield: 18 (1½ oz) waffles

Ingredients

2   egg whites, stiffly beaten
1¼ cups Whole Grain Spelt flour
½   cup + 2 Tbsp White Spelt flour
½   cup granulated sugar
3   tsp baking powder
1   tsp salt
¾   cup milk
2   egg yolks, lightly beaten
¼   cup + 2 Tbsp vegetable oil
1   tsp vanilla
¼   cup Spelt sprouts
¼   cup fruit bits

1. Heat waffle maker; oil grids (or not) according to individual waffler instructions. Suggested Browning level is 3 to 4 for first batch.

2. Combine the flours, sugar, baking powder and salt in mixing bowl; whisk. Add the milk, beaten egg yolks, oil and vanilla; mix just enough to blend ingredients. Stir in the Spelt sprouts and fruit bits. Fold in the egg whites.

3. Pour into grids according to instructions. These waffles require a slightly longer baking time so Browning level may need to be increased on your waffler. When done, place on wire rack to keep crisp. If making a whole recipe prior to serving, place wire rack on baking sheet and set in slow 200° F oven. Cool leftover waffles completely. Freeze in plastic bag.

Chocolate Walnut Waffles

Blood Type: A, B, AB (O make with water or nut milk)
Prep time: 10 min • Cook time: 25 min • Yield: 18 (1½ oz) waffles

---

Ingredients

2   oz unsweetened baking chocolate, melted
2   egg whites, stiffly beaten
1¼   cups White Spelt flour
¾   cup Whole Grain Spelt flour
½   cup granulated sugar
3   tsp baking powder
1   tsp salt
¾   cup milk
2   egg yolks, lightly beaten
¼   cup + 2 Tbsp vegetable oil
1   tsp vanilla flavoring
½   cup walnuts, finely chopped

1. Melt chocolate. Set aside to cool. Beat egg whites. Set aside. Heat the waffler and oil grids (or not) according to individual waffler instructions. Suggested initial Browning level is 2 to 4.

2. Combine the Spelt flours, sugar, baking powder and salt in mixing bowl. Whisk. Blend the milk and egg yolks; stir in to dry ingredients just enough to moisten all ingredients. Add the cooled melted chocolate and the oil. Stir in the vanilla and walnuts. Fold in the egg whites.

3. Pour into grids according to amount specified by individual waffler. When done, place on wire rack to keep crisp. Adjust Browning level if necessary. If making a whole recipe prior to serving, place waffles on wire rack, place rack on baking sheet and set in slow 200° F oven. Cool leftover waffles completely. These freeze well. Simply cool completely and store in plastic freezer bag.

BEYOND BRUNCH serving suggestions: Serve Chocolate Walnut Waffles with chocolate sauce and fresh strawberries or topped with **Batangas Bananas** (see *Sweet Toppings* section) as a dessert.

Chocolate Waffle Ice Cream Sandwich: By adjusting the baking powder (½ to 1 tsp less) and cooking them slightly longer, these make great wafers for ice cream sandwiches. Soften the ice cream by letting it sit at room temperature about 15 minutes. Spoon about ⅓ of a cup ice cream on top of a waffle with waffle design side down. Place second waffle, design side up, over ice cream and gently press and turn it to even the ice cream. Wrap with plastic and store in plastic bag or container with tight lid in freezer.

Basic Baking Powder Biscuits

Basic, old-fashioned recipe for fluffy, high biscuits made with oil not butter. Use as dumplings or transform to Rosemary and Cheese Drop Biscuits for evening meals. Make as shortcake for fresh fruit.

Blood Type: A, B, AB (O sub soy milk or water) • Prep time: 10 min • Cook time: 12–15 min • Yield: 1 dozen (2½")

Ingredients

2¼ cups + 1–2 Tbsp White Spelt flour
½ cup Whole Grain Spelt flour
4 tsp baking powder (3 tsp at altitudes above 5000'; 2½ above 6000')
½ tsp salt
4 Tbsp vegetable oil
¾ cup milk (soy milk or water may be substituted but taste and texture will change somewhat)

1. Preheat oven to 425° F. Combine the Spelt flours, baking powder and salt in large mixing bowl; whisk to combine. Add oil and cut in until mixture resembles coarse crumbs. Add the milk and stir just enough to wet all ingredients and dough forms around paddle (mixer or processor) or spoon (by hand).

2. Turn dough out onto surface lightly sprinkled with White Spelt flour. Knead gently about 10 times. Pat or roll out to ½" thickness and cut to size. Place an inch apart on ungreased baking sheet. For biscuits with softer crust, set next to one another in 8-inch x 8-inch pan or bake in 10" pie pan or ovenproof skillet.

3. Place on middle rack in preheated hot oven (425° F) and bake for 12–16 minutes until tops are golden brown and crisp.

Drop Biscuits: Use additional 2 Tbsp milk (soy milk or water) and drop by heaping tablespoonfuls onto parchment-covered or lightly oiled baking sheet. Bake as directed.

Rosemary and Cheese Drop Biscuits: Add 1 cup shredded semi-soft Mozzarella cheese, 1 tsp ground celery seed, 1 tsp ground rosemary to the dry mixture. Change oil to 5 Tbsp oil, change milk (soy or water) to ¾ cup + 2 Tbsp. Use parchment or lightly grease the baking sheet. Bake 15 minutes or until golden brown. Recipe makes 16 2-inch+ biscuits.

Shortcake: Add 2 Tbsp granulated sugar, an additional ½ tsp salt and use 5 Tbsp oil in the recipe. Pat or roll out to ¾ inch thickness. Bake 12–14 minutes. Let cool slightly and split with 2 forks as you would an English Muffin. Scoop out some of the crumb. Spoon fresh fruit mixed with sugared water onto shortcake. Makes 8 2½" (2½ oz each). Freeze leftovers for quick use another day.

Breakfast Biscuits To Go

Part of the idea of turning your kitchen into your favorite restaurant is to make healthful food fast when need arises. By baking Spelt biscuits and using turkey products, here is one good way to go.

Blood Type: AB, B, A (use Mozzarella); O (make biscuits with soy milk or water and use Mozzarella)
Prep time: 20 min • Cook/assemble time: 10 min • Yield: 4 (5 oz Breakfast Biscuits)

BISCUITS IN THE U.S. "Biscuits" in the U.S. are quite similar to what "scones" are to the rest of the world. Scones are generally considered in the U.S. as a food from the British Isles where, in turn, "biscuits" are like U.S. cookies (thin, sweet with a bit of crunch).

Ingredients

1   recipe Basic Baking Powder Biscuits
½   pkg Turkey Breakfast Patties (4 patties)
or 6 oz (8 slices cut in half) Turkey Bacon
4   eggs
4   slices (8 oz) soft Mozzarella or Cheddar cheese

1. Preheat oven to 425° F. Make one recipe of biscuits. Pat or roll out to ½ inch thickness and cut into 2½ inch diameter biscuits. Place on ungreased baking sheet and bake 14 minutes (not too crisp). Remove from pan and set on wire rack.

2. As biscuits are baking, follow directions on package for cooking turkey patties or bacon by stovetop method. (Microwave or stovetop is generally 6–8 minutes.) Place a 10", preferably nonstick, skillet on medium heat. To cook bacon so it is crisp, heat pan with 1 Tbsp vegetable oil and then cook bacon (about 6–8 minutes patties or bacon). Remove from pan; set aside on platter and keep warm.

3. Spray pan with cooking spray or add sufficient oil to coat bottom of pan. Grease 4 egg/muffin rings and place in skillet set on medium heat. Crack eggs directly into rings and poke 2–3 holes in each yolk so it breaks. Cook until egg is firm but not dry. Remove ring, flip egg, and cook until firm. Place a slice of cheese on top of the egg and cook about 30 seconds longer, just until cheese starts to melt. Remove eggs from skillet and set on a platter with turkey.

4. Slice each fresh biscuit in half. Place egg with cheese on bottom half of biscuit; next add patty or half-strips of bacon in an X. Top with remaining biscuit half. When all four are finished, wrap each in wax paper. Put in small paper bags with a couple of paper napkins and away you go. Freeze remaining biscuits to use another day with the remaining patties or bacon. Or make 8 Breakfast Biscuits and refrigerate what isn't consumed and eat the next day. Simply remove wax paper, place Breakfast Biscuit in paper towel and heat in microwave on high for 20 seconds.

Lively Vegetable and Goat Cheese Scramble in Spelt Tart Shell

A layered, colorful blend of fresh vegetables, peppers, egg and cheese served in a Spelt tart. (For tart shell recipe see **Pastry and Pie Crust Chart** in *Pastries, Pies and Other Sweet Delights* section.)

Blood Type: okay A, B, AB, O (A, AB sub pimento for red peppers; A, O use Pecorino Romano)
Prep time: 10 min • Cook time: 25–30 min • Yield: 4 6-oz servings

Ingredients

4 4" baked Spelt Tart shells (1 recipe 8–9" Mixed Flour or White Single Crust)
3 Tbsp Olive or other vegetable oil
½ medium-size red onion (1 cup), chopped
4 oz roasted red peppers, drained or pimento
2 oz soft crumbled goat cheese
3 oz fresh baby spinach (3 cups), chopped
½ tsp paprika or Dash seasoning (optional)
¼ tsp powdered garlic
2 Tbsp grated Asiago or Pecorino Romano cheese (cheese optional)
4 eggs, room temperature, beaten

1. Set a large skillet over moderate heat; add 1 Tbsp olive oil and let pan warm.

2. Sauté the red onions until soft. Add garlic powder and stir in chopped peppers.

3. Sprinkle goat cheese crumbles evenly over onions and peppers then cover the mixture with chopped baby spinach and 1 Tbsp of the grated cheese. Drizzle with 2 Tbsp olive oil. Reduce heat and let cook, covered, 15–20 minutes until spinach is tender and goat cheese begins to melt. Warm the tart shells in slow oven (250° F).

4. Pour beaten eggs over the top of the skillet mixture and sprinkle with paprika or Dash. Cook for 3–4 minutes until set. Gently fold in the eggs. Spoon the mixture into warmed baked tart shells and sprinkle with the remaining finely grated cheese. Serve warm. For Mexican flavor, add spiced shredded beef to mixture or mix in chopped Italian Hot Turkey Sausage.

Quiche

A lovely Quiche Lorraine with optional spinach and the traditional sprinkle of nutmeg. (For the pie shell recipe, see **Pastry and Pie Crust Chart** in *Pastries, Pies and Other Sweet Delights* section.)

Blood Type: B, O (A, AB sub oil) • Prep time: 20 min • Cook time: 55–60 min • Yield: 8 servings

Ingredients

1   recipe 8–9" Mixed Flour or White Spelt unbaked pie shell
1   medium sweet onion (about 1¼ cups), finely chopped
2   Tbsp butter or 1½ Tbsp vegetable oil such as Light Olive
1   cup fresh baby spinach, chopped (optional)
1¼ cups semi-soft mozzarella, coarsely grated
1   Tbsp Whole or White Spelt flour
3   eggs, room temperature
½   tsp salt
½   tsp ground black pepper or pepper medley (optional)
¼   tsp freshly ground nutmeg (optional)

1. Preheat oven to 400° F (375° F if using glass or ceramic dish). Prick the unbaked crust in many places, bottom and sides, and bake 5 minutes. Remove from oven; set aside.

2. Place a sauté pan over medium heat; add the butter or oil; sauté the onions until just about tender. Stir in the chopped spinach and continue cooking until onions become tender and translucent (3–5 minutes). Drain any excess liquid from the pan and spoon onions and spinach into the unbaked pie shell, spreading evenly across the bottom.

3. Toss the cheese and flour together; sprinkle over the onions and spinach.

4. Beat the eggs until they are well blended but not frothy; stir in the milk, salt, pepper, nutmeg and blend. Pour the mixture over the onions.

5. Bake in preheated hot (400° F) oven for 20 minutes; reduce the heat to 300° F. Bake an additional 35–40 minutes. Test by inserting toothpick or knife into center. If it comes out clean, the Quiche is done. Remove from oven. Cut into wedges and serve hot; let it cool to enjoy for brunch or buffet; chill and take on a picnic or for lunch the next day.

The fanciful painted egg with Spelt sprouts represents a long tradition. The Ukraine, Hungary and adjoining areas have a long tradition of painting eggs—often with depictions of grain. Painting eggs goes very far back in human time. Symbolizing rebirth, red eggs were placed in human flatbread forms thousands of years ago. The Danish Modern in the Morning Menu would have been braided in Medieval Times and painted eggs inserted in the coils. Eggs were also offerings. The Frittata with Ricotta was an ancient offering to the gods and a popular dish in Roman times.

Frittata with Ricotta and Herbed Spelt Crumbs

Simple and ancient dish with custard-like texture and classic ingredients, including herbed Spelt crumbs. Like Quiche, serve it warm or at room temperature for brunch or a light evening meal. Vary the taste by using breadcrumbs from the Roman, Calabrese or Brundisi Pesto Breads and fresh herbs such as summer savory, lemon thyme, italian parsley, basil or tarragon.

Blood Type: A, B, AB (O avoid because of Ricotta cheese)
Prep time: 10 min • Cook time: 20–25 min • Yield: 8 servings

Ingredients

1½ cups dried Spelt bread crumbs
¼ cup Olive or other vegetable oil
3 tsp dried, crushed herbs (basil, tarragon, savory or a mixture to taste)
1 pound (1¾ cups + 1½ Tbsp) ricotta cheese
6 eggs, room temperature
4 Tbsp finely grated Pecorino Romano or semi-soft Mozzarella cheese
2 Tbsp fresh basil, tarragon, savory or other herbs, chopped (optional)

1. Preheat oven to 350° F. Place a nonstick 10-inch ovenproof skillet over medium heat. Add 2 Tbsp of the olive oil to the pan and heat. Add the breadcrumbs and toast, stirring frequently, until lightly browned. Stir in the dried herbs. Remove from heat; set aside. Wipe skillet with paper towel. Reduce heat to moderately low; add remaining 2 Tbsp oil.

2. With mixer or food processor, cream the ricotta until it is light and smooth. Set aside. In separate bowl, lightly beat the eggs with 2 Tbsp of the finely grated cheese. Stir in fresh chopped herbs. Combine the ricotta and eggs; blend well.

3. Add half the herbed breadcrumbs to skillet and spread evenly over bottom. Gently pour the ricotta and egg mixture into the pan. Cook, without stirring, on moderately low heat until the eggs are just about set (10–15 min). Time will vary because of ricotta cheese. Edges should shrink a bit from the sides and top should be gelling.

4. Place skillet on middle rack of preheated oven (350° F); cook for 3 minutes or longer (until set). Remove from oven and sprinkle remaining breadcrumbs and 2 Tbsp remaining cheese over top of frittata. Return to oven and bake another 3 minutes until crumbs are deep golden brown, cheese slightly melted and Frittata is completely set. Remove from oven. Using a plastic spatula, loosen edges and slide onto a warmed platter or serve directly from skillet. Cut into wedges. Serve warm or at room temperature.

Breakfast Burrito

What could be easier than pulling a Spelt tortilla from the freezer and filling it with eggs and sausage?

Make tortillas ahead of time to have on hand for just such a meal on the run (15 minutes max).

Blood Type: A, B, AB, O

Spelt Flour Tortillas 6–7" diameter (see recipe under *Many Small Things* section).

Cook a package of Turkey Sausage Breakfast Links. Scramble two eggs. Chop two links and fold into the scrambled eggs. Spoon onto tortilla and roll up. Wrap paper towel around bottom of Burrito and go. Refrigerate or freeze the remainder of the sausage and use another day.

Chiles Rellenos

Traditional Southwest dish generally served with Enchilada Sauce over the Rellenos and beans and warm tortillas on the side. With a little planning, this is a mouth-watering meal especially for Brunch. (See the *Many Small Things* section for Enchilada Sauce Sabrosa and Spelt Flour Tortillas.)

Blood Type: Not rated • Prep time: 10 min • Cook time: 30–40 min • Yield: 18

Tip: This recipe uses canned mild green Chiles, 18 count to the can (9 large whole green Chiles cut in half). The count varies with the brand. A good rule of thumb is 2–3 of these canned chiles per egg so you can adjust the recipe if need be.

Ingredients

¾   cup White Spelt or Whole Grain Spelt flour
1   can (27 oz) whole green Chiles, mild
1¼ to 1½ pounds semi-soft Mozzarella or Monterey jack cheese grated or cut into thin strips to fit into Chiles
8   eggs, room temperature, separated yolks and whites
1½ tsp baking powder
½   tsp salt
1   Tbsp milk
Canola or other vegetable oil for frying

1. Place ¾ cup Spelt flour in a small bowl. Set aside. Rinse Chiles and put in colander to drain. Pat dry. Gently stuff each Chile with cheese by inserting the cheese strip or spooning grated mixture into Chile. If the Chile splits as you are stuffing it, do not lose heart. Be as careful as you can, but, in cooking, the coating will act as a seal. Roll each stuffed Chile in the flour and set on rimmed baking pan.

2. Place a large skillet with ¼ inch of oil in it over medium high heat. Preheat oven to 200° F.

3. In a mixing bowl, combine the egg whites with the baking powder and salt. Beat whites until they are stiff. Set aside.

4. In a separate bowl, beat the egg yolks. Add milk. Stir. Add the egg yolk/milk mixture to the stiff egg whites and gently, briefly, fold in.

5. Take a floured, stuffed Chile and dip into the batter to coat. Place in skillet. Repeat procedure without overcrowding (5–6 at a time in a large 12" skillet works well). Cook until golden brown on one side (about 4–5 minutes); turn with spatula and cook until the other side is brown and cheese melts. Add additional oil to the pan as needed. If the batter thins towards the end of the recipe, set a stuffed Chile in the skillet and simply spoon batter over it.

6. Remove each Chile from the skillet and place on warmed platter in preheated oven (200° F) to keep the Rellenos warm until serving.

7. Pour warm Enchilada sauce over each Relleno. Serve with a side dish of refried black or pinto beans and warm Spelt tortillas. If there are leftovers, place in airtight container and refrigerate. Reheat in oven or microwave.

Huevos Rancheros
(Mexican Ranch-Style Eggs)

Enjoy this classic Mexican breakfast dish with your own homemade Spelt Tortillas. Traditionally, Huevos Rancheros are served with a scoop of refried pinto beans on the fresh tortilla then topped with eggs and Enchilada Sauce spooned over all. It is heavenly.

Blood Type: B, O (A, AB eat without the enchilada sauce and sprinkle Longhorn cheddar on top)
Prep time: None • Cook time: 15 min • Yield: 4 servings

Ingredients

1   recipe Enchilada Sauce Sabrosa (see under *Many Small Things*)
4   6–7" Spelt flour tortillas, White or Whole Grain (see under *Many Small Things*)
8   eggs, room temperature
¾   cup Mozzarella or Longhorn Cheddar, grated
oil for cooking

1. Spray a 10" nonstick skillet with cooking spray or oil sufficient to coat bottom; place over medium heat. Place tortillas, one at a time in skillet, let warm on one side, flip and warm the other. Place in folds of a towel to keep warm. Heat the Spelt Enchilada Sauce. Prepare refried beans.

2. Add oil to the pan and fry the eggs over easy or over medium according to taste. Spoon beans over tortilla; then the eggs (2 per tortilla). Ladle Enchilada Sauce over all. Sprinkle grated cheese over all. Serve hot.

Empanadas De Fruta
(Baked Fruit Turnovers)

Fruit empanadas are ideal for portion control, they are easy to make and they bake while you do other things. In about an hour, you have a swell alternative to pies and other desserts. So instead of avoiding pie or buying turnovers in the frozen food section or fast food restaurant, make your own dainty and delicious Empanadas de Fruta.

Blood Type (Apple Turnovers): A, B, AB, O. Use spices according to Blood Type.
Prep time: 25 min • Cook time: 20–25 min • Yield: 16 empanadas (2 oz each)

May I suggest: Instead of using mushy, over-sugared bland canned fruit, use fresh fruit in season or the many varieties of fruit now sold frozen year round. Try mashed acorn squash with a little brown sugar and raisins or use those leftover sweet potatoes.

Empanadas De Manzana (Apple Turnovers)
Ingredients

1   recipe 9–10" Mixed Spelt Flour Double Crust (formed into 16 balls)*

*See *Pastry/Pie Crust Chart* under **Pastries, Pies and Other Sweet Delights** Section.

3   Granny Smith or other large baking apples (4 cups apple slices)
2   tsp lemon juice
1½   Tbsp White Spelt flour
1½   Tbsp Whole Grain Spelt flour
⅓   cup brown sugar, firmly packed
1   tsp cinnamon or mace
1   tsp nutmeg or cardamom
2   Tbsp + 1 tsp Light Olive or other vegetable oil
¾   cup water
1   egg lightly beaten with 1 tablespoon cool water
Turbinado sugar for sprinkling (optional)

1. Wash apples; pat dry. Peel and core. Cut into small, thin sections. Place in bowl. Stir in lemon juice. In separate bowl, combine the flours, brown sugar and spices. Whisk together. Set aside.

2. Place a 10" skillet on medium heat and warm the oil. Add the apples to pan and sauté 7–8 minutes, stirring frequently. Sprinkle with the flour/sugar/spice mixture and stir. Slowly add ¾ cup water; stir into mixture and cook, stirring frequently, until apples soften and paste forms and most of liquid is absorbed. Remove from heat.

3. Preheat oven to 425° F. If using two pans to bake recipe at one time, adjust racks so one is on bottom and the other is 2 rungs above. Single pan: bake on middle rack.

4. Pat or roll a dough ball into 4" diameter circle about ⅛" thick. Make as thin as you can; they will hold up and be lovely crisp when done. When working with Whole Grain Spelt, the edges tend to be rough. That's okay. Trim to round configuration with sharp knife or leave as is until crimping.

5. Lightly grease 2 large baking pans or preferably cover pan with parchment. Place the dough round(s) on pan and spoon a heaping tablespoonful of the apple mixture slightly off center of one side of dough round.

Fold edge over to form a half moon. Seal edge with fingers or tines of fork, trimming if necessary. Brush Empanada with egg/water. Puncture top in 2–3 places using sharp knife or tines of fork so steam can escape during baking. Sprinkle with Turbinado sugar (optional).

6. Place pan(s) in preheated hot (425° F) oven and bake 20–25 minutes until golden brown and juice is bubbling through vents. If using 2 pans, switch pans at 12 minutes. Remove Empanadas to wire racks to cool slightly before eating. Serve hot, warm or cool. Wrap cooled Empanadas individually in plastic. Freeze leftovers in airtight container or freezer bag. They will stay fresh for a month or more. Remove one from freezer; wrap in paper towel and microwave on high about 15 seconds. Or take on picnic/trip and let thaw as you travel.

More Empanadas De Fruta ...

Blood Type: A, B, AB • Prep time: 20 min • Cook time: 20–25 min • Yield: 16 4" empanadas

EMPANADA DE PINA Y QUESO
(Pineapple with Ricotta Empanada)

Ingredients

1   recipe White Spelt 9–10" Double Crust pastry (formed into 16 balls)
1½ cups ricotta
2   cups fresh, fine diced pineapple (drain and reserve 2 Tbsp juice)
or 20 oz can crushed pineapple (drain and reserve 2 Tbsp juice)
1   egg white beaten with 1 Tbsp cool water
Confectioners' sugar for dusting (optional)

1. Preheat oven to 425° F. Keep pastry balls covered. Grease two large baking sheets or preferably cover with parchment. Drain ricotta.

2. Blend ricotta with 2 Tbsp of reserved pineapple juice until cheese is smooth and creamy (about 5–7 minutes). Stir in the finely diced pineapple. Place bowl in refrigerator as you are rolling out pastry.

3. Roll or pat each ball of pastry into 4" disk. Place on baking pan. Keep covered with damp towel or plastic wrap while making the rest, 8 to a pan. Remove cheese/pineapple mixture from refrigerator and spoon a heaping tablespoonful of filling slightly off center onto a dough round. Fold the other half of the round over the filling to make a half moon. Crimp edges with fingers or tines of fork, trimming if necessary. Brush Empanada with egg white/water. Puncture top in 2–3 places using sharp knife or tines of fork.

4. Place pan(s) in preheated hot (425° F) oven and bake for 20–25 minutes until Empanadas are light golden brown and juice is bubbling through some of the vents. If using 2 pans, switch racks at 12 minutes. Remove to wire racks to cool. If baked on parchment, sprinkle the Empanadas with Confectioners' sugar. If not, place paper towels under the racks for sprinkling. Let cool 10 minutes before eating. When completely cool, wrap individually and freeze.

Blood Types: A, B, AB

RASPBERRY FILLING (Variations: A, B, AB Blackberry; A, B, AB, O Blueberry)

1   recipe 8–9" White Spelt Flour Double Crust formed into 12 balls
2   cups ricotta, drained
¼   cup granulated sugar
1½ cups raspberries, partially thawed or fresh
1   egg white beaten with 2 tsp cool water
Confectioners' sugar for dusting (optional)

Beat ricotta with sugar until smooth. Stir in berries (the berries should still be firm, not mushy). Follow recipe for Pineapple/Ricotta Empanadas but roll out balls to 5" disks and fill with 1½–2 tablespoonfuls of filling. Makes 12 (2.5 oz each).

New Braunfels, Texas Custard Toast
A Breakfast Confection

This fragrant, delicious Texas-size French Toast is an old Horn Ranch family recipe for using day-old bread. It takes advantage of Spelt's superior ability to absorb moisture and flavors.

Blood Type: A, AB (sub goat's milk); B (sub cardamom for cinnamon), O (avoid because of milk)
Prep time: 5 min + 1 hr soaking • Cook time: 10 min • Yield: 4 4-oz servings

Ingredients

4   pieces Classic White Spelt bread, day old, ¾ inch slices
1   cup milk (do not substitute soy or rice milk)
3   eggs
¼   tsp ground cinnamon
¼   tsp nutmeg, freshly grated
¼   tsp vanilla or almond flavoring
Butter or oil for cooking

1. Set out a 9" x 13" or 10" x 6" oblong cake pan. If dimensions are much larger, turn bread more frequently while soaking. Take care while turning because wet bread is fragile.

2. Thoroughly blend milk, eggs, spices and vanilla.

3. Arrange slices of Spelt bread in the pan; pour liquid over bread. Soak for half an hour; turn and soak other side for additional half hour.

4. Put 2 Tbsp butter or 1½ Tbsp oil in a 12" skillet and set over moderate heat. Let warm.

5. Place the bread in the warmed skillet and cook 4–5 minutes until surface caramelizes and turns shiny, golden brown. Carefully turn and cook other side an additional 4–5 minutes.

Serve warm with maple syrup or fresh berries in season.

Cheese And Pineapple Danish Modern
(Cheese Danish)

**Blood Type: Not rated • Prep time: Filling takes 10 minutes; bread including rising about 90 minutes
Cooking time: 30–35 minutes • Yield: 1 filled loaf (16 servings)**

Here is a bright-tasting, delectable Cheese Danish made from Spelt. Pineapple juice infuses the dough, which is sealed and scalloped to create a beautiful light, high and flavor-filled delight.

Ingredients

1   recipe of Auld Lang Syne (Remembrance) Bread dough taken through first rise. Deflate according to recipe; turn out onto lightly floured surface.

Filling:

2   (16 oz) packages cream cheese, room temperature

1½ tsp almond extract

1   egg (separated), yolk for filling

½   cup granulated sugar

1½ cups pineapple, chopped, drained but not dry (reserve the juice)

Brushing/Sprinkling

egg white plus two Tbsp pineapple juice, lightly beaten

2   Tbsp turbinado sugar

1. Divide dough into 2 equal portions. Cover; let rest 15 minutes while making filling.

2. Preheat oven to 375° F. Set out large rimmed baking pan and cover with parchment (preferable) or lightly oil pan. Combine cream cheese, almond extract, egg yolk and sugar in mixing bowl; blend until creamy.

3. Roll or pat out one portion of the dough into a 6-inch by 14-inch rectangle. Place dough on pan. Gently spread the cream cheese mixture equally over the dough, leaving ½ inch all the way around for sealing. Sprinkle the pineapple evenly over the cheese mixture.

4. Roll the other half of the dough into a 6-inch by 14-inch rectangle. Place over the bottom cheese-covered portion. Seal the edges all the way around by crimping with your fingers. Make indentations to form rounded scallops in the dough as you seal it so the edge has a wavy appearance.

5. Prick the dough with the tines of a fork 6 times per side and four times along the center so that steam may escape and the juices bubble through the top. Let rise, covered with plastic wrap lightly sprayed with oil, in a warm (80°–85° F), draft-free place for 15–20 minutes. Test by inserting a finger into dough; if indentation remains, bread is ready for baking.

6. Gently brush the top with egg white/pineapple juice. If the tiny holes from the fork tines have sealed during the rising process, gently prick through them again. Sprinkle the top of the dough with turbinado sugar.

7. Bake on center rack of preheated hot (375° F) oven for 30–35 minutes or until the top is golden brown and juices are bubbling through top in several places. Remove from oven and lift parchment directly to wire rack for bread to cool before serving.

Beignes
(New Orleans Style French Doughnuts)

This is a recipe shared with me a long time ago by an old friend and fine home cook, who lives on a bayou not far from New Orleans. Together over the years we have enjoyed many of these doughnuts in the Big Easy as we watched the ships go by. Now they are adapted to Spelt and remain one of the best doughnuts on earth. The puffy popular Mexican Sopaipilla comes from the French Beigne, also known as Crescentines. New Orleans is not as it was, yet this classic recipe remains.

Blood Type: Not rated • Prep time: About 1 hr 15 min • Cook time: 20 minutes • Yield: 36

Ingredients

¾ cup milk
¼ cup granulated sugar
¾ tsp salt
½ tsp mace or freshly ground nutmeg (optional)
2 Tbsp warm water (110°–115° F)
1 package active dry yeast
2 Tbsp vegetable oil (Light Olive oil or canola)
1 egg, room temperature
3½–4 cups White Spelt Flour
oil for frying
Confectioners' sugar or granulated sugar/ cinnamon mixture for sprinkling
Paper bag

1. Heat milk until it bubbles around the edges but does not boil. Remove from heat. Add the sugar, salt and spice. Set aside and cool mixture until lukewarm.

2. Add warm water to a small bowl; sprinkle yeast over water. Stir to dissolve. Let sit for five minutes until yeast is creamy and foamy.

3. In a large mixing bowl, combine lukewarm milk mixture with the yeast, oil and egg. Blend.

4. Add two cups of the White Spelt flour; mix (stand mixer) on low speed for a minute or beat by hand. Gradually add the remaining 1½ cups of the Spelt flour while continuing to mix (low speed, stand mixer) for about two minutes until soft dough forms.

5. Turn dough out onto a floured surface and briefly knead by hand, incorporating additional flour to make the dough smooth but not dry. Form into a ball; place in an oiled bowl, turn to coat all sides. Cover with plastic wrap or lid. Set in warm (80°–85° F), draft-free place until dough doubles in volume. Check at 30 minutes. Do Fingertip Test.

6. Turn dough out onto floured surface and knead gently for about two minutes so it is firm enough to roll. Add more flour to surface. Roll the dough into a rectangle (12" x 18"). With pastry scraper or sharp knife, cut rolled dough into 36 2" x 3" rectangles.

7. Cover dough with plastic wrap or damp tea towel; let rise for 20 minutes. During this rising time, add 2½ to 3 inches of oil to large saucepan (or sufficient oil for deep-fat fryer). Heat to 375° F.

8. Slide pastry scraper under a rectangle of
    dough; place dough in hot oil. Repeat
    process, frying a couple at a time. They
    will puff up and turn golden brown within
    about 20 seconds. Remove with slotted
    spoon and place on several layers of paper
    towels laid over a wire rack. While still
    hot, gently drop Beignes into a paper bag
    and shake in Confectioners' sugar or a
    mixture of cinnamon/granulated sugar
    until coated or use sugar shaker as they
    do in New Orleans. Serve them hot.

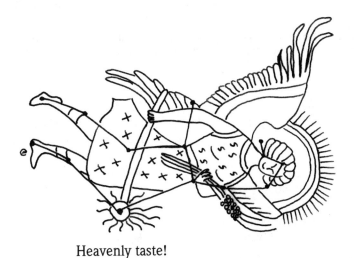

Heavenly taste!

Bagels (Water Bagels)

The Bagel is a dense, moist and chewy lean bread. You will find all those characteristics, plus exceptional natural flavor, in Spelt Water Bagels. Traditionally bagels are handmade so no two are alike; they are boiled (hence the word "Water" with the bagel) and then baked. That's the method used here. In keeping with tradition—and waistline considerations—these are a little smaller than the giant 6 to 8 oz bagels found at bakeries nowadays but the varieties you can make are many. Spread the Basic Wheat Bagel with homemade yogurt cheese (see recipe) instead of cream cheese. Use different toppings within the same recipe such as the traditional kosher salt, poppy seeds or celery seeds or see *Topping and Filling Many Small Things* for more ideas (*Many Small Things* section)

Tip: Please read the recipe thoroughly—twice—and take the time to assemble all the tools you need to make the process easier. Once you get the hang of it, you will have a hard time keeping a supply of Spelt bagels on hand.

Blood Type: A, B, AB, O • Prep time: Dough about 60 minutes including rising times; forming 10 min. Cook time: boiling 6 min per batch; baking 35 min. • Yield: 12 (3½–4-ounce plain bagels)

Ingredients

1   package active dry yeast
1¼ cups warm water (110°–115° F)
3   Tbsp granulated sugar
1   Tbsp salt
3–3¼ cups White Spelt Flour
1   cup Whole Grain Spelt Flour
Additional flour for kneading
Additional granulated sugar for boiling water
1   egg beaten with 2 tsp tepid water

In advance: Set out a stockpot or large saucepan, slotted spoon, large baking sheet, wire racks covered with a thick towel (a bartender's towel works very well).

1. Add 1¼ cups + 1 Tbsp warm (110°–115° F) water to a large mixing bowl. Sprinkle yeast over the water; stir to dissolve. Let stand for 10 minutes until yeast is creamy and foamy.

1a. *Stand Mixer:* To the yeast, add the sugar, salt, 2¼ cups of the White Spelt flour and 1 cup Whole Grain Spelt flour. Beat with paddle on speed 2 for about 1½ minutes until dough becomes smooth and long strands cling to paddle and sides of bowl. Add 1 cup White Spelt flour in ¼ cup increments and mix 30 seconds on speed 2. If dough seems dry, add water by the teaspoon. Change to dough hook and knead on lowest speed for about 1–1½ minutes until dough forms a ball and begins to clean sides of bowl. The dough should be soft and slightly sticky.

By Hand: To the yeast, add the sugar, salt, 2¼ cups of the White Spelt flour and 1 cup Whole Grain Spelt flour. Stir to form wet dough. Gradually add the remaining White Spelt flour and mix until dough becomes too stiff to stir, scraping down sides of bowl with spatula. The dough should be soft and slightly sticky.

2. Turn dough out onto surface floured with White Spelt. Knead briefly, with gentle strength, working flour in by sprinkling a little flour over the dough, sprinkling flour under dough and using pastry scraper to keep dough from sticking. Form into soft

ball and place dough in clean lightly oiled bowl. Cover with plastic wrap or lid to keep dough from drying out. Set in warm (80°–85° F), draft-free place and let dough rise for 30–40 minutes until it has just about doubled. Do Fingertip Test.

3. Depress the dough by pressing it lightly with the heel of your hand and knuckles (loose fist). Use a spatula to turn edges onto top of dough. Turn dough out onto lightly floured surface. Cover; let rest 15 minutes (10 minutes at altitude above 4000'). Add 4 quarts water to a stockpot or large saucepan. Add a Tbsp of granulated sugar to the water (this gives the bagels a shine but does not affect the taste) and bring to rolling boil; reduce heat so water is simmering.

4. Divide the dough into 12 pieces. Form each piece into a ball without working it too much. Gently poke your thumb through the center and form bagel by plying the dough around your thumb to round the dough. Leave a ½ inch wide hole in center. Place the bagels on a large floured baking sheet. Cover. Let rise 15 minutes (they should increase in volume by half to ¾).

5. Set out wire rack(s) covered with a towel near the stove. Preheat oven to 375° F and adjust rack to center position. Cover pan with lightly sprayed parchment paper or lightly grease a large baking sheet and sprinkle it with White Spelt flour.

6. Place bagels in the bubbling water, 4 at most so they are not crowded and have room to steam. Without covering, simmer for 3 minutes. If they stick to the bottom give them just a slight nudge; they will float to the top on their own. Turn with slotted spoon, simmer another 3 minutes. Remove and set steamed bagels on towel to drain. Repeat until all are boiled and completely drained (bottoms should no longer be sticky).

7. Place bagels on baking sheet and bake in hot oven (375° F) for 10 minutes. Remove from oven; turn. Brush with mixture of egg beaten with 1 Tbsp tepid water. **ADD TOPPINGS** (optional). Bake for additional 25 minutes or until shiny golden brown. Remove and place on wire rack. Do not cut until the bagels are cool or you will have a gummy mass to contend with instead of a great bagel.

Bagel Toppings. You can make different varieties within a single 12-bagel recipe. When the bagels are turned and brushed with egg/water, sprinkle top with coarse sea salt and dried onions, sesame or poppy or other seeds such as ground sunflower seeds or pumpkin seeds or with finely grated hard cheese like Pecorino.

Greek Topping (Spinach/Feta/Pine Nuts)

For 6 bagels: Set a small skillet on medium heat and add 2 teaspoons olive oil to the pan. Add 1 cup chopped fresh baby spinach and cook for several minutes until spinach is soft. Spoon 1½ Tbsp chopped spinach over bagel and sprinkle with pine nuts and feta cheese. Drizzle very lightly with olive oil. Continue baking as above.

Sprouted Wheat Bagels: Start ahead of time by sprouting Spelt (3 day germination is excellent). Add ½ cup Spelt Sprouts to dough. To incorporate sprouts: After 4 turns of the dough (see *Knead to Know*) pat dough into ½ inch thick round. Sprinkle Sprouts over surface to within 1 inch of the edges. Then fold dough over and continue to knead lightly until sprouts are evenly distributed. Form dough into ball. Continue with recipe as directed. These can also be made with Cooked Wheat Berries as in the Spelt Honey and Wheat Berry Bread and Spelt Porridge (Cooked Spelt Berries) recipes. Use the cooking liquid for the 1¼ cups liquid in the Bagel recipe.

Carns English Muffins

Traditional English muffins cooked on a griddle, these are chewy rounds with the dense but irregular texture that gives them great flavor and excellent toasting quality. The recipe uses the sponge method to develop the flavor and texture. The recipe calls for muffin/egg rings. If you haven't any rings, that's fine. Simply pat out into rounds. No cutter? Use a large, clean tuna can or cut with a sharp knife. (Please read *Knead to Know* section about working with Spelt dough to get the most out of this excellent recipe.)

Blood Type: A, B, AB • Prep time: 2–2½ hours including rising time
Cook time: 20–30 min • Yield: 10 3½" (2 oz)

Ingredients

1 package active dry yeast
¼ cup warm water (110°–115° F)
½ cup boiling water (212° F)
½ cup cow's milk or goat's milk
2 tsp salt
1 Tbsp granulated sugar
1 Tbsp vegetable oil
2 cups Whole Grain Spelt flour (divided 1, 1)
2 cups White Spelt flour (divided 1, 1)

In advance: Grease 8 muffin rings. Set out 2 skillets or one long griddle. Drop 2 tsp of oil in each of the skillets and wipe with paper towel so there is a sheen of grease on the bottoms of the skillets but no standing oil/grease. The older and better seasoned the skillet/griddle, the better.

Sponge:

1. Sprinkle yeast over ¼ cup warm (110°–115° F) water. Stir to dissolve. Let stand 10 minutes until foamy and creamy. Combine the milk, salt, sugar and oil and the ½ cup boiling water in mixing bowl. Stir. Cool to lukewarm (95° F).

2. Add the dissolved yeast and 1 cup Whole Grain Spelt Flour and 1½ cups White Spelt flour to the lukewarm mixture. Beat (stand mixer w/paddle, speed 2) for 1½ minutes; by hand beat 2 minutes until a thick batter

is formed. Cover tightly with plastic wrap or lid and set in warm, draft-free place (80°–85° F) until mixture is a lively bubbling mass that has doubled in volume (1 hr 15 min–1 hr 45 min).

Dough:

3. *Stand Mixer:* Using paddle attachment (speed 2) add the remaining cup Whole Grain flour to the sponge in ½ cup increments and ½ cup White Spelt (you may not need more). Beat on Speed 2 (1–1½ minutes) until dough starts to consolidate. Scrape down sides of bowl with spatula. Change to hook, reduce to lowest speed, and knead 2 minutes, adding White Spelt flour by the tablespoon if necessary, to form rough and sticky dough.

   By Hand: Stir sponge. Add the Whole Grain Spelt flour and beat. Add ½ cup of the White Spelt flour, scraping down sides of bowl, adding more by the ½ cup to form wet, rough dough. Beat until dough begins to ball around spoon and it becomes hard to stir. Dough should be shaggy and tacky. Scrape down sides of bowl.

4. Turn dough out onto lightly floured (with White Spelt) surface. Cover and let rest 10 minutes. Using pastry scraper to keep dough from sticking, briefly knead until

dough is smooth, not tacky, and firm and springy to the touch. Form into ball and place dough ball in clean, lightly oiled bowl. Cover tightly with plastic wrap or lid and let rise at room temperature (about 75°) in a draft-free place until just about doubled (30–40 minutes) and finger lightly pressed into dough leaves an indentation when removed. This is a very active dough; take care not to let it rise too long even if it appears not to have doubled in volume.

5. Depress dough, detaching dough from edges using plastic spatula and laying edges on top of dough. Turn out onto lightly floured surface. Pat or roll dough into a ½ inch thick circle. Cut the dough with the muffin rings leaving dough inside the rings. Or cut with large tuna can and form into muffin and cook without rings. With dough scraper or metal spatula, lift dough-filled ring onto a large floured metal baking sheet. When all are cut, cover lightly with plastic wrap sprayed lightly with oil and let rise until muffins are ¾ of way to top of ring (10–15 minutes), no higher. If not using rings, measure with ruler to gauge when they are ¾" in height. As they are going through final rise, place both skillets (or one long griddle) over medium heat and heat thoroughly.

6. Lift each muffin/ring from the bottom with metal spatula and place in skillet without crowding (4 to a skillet works well). Cook, turning every 5 minutes or so, for about 25 minutes. The reason for turning frequently is to keep them from browning too fast and assure even cooking. Adjust skillet/griddle if it gets too hot and continue to turn often. When done, the muffins will have risen to, or just about to, the top of the rings, they will be firm and well toasted to a deep golden brown, bottom and top, and will slip from the rings. The crumb will be dense but contain irregular air pockets. When cooked just right, they exhibit the characteristic break around the middle or close to the base that enables them to be split apart with two forks.

7. Cool the muffins for a couple of minutes on wire racks. Split them open and spread with butter, cream cheese, soft goat cheese and/or preserves. To save, wrap individually and store in plastic bag. Bring out, split and toast. They freeze very well and will keep for months if wrapped securely.

Sweet Muffins With Crumble Topping

Fiber and fine taste are combined in a moist, tender and light muffin with a delicate yet crunchy topping. For more muffins, try the superb Applesauce Muffins in the Section *On The Run and Working Out.*

Blood Type: B (A, AB use goat's milk) • Prep time: 5 min • Cook time: 20–25 min • Yield: 12 (1½ oz each)

Ingredients

1   cup Whole Grain Spelt flour
1¼   cups + 2 Tbsp White Spelt flour
½   tsp salt
2½   tsp baking powder
3   Tbsp granulated sugar
1   egg, room temp
1   cup cow's milk or goat's milk, room temp
½   cup vegetable oil
½   Recipe (1 cup) of Crumble Topping (see in *Sweet Toppings* section)

1. Preheat oven to 425° F. Place paper baking cups into muffin pan(s) or lightly oil the muffin pan(s) even if they are the nonstick variety.

2. In a large mixing bowl, combine the Spelt flours, salt, baking powder and granulated sugar; whisk together. Stir in the egg, milk and vegetable oil; mix just until blended and all ingredients are moist. Batter should be rough, not smooth.

3. Spoon a little less than ⅓ cup batter into each of the 12 muffin cups and sprinkle top of each with a Tbsp of Crumble Topping.

4. Bake on middle rack of preheated hot (425° F) oven for 20–25 minutes. The aroma should be tempting and the topping golden brown. Freeze any leftovers: these muffins stay fresh for weeks if stored in an airtight container with wax paper placed between layers and/or crumpled between muffins.

pelta's Cinnamon Rolls

Spelta's Cinnamon Rolls are succulent and moist and keep for several days instead of drying out like typical cinnamon rolls. Tasters rated these SSSSS (5S on the Spelt Delectable Chart) for taste and texture. Please read *Knead to Know* about working with Spelt dough if you have not worked with Spelt before.

Blood Type: Not rated • Prep/Rise/Shape time: 65–80 min • Cook time: 18–25 min • Yield: 24 rolls (3 oz each)

Ingredients

1   Recipe Brioche (Spelt Sweet Dough)
¼   cup butter, softened
½   cup brown sugar, firmly packed (divided ¼, ¼)
4   tsp cinnamon
1   cup walnuts, finely chopped (divided ½, ½)
1   cup raisins, soaked in hot water to cover and drained
1   Recipe Confectioners' Icing (below)

1. Prepare 1 recipe Brioche (Spelt Sweet Dough) through the first rising. Detach dough from edges of bowl with plastic spatula and turn edges onto top of dough. Depress dough by pressing down with lightly closed fist using gentle strength to work across and around dough (do not punch). Turn dough out onto lightly floured surface. With pastry scraper or sharp knife, divide into two equal pieces. Cover each piece with bowl and/or plastic wrap and let rest for 10 minutes.

2. Roll or pat one piece into an oblong that is ¼" thick, 12" long and about 9" wide. Using plastic spatula, spread 2 Tbsp softened butter lightly over surface. Sprinkle evenly with 2 tsp cinnamon; then sprinkle with ½ cup finely chopped nuts and ½ cup softened raisins. Roll from the long side and cut into 12 1-inch slices. Set on pan* and repeat procedure with second part of dough. *For individual rolls,* place slices, cut side down, 2 to 3 inches apart on parchment-covered or lightly buttered large rimmed baking sheet (jelly roll pan). *For softer sided, higher rolls,* place 12 rolls close together on parchment-covered or lightly buttered 13" x 9" cake pans or all 24 on one long rimmed baking sheet (jelly roll pan) where the rolls will merge with one another; slice to separate.

3. Place plastic wrap sprayed lightly with oil over the rolls or place pan with rolls in large (tented) plastic bag. Set rolls in warm (75°–85° F) draft-free place to rise. This dough rises very quickly so check at 15 minutes and 5 minute intervals thereafter by doing Fingertip Test. As they are rising, preheat oven to 375° F, adjusting racks if using two pans (one rack on the lowest rung; the other 2 rungs above).

4. Place rolls in preheated hot (375° F) oven and bake for 18–20 minutes. If using 2 long baking pans, switch the pans midway through baking. When done, the tops of the rolls should be lightly brown and sides creamy white. Remove from oven and place pans on wire racks to cool.

5. As the rolls are cooling, prepare Confectioners' Icing. For frosted rolls, allow rolls to cool almost completely before spreading thicker icing over tops. Let stand for a few minutes longer for icing to set. To store leftover rolls, place in airtight container with wax paper between layers and keep at room temperature or place in freezer.

Confectioners' Icing: To 2 cups Confectioners' sugar add ¼ tsp salt and enough milk to create initial icing. Add 1 tsp vanilla or almond flavoring. Adjust the amount of milk for consistency desired. If using parchment paper on the pans, icing will pool on it and can simply be thrown away for easy cleanup.

Pistachio Sticky Buns

These are sensational light, sweet, high and moist rolls with a caramel and toasted pistachio topping. This is fast-rising dough, a recipe you can make from beginning to end in about 2 hours. One of our testers said the Pistachio Sticky Bun is a toffee bar combined with a cinnamon roll on steroids. Another said, "Monster Munchie!"

Blood Type: Due to the nutritionally incorrect nature of this item, this recipe is not rated for Blood Types. This is for when you fall off the wagon so hard the wheels come off, too. However, you might try Light Olive oil or other vegetable oil in place of the butter. The dough is not so rich but is exquisitely tasty.
Prep time: About 1½ hrs • Cook time: 20–25 min • Yield: 18 (4-oz buns)

Ingredients

1   recipe of Brioche dough (Spelt Sweet Dough)
1   cup coarsely chopped pistachios (or other nuts such as macadamia or pecan)
⅛   tsp salt
2   cups light brown sugar, firmly packed
¾   cup real maple syrup
8   Tbsp butter (1 stick), softened (or ¼ cup + 2 Tbsp vegetable oil such as Light Olive)

1. Make one recipe of Brioche and set it to first rise according to instructions. Once it has started to rise, make the topping but first set out three 8" x 8" inch pans (preferably nonstick variety); spray them with oil or lightly grease bottom and sides. Set out 3 large plates for cooked buns.

2. Place a small skillet over medium low heat; add the coarsely chopped pistachios and stir in the salt. Toast for 7 minutes, stirring occasionally. Remove from heat; set aside.

3. Place a heavy saucepan over medium heat. Combine the brown sugar, maple syrup and butter in the pan and bring to a rolling boil. Continue to boil the mixture, stirring constantly, for 3 minutes. Remove from heat. Set aside. Sprinkle the toasted pistachios in an even layer on the bottom of each pan. Gently pour the topping over the pistachios. Set the pans aside as you prepare the buns.

4. Divide the dough into 18 pieces by cutting dough with pastry scraper or sharp knife. Dip the pastry scraper or knife in cold water to help cut the dough cleanly if necessary. Cover the dough pieces with plastic wrap or lightly floured tea towel or inside a large (tented) plastic bag and let rest for 15 minutes. Preheat oven to 400° F. Adjust oven racks so one rack is on bottom rung, next rack 2 rungs up.

5. On lightly floured surface, form each piece into a ball then gently pat and roll ball into a 7-inch long rope. Coil the rope and set on top of pistachio/syrup mixture in a pan. Continue with next coil, spacing buns about 2 inches apart as they will double in volume as they rise. Cover pan with plastic wrap sprayed with oil; continue until all 18 buns are finished and covered. Place pans in warm (75°–85° F), draft-free place to rise (20–30 minutes) until doubled. Test by gently inserting a finger into a bun in each of the pans; if the indentations remain, they are ready for baking.

6. Place in preheated hot (400° F) oven and bake 12 minutes; switch pans to different rack, rotating each pan 180° to assure even baking, and bake for additional 10–13 minutes or until buns are deep golden brown. Remove from oven. While hot, invert each pan over a large plate to cool. With spatula, scrape any topping leftover in the pan onto the Sticky Buns.

THE BAKERY

Introduction to the Breads

The Breads in *The Bakery* are made by two methods:

The Direct or Straight Dough Method: All ingredients are added to the bowl during the mixing and kneading stage. Typically the flavor of these breads or rolls comes from the addition of enrichments such as butter, milk, sugar, herbs or spices to make tender, tasty products such as sandwich breads or rolls like Classic White Spelt Bread, Brioche and Traditional Feast Rolls.

The Indirect Method (Sponge, Biga). Water, yeast and part of the flour that is going to be used in the recipe are mixed in advance and allowed to ferment. It is the first rise for this type of bread. During fermentation, the sugars and flour interact with the yeast to produce bread with greater volume, better natural flavor and more moisture. This is the basic method for making many of the free-form rustic breads such as the Compocosenza Country Wheel. These breads require minimal shaping because the fermentation process has done the work for you.

Before baking Spelt Breads, please read:

Part IV
Knead To Know About Cooking and Baking
With Spelt: Going Beyond the Basics
for information and illustrations
on working with Spelt.

Direct Method Breads
A Beginning Loaf

If it has been some time since you've made bread, or, if you are just starting out with Spelt, give this recipe a try. There is nothing to making this small, delicious loaf of bread. It has a delicate, slightly sweet taste that matches its appearance. If made with White Spelt, expect the crumb to be creamy yellow in color and have a dense, moist crumb that slices cleanly. If Whole Grain only, expect the crumb to be tan and somewhat grainer than the White. This little bread can quickly be made by hand, there is little cleanup, and in an hour you can have a small loaf, fresh and steaming, on your table for brunch or dinner. Experiment with a variety of forms to suit the occasion: a small free-form round, an 8" x 4" loaf, or 2 dainty 3½" x 6" loaves for tea in the afternoon.

Blood Type: A, B, AB (O sub soy milk)
Prep time: 5 min/30 rising • Cook time: 25 min • Yield: 1 loaf (8" x 4")

Ingredients

2 cups Spelt flour (all White or blend of Whole Grain Spelt and White, all Whole, Light, your choice)

1 pkg quick-rising dry yeast (active dry yeast will work also; give bread a little longer to rise)

2 Tbsp granulated sugar or brown sugar, firmly packed

⅛ tsp salt

⅔ cup warm goat's or cow's milk or soy milk (110°–115° F)

2 Tbsp Light Olive oil or other vegetable oil (divided 1 Tbsp, 1 Tbsp)

1. Combine flour, yeast, sugar and salt in large mixing bowl. Whisk.

2. Heat the milk or soy milk until warm (110°–115° F); stir it in along with 1 Tbsp of the oil. Continue stirring until dough forms (about 30 seconds). Turn out onto a lightly floured surface and knead until the dough is smooth and springy (about 3 minutes).

3. Place dough in a clean, lightly oiled bowl; turn so all surfaces are lightly covered with oil. Place in a warm (80°–85° F), draft-free place and let rise until about doubled in volume (25–30 minutes). Check by pressing a fingertip lightly into top of dough about ½" deep. If the indentation remains, dough is ready. Heat oven to 350° F.

4. Turn dough out of mixing bowl. Form into a round and place on baking pan; or form into loaf and place in lightly greased loaf pan. Gently brush the top (and sides if making a round) of the loaves with the remaining oil. Bake on center rack of moderate preheated oven (350° F) for 25 minutes or until bread turns golden brown and sounds hollow when tapped with your finger. Serve hot or room temperature. For variations, try serving with a fruit juice glaze or berry topping or incorporate a teaspoon of spice such as cardamom into the dough.

Speltessence Bread
Become Acquainted with Spelt Recipe

Basic Speltessence Bread—like the little black dress or a smile—goes anywhere. It is one of the simplest yeast breads of all to make and it rewards you amply. All the traditional Direct Method baking steps are here. This bread is moist, rich in taste and lighter in texture than you might think possible. Ah, the aroma. It is the smell of home and hearth. Please read *Part IV Knead to Know* for the basics of working with Spelt including directions/illustrations.

Blood Types: A, B, AB, O • Prep time: about 2 hrs • Cook time: 45–50 min • Yield: 1 loaf (1½ lb)

Ingredients

1   pkg active dry yeast
¼   cup warm water (110°–115° F)
2   Tbsp brown sugar, tightly packed
¾   cup + 2 Tbsp lukewarm water (about 95° F)
2   cups Whole Grain Spelt flour
1¼ to 1½ cups White Spelt flour (divided 1¼, ¼)
1   tsp salt
3   Tbsp Olive or other vegetable oil (divided 2, 1)

1. **Ferment.** Pour ¼ cup warm (110°–115° F) water in glass measuring cup or small bowl. Stir in the brown sugar. Sprinkle yeast over water/sugar and stir to dissolve. Let stand for 10 minutes until creamy and foamy.

2. **Mix/Knead.** Add the yeast and ¾ cups + 2 Tbsp lukewarm water to large mixing bowl. Add 2 cups Whole Grain Spelt flour and the salt.

Stand Mixer: Mix (paddle, speed 2 or next to lowest speed on your machine) to moisten flour and begin distribution of yeast. It will take about a minute to form ropy dough that clings to paddle and sides of bowl. Add 1¼ cups White Spelt flour in several increments alternating with the addition of 2 Tbsp of the oil to form smooth dough (about 1½ minutes). As dough begins to ball, change to dough hook and reduce to lowest speed. Add remaining oil and knead (about 1 minute) until dough becomes quite smooth yet moist, the oil is incorporated, the dough ball begins to clean sides of bowl. If necessary, adjust either amount of flour by the tablespoon or water by the teaspoon to achieve smooth ball.

By Hand: Beat mixture to form ropy dough that clings to bowl and spoon. Use spatula to scrape down sides of bowl. Add 1¼ cups White Spelt flour in several increments alternating with 2 Tbsp of the oil. The dough will be moist and will begin to ball around the spoon. Continue to mix, adding the remaining 1 Tbsp oil, to form smooth moist dough that becomes too heavy to mix and chases spoon around bowl. Adjust either amount of flour by the tablespoon or water by the teaspoon.

Turn out of bowl onto surface lightly floured with White Spelt. Cover with bowl and let rest 10 minutes. Knead dough by sprinkling small amounts of flour over/under dough and using pastry scraper to keep dough from sticking. (See *Knead to Know, Chapter 3 Giving Form to Spelt* for instructions/illustrations). Continue to knead until dough is smooth, moist and springy (about 8 good turns of the dough). Form into a ball and place in a clean oiled bowl. Turn to coat all sides of dough with oil.

3. **First Rise.** Cover with plastic wrap, lid or saucer and let rise in draft-free place at room temperature (75° or so) until dough is somewhat less than doubled in volume. Check at 25 minutes and five minute intervals thereafter. Test for ripeness by doing Fingertip Test: Insert forefinger about ½" into crown of dough. If indentation remains, dough is ripe. If dough springs back quickly, it is still expanding. Wait 5 minutes and test again.

4. **Degas (deflate).** Detach dough from edge of bowl with spatula and lay edges over top of dough. With a loose fist, gently work hand around bowl to deflate. Do not punch the dough! As you deflate it, it will give off a sighing sound not the whoosh that comes from punching. Turn dough out onto lightly floured surface. Round into a loose ball. Cover with bowl and let rest 10 minutes.

5. **Form/Second Rise.** Lightly oil an 8" x 4" loaf pan. Shape dough into a loaf and place in pan so ends of dough touch the ends of the pan to give support during rising. Cover with plastic wrap or place loaf pan in large (tented) plastic bag with ends tucked under pan to keep out draft. Let rise until dough just about reaches top of pan (20–30 minutes). Preheat oven to 375° F.

6. **Bake.** Bake on center rack of preheated oven for 35 minutes or until done. The crust will be reddish brown and will have shrunk slightly from edges of pan. Thump the sides; if bread reverberates with a hollow sound as when you thunk a ripe melon, the bread should be done. Remove from oven and let sit for just a moment before tipping bread out of pan onto its side. Place on wire rack to cool. If you are in doubt about its being done, thump the bottom of the loaf. If not completely baked, place back in pan or as it is and allow to bake an additional 5 minutes or until done. Allow to cool a minimum of 30 minutes before slicing. This bread freezes well. Save leftovers for croutons or breadcrumbs (see *Croutons and Crumbs*).

Molasses and Spelt No-Knead Bread

Subdued blend of Spelt and molasses creates the basis for this no-knead deeply toned and hearty bread with good oven spring. It has a chewy and slightly sweet crust that is deep chestnut in color. The delectable crust gives way to a moist crumb that is dense with some irregular holes. If bread could be said to have seasons, this bread suggests Fall—golden pumpkins, turning leaves, a fire in the hearth to take the sudden chill off the air, a sweet yeasty aroma in the kitchen. Excellent slicing and keeping qualities.

Blood Type: B; A, AB use goat's milk (O avoid because of milk)
Prep time: about 1 hr and 45 min • Cook time: 45 min • Yield: 1 large loaf (9 x 5)

Ingredients

1¾ cups milk
⅓ cup Regular or Robust molasses
1½ tsp salt
¼ cup warm (110°–115° F) water
1 package active dry yeast
2½ cups Whole Grain Spelt flour
2¼ cups White Spelt flour

1. Heat milk until it bubbles around the edges but does not boil. Pour into a large mixing bowl and stir in the molasses and salt. Let stand until lukewarm (about 95° F). In small bowl, place ¼ cup warm (110–115° F) water. Sprinkle yeast over water; stir to dissolve. Let stand 10 minutes until yeast is creamy and foamy.

2. To the milk mixture, add the yeast and stir.

Stand Mixer: Use paddle on speed 2 to beat, adding flours in ½ cup increments. Beat for 2 to 2½ minutes until the batter begins to ball and comes away from sides of bowl. Leave in mixing bowl and cover with lid or plastic wrap. Set in draft-free place (75°–80° F) and let rise until the batter has doubled in volume. It will be vigorous (bubbly) and highly elastic.

By Hand: Add the flours in ½ cup increments and beat several minutes until ball begins to form around spoon, scraping down sides of bowl with spatula. Batter will be quite stiff. Leave in bowl as above.

3. Preheat oven to 375° F. Briefly beat the dough by hand or with paddle, speed 1 (30–45 seconds). Turn into a very well greased 9" x 5" x 3" loaf pan. Cover with plastic wrap lightly sprayed with oil or in large plastic (tented) bag and set in same place to rise until it is about 1" below pan rim (10–20 minutes). This is fast rising bread so check often. Do not over-proof. Gently pop any bubbles that come to the surface.

4. Place on middle rack in preheated hot (375° F) oven and bake for 45–50 minutes. Crust will be 1½" above rim of pan and be deep chestnut brown, sides shrunken away from edges of pan and loaf should sound somewhat hollow when thumped. Turn out of pan onto side and cool on a wire rack to cool thoroughly before cutting.

Classic White Spelt Bread

The bakery smell, the real pleasure of white bread that does not taste like paper or anything at all, something that tickles your memory from the past or the lure of a pleasure yet to be experienced ... This is it, Classic White Spelt Bread. Expect a cream-colored, tender, moist and delicately sweet loaf. The crust is soft and bakes to a marbled golden brown. It slices cleanly, thick or thin, and keeps days longer than most white breads.

This is a **versatile basic bread** recipe for making loaves for sandwiches, pretty hemispheres of bread for the table, braided breads, hamburger and hotdog buns and an array of rolls. Turn leftover bread into croutons or crumbs.

Blood Type: B; A and AB use goat's milk and make with Light Olive or other vegetable oil instead of butter. Type O avoid because of milk. Soy milk is not recommended as a substitute in this recipe.
Prep time: about 2½ hrs • Cook time: 30 min • Yield: 2 loaves (about 1¼ lb each)

Ingredients

½   cup cow's milk or goat's milk
3   Tbsp sugar
2   tsp salt
3   Tbsp butter, softened (or 2 Tbsp + 1½ tsp Light Olive or canola oil)
1¼ cups warm water (110°–115° F)
1   pkg active dry yeast
6½ to 7 cups White Spelt flour

1. Microwave or on stovetop, heat milk until it bubbles around the edges but does not boil. Remove from heat source and stir in the sugar, salt and softened butter. To large mixing bowl, add 1¼ cups warm water; sprinkle yeast over water. Stir to dissolve. Allow to sit 10 minutes until creamy and foamy.

2. Add the lukewarm milk mixture to the yeast/water and add 3½ cups of the flour.

Stand Mixer: Attach paddle, beat on speed 2 for 1 minute, using spatula to scrape down sides of bowl. Add flour ½ cup at a time until soft dough forms and begins to clean sides of bowl (about 1½ to 2 minutes). Do not over beat. Turn out onto lightly floured board.

By Hand: Beat by hand until smooth. Add remainder of flour ½ cup at a time and beat until dough starts to ball around spoon and is too stiff to mix. Turn out onto lightly floured board.

Knead until smooth and elastic, which should not take many turns of the dough. Form into a smooth ball and place in buttered or oiled bowl, turning to grease all sides. Cover with lid, plate or plastic wrap and let rise in draft-free place (75°–85° F) until doubled in volume (rising time varies so check at 50 minutes and every 10 minutes thereafter). Check ripeness of dough by lightly pressing a finger about half an inch into crown of the dough; if indentation remains after pulling out finger, dough is ready.

3. With plastic spatula, loosen edges of dough and place over top then depress the dough (don't punch) by pressing down with a loose fist and working hand around the bowl several times. You will hear whooshing sounds as the air is gently expelled. Turn dough out onto lightly floured surface; cover with bowl or plastic wrap or damp towel and let rest for 15 minutes.

4. Divide the dough into 2 equal portions with pastry scraper or sharp knife. Shape each half into a loaf and place in lightly oiled 9" x 5" x 3" loaf pan. Cover; let rise in warm place free from draft until just about doubled in bulk (about 40–50 minutes). Check at 35 minutes by doing Finger Test. Preheat oven to 400° F when bread is set to rise.

5. Place bread on middle rack and bake in preheated hot (400° F) oven about 30 minutes or until done. At 15 minutes, turn each pan 180° to assure even baking.

Crust will be a marbled golden brown and bread should sound hollow when thumped. When done, turn bread out of pans and place on wire racks. Let cool 30 minutes before turning on side and slicing with long sharp knife (serrated blade not recommended for this bread).

Classic White Spelt Bread freezes very well; both taste and texture remain true for a month or more. Leftover bread? Cut stale leftover slices into large croutons and freeze for later toasting or turning into breadcrumbs.

Traditional Feast Rolls

These are tender, yeasty rolls with a delectable, slightly crisp crust. Make four or five different varieties of forms at a time and freeze them in advance for get-togethers, dinner and special occasions from Turkey Day to a rainy day when you do not feel like baking but want something to make your meal special.

Blood Type: A, B, AB (goat's milk); or B, AB use 2% (A, O avoid) • Prep time: varies
Cook time: 15 min/batch • Yield: 4–5 dozen

Special Instructions: These are terrific rolls and very rewarding to make but please read the recipe thoroughly and have everything in place. Decide in advance which forms you wish to make and divide dough accordingly when the time comes. Have utensils and pans ready because this is fast-rise dough. See *Knead to Know* section on rising and Fingertip Test and working with Spelt in general to get the very best from this recipe.

Ingredients

1¾ cups cow's milk or goat's milk
2   packages active dry yeast
½   cup warm water (110°–115° F)
½   cup light brown sugar, firmly packed
6   Tbsp Light Olive or other vegetable oil
2   tsp salt
1½ cups Whole Grain Spelt flour
5½ cups White Spelt or Light Spelt flour
2   eggs, room temperature, well beaten
Softened butter or vegetable oil for brushing rolls

1. Heat milk until it bubbles at the edges but does not boil. Set aside. Add ½ cup warm (110°–115° F) water to small bowl or measuring cup. Sprinkle yeast over water; stir to dissolve. Let stand 10 minutes until creamy and slightly foamy.

2. To a large mixing bowl, add sugar, oil and salt. Pour in the milk and stir. Let stand until lukewarm (about 95° F). Stir in the Whole Grain Spelt flour and briefly beat until blended either by hand or with paddle of stand mixer (speed 2, about 1 minute).

3. Add the yeast to the bowl and add 3 cups White Spelt flour, 1 cup at a time, and beat, by hand, or with stand mixer on low speed, with paddle, to incorporate flour (about 1 minute). Dough will begin to cohere and cling to bowl and utensil.

4. Add the beaten eggs; stir briefly. Add 2 cups White Spelt by the half-cup and mix to form soft dough; change to dough hook, adjust flour by adding by the tablespoon if necessary, and keep total mixing time to about 1½ minutes. This dough forms quickly and is easy to over mix. By hand, stir until too heavy to mix. Dough will be soft and somewhat sticky and will begin to clean sides of bowl. Using spatula to scrape down sides of bowl and utensil, turn dough out of bowl onto surface floured with White Spelt. Cover with bowl and let rest 10 minutes.

5. Knead gently and briefly, sprinkling flour over and under dough to form smooth springy large ball. Place in oiled bowl and turn to oil top. Cover bowl securely with lid or plastic wrap and place in draft-free area (75°–80° F). Let rise until just about doubled in bulk (25–40 minutes depending upon temperature). This is fast-rise dough so check at 25/30 minutes and every 5 minutes thereafter by doing Fingertip Test.

6. Detach edges from sides of bowl with spatula and place over top of dough. Gently deflate dough with palm and heel of hand working around bowl. Turn dough over and let rise again under same conditions until it is just about doubled (15–20 minutes). This dough rises quickly so monitor the rising by doing Fingertip Test.

7. Turn dough out onto lightly floured surface. Divide and shape into a variety of interesting forms that follow this recipe.

General Directions:

Divide dough into half or quarters. A quarter of the dough will make about a dozen rolls depending upon the type. Place what you are not using in well-covered bowl in refrigerator. Bring out and let come to room temperature and become springy again before forming. This usually takes about 10–15 minutes if dough has only been in the refrigerator a short while especially if kitchen is warm from oven.

Cover large baking sheet(s) with parchment and spray lightly with oil or oil the pan(s) directly. If using two large baking pans, adjust oven racks so one is on the bottom and the other rack two rungs up. If using single pan, place pan on middle rack. Some rolls require muffin pans. See individual forms.

Preheat oven to 425° F as you begin to form rolls. Brush rolls with softened butter or oil if you have not done so already (see recipes next page) and cover loosely with plastic wrap. Let rolls rise until light (10–20 minutes). Do Fingertip Test to check. Bake rolls in preheated oven for 12–15 minutes or until golden brown. If baking two pans at once, shift pans to alternate racks at 7 minutes and rotate each pan 180° to assure even browning. Remove from pan immediately. When cool, place in heavy-duty freezer bag and store until needed. These will keep a couple of months if wrapped properly.

Fun Forms

Snails

Pat/press or gently roll dough into a ¼ inch thick rectangle. With pastry scraper or sharp knife cut into strips ½ inch wide and about 4 inches long. Gently pat and roll into longer strips then coil the strip around index finger to form the snail. By rolling out longer, make a double snail. Place on baking sheet. Lightly brush with oil or softened butter. Follow general directions previous page.

Cloverleaf Rolls

Oil the wells of muffin pan(s). With pastry scraper or sharp knife divide one quarter of the dough into 12 pieces. Cut each piece into three sections, each about ¾ inch in diameter. Place three balls in each of the muffin pan wells. Lightly brush with oil or softened butter. Follow general directions.

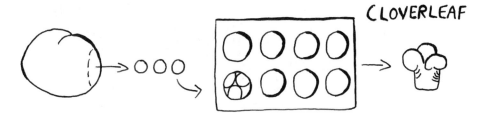

Butterflies

Pat/press or gently roll dough into a rectangle that is ¼ inch thick and 6 inches wide. Brush with softened butter or oil. Starting with the long side of dough, roll it then cut into 2 inch pieces. Use a knife handle to depress center to make two lobes. Sprinkle depression with Spelt flour to keep from melding together during rising. Follow general directions on previous page making sure to preheat oven.

Twists

Pat/press or gently roll dough to ¼ inch thickness. With pastry scraper or sharp knife, cut dough into strips that are 6 inches long and ¾ inch wide then pat/press and roll with your fingers to make a slightly longer strip (about 8 inches). Fold in half length-wise and pinch ends to seal. Twist the roll. Tuck ends under. Place on oiled pans. Lightly brush with oil or softened butter. See general directions previous page.

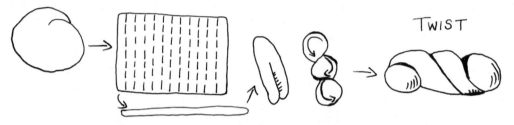

Crescents

A quarter of the total dough will make 2 rounds, 6 or more wedges each. Pat/press or roll the dough into a round that is 8 inches wide and ¼ inch thick. Brush the round with oil or softened butter. Cut the round into wedges and slightly separate each wedge to make them easy to roll. Roll the wedge starting with wide end and place on oiled baking sheet. Curve end around roll. See general directions.

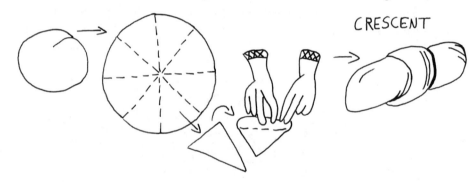

Bowknots

Pat/press or gently roll dough into ¼ inch thick rectangle and cut strips that are ½ inch wide and 4 to 5 inches long. Pat/press and roll with your fingers into 6–7 inch strips. Twist the strip and tie into a single or double knot. See general directions.

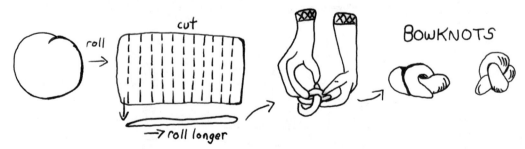

160

Brundisi Pesto Bread

A savory and subtle symphony of tastes intertwine in this rustic bread. The crust is crisp with deep sienna colored burnished crust dotted with bits of baked cheese. The crust gives way to a light, moist, slightly irregular crumb the color of antique gold flecked with the deep green of herbs. The range of tastes in this one bread makes it a good accompaniment to cheese and wine, for special croutons, as an untoasted base (panini) for cold cuts such as salmon or roast beef or for warm and fragrant bruschetta. This is a nutritionally well-balanced bread. (See cover photograph.)

Blood Type: A, B, AB, O • Prep time: 2½–3 hrs • Cook time: 30–40 min • Yield: 2 large rounds (2½ lb)

Ingredients

½ recipe (½ cup) Spinach Pesto (see *Many Small Things*)
2 pkgs active dry yeast
1½ cups warm water (110°–115° F)
1 cup Whole Grain Spelt flour
4½ to 5 cups White Spelt flour
1 Tbsp granulated sugar
2 tsp salt
1 cup semi-soft Mozzarella cheese, coarsely grated
2 Tbsp Olive oil
2 tsp celery seed, coarsely ground
1 egg yolk beaten with 2 tsp water

1. *Stand Mixer:* Warm the mixing bowl by running hot water over exterior and drying it. To the bowl, add 1½ cups warm water. Sprinkle both packages yeast over water; stir to dissolve. Let stand 10 minutes until foamy and creamy.

2. To the yeast, add the granulated sugar, salt, pesto and 1 cup Whole Grain Spelt and 2 cups White Spelt flour. With paddle attachment, Speed 2, beat 1½ minutes. Dough strands will cling to paddle and sides of bowl. Add 2½ cups White Spelt flour and change to dough hook. Knead on Speed 1 for 30–45 seconds. Moist dough will form and begin to clean sides of bowl. Make

adjustments by adding small amounts (1 tablespoon at a time of either flour or tepid water depending on consistency).

3. Add the grated Mozzarella and, continuing on speed 1, add 2 Tbsp olive oil, and continue kneading for 30–60 seconds. The dough will start to clean sides of bowl and ball around hook. It should be slightly shaggy in texture, moist and slightly sticky but not wet and tacky. Remove bowl from stand; cover with plastic wrap, a lid, saucer or damp tea towel and let rest 10 minutes.

By Hand: Warm mixing bowl and add yeast as in #1 above. Add sugar, salt, pesto and half the flour. Beat until thick batter forms and starts chasing spoon around bowl. Add remaining flour in half-cup increments then the mozzarella and olive oil. Beat until dough starts to clean sides of bowl and becomes too stiff to mix. Dough should be moist, somewhat shaggy and sticky at this stage. Scrape down sides of bowl. Cover dough with plastic wrap, a lid, saucer or damp tea towel and let rest 10 minutes.

4. **Knead/First Rise.** Gently turn dough out onto floured (White Spelt) surface. With lightly oiled hands, knead lightly for 30–60 seconds and form into a ball. Place rough side down in lightly oiled bowl. Cover. Let rise in draft-free place (75°–85° F). This

bread rises quickly and will almost double in volume: check at 25–30 minutes by gently inserting a dampened forefinger up to the first knuckle into the top of the dough. If the indentation remains in the dough when you remove finger, it is ready. If the dough springs back quickly, let it continue to rise. Check at 5 minute intervals.

5. **Second Rise.** Loosen the dough gently from sides of bowl with plastic spatula. Turn edges onto top of dough and depress the dough with a loose fist, working hand around bowl. Turn dough over, cover bowl and set it to rise in the same place again. It will take about half the time for this second proof. Check dough at 15 minutes and 5 minute intervals thereafter.

6. Gently remove dough from bowl by detaching edges with plastic spatula and turn out, top side down, onto lightly floured surface. With pastry scraper or sharp knife, divide into two equal pieces and cover both pieces with plastic wrap, bowls or damp tea towel. Let rest for 10 minutes. Gently form into two rounds, handling the dough as little as possible and using pastry scraper and light sprinklings of flour to keep dough from sticking to work surface. Choose a method below for baking. Either way, they will almost double in size (25–30 minutes) during this last proof. Preheat oven to 450° F or 400° F according to method you are going to use (see below).

Baking Stone. These are large rounds. Two do not fit on pizza-size baking stone. Solution: to use stone, place one of the rounds, covered, into refrigerator after second proof. Place other round on peel or pan to rise. Heat pizza stone in 450° F oven for 30 minutes prior to baking; turn down to 400° F to bake the bread.

Large Baking Pan (Jelly Roll Pan): Invert the pan so rim is down. Sprinkle with White Spelt flour or cover with lightly floured parchment. Set the rounds 4" apart so they have room on all sides to expand.

7. Cover rounds with plastic wrap sprayed lightly with oil or damp towels or inside a large (tented) plastic bag with ends tucked under and set them to rise in draft-free place (75°–85° F). Check at 20 minutes and 5 minute intervals thereafter. Five minutes prior to baking, make slits about 2–2½" in length, about ¼" deep, in several places on the crown(s). Slit at an angle instead of straight down into the dough. Gently brush all exposed surfaces with egg yolk/water. Sprinkle surfaces with coarsely ground celery seed. Using spray bottle, spritz oven several times at one minute intervals in advance of baking so there will be moisture for baking.

8. **Baking stone:** Reduce oven heat to 400° F. Sprinkle stone with cornmeal or Whole Grain Spelt flour. Slide round onto baking stone. Bake 30–35 minutes. Midway through baking, remove other round from refrigerator and let rise, covered. Repeat process.

Baking pan: Place pan on lowest rack in preheated hot (400° F) oven. Spray oven sides and bottom with water in advance. At 15 minutes, turn the pan so rounds are on opposite side from where they were; continue baking for additional 15–20 minutes.

When done, the bread color should be burnished deep reddish brown and sound hollow when thumped with finger on base of sides and bottom. If not, bake for an additional 5 minutes. Remove from oven and place on wire racks to cool completely before cutting or storing. This bread freezes exceptionally well. Wrap securely in plastic then in foil. Freeze. It will keep its texture/taste for more than a month.

Brundisi Pesto Rolls (Deli Style)

A modified Kaiser roll, these are large luscious pesto rolls that go well with many things from making it a sandwich roll to eating with soups, such as Cioppino or a bouillabaisse, or when salad is your main course.

Blood Type: A, B, AB, O • Prep time: about 2 hrs • Cook time: 20–25 min • Yield: 12 large rolls (about 4 oz each)

Ingredients

1   recipe Brundisi Pesto Bread (preceding page)
1   cup semi-soft Mozzarella, coarsely grated (for topping)
2   tsp celery seed, coarsely ground (for topping)
1   egg white

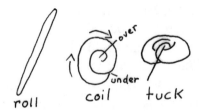

1. Follow directions for Brundisi Pesto Bread through the first rise (Step 4).

2. Gently depress dough and let rise again in same place. The second proof will take less time. Check at 20 minutes and 5 minute intervals thereafter by inserting dampened forefinger up to first knuckle into top of dough. If the indentation remains in the dough when you remove finger, it is ready.

3. Using plastic spatula, gently detach dough from edges of bowl and lay edges on top of dough. Gently depress dough with loose fist working around bowl several times. Turn out of bowl onto lightly floured (White Spelt) surface. Divide into 12–15 pieces. Let rest, covered with plastic wrap or slightly damp tea towel, for 10 minutes.

4. Form each piece into 6" lengths first by rounding dough then gently rolling and patting it with your fingers. Coil the dough by tucking one end under and bringing the other end over and through the center.

5. Place rolls on floured, rimmed large baking pan (15½" x 10½" x 1") leaving 2½ inches or more between each roll and sides of pan. Cover loosely with plastic wrap or damp towel and let rise until almost doubled in volume. Check (Finger Test) at 15 minutes and 5 minute intervals thereafter. During this rise, heat oven to 400° F. Beat egg white with 1 Tbsp room temperature water.

6. Gently brush rolls with the egg white/water. Sprinkle rolls with the ground celery seed. Sprinkle Mozzarella over the top of each roll. Place rolls in oven and bake on center rack for 20–25 minutes, turning pan around at 12 minutes so rolls bake evenly. Remove from oven and place on wire racks to cool.

These rolls freeze well. Once cooled, place in heavy-duty freezer bag and pull them out as needed. Thaw 10 minutes at room temperature or wrap in napkin or paper towel and reheat for 10 seconds on high in microwave or take directly from freezer and wrap in foil and place in preheated moderate (350° F) oven for 15 minutes.

French Bread
(Pain Ordinaire)

This is a basic and "quick" recipe for one of life's great delights: lean bread with plenty of crisp, chewy crust and a dense crumb full of the irregular air pockets that give it the renowned flavor. Traditional French bread can take a minimum of 3 fermentation (proofing) periods, the slower the better, and the best of them are made with a Whole Grain sponge and take 3 days to make. Look for a long version of Spelt French Bread in the upcoming *Spelt Healthy!* Volume III on Spelt Baking. In the meantime, I hope you will enjoy this bread. It takes about 3 hours and does not use a sponge (starter). The Whole Grain Spelt is what gives the flavor to this reliable, mouth-watering bread. For similar breads, see All-Purpose Italian Biga/Dough, Medi-Crostini, Roasted Garlic and Mozzarella Baguettes, Campocosenza. (See *Knead to Know,* Chapter 3 for directions/illustrations on forming.)

Blood Type: A, B, AB, O • Prep time: 3 hours • Cook time: 30–35 min
Yield: 2 French loaves or boules (15 oz each) or 2 American sandwich loaves

Ingredients

1   package active dry yeast
½   cup warm water (110°–115° F)
1   Tbsp sugar
2   tsp salt
1¼   cups warm water (110°–115° F)
1   cup Whole Grain Spelt flour
5   cups White Spelt flour (reserve 1 cup for kneading)
1   egg white mixed with 1 Tbsp tepid water

1. **Ferment.** Add ½ cup warm water to large mixing bowl. Sprinkle yeast over water; stir to dissolve. Let stand 10 minutes until foamy and creamy.

2. **Mix/Knead.** Add the salt, sugar and 1¼ cups warm water to the yeast. Add the Whole Grain Spelt flour and 2 cups White Spelt flour and beat.

Stand Mixer or By Hand: Speed 2, paddle for 2 minutes, several minutes by hand. As sticky dough begins to form, add 2 cups White Spelt flour, half cup at a time, and mix just until dough starts to ball and clean sides of bowl (stand mixer about a minute). Scrape the sides of the bowl with spatula. Turn dough out onto generously floured surface. The dough should be moist and slightly sticky at this point. Cover with bowl and let rest 10–15 minutes depending on your altitude.

Using pastry scraper to keep dough from sticking and sprinkling additional flour over dough if necessary, knead for several minutes to form smooth, elastic dough. Form into ball.

3. **First Rise:** Place dough in lightly oiled mixing bowl and cover with plastic wrap or lid. Set in draft-free place to rise (75°–80°) until almost doubled in volume (45–60 minutes). Check by lightly pressing a finger about ½" into crown of dough; if indentation remains dough is ready. Be careful not to let the dough go too long (go slack). It is difficult to recover the dough and you might have to begin again. So be on the safe side and check every 5 minutes after initial 45 minutes has passed.

4. **Second Rise:** Depress dough (don't punch it) with lightly closed fist working around bowl several times. You'll hear the whooshing sound of gas gently being expelled. Cover the bowl and set it in same place to proof the second time (25–35 minutes).

5. **Knead/Divide.** Detach dough from sides of bowl with plastic spatula and lay edges over top of dough. Depress dough. Turn out onto lightly floured board, smooth side down and knead for 2–3 minutes. With pastry scraper or sharp knife, divide the dough into 2 or 3 equal pieces. Cover and let rest for 10 minutes.

6. **Forming.** Keeping other pieces covered, form one piece into traditional pointed loaf or boule (sphere). (See *Knead to Know* about forming boules, bâtards, baguettes.) Set on lightly greased baking sheet sprinkled with White Spelt Flour. Or cover sheet with parchment and lightly oil and flour the parchment. Continue with other pieces. Spray loaves lightly with oil. Cover all with plastic wrap or place in large plastic (tented) bag or damp towel and let rise in draft-free place (75°–80° F) until dough is ready (25–30 minutes). Do the Finger Test because this dough does not double in volume. As you set the bread to rise, preheat oven to 450° F. (If using large baking stone, preheat oven 30 minutes in advance.) Using spray bottle, mist the interior of oven several times during the last five minutes before baking. The humidity makes a good crust and this is one way to achieve a small amount of humidity in home ovens.

7. Before placing in oven, diagonally slash each loaf 3 times (about 2½" long, ¼" deep) or slash top of rounds with a cross. Gently brush loaves with egg white/water. Spritz the oven again as bread is going in to bake. Bake at 450° F for five minutes; reduce heat to 375° F (400° F at altitudes about 4500 feet) and bake for additional 30–35 minutes until tops of loaves are deep golden brown.

Save all leftovers to make croutons and crumbs, especially herbed varieties. (See *Croutons and Crumbs.*)

French Rolls

Delicious French rolls with a crisp, shiny, chewy crust and moist, dense crumb. They make wonderful buns for special burgers such as mushroom and onion burgers and make fine submarine sandwich rolls. Excellent with Roasted Garlic in *Many Small Things* or Aioli (Garlic Mayonnaise) under *Sauces*.

The ratio of flours can easily be varied so there is more Whole Grain Spelt or use Light Spelt instead of White. (See *Knead to Know,* Chapter 3 for directions/illustrations on forming types of rolls.)

Blood Type: A, B, AB, O • Prep time: 1½–2 hrs • Cook time: 20–25 min • Yield: 12–16 French rolls

Ingredients

1   recipe French Bread (see previous pages)
1   egg white lightly beaten with 1 Tbsp tepid water

1. Make one recipe of French Bread dough and follow recipe through second rise (Step 4).

2. Depress the dough with your fingers and remove dough from sides of bowl with a rubber spatula, gently turning the edges onto the top of the dough. Turn dough out onto a lightly floured surface and knead for a couple of minutes by hand.

3. Divide the dough into 12–16 pieces; cover and let the dough rest for 8–10 minutes on lightly floured surface.

French Rolls: Form each piece into a ball then form into an oval with slightly tapered ends.

Subs: Divide dough into 8 pieces and form into oval with slightly tapered ends.

Buns: form into 8–10 balls then flatten by patting them out.

4. Place each roll on lightly greased baking sheet, leaving 2½ inches between each for crustier rolls. Cover rolls with plastic wrap or set in large (tented) plastic bag or slightly damp tea towel and let rise in a warm place (80°–85° F) free from draft until the rolls are about doubled in size (30–40 minutes).

French Rolls or Subs: Midway through this last rising, slash the top of each roll at an angle ¼ inch deep, 1½–2" long.

Buns: Do not slash.

5. Preheat the oven to 450° F and place a small pan with 1" boiling water in it on bottom of gas oven, on the topmost rack for electric ovens, or spray interior of oven three times in the last several minutes before baking. These methods help to give the rolls the desirable chewy, crusty crust.

6. When rolls have about doubled in size, re-slash the tops if they have filled in during rising. Gently brush the rolls with egg white/water mixture.

7. Place rolls in preheated hot (450° F) oven on middle rack for *five* minutes; then lower the heat to 375° F (400° F for altitudes above 4500 feet) and continue baking for 20–25 minutes or until the rolls are shiny deep golden brown and they pass the thump test. (Thump one of the rolls; if it sounds hollow, it is done.) Eat fresh or freeze and take out when needed.

French Breadsticks

There is a variety of recipes in *Spelt Healthy!* that make good breadsticks that you might not have thought of trying, for example, the Brundisi Pesto Bread and the All-Purpose Italian recipe. This excellent recipe for "Sticks" is from the basic French Bread recipe. The slight alteration in the French Bread recipe makes them slightly softer with excellent taste and keeping qualities. Be experimental with toppings and seasonings and make a variety of breadsticks in one batch, just like individual pizzas. The size can be varied, for example making fewer ultra-long breadsticks or many more shorter, pencil-size sticks. You will get the hang of it quickly as you do it. These are fun and easy! Try the Dynamite Stick for jazzing up a menu.

Blood Type: A, B, AB, O • Prep time: Varies • Cook time: 30–35 minutes • Yield: 24 or more

Ingredients

1   recipe French Bread with the following alteration: use 2 cups Whole Grain Spelt and 4 cups White or Light Spelt flour
1   egg white, room temperature, mixed with 1 Tbsp water
Variety of seasonings, herbs, cheeses and seeds
Finely grated hard cheese such as Pecorino Romano, Kasseri or Asiago
Herbs or seeds such as cumin, celery seed
Seasonings such as cayenne, garlic salt, crushed rosemary

1. Follow the French Bread recipe through the first rise (Step 3). Organize seasonings/toppings as dough rises. With spatula, detach edges of dough from sides of bowl and fold edges onto top of dough. Turn dough out onto lightly floured surface. Pat and press into an 18-inch by 12-inch rectangle. Lightly sprinkle with White Spelt flour. Cover with plastic wrap and let rest for 10 minutes.

2. Oil two large baking pans or cover with parchment paper and lightly oil the paper. Breadsticks take much room so you might consider turning the pans over so breadsticks are placed on bottom, which gives them more room for rising. Or remove your oven racks and put heavy duty foil over each up to about 1½–2 inches of edges to allow for air circulation. Spray the foil well.

3. Using a pastry scraper or sharp knife cut the dough in half vertically—long edge to long edge. Then cut each half horizontally into 12 strips or to desired size. (They can be cut vertically for longer sticks. See illustration.) Pat/press and roll each strip into breadstick. If dough is too soft, gently roll into a ball and work gently into a breadstick by pushing/rolling between fingers without overworking dough. Place each stick on pan and leave some room between them for expansion during rising and baking. Spray sticks lightly with oil. Cover with plastic wrap. Let rise on pans or racks until dough is springy but not doubled (25–35 minutes, sometimes sooner depending on temperature).

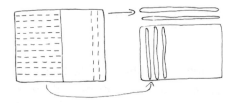

4. Preheat oven to 350° F. Adjust oven racks; one on bottom, other two rungs up. Gently brush each strip with egg white/water mixture. Sprinkle a variety of herbs, seeds, cheeses and seasonings over breadsticks. For example, deftly sprinkle a dozen sticks with finely grated cheese and sprinkle with cayenne for a **Dynamite Stick.** Sprinkle with crushed rosemary and salt. Sprinkle with cumin or celery seed and garlic.

5. Place pan(s) in preheated moderate (350° F) oven and bake for 15 minutes. Alternate pans/racks at 15 minutes. Rotate pans 180° for even baking. Bake an additional 15 minutes or until light golden brown. For crisper breadsticks, bake additional 10 or so minutes. Remove from oven and store upright in paper bag or place in a basket or other container for serving fresh.

Challah (Egg Bread)

Traditional airy egg bread, braided and sprinkled with seeds. Saffron or Mexican Safflower flecks the dough with golden red bits of color. Refer to *Knead to Know,* Chapter 3 for forming and braiding. See also *Speltoids,* Chapter 3, for factoids on Challah's long history.

Blood Types: A, B, AB, O • Prep time: about 1½ hrs • Cook time: 20–25 min • Yield: 2 braids

Ingredients

¾ cup warm (110°–115° F) water
2 packages active dry yeast
¼ cup + 1 Tbsp Light Olive oil or other vegetable oil
4 eggs, room temperature
2 cups Whole Grain Spelt flour
2½ cups White Spelt flour (+ additional for kneading)
2 Tbsp granulated sugar
1 tsp salt
1 tsp crushed saffron or Mexican safflower (optional)
Or sprinkle with turbinado sugar
1 egg white mixed with 1 Tbsp tepid water

1. **Ferment/Mix/Knead.** Pour ¾ cup warm water into large mixing bowl. Sprinkle 2 packages yeast over top; stir to dissolve. Let stand 10 minutes until creamy and foamy. Add 2 cups Whole Grain Spelt flour, sugar, salt and saffron (optional). Mix briefly. Add the oil and eggs.

Stand Mixer: On lowest speed with paddle attachment, blend ingredients until moist and incorporated (about 1 minute). On speed 2, gradually add 2 cups White Spelt flour to form soft, sticky dough. Scrape down sides of bowl with spatula; change to dough hook. On lowest speed, gradually add ½ cup of White Spelt to form sloppy, sticky dough (2 minutes). Turn out onto lightly floured board.

By Hand: Stir to blend and moisten all ingredients, using spatula to scrape down sides of bowl. Stir in 2 cups White Spelt flour to form sticky loose dough that grabs at the spoon. Turn out onto lightly floured surface and add additional White Spelt by sprinkling it over and under dough.

Knead. Knead several minutes to form a dough that is pliable and smooth, using pastry scraper to keep this very sticky dough from catching on surface and tearing dough. Sprinkle additional flour over and under dough as you work.

2. **First Rise.** Form a soft ball and place in clean, lightly oiled bowl and cover tightly with plastic or lid to prevent dough from drying. Set in draft-free place (75°–80°) to proof until just about doubled in volume (25–40 minutes). Test by inserting moistened fingertip ½" into crown of dough. If impression remains, dough is ripe. There should be some bubbling under skin of dough.

3. **Knead/Divide/Rest.** Detach dough from edges of bowl and lay over top of dough. Turn out onto lightly floured surface and gently knead to remove air bubbles out to edge of dough. Divide dough in half. Divide each half into 3 portions. Cover well and let dough rest 10 minutes.

Place parchment paper on large rimmed baking pan (17" x 12" is optimal) or two smaller baking pans. Dust with Whole Grain Spelt. Or lightly grease pans and dust with flour.

4. **Form Braids:** Roll and pat one ball into a rope that is 12" long. Do the same with two other balls. Sprinkle ropes with Whole Grain Spelt flour; it will help keep the strands from blending into one another when braided. Place them side by side on pan across the narrow axis if using a large jellyroll pan. Again, dust ropes with Whole Grain Spelt to keep them from bleeding into one another. Braid the ropes, pinching ends closed and tucking them under and snugging ends against pan. Repeat with other half of dough to form second braid.

Note: Almost any pan will do for braided bread. Just adjust the length of ropes to the pan, such as large loaf pans. Or make free-form braid to place in center of a baking pan.

5. **Second Rise and Preheat Oven.** Cover braids with plastic wrap lightly sprayed with oil or set in large (tented) plastic bag or cover with damp towel. Let rise until dough has expanded by ½–¾ (20–25 minutes). Test by inserting finger into dough as above. Size alone is not an accurate indicator of ripeness of Spelt dough. The dough will expand considerably during baking. Preheat oven to 400° F.

6. **Brush/Bake.** Gently brush the braids on all surfaces with egg white mixture. Sprinkle with sesame, poppy or other seeds (optional). To make sweet breakfast bread, sprinkle with turbinado sugar. Place in preheated (400° F) oven and bake for 20–25 minutes. High altitude: bake at 425° F. Ten minutes into baking, turn pan 180° for even baking. When baked, the Challah will sound hollow when tapped and surface will be variegated and shiny golden brown. Remove from pans and place on wire racks to cool.

Cardamom Gold Pumpkin Bread

This is a sweet and spiced yeast bread with raisins or currants. The toffee-like topping is optional but makes an exquisite finish. Best if refrigerated overnight for deep flavor to fully develop.

Blood Type: A, B, AB use goat's milk or soy milk; O use soy milk
Prep time: about 1½ hrs • Cook time: 30–35 min • Yield: 1 large or 2 smaller loaves

Ingredients

½ cup cow's milk or goat's milk or soy milk (texture and taste will change somewhat with soy)

½ cup canned pumpkin (plain pumpkin not pumpkin pie filling)

2 Tbsp vegetable oil

2 Tbsp brown sugar, tightly packed

1 tsp salt

1 tsp cinnamon, ground

1 tsp cardamom, ground

½ tsp ground ginger

1 package active dry yeast

¼ cup warm water (110°–115° F)

2¾ cups White Spelt Flour (divided 1½, 1¼)

1 cup Whole Grain Spelt flour (divided ½, ½)

2 eggs, room temperature

¾ cup raisins or currents (softened)

Butter-Nut Topping (optional)

Melted butter or oil for brushing tops of loaf (loaves)

1. **Mix/Ferment/Knead.** Heat milk until it bubbles but does not boil. Transfer to a large mixing bowl. Add pumpkin, oil, brown sugar, salt, cinnamon, cardamom and ginger. Whisk to blend. Set aside and cool mixture to lukewarm (about 95° F).

2. Pour ¼ cup warm water (110°–115° F) into a small bowl. Sprinkle yeast over water; stir to dissolve. Let stand for 10 minutes until it is creamy and foamy.

3. Add yeast to mixture in large bowl. Add 1½ cups White Spelt Flour, ½ cup Whole Grain Spelt flour and eggs to milk mixture.

Stand Mixer: Beat with paddle (speed 2) for 60–90 seconds until long ropy strands form and attach to paddle and sides of bowl. Add raisins to batter; mix just enough to incorporate. Add remaining 1¼ cup White Spelt Flour in several increments and the remaining ½ cup Whole Grain Spelt flour and continue to beat with paddle on speed 2 for 30 seconds. Change to dough hook and knead (speed 1) until dough starts cleaning sides of bowl (about a minute). Do not over beat or dough will go slack. Turn out onto lightly floured surface and knead until dough is smooth (2–3 minutes by hand).

By Hand: Beat until smooth, scraping down sides of bowl. Stir in raisins and Spelt Flours a half cup at a time. Mix until batter becomes too stiff to stir and starts cleaning sides of bowl. Turn out onto lightly floured surface and knead until smooth.

4. **First Rise.** Place dough in a large lightly oiled bowl, turning to oil all sides. Cover with plastic wrap, saucer or lid. Set dough in a warm (75°–80° F) draft-free place until doubled in volume (30–40 minutes). Dough rises quickly so test for ripeness at 30 minutes and 5 minute intervals thereafter. Test by inserting finger about ½" in top of dough; if indentation remains when finger is pulled out, dough is ready.

5. **Divide/Rest.** Depress the dough with loose fist using plastic spatula to remove dough from sides of bowl and fold over top as you go. Turn out onto lightly floured board and divide if making 2 8" x 4" loaves. Cover with plastic wrap or damp cloth and let dough rest 7–10 minutes.

6. **Shape/Second Rise.** Shape into loaves and place in lightly greased 9" x 5" x 3" loaf pan or two 8" x 4" pans. Cover with plastic wrap or damp tea towel or place in large (tented) plastic bag and let rise until *almost* doubled (about 25–30 minutes).

7. **Preheat Oven/Topping (optional)/ Brush with Butter/Oil.** Fifteen minutes into the last rise, preheat oven to 375° F and make topping below (optional). Gently brush top of loaf (loaves) with melted butter or oil, or spoon TOPPING over loaf (loaves).

8. Place bread on dark baking pan if made with topping (in case of drips). Otherwise, set pan(s) to bake on middle rack of preheated hot (375° F) oven for 30–35 minutes or until done. Test with toothpick or skewer inserted in center of loaf (loaves); if it comes out clean, the bread is done. Remove from oven to wire rack and cool 10 minutes then tip (Non-Topping recipe) out of pan(s) and let cool completely before cutting. Leave bread with topping in pan to cool completely. Refrigerate overnight for best flavor.

HONEY BUTTER-NUT TOPPING

Ingredients

¼ cup butter, softened
⅓ cup light brown sugar, tightly packed
¼ cup fluid honey
½ cup walnuts or pecans, finely chopped

Whip the butter, brown sugar and honey until fluffy and light, adding a few drops of warm water if it is too thick. Spread evenly over the dough and sprinkle with the chopped nuts.

Dark Rye Bread

Beautiful, clean-slicing rye with burnished chestnut brown crust and dense moist, chewy crumb redolent with flavor. Make rounds, loaves or cocktail loaves. (See cover photograph.)

Blood Type: A, AB • Prep/Proof time: 2½–3 hrs • Cook time: 45–55 min • Yield: 2 loaves (1 lb 3 oz each)

Ingredients

1 cup milk
2 Tbsp butter, softened
¼ cup Robust molasses (dark)
4 tsp salt
2 Tbsp caraway seeds
¾ cup warm water (110°–115° F)
2 pkgs active dry yeast
2 cups Medium Rye Flour
1 cup Whole Grain Spelt Flour
2¼ cups White Spelt Flour (+ additional for kneading)
1 egg mixed with 1 Tbsp tepid water

1. **Mix/Ferment.** Stovetop or microwave: heat milk until it bubbles but does not boil. Stir in softened butter, molasses, salt and caraway seeds. Cool to lukewarm (about 95° F). Pour ¾ cup warm water into large mixing bowl. Sprinkle 2 packages yeast over top; stir to dissolve. Let stand until creamy and foamy (10 minutes).

2. **Mix/Initial Knead.** Add the milk/molasses mixture to yeast in the large mixing bowl. Stir in the Rye flour.

Stand Mixer (Paddle): Beat on speed 2 until ingredients are thoroughly incorporated (30–45 seconds). Add the Whole Grain Spelt flour and 1 cup White Spelt Flour and mix (speed 2) until dough becomes ropy (about a minute). Gradually add 1¼ cups White Spelt Flour. As rough dough forms, change to dough hook and knead (about 2 minutes) on low speed. Resist the temptation to adjust either liquid or flour measure at this time. Rye absorbs water at a different rate than Spelt.

By Hand: This is a very stiff dough. After adding the Rye flour, beat until ingredients are moist and thoroughly incorporated. Add the Whole Grain Spelt flour and beat, scraping down sides of bowl continually. Gradually add 1¼ cups White Spelt Flour and beat until dough is too stiff to work. Turn out onto lightly floured board to work in the remaining White Spelt flour.

3. **Rest/Knead.** Let dough rest, covered, for 10 minutes. The dough will be moist and sticky at this stage. Knead by hand 2–3 minutes to form smooth, moist dough. Mist hands with water or dust with flour and/or pick up dough to knead it to prevent incorporating too much flour. Form into a ball. Place in clean, oiled bowl and turn dough to oil all sides.

4. **First Rise.** Cover tightly with plastic wrap or lid or damp towel. Place in draft-free place (75°–80° F) to let rise (60–75 minutes). Check by gently but quickly inserting a moistened finger ½" into the crown of the dough. If the impression remains in the dough, it is ripe.

5. **Degas/Knead/Divide/Rest.** Dust hands with flour. Gently deflate dough by pressing a loose fist into dough and working around bowl. Detach dough from edges of bowl with plastic spatula and place on top of dough. Turn out onto lightly floured surface and knead briefly. Divide into two equal portions. Cover and let dough rest 10 minutes.

6. **Forming/Second Rise/Preheat Oven.**

(See *Knead to Know*, Chapter 3 for illustrations/directions on forming breads.)

American Rye Loaf. Form one portion of dough into a 9" long oval so dough touches ends of lightly oiled 9" x 5" loaf pan. Repeat with other portion or form other into a round (see below).

OR form into smaller **Cocktail Loaves** by placing in 4 oiled 5½" x 3¼" x 2¼" pans.

Cover loaves with plastic wrap or damp tea towel or set both pans within a big plastic bag that is tented and ends tucked under. Set in same draft-free place until about doubled in volume (45–60 minutes; cocktail loaves less time). Preheat oven to 375° F. Gently brush top of loaves with egg white/water mixture. Make slashes (¼" deep, 1½" long) in three places along the top of each large loaf. One slash if making cocktail loaves.

Hearth Round. Form each portion of dough into a smooth ball; place each on a lightly oiled 8" pie pan. Cover with plastic wrap and set in same place to proof until rounds expand to about ¾ volume (45–60 minutes). Score a # sign a little less than ½" deep into the top of each round. Brush or wipe entire exposed surface with egg/water mixture. Press caraway seeds into loaf if desired (optional).

Preheat oven to 375° F 30 minutes into this second rise.

7. Place pan(s) on center rack of preheated moderately hot (375° F) oven and bake for 25 minutes. Switch pans to opposite sides and rotate each 180° to assure even baking. Bake 20–25 minutes longer until crust is shiny, chestnut brown and bread sounds hollow when tapped. Remove from oven and tip loaves out of pan to cool on wire rack. Cool loaves and rounds completely before slicing with sharp knife with non-serrated blade. This bread has excellent keeping properties fresh or frozen.

Brioche
(Spelt Sweet Dough)

This is the short method for Sweet Dough. This recipe contains *both* Whole Grain and White Spelt. Together they provide a sweetness and depth of taste often lacking in even the richest of white flour Brioches that undergo initial fermentation and refrigeration. Spelt makes delicate, fine dough for Pane Brioche, holiday breads and an array of delicate rolls.

Blood Type: B; A, AB use goat's milk; A, AB use oil instead of butter. O avoid because of milk. Do not substitute soy milk for milk in this recipe. Note: the butter makes this dough more delicate and cakelike. • Prep time: about 50–60 min • Cook time: Varies according to recipe. • Yield: 3 lb wet dough; 2 lb 12 oz baked, cooled weight

Ingredients

1 cup milk
½ cup light or dark brown sugar, firmly packed
1¼ tsp salt
½ cup (1 stick) butter, room temperature or ¼ cup + 2 Tbsp vegetable oil especially Light Olive or canola
¼ cup warm water (110° to 115° F)
2 pkgs active dry yeast
3 eggs, room temperature
4 cups White Spelt flour (+ ½–1 cup for kneading)
2 cups Whole Grain Spelt flour

1. **Initial Mix.** In microwave or on stovetop, heat milk until it bubbles around the edges; do not boil. Remove from heat source and stir in sugar, salt and butter. Cool to lukewarm (about 95° F).

2. **Ferment.** Warm a large mixing bowl by running under hot water. Dry off. To the warm bowl, add ¼ cup warm water and sprinkle the yeast over the water. Stir to dissolve. Let sit for 10 minutes until creamy.

3. **Mix/Knead.** Add the milk mixture to the yeast. Add the eggs, 2 cups White Spelt flour and 1 cup Whole Grain Spelt flour.

Stand Mixer: Using paddle (speed 2) beat until mixture is smooth (about 1½ minutes). Add remaining cup Whole Grain flour; mix very briefly to form soft dough. Change to dough hook and, mixing on lowest speed, add 2 cups White Spelt flour a half-cup at a time. Knead until soft dough begins to ball and clean sides of bowl (1½ minutes). The dough should be slightly sticky at this stage. Turn out onto surface generously floured with White Spelt. Lightly knead to form soft, smooth dough.

By Hand: Stir the milk mixture, yeast, eggs, 2 cups White and 1 cup Whole Grain Spelt until ingredients are thoroughly incorporated. In half-cup increments, gradually beat in 2 cups White Spelt and 1 cup Whole Grain Spelt until soft dough forms. The dough should be slightly sticky. Turn out onto surface generously floured with White Spelt. Lightly knead to form soft, smooth dough

4. **First Rise.** Place dough rough side down in lightly buttered or oiled boil and turn to grease the top. Cover with plastic wrap, lid or damp towel; let rise in warm (80°–85° F) draft-free place until doubled in volume (30–40 minutes). Test at 25–30 minutes by lightly pressing a finger ½" into crown of dough and removing it. If impression remains, dough is ripe.

Please note Brioche dough rising is traditionally retarded by placing in refrigerator to develop flavor. This can also be done with Spelt; however, it rises quicker than wheat so refrigerator times will be significantly shorter.

5. **Degas/Divide/Rest.** Depress dough, working around bowl with loose fist and using plastic spatula to loosen edges from sides of bowl. Turn out onto lightly floured surface. With pastry scraper or sharp knife, divide dough according to any traditional recipes you may be using for bread, rolls, etc. Let dough rest, covered, 10 minutes and proceed with recipe such as those calling for Brioche forms, pastries and others such as *Brioches with Hint of Lemon* that follows.

Brioches with Hint of Lemon

Delicate sweet rolls with the characteristic topknot. Easy to make in muffin pan cups; they bake in 10 minutes. There is no initial fermentation and refrigeration required for this recipe as in traditional Brioche recipes.

Blood Type: See Brioche • Prep time: about 2 hrs • Cook time: 10 minutes • Yield: 18 rolls (2 oz)

Ingredients

1   recipe Spelt Sweet Dough made with 1 tsp freshly grated lemon zest added with eggs (See previous pages for recipe)

1. Follow directions for making Spelt Sweet Dough through the first rise and turning out on lightly floured board.

2. Lightly knead the dough. Divide the dough into 2 unequal portions: ⅔ and ⅓. Divide each portion into 18 pieces. Let the dough rest, covered, for 10 minutes. Grease 18 muffin pan cups.

3. Shape the larger ⅔ portion into balls about 2" in diameter. Set balls in muffin cups and make an indentation on the top. Shape the small ⅓ portion of the dough into 18 small smooth balls. Place on top of the large balls in muffin cups. Preheat oven to 425° F.

4. Brush the Brioches with oil or butter; cover loosely with plastic wrap. Let rise until just about doubled in volume (15–25 minutes). Do not allow to rise too long.

5. Place on middle rack of preheated hot (425° F) oven and bake for 10 minutes or until golden brown. Remove from pan immediately and set on wire rack to cool.

Pao Doce
(Massa Sovada or Portuguese Sweet Bread)

I consider Pao Doce one of the world's great breads: fine textured, with a suggestively sweet thin crisp crust and a dense, even, fine almost velvet crumb that is exceptionally moist and flavorful.

The first time I ate Pao Doce was many years ago when a member of my Portuguese class brought one made by his Portuguese mother for the class to enjoy. We ate it as he explained its place as one of the centerpieces in festivals especially at Easter. That same tradition still echoes through certain regions of Spain where fine White Spelt flour was, and is, used in festival breads and for special occasions and is sold as a gastronomic delight in the region of Asturias (read more about it in Part II: *Speltoids, Chapter 2 Spelt Time*). It remains one of my favorite breads. When I first made it with Spelt, tears came to my eyes and I understood right then and there why Spelt ranks as a gourmet flour.

Pao Doce (literally "sweet bread") is a member of the Massa Sovada (Portuguese for "sweet dough") family that includes Brioche and Pannetone. (See upcoming Volume 3 in the Autumn Rose Press *Spelt Healthy!* series for more specialty breads like Pannetone.) Serve as you would pound cake or enjoy a piece on its own, simply, with a cup of chamomile tea.

Please read the chapter *Knead to Know* and then read the recipe completely and decide ahead of time the form(s) you want to make. (See cover photograph for braided Pao Doce.) The coiled form you cut like a cake but slice under the rim (a cap) saving the "lid" with raisins for the last sweet bite. This bread freezes extraordinarily well. Instead of raisins or currents use candied fruits such as cherries and slivered almonds or crushed pine nuts and knead in gently immediately prior to first rise.

Blood Type: Not rated • Prep time: about 2½ hrs • Cook time: 35–40 min • Yield: 2 loaves (about 1½ lb each)

Ingredients

2   pkgs active dry yeast
¼   cup warm (110°–115° F) water
1   tsp granulated or brown sugar (brown sugar preferable)
1   cup granulated sugar
6½ to 7 cups White Spelt flour
1   tsp salt

1   cup warm (110°–115° F) cow's milk (goat's milk is highly recommended for the superb sweet flavor and texture it gives to this fine bread)
3   eggs, room temperature
¼   pound (1 stick) unsalted butter, room temperature
2   Tbsp softened butter (for bowl and pans)
1   egg, lightly beaten

Coils: 1 Tbsp raisins or currents (soaked in hot water, drained, cooled) and turbinado sugar for sprinkling

Braids: ¼ cup raisins or currents (soaked in hot water, drained, cooled) and ½ cup turbinado sugar

1. **Ferment.** In small bowl or glass measuring cup, add yeast and 1 tsp granulated or brown sugar to ¼ cup warm water; stir to dissolve. Allow to stand 10 minutes until creamy and foamy. Heat milk until it bubbles around the edges but does not boil; let cool to lukewarm (about 95° F).

2. **Mix/Initial Knead.** In large mixing bowl, combine 1 cup granulated sugar, 4 cups White Spelt flour and salt. Whisk to combine. Pour in the yeast and the warm milk; drop in the eggs.

Stand Mixer: Attach whisk. On speed 2, combine the above ingredients (about 30 seconds). Change to paddle, speed 2, beat in one stick soft butter, adding 2–2½ cups White Spelt flour ½ cup at a time to form a soft ball (about 1½ minutes). Change to dough hook and, on lowest speed, knead to form very soft dough that cleans sides of bowl (45 seconds). Be very careful—*do not overmix* this dough. It develops quickly. At this stage this should be a soft and slightly sticky dough. Turn soft dough onto surface lightly sprinkled with White Spelt flour.

By Hand: Mix the above ingredients to uniform moistness, scraping down sides of bowl to incorporate all ingredients evenly. Beat in the softened butter to form a smooth dough, gradually adding remaining White Spelt flour. The smooth, heavy dough will wrap around the mixing spoon. Scrape down sides of bowl and transfer dough to surface sprinkled with White Spelt flour.

3. **Rest/Knead/First Rise.** Turn out onto lightly floured surface. Cover dough with bowl and let dough rest 10 minutes. Knead gently until smooth and elastic, sprinkling a small amount of flour over dough as necessary and using pastry scraper to keep dough from sticking. **(If making Braided Bread, sprinkle softened currents or raisins on the surface of the dough to within an inch of the edge. Gently knead in.)** Shape dough into a ball and place, smooth side down, in a lightly buttered or oiled bowl, turning to coat all sides. Let rise at room temperature (75° F) in a completely draft-free place until the dough *more* than doubles in bulk (check at 30 minutes and 10 minute intervals thereafter). Please do not let it go too long or it will go slack and become very difficult or impossible to recover.

4. **Degas/Rest/Divide.** Loosen edges with plastic spatula and place over top of dough; depress dough (do not punch) with loose fist, working around bowl several times, and turn out, rough side down, onto lightly floured surface. Let rest 10 minutes. Divide into 2 pieces with dough scraper or sharp knife being careful not to tear the dough.

5. **Form:**

Round Loaves: Gently form each piece into a round about 8" across. Place in lightly buttered pie pans. Cover with buttered or oil-sprayed plastic wrap or set in large (tented) plastic bag and let rise in same draft-free place until more than doubled (check at 30 minutes and 5 minute intervals thereafter). Preheat the oven to 350° F. Brush the top of each loaf with the beaten egg. Place on middle rack and bake until loaves are shiny, golden brown and crusty (about 35 minutes). Test for doneness by thumping the bottom of loaves; they should sound hollow.

Snail (Caracois). This is a very old form one of my Portuguese teachers told me was created to mimic the famous Chambered Nautilus that appears in so much Mediterranean art from antiquity. In reality, coiling is one of the great methods for giving bread added height and dramatic presentation as the coils are not visible after baking.

To coil, roll each piece of dough into a rope about 1½" in diameter. Set the rope in a buttered pie plate or, preferably larger round pan, and form a coil leaving space between the coils (and the edge of pan). Cover with buttered or oiled plastic wrap or in large (tented) plastic bag with ends tucked under and set in same draft-free place to rise (40–45 minutes). Very gently brush the coils with beaten egg and set half of the raisins in the center before baking. Sprinkle top and sides with turbinado sugar. Bake on center rack in preheated moderate oven (350° F) for 30–35 minutes. The bread will rise about 4" above the pan and be a shiny, striated golden brown when done. The center with raisins will form a small cap. Cool completely before serving. Slice as you would a cake, under the rim, leaving the "cap" for last.

Braided Bread. (See cover photograph.) Before you finish kneading the bread before its first rise, sprinkle the soaked, drained raisins or currents over the dough to within an inch of the edge. Gently knead in before forming the dough into a ball for the first rise. Place in lightly buttered or oiled bowl, turning to coat all edges. Cover tightly with plastic wrap or lid and let the dough rise until more than doubled in bulk (check at 30 minutes and 10 minute intervals thereafter). With plastic spatula, loosen edges of dough and place them on top surface. Gently depress dough and turn out onto lightly floured board. Divide in two and let rest, covered, 10 minutes.

Divide each portion of the dough into 3 pieces using pastry scraper or sharp knife Be very careful not to tear the dough. Form (pat/press but do not pull) each of the three pieces into ropes about 8"–10" long. If the dough resists, let it rest (covered) for 10 minutes and begin again. Sprinkle each of the ropes with White Spelt Flour (or Confectioners' sugar) to keep them from "bleeding" together. Braid the 3 strands, turning the edges under and sealing them. Repeat with the other half of the dough.

Place on lightly buttered or parchment covered (preferable) large, rimmed baking sheet allowing several inches between each loaf if using a single pan. Cover with lightly buttered or oiled plastic wrap or inside a large plastic bag that is tented and ends tucked under and set in same draft-free place to rise until just about doubled in bulk (check at 30 minutes and 10 minute intervals thereafter). Gently brush each braid with the beaten egg and sprinkle with ½ cup turbinado sugar. Set in preheated moderate oven (350° F) and bake for 30–35 minutes. The bread will expand considerably during baking and present a shiny, golden finish when done. Let cool completely before serving.

Make ahead of time and freeze cooled loaves by wrapping securely in plastic wrap and then wrapping in foil. Let thaw at room temperature.

Indirect Method Breads
Spelt Wheat Berry and Honey Bread

Spelt has character just like fine wine. In *Spelt Wheat Berry and Honey Bread* its character is fully developed through a combination of Spelt flours, Spelt Berry water, and fermentation (sponge method) to produce wonderfully complex flavors and baking aromas. This method accentuates the natural sweetness and slightly nutty taste of Spelt. There is contrast between the moist dense crumb and soft crunch of Spelt Berries. All of these things combine to make one of the most delicious and nutritious of breads. (Please review *Knead to Know* chapter on working with Spelt breads.)

Blood Type: A, AB, B, O • Prep time: about 3 hrs • Cook time: 50–60 min • Yield: 2 loaves (1 lb 5oz each)

Ingredients in Advance:
1 cup *boiled* Spelt wheat berries
1¼ cups Spelt Berry water (lukewarm)

Sponge
2 pkgs active dry yeast or 4¼ tsp bulk active dry yeast
½ cup warm (110°–115° F) water
1¼ cups lukewarm (95° F) Spelt berry water
5 Tbsp fluid honey
1½ cups Whole Grain Spelt flour
1 cup White Spelt flour

Dough
2½ cups White Spelt Flour (+ additional for kneading)
1 cup Whole Grain Spelt flour
¼ cup Light Olive oil or other vegetable oil
1½ tsp salt

1. **Spelt Berries.** Soak the berries overnight in a large bowl with 3 inches of water to cover or start cooking the berries several hours before you start the bread. Place ½ cup Spelt Berries in a saucepan with 3 cups of water and boil for 10 minutes. Remove from heat and take 1¼ cups of the water and set aside. Let berries stand for 10 minutes then simmer for additional 1 to 2 hours adding water as needed until berries soften and most of the water is absorbed. Drain any remaining liquid and strain the berries in a colander. Set aside to cool.

2. **Ferment (Sponge)/Rise.** Add ½ cup warm water to a small bowl; sprinkle yeast over top. Stir to dissolve. Let stand 10 minutes until creamy and foamy. In large mixing bowl, combine honey with 1¼ cups *lukewarm* (about 95° F) Spelt Berry water. Add yeast and 1½ cups Whole Grain Spelt flour and 1 cup White Spelt flour. *By hand:* Beat well for several minutes, scraping down sides of bowl with plastic/rubber spatula, to thoroughly mix and moisten all ingredients. *Stand Mixer:* Beat with paddle, speed 2, about 2 minutes. Cover with plastic wrap, saucer or lid. Set in draft-free place (75°–85° F) and proof (35–40 minutes). The sponge will be a lively, viscous mass that climbs up the bowl and more than doubles.

3. **Dough Mix/Knead.** Add oil and salt to the sponge. *By Hand:* Mix in oil and salt and gradually add flour, stirring until dough begins to ball around spoon, and clean sides of bowl. *Stand Mixer:* Using paddle, beat on speed 2 for 1 minute; gradually add 2–2½ cups White Spelt flour and 1 cup Whole Grain flour and mix (1 minute). As the dough stiffens, change to dough hook and decrease to lowest speed. Knead for a minute. Dough should be somewhat wet and sticky. Scrape down sides of bowl.

4. **Knead/Add Berries.** Turn out onto floured surface. Cover and let rest 10 minutes. Knead lightly, using pastry scraper to keep dough from sticking and sprinkling White Spelt flour over/under dough. The berries add a portion of the flour ratio; do not incorporate too much flour as this is wet dough. Instead, dust your hands with flour or mist them with cool water. Pat out into a rectangle ½ inch thick. Sprinkle Spelt Berries over dough to within ½" of the edges. Knead in, very lightly, as both Whole Grain Spelt and the Berries are rough and will tear dough with excess handling. Form into a moist ball. Place in clean oiled bowl. Cover.

5. **First Dough Rise:** Set in warm place (80°–85° F) to rise until almost doubled (40–50 minutes). Test by pressing a floured finger lightly into the crown of the dough about ½". If indentation remains, dough is ripe.

6. **Degas/Divide/Rest.** With plastic spatula, detach dough from edges of bowl then depress dough with loose fist (do not punch), working hand around bowl several times. Turn out onto lightly floured surface and divide into 2 equal portions with pastry scraper or sharp knife. Cover the dough with plastic wrap or damp towel and allow to rest 10 minutes.

7. **Form/Second Dough Rise:** Form into symmetrical loaves. (See *Knead to Know,* Chapter 3 for illustrations/directions on forming.) Place in 2 well-oiled, 9" x 5" x 3" loaf pans with dough touching each end of the pan for support as it rises. Slightly flatten dough so it almost touches the long edges of the pan. Cover with plastic wrap sprayed with oil or set in large (tented) plastic bag with ends tucked under pan and set in same place until almost doubled (40–50 minutes). Watch carefully so bread does not over-proof and go slack. Check at 40 minutes by doing Finger Test to gauge dough tension. Midway into this last rise, preheat oven to 350° F.

8. **Bake.** Place bread on lower rack of preheated moderate (350° F) oven. Bake 50–60 minutes until bread is a deep golden brown, the edges have shrunk slightly from sides of pan and it sounds hollow when thumped. Remove from oven and tip out onto wire racks to cool completely before cutting or storing.

Light Rye Bread

This basic recipe for Light Rye Bread uses the sponge method for fermenting Rye and Spelt, both heavy flours, to create better taste and texture. The flavor develops more fully (sweeter deeper notes characteristic of the ryes) if the sponge is made the night before and then refrigerated. This slightly sweet and pliable bread slices perfectly, keeps well and is excellent for grilled sandwiches, such as Patty Melts.

Note: This is a Stand Mixer recipe because of the very stiff dough.

**Blood Type: A, AB, O • Prep time: 3–4 hrs minimum fermentation; 2–2½ hrs dough
Cook time: 35–45 min • Yield: 2 loaves (about 1 lb 5oz each)**

Ingredients

Sponge
1   pkg active dry yeast
1   cup lukewarm water (95° F)
1   cup medium weight Rye flour

Dough
¾   cup + 2 Tbsp boiling water
1   cup dark brown sugar, firmly packed
2   Tbsp butter (or 1½ Tbsp vegetable oil)
2   tsp salt
2   Tbsp caraway seed
½   cup medium weight Rye flour (as above)
2   cups Whole Grain Spelt flour
3–4 cups White Spelt flour

1. **Sponge:** Into large mixing bowl, pour 1 cup of lukewarm water (about 95° F). Sprinkle yeast over water. Add 1 cup medium weight Rye flour; blend thoroughly. Cover the sponge with plastic wrap or lid. Let ferment 3–4 hours at 70°–75° F until sponge rises and falls.

If you are not present for the rise and fall, you will see where the sponge has bubbled up and dried against the sides of the bowl. The sponge leaves tracks for you to follow. The mixture will look like a "sponge" and you will understand how it got its name. It will be a viscous mass with many bubbles and holes and it shakes like gelatin. At this stage, proceed with dough or place sponge, covered, in refrigerator overnight, and let come to room temperature before using in dough.

2. **Dough:** Place ¾ cup + 2 Tbsp water in a small saucepan; bring to the boil. Add the sugar, butter, salt and caraway seed to the water. Stir until sugar is in solution and butter melts. Let mixture cool. This will soften the seeds and infuse their flavor into the liquid.

Spoon the Rye sponge into large mixing bowl. Attach paddle to Stand Mixer, and, at lowest speed, alternately add the flours in ½ cup measures and the brown sugar/butter/seed mixture (about 1½ minutes). Change to the dough hook. Knead until dough begins to smooth and clean sides of bowl (about 2 minutes). The dough should be stiff and rather sticky at this stage.

3. **Rest/Knead.** Turn dough out onto floured (White Spelt) surface. Cover with bowl; let dough rest 15 minutes. Form into rough ball and then begin to knead until dough is smooth and elastic, moist but not sticky. Form dough into a ball. Rub your hands with vegetable oil and rub dough ball lightly all the way around with oil. Place in clean bowl. Cover with lid or plastic wrap sprayed lightly with oil.

4. **First Dough Rise.** Set dough out at room temperature (75°–80° F) in a draft-free place until the dough approximately doubles in volume (60–80 minutes). Check dough at 55 minutes by pressing a fingertip ½" into crown of dough. If impression remains after taking finger out, dough is ripe. If dough springs back quickly, let it continue rising. Check at 10 minute intervals. Over-proofing can produce a dry and gummy vs. moist and chewy loaf.

5. **Degas/Knead/Divide/Rest.** Depress the dough with a loose fist (do not punch) working around the bowl several times to expel air. With plastic spatula, detach dough edges from side of bowl and place over top of dough. Turn dough out, bottom side up, and knead briefly. With pastry scraper or sharp knife, divide the dough into 2 equal portions. Cover; let rest 10 minutes. Grease 2 loaf pans (8" x 4").

6. **Second Dough Rise.** Shape into loaves and place in the greased pans with dough touching ends of pan. Gently brush the top of each loaf with vegetable oil for a softer crust. Set pans in large plastic bag or cover loosely with plastic wrap sprayed with oil. Place in same (75°–80° F) draft-free place until the dough has just about doubled in volume (50–60 minutes) and rounds above the pan. Use Fingertip Test to check at 50 minutes and 5 minute intervals thereafter. The bread will rise slightly more in the oven, so take care not to over-proof. Midway through second rise, preheat the oven to 350° F.

7. **Bake.** Place on middle rack of moderately hot (350° F) oven and bake for 35–45 minutes. Crust will be deep golden brown, the loaves should sound hollow when thumped and the bread will have shrunk from edges of pans. Tip loaves out of pans onto wire racks and let cool completely before cutting with sharp, non-serrated slicing knife.

Roman Bread

This deep sienna colored Roman Bread is a link to the ancient past. Archaeologists at Herculaneum and Pompeii found baked loaves like this perfectly preserved in the ashes from the volcanic eruption of Mt. Vesuvius in A.D. 79. See cover photograph of stacked rounds of Roman Bread; the top round was cut with a Roman pugio (soldier's knife). The flour, herbs, salt and olive oil are all traditional Roman ingredients. The recipe here calls for Whole and White Spelt but easily converts to all Whole Grain Spelt or Whole Grain mixed with Light Spelt.

Roman Bread makes one large wheel, 2 rounds or 4 Focaccia rounds by adding toppings from the *Many Small Things* section. Or make the traditional Roman Bread by simply brushing with oil and sprinkling with chopped green onions or crushed rosemary and salt or seasonings in this recipe.

The crumb is tan and fairly dense yet moist with some irregular large air pockets. It slices well especially when scored in advance as the Romans did. The aroma while baking is sensuous. Serve with fish, salad or meat dishes. For a touch of authenticity, dip a wedge in oil and garlic (see recipe for Aglio e Olio under *Sauces* or eat with Roasted Garlic and Grilled Kasseri Cheese both under Beginnings in *Many Small Things*).

Blood Type: A, B, AB, O • Prep time: 2 hrs including rise time • Cook time: 35 min • Yield: 2 rounds (14 oz each)

Ingredients

Sponge
¼   tsp active dry yeast
¼   cup warm (110°–115° F) water
1¼ cups warm (110°–115° F) water
1   Tbsp dark brown sugar
1   cup Whole Grain Spelt flour
1½ cups White Spelt flour

Dough
1   pkg active dry yeast
¼   cup lukewarm water (110°–115° F)
1   Tbsp brown sugar
1   Tbsp Olive oil
2   Tbsp rosemary, dried and freshly ground (divided 1, 1)
2   tsp celery seed, freshly ground (divided 1, 1)
2   tsp sea salt (divided 1, 1)

1½ tsp garlic, powdered or 1 tsp minced fresh garlic
1   tsp thyme
1   tsp dried onion
1   cup Whole Grain Spelt flour
1½ cups White Spelt flour
1   egg white mixed w/1 Tbsp tepid water

1. **Ferment (Sponge).** Place ¼ cup of warm water in a large mixing bowl and stir in a Tbsp of brown sugar. Sprinkle ¼ tsp yeast over water. Stir to dissolve. Let stand 5 minutes until yeast becomes creamy and starts to bubble. To the yeast, add 1¼ cups warm water, 1 cup Whole Grain Spelt flour and 1½ cups White Spelt flour. Beat for several minutes by hand or 2 minutes (Stand Mixer, paddle, speed 2) until ropy thick batter forms. Cover bowl loosely with plastic wrap, lid or damp towel and set in

draft-free place (75°–85° F) until mixture doubles and bubbles actively (30–45 minutes).

2. **Dough/Mix/Initial Knead.** Place ¼ cup warm water in measuring cup or small bowl. Sprinkle 1 package yeast over top; stir to dissolve. Let stand 10 minutes until creamy and foamy. Add to the sponge. Stir in the olive oil, 1 Tbsp of the ground rosemary, 1 tsp of the ground celery seed, 1 tsp of the salt and all the garlic, thyme and dried onion. Add 1 cup Whole Grain Spelt and 1½ cups White Spelt, a half cup at a time.

   By Hand or *Stand Mixer* with paddle attached, mix 1½ minutes, longer by hand, scraping down sides of bowl, until dough begins to leave sides of bowl. Change to hook; knead 30–45 seconds. Dough will start to ball around hook *(Stand Mixer)* and pull away from sides of bowl. The dough should be somewhat sticky at this stage.

3. **Rest/Knead/First Dough Rise.** Turn out onto floured surface. Cover; let rest 10 minutes. Knead lightly for several minutes, using pastry scraper to keep dough from sticking and sprinkling additional flour over/under dough until it becomes moist and elastic. Form into soft ball. Rub dough lightly with olive oil and place in clean bowl. Cover and let rise in warm (80°–85° F), draft-free place until about double in volume (30–40 minutes). Check at 30 minutes by inserting moistened finger gently into the dough to ½"; if indentation remains when finger pulled out, dough is ripe.

4. **Degas/Divide/Rest.** Depress the dough with a light fist (don't punch), using a plastic spatula to detach dough from sides of the bowl. Turn out onto lightly floured surface. Dough should be springy and slightly sticky at this stage. If making two rounds, divide dough in half with pastry scraper or sharp knife. Cover and let rest 10 minutes. Preheat oven to 450° F.

5. **Form.** Form dough into ball(s) and place on lightly oiled baking sheet or in individual pie pans. For Focaccia rounds, flatten into circle(s) about 1 inch thick and add Toppings. For Roman rounds, gently brush with egg white/water then sprinkle surface with mixture of 1 Tbsp rosemary, 1 tsp ground celery seed and 1 tsp salt.

6. **Score.** Score each round about ½" deep to make 8–10 sections. Dust scores with Whole Grain Spelt flour. Cover dough with oiled plastic wrap or in large (tented) plastic bag and set in warm (80°–85° F), draft-free place until almost doubled in volume (25–35 minutes). If scored lines have filled in during rise, lightly rescore. Check oven heat.

7. **Bake.** Spritz interior of oven several times during five minutes preceding baking. *Reduce* temperature to 425° F. Place on middle rack. Bake for 25–30 minutes or until done and bread is a deep golden brown, almost mahogany in color. Thump the bread. If it sounds hollow and color is right, it is ready to come out of the oven. Remove to wire rack for cooling. Cut into wedges and serve.

Calabrese Bread

A dark toasty crust invites you into the deep taste of Whole Grain Spelt. The herbs and cheese hark back to ancient days of making bread. This is sumptuous aromatic bread that sustains life and nourishes the spirit.

Note: Stand Mixer recipe

Blood Type: A, B, AB, O • Prep time: 4 hrs fermentation + 80 min
Cook time: 40–50 min • Yield: 2 loaves (total 3 lb)

Ingredients

Sponge

½   tsp active dry yeast
¼   cup warm (110°–115° F) water
1½ cups tepid water
2½ cups Whole Grain Spelt flour
½   cup White Spelt flour

Dough

1   package active dry yeast
¼   cup warm (110°–115° F) water
1½ cups tepid water
2   tsp salt
2   cups Whole Grain Spelt flour
3 to 3½ cups White Spelt flour (this may vary depending on the White Spelt)
1   tsp freshly ground fennel seed
2   tsp savory, dried and crushed
1   tsp thyme, dried and crushed
1   cup loosely packed Pecorino Romano cheese, coarsely grated (2.5 oz)

1. **Ferment (Sponge) First Rise.** Pour ¼ cup warm water into small bowl; sprinkle ½ tsp yeast over top. Stir to dissolve. Let stand 5 minutes. Add yeast to a very large mixing bowl or large, tall plastic pitcher (the sponge will rise significantly) and add 1½ cups tepid water. Stir in 2½ cups Whole Grain Spelt flour to make a thick batter. Cover with plastic wrap or a lid and set in draft-free place (70°–75° F) for 2 hours. Uncover sponge and stir in ½ cup White Spelt flour. Cover the sponge and let sit in same place for additional

2 hours. At the end of this time, the sponge will have quadrupled its size and should be just starting to slow and sink. It should be a thick, active, bubbly blob. If making late in day, refrigerate overnight and set out for 15 minutes in morning and use immediately in dough.

2. **Dough Mix/Knead:** Spoon sponge into large mixing bowl (Stand Mixer bowl). Sprinkle yeast over ¼ cup warm water; stir to dissolve and let stand 5 minutes until foamy. Add the yeast, 1½ cups tepid water, 2 tsp salt, 2 cups Whole Grain flour and 1 cup White Spelt flour. Beat to form a thick batter (Paddle; Speed 2 for 1½ minutes). Add the herbs and the coarsely grated cheese and add 2 cups White Spelt flour by the half cup measure. Mix briefly. (*Stand Mixer:* paddle, 1 minute, then change to dough hook, work on lowest speed, about 1 minute). Knead only until dough starts cleaning sides of bowl. The dough should be wet and slightly rough. Turn out onto lightly floured (White Spelt) surface. Let dough rest, covered, for 10 minutes. Using pastry scraper and sprinklings of White Spelt flour, knead dough lightly until springy and smooth which should require only 5–6 turns of the dough. Form into a ball.

3. **Divide/Shape:** Divide dough and form 2 equal pieces. Let dough rest, covered, 10 minutes. Gently form into boules (balls)

or into loaves. (**For bread bowls or small boules, see below.**) Gently place shaped dough on lightly greased/floured parchment set on baking sheets or directly on oiled and floured baking sheet(s). If you wish to give the large boules support, use lightly oiled and floured 9" pie pans or paper forms. Baking stone: Set dough on oiled/floured peels and sprinkle stone with Whole Grain Spelt flour in advance. Most baking stones do not accommodate 2 of these loaves so retard the rise of one by placing in tented plastic bag in refrigerator. Set out to finish rising about midway through baking.

4. **Rise:** Cover bread loosely with plastic wrap sprayed with oil or, preferably, set inside large plastic (tented) bags and proof (70°–75° F) until just about doubled in volume (45–60 minutes). Do not rely on looking at the dough to gauge whether it is ripe. Test by pressing a finger ½" into the crown of the dough and removing it. If the impression remains, the bread is ripe for baking. If it springs back quickly, check again in 5–10 minutes.

Midway into the rising process, preheat oven to 450° F (baking stone: heat 30 minutes in advance at 475° F for baking stone; reduce to 425° F for baking). Five minutes before baking, mist interior of oven with tepid water several times OR place shallow pan on the topmost rack of oven and carefully add ½" boiling water to it, just enough so it will evaporate during the first 10 minutes of baking. Misting/boiling water provides the humidity, which gives this bread such a lovely crust. Do not spray oven door or light. Do not mist oven with baking stone, instead using pan of water as described above.

5. **Baking:** Slash top of boules with a cross about ¼" deep, keeping razor or other tool at an angle to the bread. For loaves, slash diagonally across top of loaves making quick decisive slashes at an angle ¼" deep, 2½"–3" long in several places along loaf. *Reduce* heat to 425° F.

Baking stone: Slide loaf onto baking stone. Pan breads: Place bread on lowest rack, and bake in preheated hot (425° F) oven for 10 minutes. Turn bread around 180° to assure even baking. Reduce heat to 375° F (400° F above 4500 feet) and bake for additional 30–40 minutes until bread is a deep golden chestnut brown and sounds hollow when thumped with a finger. Remove from oven and place on wire racks to cool for at least a half hour before slicing.

BREAD BOWLS OR BABY BOULES. This recipe makes wonderful bread bowls that people will talk about long after they have eaten the salad. The good thing is you can reprise that "fete" with others by freezing the bowls after baking and letting them heat up as you prepare what goes in them. (See *Knead to Know*, Chapter 3 for illustrations/directions for forming.)

Recipe makes 6–8 large bread bowls or free-form rounds that are perfect dinner-for-two loaves (baby boules). Each is about 8 oz. Texture is a bit like sourdough, irregular holes and a thin crisp and chewy crust, full of flavor, inviting.

Bake bowls/baby boules for 10 minutes at 425° F; reduce heat to 375° F and bake for additional 25 minutes. Be sure to spritz oven 3–4 times in advance as directed above. The rolls will rise a couple inches in the oven and be about 5" in diameter.

Campocosenza Rustic Wheel or Rounds

Campocosenza is free-form rustic bread with a chewy and flavorful crust and dense, moist somewhat chewy crumb that has irregular air pockets to give it a slightly tangy taste. This bread has personality. It will vary with the type of flour sift so that occasionally large flecks of bran will dot the beautiful crust or it will be more/less tangy. This is a very good and forgiving recipe for experimenting with Spelt like using the opposite ratio of flours (more Whole Grain/less White) or adding green olives, roasted peppers, garlic or cheeses. It is panini bread and is perfect for bruschetta or other grilled sandwiches. Let me know how it turns out for you (spelthealthy.com).

Blood Type: A, B, AB, O • Prep time: Varies • Cook time: 25–40 • Yield: 2 loaves (about 1½ lb each)

Ingredients

Campocosenza Biga (Starter)
Makes about 2 cups (about 22 oz/616 gr)
¼   tsp active dry yeast
¼   cup warm (110°–115° F) water
1   cup tepid water
2½ cups Whole Grain Spelt Flour

Dough
1   pkg active dry yeast
¼   cup warm (110°–115° F) water
1¼ cups tepid water
2   tsp salt
4 to 4½ cups White Spelt Flour (amount varies with the flour)
1   cup Whole Grain Spelt flour

1. **Ferment (Sponge) First Rise.** Add ¼ cup hot water to large mixing bowl. Sprinkle the yeast over water; stir to dissolve. Let stand 5 minutes. Add 1 cup tepid water to the bowl and stir in 2½ cups Whole Grain Spelt flour. *Stand Mixer:* paddle, speed 2, beat 2 minutes. The batter should be rubbery and ropy. *By Hand:* Beat until a thick, sticky batter forms.

Cover bowl tightly with plastic wrap. Set in cool draft-free place (70°–75° F). Allow sponge to rise until it more than doubles (2–3 hours; varies with altitude and temperature). It should be bubbly and viscous. You will see dried tracks of this activity on sides of bowl, like high water marks on a wall.

2. **Dough Mix/Knead.** In small bowl or glass measuring cup, sprinkle 1 package yeast over ¼ cup warm water. Stir to dissolve. Let stand 10 minutes until foamy and creamy. Measure out one cup of sponge (10–11 oz/ about 300 gr) and place in large mixing bowl. Discard the remaining sponge or save for later use (see below). Add the dissolved yeast, 1 cup (minus 2 Tbsp) tepid water. Briefly beat mixture to break up sponge and uniformly distribute it in the liquid. Then add 2 tsp salt, 2½ cups of the White Spelt flour and 1 cup Whole Grain Spelt flour.

Stand Mixer: Attach paddle and mix on speed 2 (1 minute). Add 2 cups White Spelt by half cup measures and mix about 1 minute just until ingredients are incorporated and soft dough begins to form. Scrape down bowl, change to dough hook, and knead on low speed for 2 minutes, adjust dough by adding White Spelt by the Tbsp if needed or reserved water by the tsp to form slightly tacky dough that begins to ball and clean sides of bowl.

By Hand: Beat until batter thickens, scraping down sides of bowl. Gradually add 2 cups White Spelt flour and ¾ cup of the Whole Grain Spelt flour. Adjust dough by adding reserved water by the tsp or adding flour by the Tbsp. Mix until dough starts cleaning sides of bowl, begins to ball and becomes too stiff to mix with spoon.

Turn out onto lightly floured board. Cover; let dough rest 10 minutes. Form into rough ball and knead with gentle strength, sprinkling flour over dough and using pastry scraper to keep dough from sticking. After 4–6 turns of the dough, the dough should be smooth and springy to the touch. Form into a ball.

3. **First Dough Rise.** Place in lightly oiled bowl; cover tightly with plastic wrap or lid. Let rise at room temperature (75°) until almost doubled (60–75 minutes). Test by inserting floured forefinger into dough; if impression remains, dough is ripe. Test often; do not over-proof.

4. **Divide/Rest.** Detach edges from bowl with plastic spatula. Turn dough out, top side down, onto lightly floured board without deflating it first. Dough should be slightly sticky at this point. With pastry scraper or sharp knife, divide into two portions or form into one soft ball. Let rest, covered, 10 minutes.

5. **Form/Second Rise**. Shape into one large sphere to form wheel or form each portion into a firm ball and set on pan(s) to rise. Lightly cover with plastic wrap sprayed with oil for 30–45 minutes. Check dough by using Fingertip Test at 30 minutes and 5 minute intervals thereafter. This is important because the bread does not swell and expand to double its volume. It will spring in the oven.

Boules (Balls): Lightly grease 2 9" pie pans or set dough in paper forms. Or turn a large rimmed baking pan upside down; cover with parchment paper and sprinkle with White Spelt flour or simply lightly grease and dust the bottom. This method gives the bread room to expand during baking to form a lovely wheel or completely free-form rounds or loaves.

6. **Preheat/Slash.** At the beginning of the second rise, heat oven to 425° F. During the last five minutes prior to baking, spritz the interior with water (avoiding oven light). Just prior to baking, slash *boules* (balls) in a cross fashion across crown (¼" deep). Slash the *loaves* at an angle, diagonally about ¼" deep, about 2½" in length in three places across top.

7. **Bake.** Place bread in preheated 425° F oven for 10 minutes. Reduce oven to 375° F (400° F at altitudes above 4500 feet) and bake an additional 30–35 minutes (two rounds; the wheel will take longer) or until loaves are deep golden brown and make a hollow sound when thumped.

Note on Saving Campocosenza Sponge: The recipe takes only half the ferment. Freeze the remainder for the next baking. Allow to defrost at room temperature several hours until bubbling activity resumes.

To Refresh (continue your sponge instead of throwing it away and starting over): Add 1 cup Whole Grain Spelt flour and ½ cup tepid water to the remaining ferment. Mix well. Allow to stand at cool room temperature for 2 hours and then freeze. (A shorter second fermenting time can produce a bread with more tang.) Let it defrost per above instructions. Through this cycle of refreshing the sponge; freezing it; refreshing it and allowing it to ferment again, you develop your own starter from that initial ¼ tsp of active dry yeast. It develops its own unique flavors for your own, signature bread. Freeze the leftover starter and begin the cycle anew unless the flavor begins to dissipate or activity decreases at which time you can choose to re-invigorate it with a slight amount of yeast or variations on the flour/water ratios.

All-Purpose Italian Biga/Dough

Develop the taste you want in your own Italian food recipes by using the biga (starter) recipe. This basic dough makes loaves, rounds, submarine sandwich rolls, pizza, focaccia, bruschetta, calzones and breadsticks. Use leftover bread for croutons and seasoned breadcrumbs. This is a soft dough, one that requires very little handling to get the best from it. (See cover photograph.)

Blood Type: A, B, AB, O • Prep time: Varies • Cook time: Varies • Yield: 3 lb wet dough

Baking Note: The biga (starter) requires 5–6 hours minimum to ferment in advance of making dough. Like many ferments, this one is best when made the evening ahead of baking, allowed to ferment at room temperature a couple of hours, add additional flour/water, then placed in refrigerator overnight and brought to room temperature prior to baking. This method makes baking easy because it is done in stages (the Indirect Method).

In Advance:

See *Many Small Things* for Toppings and Fillings
See *Pasta, Pizza, Flatbreads* section for Focaccia, Calzones, Pizza directions
Refer to *Knead to Know©* section on Forms and how to bake with Spelt flours

API Biga (Starter)

Makes about 2 cups (about 14 oz/375 gr)
Make in advance

½   tsp active dry yeast
¼   cup warm water (110°–115° F)
¾   cup tepid water
1½ cups White Spelt flour (divided 1, ½)
1   cup Whole Grain Spelt flour

Sprinkle ½ tsp yeast over ¼ cup warm water in small bowl. Let stand 5 minutes until creamy. Pour ¾ cup tepid water into large mixing bowl; add the yeast and gradually mix in the White and Whole Grain Spelt flours. Beat well. The biga will be thick and stiff but will soften and become viscous and lively as it sits. Cover biga securely with plastic wrap or lid; let stand 4 hours at room temperature (75° F). Stir in ½ cup White Spelt flour and ¼ cup tepid water. Let stand at room temperature an additional hour or more (until active and bubbling). Use in dough at the end of the 5–6 hour proof (fermentation) period or

refrigerate overnight for use the next day. Bring to room temperature and allow time for fermentation activity to resume (active bubbling).

API Dough

2   cups biga
1¾ tsp active dry yeast
¼   cup warm (110°–115° F) water
1¼ cups tepid water (divided 1, ¼)
2   tsp salt
1   cup Whole Grain Spelt flour
3¼ to 4 cups White Spelt flour (varies with the White Spelt flour)

1. **Mix/Knead.** In large mixing bowl, sprinkle 1¾ tsp yeast over ¼ cup water. Stir to dissolve. Let stand 5 minutes until creamy.

   Stand Mixer: Attach the paddle. Run on speed 2. Add the biga and 1 cup tepid water to the mixing bowl. Mix briefly to break up biga (about 30 seconds). Add the Whole Grain flour and 2 cups White Spelt flour and mix on next to lowest speed (speed 2) until rough dough begins to form (about 30 seconds). Add salt to the remaining ¼ cup water, stir to put salt into suspension, then add to bowl. Gradually add 1¼ to 1½ cups White Spelt flour to form soft and sticky dough (1½ minutes). Scrape down sides of bowl with plastic/rubber spatula. Change to dough hook and on lowest speed, add White Spelt by the Tbsp if necessary to adjust consistency and form a soft and sticky dough that begins to ball and clean sides of bowl (about 1 minute). Do not overmix. This should be soft, moist, tacky dough when it comes out of the mixing bowl. Turn out onto surface sprinkled with White Spelt flour. Cover dough and let rest 10 minutes.

By hand: Vigorously mix the yeast and biga with 1 cup tepid water. Add the Whole Grain flour and 2 cups White Spelt flour to form rough dough. Add salt to the remaining ¼ cup water, stir to put salt into suspension, then add to the bowl. Gradually add 1¼ to 1½ cups White Flour and beat until soft dough forms. Adjust consistency by adding White Spelt by the Tbsp if necessary. Scraping down sides of bowl, mix until dough begins to ball and chase spoon around bowl and is too heavy to mix. Dough should be sticky, soft and very moist. Turn out onto surface sprinkled with White Spelt flour. Cover dough and let it rest 10 minutes.

2. **Knead/First Dough Rise.** Form into a loose ball then briefly knead by hand until elastic but still slightly tacky. Place in lightly oiled bowl. Cover and let rise in a draft-free place at cool room temperature (70°–75° F) for 40–50 minutes. Check dough tension by lightly pressing finger into crown of dough; if impression remains when finger is removed, dough is ready. The dough will have some large bubbles beneath the skin.

3. **Degas/Divide.** Using plastic spatula, detach dough from edges of bowl and lay on top of dough. With loose fist, gently deflate dough by working hand over surface several times. Do not punch down dough or press hard. Remember, the purpose of the ferment (biga) is to develop dough. It should be handled as little as possible so the gases are not expelled. Dough should be

very springy at this stage. Form into a loose ball and divide according to recipe for pizza dough, rolls, etc. Let dough rest, covered, 10 minutes before forming and second, last rise as with rolls, or bake as with pizza dough. See roll forms below.

Submarine Rolls: (Makes 8–10)
Form into balls. Form into pointed rolls by gently patting and pressing dough into torpedo shape (see *Knead to Know©* section on forms). Place on parchment covered large rimmed baking pan sprinkled with White Spelt flour or on lightly greased and floured rimmed pan. Leave 2–3 inches between. Sprinkle lightly with White Spelt flour and cover loosely with plastic wrap or place in large (tented) plastic bag to rise until almost doubled in size (15–20 minutes). During last five minutes of rise, make 2" long, ¼" deep slash (at an angle to the dough) along the tops of the rolls. Spritz oven several times. When oven has reached temperature and rolls are ready (do Fingertip Test) bake on center rack of preheated hot (425° F) oven for 15–20 minutes or until deep golden brown. Take one out and thump it; it should sound hollow.

Focaccia: (Makes 2 [13" x 9"])
See **Country Oven Focaccia** directions for forming and topping. Note this bread requires much "dimpling" because it forms bubbles.

Pizza:
See Country Oven Pizza Dough makes 8 individual size (10 inch) pizzas or 3 medium size. Form into balls, then pat/press into place for free-form individual pizzas, for deep dish pizza forms or for large pan pizza.

Calzones: (Makes 12–18)
See **Country Oven Calzones**

Makes baguettes, bâtards, ciabatta, boules (see next page for **Roasted Garlic and Mozzarella Baguettes**).

Roasted Garlic and Mozzarella Baguettes

Instead of the usual garlic bread, you might try a different kind based on the All-Purpose Italian Biga/Dough recipe. These six baguettes have a crunchy chewy crust flecked with baked cheese and a hint not a blast of garlic. The roasted garlic and the cheese "melt" into the crumb and add moistness to it. Their complementary flavors intertwine with the fermented Spelt. The crumb has large irregular holes and an occasional shine. The bread is delicately full of flavors that accent pasta, grilled steak or fish, or a fine salad.

Preparation Tip: Please read recipe thoroughly. This is a biga (fermented) bread that takes 2 days to prepare. Actual time spent in handling the dough is less than 30 minutes. The Spelt and other ingredients do the actual work. Organization and gentle handling are the keys to this wonderful bread.

Blood Type: A, B, AB, O • Prep time: Varies • Cook time: 25/25 • Yield: 6 small baguettes (8 oz each)

Ingredients

1   recipe All-Purpose Italian Biga (see preceding recipe)

Dough

2   cups biga (14 oz/375 gr)
1¾ tsp active dry yeast
¼   cup warm (110°–115° F) water
1½ cups tepid water (divided 1¼ and ¼)
2   tsp salt
1   cup Whole Grain Spelt flour
3¼ cups White Spelt flour + additional for kneading
1   recipe (¼ cup or 2 oz) Roasted Garlic, cooled (see recipe under *Many Small Things*)
1   cup (4 oz) low moisture Part Skim Mozzarella cheese, coarsely grated

1. **In Advance.** Make the biga according to recipe and leave in refrigerator overnight until baking the next day. Make the roasted garlic and allow it to cool or make in advance and leave in refrigerator overnight along with biga.

2. **Mix/Knead Dough**: Sprinkle 1¾ tsp yeast over ¼ cup warm water in small bowl. Stir to dissolve. Let stand 5 minutes until creamy. Meanwhile, add the cold biga and

1¼ cups tepid water to large mixing bowl. Beat by hand to break up biga or with Stand Mixer (paddle, speed 2, about 2 minutes). Add the yeast and 2 tsp salt dissolved in the remaining ¼ cup water. Add the Whole Grain Spelt flour and 2 cups White Spelt flour.

Stand Mixer: With paddle, speed 2, beat until rough dough begins to form (1 minute). Scrape down sides of bowl. Change to dough hook. On lowest speed, add 1 cup of the remaining White Spelt flour in ¼ cup increments. Continue to knead, adding the remaining ¼ cup White Spelt flour (1 minute). Add the garlic and the cheese and knead an additional minute. The dough will be a wet, sticky mass. Scrape onto floured surface.

By Hand: Mix ingredients, scraping down sides of bowl. Beat until rough wet dough begins to form. Add the cheese and garlic. Add the remaining White Spelt flour and stir until the dough becomes too heavy to mix. Scrape sides of bowl and turn out wet, sticky mass onto floured surface.

3. **Rest/Knead/First Dough Rise.** Cover dough and let it rest 10 minutes. Knead to form smooth and somewhat dry dough (4–5

minutes). Use pastry scraper to keep dough from sticking and sprinkle additional flour over and under dough as you knead. The dough should be soft not firm so resist incorporating excess flour into the dough. Form into soft ball and place in an oiled bowl. Cover tightly with plastic wrap or lid. Let rise at moderate room temperature (75° F) for 55–75 minutes until not quite doubled in volume. Check at 55 minutes by inserting a moistened or floured finger into the crown of the dough in two places. If dough springs back quickly and indentations remain, let dough proof longer. Check every 10–15 minutes. When ripe, the dough will feel light yet springy and have bubbles on and under the surface.

4. As the dough is entering its last 20 minutes of rising, prepare two large rimmed baking pans (jelly roll pans, 15^1/$_2$" x 11^1/$_2$" x 1" or larger). Cover the backs of the pans with parchment and sprinkle liberally with White Spelt flour. If not using parchment, oil the pans and sprinkle liberally with flour. Preheat oven to 500° F. If using baking stone, place in oven to heat a half hour before end of the rising period.

5. Very gently turn the dough out onto a surface floured with White Spelt. Sprinkle the surface of the dough with a little White Spelt. With a pastry scraper or sharp knife, smartly divide the dough into two equal portions taking care not to expel gas from the dough by rough handling or tearing the dough. Divide one portion of the dough into 3 pieces (or 2 for larger baguettes) again taking care not to deflate the dough. Dip the knife or scraper into cool water for ease of cutting. Repeat with the second half of the dough.

6. Carefully lift one segment of the rather floppy dough and place on prepared baking sheet. Very gently pull the dough so it is the length of the pan. Place three segments on the back of one rimmed pan allowing equal space between them for expansion in oven. Repeat on second pan with the next three segments of dough. Dust with flour or lightly spray the loaves on one pan with oil and place in a large plastic bag (slightly tented to keep dough from sticking) and set the pan in the refrigerator to retard rising while the other loaves are baking.

7. Open the oven and spritz the walls and back of oven with a spray bottle containing room temperature water. Be certain not to spray light or oven door. Spritz twice more. Slide the parchment with bread on it onto baking stone or, if using pan method, set pan on lowest rack. Reduce oven heat to 475° F. Bake for 10 minutes. Open oven door and turn pan 180° so baguette that was in front is now in the back to assure even baking. Bake an additional 15–20 minutes until crust is lovely golden brown (sienna). Meanwhile remove the second pan from the refrigerator and uncover.

8. Remove baked baguettes from oven and place on wire racks to cool. Turn oven to 500° and spritz oven once. Close door. Spritz twice more. Let oven heat. When it comes to temperature, place bread in oven. Reduce heat to 475° F. Bake for 10 minutes; rotate pan. Bake for 15–20 minutes as above. Remove from oven and place on wire racks to cool with the others.

Medi Crostini Bread

One of my favorites, Medi Crostini is a very crusty, flavorful and chewy rustic bread for all the uses for which *Crostini* is staple fare. In our household there are many—from dipping to topping to eating as garlic toast and for grilling. Once you get the hang of it, it is easy to make. The ferment does the work, along with the timer—not you. The actual time you work directly with this bread is about 20 minutes. The aroma while baking is complex with a sweet and slightly sour chord, redolent of sea air, yeast and grain acting in harmony. (See cover photograph.)

Blood Type: A, B, AB, O • Prep time: Varies • Cook time: 35 minutes
Yield: 2 dense loaves (about 2¾ lb dry weight)

Medi Crostini Biga (Ferment) Makes 2 cups (about 19–29 oz/500 grams)
½ tsp active dry yeast
¼ cup warm (110°–115° F) water
¾ cup tepid water
1 cup Whole Grain Spelt flour
1½ cups White Spelt flour

Dough
1¼ tsp active dry yeast
¼ cup warm (110°–115° F) water
1½ cups tepid water
1½ cups (375 grams) Biga (weigh instead of measure for accuracy)
4 to 4½ cups White Spelt flour (+ additional for kneading; will vary with the flour)
½ cup Whole Grain Spelt flour
1 Tbsp salt

Make Biga In Advance: Spelt Biga must be made ahead of time. The long fermentation time is what gives the slight tang and flavor to Medi Crostini and keeps it fresh much longer.

1. **Biga:** Into a medium mixing bowl, pour ¼ cup warm water and sprinkle yeast over top. Let stand until creamy and foamy (10 minutes). Stir in the tepid water and add the flour, ½ cup at a time.

Stand Mixer: Beat with paddle, 2 minutes, lowest speed until soft sticky dough forms.

By Hand: Beat vigorously for several minutes.

Place in large lightly oiled bowl or tall lightly oiled plastic pitcher and cover with plastic wrap or a lid. Let rise at cool to moderate room temperature (70°–75° F) for 6–8 hours during which time the Spelt biga will rise and fall. The dried tracks on the edges of bowl will show that it has climbed considerably. Refrigerate overnight and add directly to this recipe the next morning. It will be a gluey stringy mass best weighed on kitchen scale instead of measured in a cup. You can also freeze the biga after its fermentation period. Let it stand at room temperature for several hours and wait for it to become active prior to incorporating in recipe. It will be bubbly and look like a "sponge". Weigh the biga (13.5 oz/375 gr) instead of simply measuring it (1½ cups) because of its rubbery consistency.

2. **Mix/Knead.** Pour ¼ cup warm water into a small bowl or glass measuring cup. Sprinkle 1¼ tsp yeast over the water; stir to dissolve. Let stand for 10 minutes until creamy and foamy. In large mixing bowl, combine 1½ cups Spelt biga (about 13.5 oz/ 375 gr), the yeast and 1½ cups tepid water.

Stand Mixer: Attach paddle, and mix on speed 2, until the biga mixture becomes smooth (about

1 minute). Stir in 1 Tbsp salt. Add the Whole Grain Spelt flour and 2 cups of the White Spelt and mix (1 minute) then gradually beat in remaining White Spelt flour. Change to dough hook and working on lowest speed, knead (1 minute) to form smooth, sticky, rubbery dough that starts to ball around the hook and clean sides of bowl. Turn out onto surface generously floured with White Spelt flour.

By Hand: Beat to form smooth mixture. Mix 1 Tbsp salt and the Whole Grain Spelt flour. Add 2 cups White Spelt flour and beat vigorously to incorporate then slowly beat in White Spelt flour by the ½ cup measure to form a smooth dough. It will be heavy and may require using your hands to mix completely and form the desirable sticky, smooth and rubbery dough. Scrape down the bowl completely and turn mass out on surface generously covered with White Spelt flour.

3. **Rest/Knead.** Allow the dough to rest, covered, for 10 minutes. Knead gently, using pastry scraper to keep dough from sticking and sprinkling flour under/over dough to form a smooth, moist, springy dough that has bubbles beneath the surface. While dough is resting, prepare a large rimmed baking pan by covering it with parchment and sprinkling it with White Spelt flour or lightly oiling and flouring pan. If using baking stone, set parchment on peel and dust with flour for rising and ease of transferring to stone.

4. **First Rise.** Place the dough into a lightly oiled bowl then cover with plastic wrap or lid. Let rise in a draft-free cool place (70° F) until about doubled in volume. The time will vary according to temperature, barometer, etc. so check at 50 minutes and 15 minute intervals thereafter by pressing a moistened finger into the crown of the dough in a couple of places (Fingertip Test). I have let this bread rise at 70 degrees for 2 hours, twice as long, and it comes up

beautifully. The point is, the longer it takes to rise, the better the flavor—but do not let it go overlong or the bread will be gummy inside and won't expand as it should. When ready, there will be bubbles under the surface and the Finger Test should produce indentations that do not fill in when you remove finger.

5. **Degas/Divide/Rise.** Using a spatula, gently loosen the dough from sides of the bowl and gently turn out onto lightly floured surface. With pastry scraper or sharp knife, divide dough into two equal portions. Shape each portion into a ball, then pat/press and form into an oval and then a fat torpedo. You will occasionally hear the bubbles pop. That's okay as long as you are not forcing too much air from the dough. If it resists forming, let the dough rest, covered, for 5 to 10 minutes. If it is overworked, it will not bloom.

After the loaves are formed, use a razor blade or other slashing tool, and slash about ¼" deep along the fattest part of the torpedo-shaped loaves taking care not to expel too much air from the loaves. Set slashed side down on prepared baking sheet (Step 4 above).

Cover with plastic wrap or, better, set in large (tented) plastic bags with ends tucked under pan. Let rise in same draft-free cool place for 25–35 minutes until just about doubled in volume. Do Fingertip Test at 25 minutes to check. There will be bubbles under the skin. Once the bread is set to rise, preheat oven to 425° F. (If using a baking stone, preheat oven with stone in it thirty minutes at 475° F before baking. Note: Many baking stones are too small to fully accommodate 2 large rounds. Retard the rise of one by placing in refrigerator in large (tented) plastic bag and bringing out to finish rising about midway through baking.)

Spritz the oven several times in the last five minutes before baking or place pan with ½" boiling water (sufficient so it will evaporate during first 10 minutes of baking) on the topmost shelf. Place oven rack in center for pan bread. Sprinkle baking stone with Whole Grain Spelt flour if not using parchment.

6. **Reslash/Bake.** Reduce heat to 400° F (leave at 425° for altitudes over 4500 feet). Carefully turn the dough over. If slash has closed during the rising period, firmly but gently slash again taking care not to slash too deeply and expel the gasses that cause the loaves to bloom. Baking Stone: Gently and deftly as you can, slide loaves onto stone. Bake loaves in preheated hot (400° F) oven for about 35 minutes. Crust will be palomino in color. Thump loaf with a finger to test for doneness; if it sounds hollow. If not, place back in oven and bake an additional 7–10 minutes. Remove from oven; allow to cool on wire racks. Slice with sharp knife. Wrap sliced bread in foil and keep at room temperature. To freeze whole or partial loaf, wrap in foil and then securely wrap in plastic wrap.

Preserving your Medi Crostini Sponge:
About ¾ of sponge is used in the recipe itself. You can throw it away or refresh your sponge (now about 6 ounces) and let it develop flavor for another day. Over time it will develop wonderfully unique flavors and a tanginess akin to sourdough.

To refresh your Medi Crostini Sponge:
Sprinkle ¼ tsp active dry yeast over ¼ cup warm water. Stir to dissolve and allow to stand 10 minutes until creamy and room temperature. Add yeast and ¾ cup tepid water to the existing sponge. Stir in ¾ cup Whole Grain and 1¼ cup White Spelt flours. Beat vigorously with spoon until the new ingredients are blended.

Let stand, covered with lid or plastic wrap, at room temperature for 4–6 hours. Place in airtight container and freeze. To use, let stand at room temperature for several hours until bubbly and active again.

Pan Andrea
Festival And Wedding Bread

Recipes are heirlooms. Pan Andrea is a recipe I created as a wedding gift for two people I cherish. It is a recipe designed for them that they in turn may pass on, amended, to their children.

Pan Andrea makes a stunning large shiny wheel of bread much like traditional Greek Wedding breads. The large, round wheel is a shape of antiquity; it is a sign of those times when the dough was placed in large terracotta bowls to both rise along the way and bake upon arrival much like the Roman Bread or Campocosenza breads in this book. Pan Andrea has a crisp, chewy sugary crust and a delectable subtly sweet, spiced flavor that lingers on the palate. The crumb is moist and filled with irregular air pockets that trap the flavor. With the soft bits of sweet fruit and nuts, there is a range of intriguing tastes and textures in this single bread. By scoring the bread in advance of baking and sprinkling with sugar, as the bread bakes a shiny star pattern emerges. The star can be made to sparkle even more by sprinkling additional sugar on the bread when it comes out of the oven.

Blood Type: A, B, AB, O (O omit the nutmeg) • Prep time: Biga 6 hrs; 2 hrs prep/rise
Cook time: 40–50 • Yield: 1 wheel (about 3½ lb)

Baking Note: The entire Pan Andrea recipe, Biga and dough, requires only 1 package active dry yeast in case you do not have bulk yeast on hand. It is the fermentation process that makes this bread expand so beautifully.

Ingredients

Pan Andrea Biga: Makes 2¼ cups (20 oz/ 560 gr)

½ tsp active dry yeast
¼ cup warm (110°–115° F) water
1 cup tepid water
½ cup Whole Grain Spelt flour
2 cups White Spelt flour (divided 1½, ½)
2 Tbsp tepid water

Dough

1½ cups biga (12 oz/340 gr) (best weighed not measured)
1¾ tsp active dry yeast
¼ cup warm (110°–115° F) water

1½ cups tepid water
4   cups White Spelt flour (plus additional for kneading; will vary according to flour)
1   cup Whole Grain Spelt flour
2   tsp salt
1   tsp freshly grated lemon zest
1   cup dried pineapple bits, minced
2   Tbsp White Spelt flour
1   cup almonds, finely chopped
½   tsp cardamom, ground
¼   tsp coriander, ground
¼   nutmeg, freshly ground
1   egg white
Turbinado sugar for sprinkling

In Advance, Prepare the Biga

1. **Pan Andrea Biga:** Sprinkle ½ tsp active dry yeast over ¼ cup warm water in large mixing bowl; stir to dissolve. Let stand 5 minutes. Add 1 cup tepid water and stir in ½ cup Whole Grain flour and 1½ cups White Spelt flour. Beat mixture to form thick batter (Stand Mixer with paddle about a minute and a half). Cover bowl with plastic wrap or lid. Let stand at room temperature 4 hours. The sponge should be bubbling actively. Add remaining ½ cup White Spelt flour and 2 Tbsp tepid water. Lightly beat. Cover and let stand at room temperature two more hours or until bubbly. Freeze Biga if intending to use at a later time and let stand several hours before using in recipe to give it time to activate (become bubbly).

Dough Preparation

2. **Prepare other ingredients.** In medium bowl, cover the dried pineapple bits with 2 inches hot water to cover. Let stand 15 minutes. Drain. Place in small bowl; mix with 2 Tbsp White Spelt flour and stir so fruit is completely dusted with flour. Set aside. Mix egg white with 1 Tbsp water. Set aside.

3. **Mix/Knead.** Pour ¼ cup warm (110°–115° F) water into a small bowl. Sprinkle 1¾ tsp yeast over top; stir to dissolve. Let stand 5 minutes until creamy. Place 1½ cups (12 oz/340 gr) Biga in large mixing bowl. (Please note: It is best to measure the Biga by weighing on a kitchen scale instead of measuring in a cup. It is very rubbery and squirms to get out of the measuring cup making an accurate measure difficult.)

Into the bowl with Biga, add the yeast and 1½ cups tepid water, salt, spices, lemon zest and Whole Grain Spelt flour. By Hand or Stand Mixer (paddle, low speed, 1 minute), mix briefly to break up Biga and smooth mixture. Add the White Spelt flour (paddle, lowest speed, about 1 minute) to form soft dough. Change to dough hook and knead 1 minute (lowest speed). Add pineapple and almonds; knead briefly, only until incorporated. Dough will be cleaning sides of bowl and form a soft, sticky ball at this point. Turn out onto lightly floured surface. Let dough rest, covered, 10 minutes. Knead briefly, sprinkling dough with flour and using pastry scraper to keep dough from sticking. Dough should be soft but elastic and a little sticky.

4. **First Dough Rise.** Form dough into a soft ball and place in large lightly oiled bowl. Cover with plastic or a lid and let rise at room temperature (75° F) for 30–40 minutes. Test for ripeness by inserting moistened finger about ½" into crown of dough; if impression remains after removing finger, dough is ripe. There will be bubbles under skin of dough.

5. **Knead/Form.** Using plastic spatula to detach edges of dough from bowl, turn edges onto top of dough. Turn out onto lightly floured surface and knead lightly. Bubbles will pop. Keep going, gently. Form wheel and set on parchment-covered or lightly greased pan dusted with White Spelt flour.

6. **Second Dough Rise/Preheat Oven.** Cover with very large bowl or plastic wrap and place in draft-free place (70°–75°) for 35–45 minutes. The dough will expand by about half its volume so check for maximum rise by using Fingertip Test. Gauging by size alone will not determine ripeness of dough. Much expansion will occur during baking. After setting the bread to rise, preheat oven to 450° F.

7. **Brush with Egg/Water/Score.** Gently brush the entire exposed surface of the wheel with egg white/water mixture. Score the wheel about ¼" deep with sharp knife to create 14–16 triangles or more for

serving (bread can be resliced after baking to make far more wedges). Sprinkle with turbinado sugar. Spritz interior of oven with tepid water several times during the last five minutes before baking or set a pan with ½" boiling water on topmost shelf (should only be enough water that it all evaporates during first 10 minutes of baking).

8. **Reduce** oven temperature to 425° F. **Bake.** Place bread on bottom rack of preheated hot (425° F) oven and bake for 10 minutes. Reduce heat to 375° F and bake 40–50 minutes longer or until done (longer for higher altitudes). Bread will expand significantly in oven and develop a deep golden variegated sheen while baking. Thump wheel on sides and bottom; if it sounds hollow, remove from oven and place on wire rack to cool completely (2 or more hours) before slicing with sharp knife.

Bread Machine Recipes

Speltessence Bread

Rosemary Cheese Bread

Seattle Supreme Sandwich Loaf

Bread Machine Recipe
Speltessence Bread

This is a basic, get-acquainted with Spelt recipe with its counterpart under *Direct Method Breads.* This is the little black dress or the smile, the go anywhere, do anything bread from sandwich loaf to croutons and crumbs.

Blood Type: A, B, AB, O • Prep time: 5 min • Cook time: varies with machine • Yield: 1½ lb loaf

Ingredients

1	cup tepid water
2	Tbsp Olive oil or other vegetable oil
1	tsp salt
1	Tbsp dark brown sugar
2	cups Whole Grain Spelt flour
1½	cups + 2 Tbsp White Spelt flour
1½	tsp active dry yeast

Add ingredients according to your bread machine instructions. All are different with respect to cycles. Speltessence will vary in the bread machine according to type of flour yet this recipe should produce a tender, moist, fine slicing loaf with reddish brown crust. Suggested settings (guideline only) because machines differ: Whole Wheat, Medium Crust, Loaf Size 1½ lb.

Bread Machine Recipe
Rosemary Cheese Bread

Rosemary Cheese Bread is a relatively moist loaf with irregular holes in the crumb that trap the many flavors of this Mediterranean type bread. It is a good basic recipe for making seasoned croutons or crumbs. Try quartering a slice into toast triangles. Top with finely grated Pecorino Romano or Asiago, broil briefly and serve with salads, fish or as an accompaniment to soup.

Blood Type: B, AB • Prep time: 5 min • Cook time: Varies with machine • Yield: 1 loaf (1 lb 6 oz cooled weight)

Ingredients

½   cup + 2 tsp warm (110°–115° F) water
1   Tbsp vegetable oil especially Olive or canola
1   egg, room temperature
2   Tbsp granulated sugar
1   tsp salt
2   tsp crushed rosemary
1   tsp celery seed
½   tsp garlic powder
2   cups White Spelt flour
1   cup Whole Grain Spelt flour
¼   cup nonfat dry milk
1   cup semi-soft Mozzarella cheese, grated
1½ tsp active dry yeast

1. Add the above ingredients in the order given according to your Bread Machine instructions. Generally they follow the above listing starting with liquid ingredients first and yeast last.

2. Remember to make a little well in the top-most ingredients so you are sprinkling most of the yeast onto the dry milk granules and not just the Mozzarella.

3. Suggested settings are Whole Wheat, Medium Crust, 1½ lb loaf. The settings vary according to machine. These are initial guidelines only.

Bread Machine Recipe
Seattle Supreme Sandwich Loaf

Moist, light, tender and delicious, Seattle Supreme bread has excellent cutting and keeping qualities.

Blood Type: A, B, AB • Prep time: 5 min • Cook time: varies with machine • Yield: 1½ lb loaf

Ingredients

- ⅓ cup plain goat's milk yogurt (no substitutes)
- ¾ cup tepid water (90° F or slightly less)
- ⅓ cup fluid Light to Light Medium Honey such as Clover honey
- 2 Tbsp Light Olive or other vegetable oil such as canola
- 1 tsp salt
- 2¾ cups White Spelt flour (Vita-Spelt recommended for this recipe)
- ¾ cup Whole Grain Spelt flour
- 1¼ tsp active dry yeast

Add ingredients according to your bread machine instructions. All are different with respect to cycles. I do not normally use the Whole Wheat Rapid cycle but it works for this particular bread. These are the settings where I get the best results for the Seattle Supreme Loaf: Whole Wheat Rapid, Medium Crust, Loaf size 1½ lb. This is a guideline only. All machines are different.

WHAT TO DO WITH BITS OF BREAD ... CROUTONS AND CRUMBS

Croutons and Crumbs

Dressing/Stuffing

Dressing Sticks

Croutons and Crumbs

Croutons are often an afterthought, something taken from a bag and dropped on salads to provide some heft and crunch but generally add very little flavor or nutrition. You are in for a pleasant surprise with Spelt croutons. They are anything but hard or ho-hum. They make **Caesar** sing.

Variety of Taste and Texture

Flip through the pages and see the variety of breads in *Spelt Healthy!* Calabrese Bread makes sensational croutons because of the herbs and cheese. Brundisi Pesto Bread and Roman Bread are full of flavors accentuated with toasting. The various Italian and French breads make ideal croutons and breadcrumbs. When you toast them for your next Caesar Salad, be prepared for people to ask for more. Speltessence Bread (Direct Method or Bread Machine recipe) provide some basic easy crumbs.

Not Just for Salads Anymore

✳ Add Spelt croutons to soups like the Minestrone di Farro or to your own favorite recipes.

✳ Spelt makes dressing or stuffing delicious and nutritious. Try stuffing a game hen with Spelt Wheat Berry Bread for a delightful change. Dressings are not just for Turkey Day anymore. (See Dressing/Stuffing and Dressing Sticks to follow).

✳ Sweeten the croutons and use them as a base for puddings, as the bread in bread pudding, or turn them into crunchy toppings for desserts or making a Peach Betty. Or use sweet dough recipes like Brioche or Pao Doce as a sweet soft or crisp crouton base for unusual desserts. Cut the leftover sweet bread into strips, sprinkle with cinnamon and sugar, for breakfast. (See more on Sweet Croutons below.)

✳ Slice the bread into 1" cubes and turn it into a toasted delight for dipping or serving with crudités. You may be surprised how fast they disappear at a party while the celery wilts.

Tips for Leftover Bread ("Day Old")

Slice it, cube it … small (¼"), medium (½"), large (¾–1"). Use the cubes or freeze them so you always have a choice of croutons on hand for any occasion.

STOVETOP METHOD for Basic Spelt Croutons (About 10 minutes)

Slice and cube leftover bread. Place a skillet or sauté pan over medium high heat. Add olive oil, about ¼ cup for 2 cups croutons, and toast the croutons, tossing and turning, until they are crisp and golden brown. The garlic and/or herbed Spelt Croutons below are also easy to make on stovetop even with the addition of cheese.

OVEN METHOD Garlic and/or Herbed Italian Spelt Croutons

(About 10 minutes)

Preheat oven to 350° F.

Slice and cube leftover bread. Combine ¼–⅓ cup Olive oil, 2–3 large cloves garlic (mashed) or 1 tsp garlic powder, 2–3 tsp dried herbs (such as thyme, basil, parsley, tarragon or other mixture to suit the recipe you are making) in a bowl and stir. Add the croutons and toss. Spread on rimmed baking pan and bake for 10–12 minutes tossing once during baking. *Cheese:* Grate 2 Tbsp to ¼ cup hard, grating cheese such as Romano, Parmesan, Kasseri Greek, Pecorino Romano or Asiago and add to the bowl with oil, garlic and herbs. Spread on rimmed baking pan and bake for 10–12 minutes tossing once or twice during process.

Sweet Croutons

Sweet croutons for Betties, puddings, or with yogurt and fresh fruit are a good addition to the larder. Make them from Classic White or Speltessence, A Beginning Loaf, Cardamom Gold Pumpkin Bread, Pao Doce or from Spelt Sweet Dough (Brioche). Combine Light Olive oil or canola oil with granulated or brown sugar. Or add spices such as cinnamon, nutmeg, allspice or a mixture such as pumpkin pie spice. Brush oil/sugar/spice mixture on both sides of the bread. Spread out evenly on rimmed baking pan and bake on middle rack of moderate (350°) oven for 10–12 minutes. Cut into cubes when cool. Use that day or freeze.

Breadcrumbs

There are so many recipes containing breadcrumbs, it is important to have them on hand. One of the things you will find about Spelt is that it stays moist much longer than bread you commonly buy in the store. This is one of the reasons it makes terrific crumbs that take to toasting.

Use a processor fitted with metal blade to turn Spelt bread into semi-fine crumbs. As the crumbs age and dry, you can process them again to make the crumb smaller. With the lean breads such as French and the various Italian breads such as Medi Crostini, let the bread dry and then use a box grater to get fine crumbs. Freeze the crumbs to have on hand whenever you need them. Toast the crumbs quickly in the skillet or oven for making the dried crumbs called for in recipes. Add herbs when you toast them to create flavors that accent the particular food you are making. Almost any recipe in the book will do for breadcrumbs for everything from piquant Falafel to Coated Pan Fried Fish Fillets to inclusion in Meatballs, either Classic or delicate Shrimp.

Dressing/Stuffing

This is a moist, delicious basic stuffing for turkey, chicken, game hen, fish or as a side dish. It is easy to make and contains vegetables for nutrition and added flavor and liquid. It is versatile—experiment by adding fruit such as apples or berries. This recipe will provide stuffing for a 9–12 pound turkey. The recipe halved will stuff four game hens or fish. The texture and liquid absorption capacity of the stuffing will vary according to the type(s) of Spelt bread used. I encourage you to combine types. It makes for exceptional dressing/stuffing.

Blood Type: A, B, AB, O (A, AB use oil instead of butter)
Prep time: 20 min • Cook time: varies. If baked alone 35–40 min. • Yield: about 8 cups

Ingredients

½ cup butter or ¼ cup + 2 Tbsp vegetable oil
1½ cups celery, diced (4 oz, several stalks)
1 cup sweet onions, chopped
2 cups fresh baby spinach, chopped (optional)
6 cups dried Spelt bread cubes
1 egg, room temperature, beaten
2 tsp ground rosemary
2–3 tsp dried, chopped sage or ½ to 1 tsp ground
1 tsp dried, chopped thyme
½ tsp marjoram
1 tsp ground black pepper
1 Tbsp celery salt or
  2 tsp celery seed, ground and 1 tsp salt
or Use Poultry Seasoning in place of the above
2 to 3 cups hot water, turkey stock or low sodium vegetable bouillon

1. In a large skillet, melt the butter and/or heat oil over medium low heat. Add the celery and the onions; sauté until tender but not soft. Stir the herbs into the sauteed vegetables. Add the chopped spinach (optional) and stir, cooking about a minute until the spinach slightly wilts.

2. Place bread cubes in a large bowl.

3. Pour the ingredients from the skillet onto the bread cubes. Stir.

4. Slowly add two cups water or stock over bread cubes and mix until bread absorbs the moisture, the cubes start to break down, and the dressing starts to hold together. Stir in the beaten egg; adding liquid if necessary to bind the stuffing. If using oil, drizzle a little more over dressing and stir until incorporated. The mixture should be moist and aromatic and will become even more moist and flavorful as it cooks and the Spelt absorbs the liquids and herbs.

Stuff the turkey or other fowl/fish according to your recipe. As an alternative, stuff the bird(s) with a sweet onion or apple(s) and place the dressing in a 13" x 9" pan, lightly greased. Place on center rack of moderately warm (350° F) oven for 35–40 minutes or until the top is lightly brown and crisp.

Dressing Sticks

Dressing Sticks are easy to make and quick to cook. They are terrific for portion control and a tidy way of serving dressing with a variety of foods other than turkey.

Blood Type: A, B, AB, O (B, AB use turkey or vegetable broth) • Prep time: 15 minutes • Cook time: 20 minutes
Yield: 7–8 two-ounce sticks depending on vegetables and type of Spelt bread used

Ingredients

4   cups stale, coarse Whole Grain or Whole/White Spelt crumbs
2   Tbsp Italian Parsley (flat-leaf parsley) or fresh baby spinach, finely chopped
4   Tbsp white or brown onion, finely chopped
⅓   cup celery, finely diced (optional)
1   tsp ground celery seed
½   tsp salt (use 1 tsp celery salt in place of seed and salt)
    or substitute Dulse granules
¼   tsp pepper, freshly ground (optional)
½   tsp dried, crushed thyme
½   tsp dried, crushed marjoram
½   tsp ground sage
1   tsp rosemary, dried and crushed or 1 Tbsp fresh
1   egg, slightly beaten
½   cup hot chicken/turkey broth or vegetable broth or plain hot water
3   Tbsp Olive or other vegetable oil

1. Preheat oven to 350° F. In large bowl, toss the breadcrumbs, parsley, onion, celery, salt, pepper and herbs.

2. Add the beaten egg and the oil. Stir and slowly add the water until the mixture moistens and starts clumping together.

3. Shape dressing into big fingers, about 4½" x 1¼" x ½". Set sticks on oiled cookie sheet and bake in preheated moderate oven for 15 minutes or until the sticks crisp and start to brown. Serve warm.

THE BREAD BASKET

**Quick Breads and Batter Breads
(Breads made without Yeast)**

**Blueberry and Whole Grain Spelt
Coffeecake with Crumble Topping**

Dove's Farm Soda Bread

Cherried Plum Bread

Carrot Nut Bread

Gingerbread

Chocolate Variety Bread

Zucchini Bread

Blueberry and Wholegrain Spelt Coffeecake
with Crumble Topping

Designed for all Blood Types, this is an easy-to-make coffeecake that features the full-bodied texture and natural sweetness of Whole Grain Spelt. Use rolled Spelt or rolled oats in the topping to complete this wholesome delight.

Blood Type: A, B, AB, O • Prep time: 10 min • Cook time: 25–30 min • Yield: 10 servings (2.5 oz each)

Ingredients

1 recipe Crumble Topping (see *Sweet Toppings*)
1 cup frozen blueberries
2 tsp granulated sugar
¼ cup vegetable oil
1 egg
½ cup soy milk (or milk)
1¾ cups Whole Grain Spelt Flour
¾ cup brown sugar, tightly packed
2 tsp baking powder
½ tsp salt

1. Preheat oven to 350° F. Take blueberries from freezer. Lightly coat with 2 tsp granulated sugar. Set aside. In large mixing bowl, combine and lightly blend the oil, egg and soy milk.

2. In separate bowl, combine the Whole Grain Spelt flour, brown sugar, baking powder and salt. Whisk. Add to the wet ingredients and mix just enough to incorporate and moisten all ingredients. Do not over beat.

3. Add the frozen blueberries; stir into the batter. Spoon mixture into lightly sprayed or oiled 9" pie pan, preferably nonstick, or use lightly oiled glass pie plate.

4. Sprinkle Crumble Topping evenly over dough. Bake in preheated moderate oven (350° F) for 25–30 minutes or until done. If using glass plate, check at 20 minutes. Test by inserting wooden toothpick or skewer into center. If it comes out clean, coffeecake is cooked. Remove from oven and place on wire rack to cool 10 minutes before slicing into wedges and serving. This coffeecake freezes very well.

Dove's Farm Soda Bread

Courtesy of Dove's Farm, Great Britain, it is fitting this recipe be here as people in the British Isles have been cooking with Spelt since the Iron Age. I encourage you to read more about Spelt at the Dove's Farm website (see Appendix 2—Spelt Resources). This is a traditional and nutritious Whole Grain Spelt round with salty taste. It is designed to eat fresh from the oven with soups and stews. Easy to make, quick to cook, you can have this on your table in an hour from start to finish.

Blood Type: A, B, AB (A and AB use goat's milk) • Prep time: 5 min • Cook time: 35 min • Yield: 1 round

Ingredients

2½ cups Whole Grain Spelt flour
2   tsp salt
2   tsp cream of tartar
1   tsp soda
1   cup milk, room temperature

1. Preheat oven to 425° F. In large mixing bowl, combine the flour, salt, soda and cream of tartar. Whisk ingredients together.

2. Stir in the milk and mix until soft dough forms (less than a minute). Sprinkle additional flour over dough and shape into a smooth ball. Place on an oiled or greased baking pan.

3. With sharp knife or razor blade, cut a cross (1") into the top of the round. Cover the round with a round stainless steel or glass bowl.

4. Allow oven to finish preheating to 425° F. Place bread in oven and bake for 35 minutes.

5. Remove from oven and place on wire rack to cool for 10–15 minutes before slicing and serving.

Cherried Plum Bread

The aroma of Cherried Plum Bread perfumes the air as it bakes; the taste lingers delightfully on the tongue.

Blood Type: Not rated • Prep time: 15 min • Cook time: 50–55 min • Yield: 2 8" x 4" loaves

Ingredients

1   cup brown sugar, tightly packed
1   cup Whole Grain Spelt flour
2   cups White Spelt flour (4.5 oz cup)
1   tsp baking soda
¼   tsp baking powder
½   tsp salt
2   Tbsp butter, melted
1   large egg, room temperature, well beaten
1   cup dried/reconstituted plums or with good moisture content, finely diced, firmly packed*
½   cup black cherry juice or reconstituted cherry concentrate
1   cup plain goat's milk yogurt or other plain yogurt without additives
1   tsp cherry flavoring

Tip: Place dried plums (should be the kind that are moisture packed) in freezer an hour ahead of baking. This will make them easy to dice in food processor or by hand.

1. Preheat oven to 375° F. Oil or lightly grease 2 8" x 4" loaf pans (preferably non-stick variety). In a large mixing bowl, combine the brown sugar, Spelt flours, baking soda, baking powder and salt. Whisk.

2. Stir the melted butter and well-beaten egg into the dry ingredients. Add the finely diced dried plums, cherry juice, yogurt and cherry flavoring. Mix well but do not over beat. This should be rough and fairly stiff batter.

3. Spoon the batter into prepared 8" x 4" loaf pans. Bake in preheated moderate oven (375° F) for 50–55 minutes. Test by inserting a wooden toothpick into center of each loaf. If it comes out clean, bread is done.

4. Remove loaves from oven and place on wire racks to cool for 10 minutes; tip out and let loaves cool directly on racks. When cool, wrap securely in plastic wrap and place in refrigerator to chill overnight before cutting to allow the flavors to fully develop and make for clean slicing. This perfumed bread is very much worth the wait.

Carrot Nut Bread

Orange-brown loaf with delicate sweet undertones.

Blood Type: A, B, AB, O • Prep time: 20 min • Cook time: 60 min* • Yield: 1 loaf

*Refrigerate overnight and then slice for best results.

Ingredients

1   cup (5 oz) raw baby carrots, finely grated
1   cup brown sugar, tightly packed
1   tsp baking soda
1   Tbsp vegetable oil
¾   cup boiling water
2   eggs, room temperature, lightly beaten
2½   tsp baking powder
1   tsp salt
1¼   cups White Spelt flour
1   cup Whole Grain Spelt flour
1   cup walnuts, chopped (if chopping in food processor, use one Tbsp out of the cup of Whole Spelt Flour and process with the nuts)

1. In large mixing bowl, combine the grated carrots, sugar, soda and oil. Pour the boiling water over ingredients; stir only to mix then set aside until cool. In separate smaller bowl, whisk together the Spelt flours, baking powder and salt.

2. Add the beaten eggs to the cooled carrot/sugar mixture. Preheat oven to 350° F.

3. Add the dry ingredients to the carrot/sugar/egg mixture; stir. Fold in the chopped walnuts.

4. Lightly oil or grease an 8" x 4" loaf pan (preferably non-stick). Pour batter into the prepared pan, and allow the mixture to stand for five minutes.

5. Bake on middle rack of preheated moderate oven (350° F) for 60 minutes or until bread tests done. Remove to wire rack and turn out of pan for loaf to cool on wire rack. When completely cool, wrap whole loaf well in plastic wrap and keep in refrigerator overnight. It will slice thinly and cleanly in the morning and is well worth the wait. Excellent with breakfast and brunch or with salads. It is also a lovely little tea-in-the-afternoon bread.

Gingerbread

Ginger and Spelt are perfect companions, each bringing out the best in the other. This is a moist flavorful Gingerbread with a somewhat open crumb structure. You can replace milk and butter with soymilk and oil and still enjoy fine bread that tastes like Grandmother's did lo those many years ago.

Blood Type: A, B, AB, O (B, AB use cloves instead of allspice; oil for A, AB; O use soymilk)
Prep time: 10 min • Cook time: 30 min • Yield: 16 servings

Ingredients

1½ cups dark brown sugar
½   cup Robust molasses
¼   cup melted butter or 3 Tbsp vegetable oil
1   egg, beaten
1   cup milk or soymilk
2   cups + 2 Tbsp White Spelt flour
1   cup Whole Grain Spelt flour
1   tsp baking soda
½   tsp salt
1   tsp ginger
½   tsp cloves or allspice
Turbinado or brown sugar for sprinkling

1. Preheat oven to 350° F. Spray oil or lightly grease a 13" x 9" x 2" baking pan (preferably non-stick variety). In medium bowl, combine the Spelt flours, baking soda, salt and spices. Whisk together and set aside.

2. In large mixing bowl, combine the brown sugar, molasses, butter or oil, and the beaten egg. Blend well, scraping down sides of bowl with plastic spatula. Gradually and alternately, add the dry ingredients and the milk to the sugar/molasses mixture and beat until ingredients are thoroughly incorporated, scraping down sides and along bottom of bowl with spatula several times to assure even distribution of ingredients.

3. Pour into prepared baking pan. Sprinkle with turbinado or brown sugar. Place on center rack of preheated moderate (350° F) oven and bake for 30 minutes. Top will be shiny reddish gold and sides will have shrunk slightly from edges of pan when done. Test by inserting a wooden toothpick into center; if it comes out clean, remove from oven. If not, bake an additional 5 minutes.

4. Remove from oven and place on wire rack to cool 10–15 minutes before cutting into squares or bars and serving warm.

Chocolate Variety Bread

My mother's moist luscious recipe adapted to Spelt. Make it with zucchini or bananas and vary the flavorings for variety bread with good slicing qualities and rich taste.

Blood Type: B, O Banana or Zucchini Version; A, AB Zucchini Version • (O use mace instead of nutmeg; AB sub cinnamon for allspice; B sub 1 tsp cardamom for cinnamon or allspice)
Prep time: 15 min • Cook time: 50–55 min • Yield: 2 9" x 5" loaves

Ingredients

3 large eggs, room temperature, lightly beaten
¾ cup vegetable oil
2 cups granulated sugar
2 tsp vanilla (or Kirsch, cherry, almond or mint flavorings)
2½ cups White Spelt flour
1 cup Whole Grain Spelt flour
2 tsp soda
1 tsp salt
½ tsp baking powder
½ cup cocoa powder
1 tsp mace or nutmeg
½ tsp allspice or cinnamon
½ tsp cloves (optional)
½ tsp ginger (optional)
2 cups coarsely grated zucchini (2–3 medium zucchini)
or 2 cups mashed ripe bananas (3–4 medium bananas)
1 cup chopped, toasted walnuts or other nuts (pine nuts, almonds, pistachios)
Confectioners' sugar for dusting (optional)

1. Preheat oven to 350° F. If using glass or ceramic, preheat to 325° F. Lightly oil or grease two 9" x 5" loaf pans and line bottoms with parchment or dust with flour.

2. In large mixing bowl, combine the lightly beaten eggs, oil, sugar and vanilla.

3. In separate bowl, whisk together the Spelt flours, soda, salt, baking powder, cocoa and spices.

4. By hand or with mixer on slow speed, alternately add the dry ingredients and grated zucchini (or bananas) to the egg/oil/sugar mixture. Do not over mix. Stir in the chopped nuts.

5. Spoon the batter into prepared loaf pans. Place on center rack of preheated moderate (350° F metal/325° F glass) oven and bake 55–60 minutes. Test by inserting toothpick into center of each loaf. If it comes out clean and sides of bread have shrunk slightly away from side of pan, the bread is finished baking.

6. Remove from oven and place on wire racks to cool for 10 minutes. Gently tip loaves out onto wire racks. Once cool, sprinkle with Confectioners' sugar (optional), and wrap securely in plastic wrap and refrigerate overnight so bread slices cleanly and flavors fully develop.

Zucchini Bread

Spelt is a natural for Zucchini and other quick breads because it holds moistness and adds its own sweet slightly nutty taste to the mix. This bread is redolent with complex texture and flavor: subtly spiced with deep sweet sugared undertones that come through immediately when you bite through the crisp exterior and into the dense moist crumb.

Blood Type: A, B, AB, O (B sub cardamom for cinnamon; B, AB use cloves instead of allspice; O use mace instead of nutmeg)
Prep time: 20 min • Cook time: 55–60 min • Yield: 2 large 9" x 5" loaves

Ingredients

2   cups (2 medium) fresh zucchini, unpeeled, coarsely grated
1   cup raisins, soaked in hot water 15 minutes and drained
2½ cups White Spelt flour
1   cup Whole Grain Spelt flour
1   tsp soda
1   tsp salt
1   tsp baking powder
2   Tbsp cinnamon
1   tsp freshly grated nutmeg
¼   tsp cloves or allspice (optional)
4   eggs, room temperature, lightly beaten
1½ cups granulated sugar
½   cup dark brown sugar, firmly packed
1   cup Light Olive, canola or other vegetable oil
2   tsp grated lemon zest
1   cup toasted walnuts, coarsely chopped

1. Preheat oven to 350° F. Spray or oil two 9" x 5" loaf pans and dust with flour. Line bottoms of each pan with parchment or dust with additional flour. Place the grated zucchini in a colander. Mix the raisins with 1 Tbsp of the Whole Grain Spelt flour. Stir to coat. Set aside.

2. In medium mixing bowl, combine the Spelt flours, soda, salt, baking powder and the spices. Whisk together and set aside.

3. In large mixing bowl, combine the lightly beaten eggs, granulated and brown sugars, oil and lemon zest and blend, occasionally scraping down sides of bowl with plastic/rubber spatula.

4. Gradually and alternately, add the dry ingredients and the zucchini to the egg/sugar/oil mixture, stirring just until all ingredients are thoroughly incorporated. Stir in the toasted chopped nuts and the raisins. Pour batter into prepared pans.

5. Place on middle rack of preheated moderate (350° F) oven and bake for 55–60 minutes. The tops should be deep golden reddish brown and sides will have shrunk slightly from edges of pan. Test by inserting wooden skewer or toothpick into crown of each loaf. If it comes out clean, loaves are ready to remove from oven. Place on wire racks to cool for 10–15 minutes. Tip out of pans and turn loaves on sides. Allow to cool completely before cutting. Wrap securely in plastic wrap and place in refrigerator overnight. Slice the next day for best results.

SUGGESTIONS FOR SPECIAL SANDWICHES

Patty Melt on Rye with Caramelized Onions made on
Light or Dark Spelt Rye

Hamburgers with Grilled Tomatoes and Specialty Hot Dogs or Sausages
on Classic White Spelt Buns, Rosemary Cheese Bread or on Brundisi
Pesto Bread spread with Garlic Mayonnaise (Aioli)

Hoagies or Subs with Classic Spelt Meatballs
on All-Italian Submarine Rolls or French Rolls

Grilled Chicken or Turkey with Roasted Vegetables
on Brundisi Pesto or Calabrese Bread, Roman Bread made as
Bruschetta or Wrapped in Spelt Tortillas

Deli Sandwiches, Open-Faced Panini or Bruschetta or Other Grilled
Sandwiches on slices of bread from the Campocosenza Wheel,
French Bread (Bâtard) or Roasted Garlic and Mozzarella Baguettes

Tuna, Chicken or Classic Egg Sandwich on Speltessence,
Seattle Supreme Sandwich Loaf, Spelt Wheat Berry and Honey Bread
or on a Brundisi Pesto Roll or Wrapped in Challah

A Plain Ole Peanut Butter and Really Good Fruit Preserves Sandwich?
Try it on Spelt Wheat Berry and Honey Bread or Speltessence

For Dipping into Sauces, for Topping
Medi Crostini, French Bread, Roman Bread, French Breadsticks
Or putting sauces and salads into ...
Bread Bowls made from Calabrese or Brundisi Pesto or
French or All-Italian or Classic White

Tea Sandwiches with Cardamom Gold Pumpkin Bread,
Cherried Plum Bread, Carrot Nut Bread, Zucchini Bread or Rosemary
Cheese Bread or the Many Fun Forms of Traditional Feast Rolls

Don't Forget the Char Shiu Bao ...
the Ready-Made Chinese Steamed Bun Sandwich

Falafel or Meat in Pita Pocket with Tsatsiki Sauce

Meet Maximo,

The Mighty Meatball!

Classic Meatball
Beef or Turkey

New Swedish Meatballs

Sopa de Albondigas
(Meatball Soup)

Sopa de Albondigas con Camarones
(Shrimp Meatball Soup)

Classic Meatball
Beef or Turkey

Roll large for spaghetti or submarine sandwiches or small for appetizers or side dishes. Spice 'em up or dress 'em down, use fresh herbs or different types of bread. Very simple to make and freeze.

Blood Type: Beef B, O / Turkey A, B, AB, O / Lamb B, AB, O
Prep time: 30 min • Cook time: 30–40 min • Yield: 6–7 dozen

Ingredients

1 pound turkey or beef, finely ground
½ cup onions, finely diced
2 tsp garlic, minced or 1½ tsp powdered
1 tsp salt
1 tsp ground rosemary
½ tsp ground thyme or 1½ tsp crushed
½ tsp ground marjoram or 1½ tsp crushed
¼ cup dried, fine Spelt breadcrumbs (Whole Grain, White or mixed)
½ cup semi-soft Mozzarella cheese, grated
¼ tsp red pepper, powdered or black pepper to taste (optional)
1 tsp Olive oil
vegetable oil for cooking

1. Place all ingredients in a large bowl or stand mixer with paddle and mix until thoroughly blended.

2. Heat vegetable oil in large skillet placed over medium heat.

3. Form the meat into balls about 1¼" to 1½" in diameter or desired size.

Stovetop: Brown meatballs on all sides in skillet. Drain on paper towels.

Oven Baked: The meatballs will exude some juice so place on wire racks set over large baking pans or on broiler rack set over broiler pan. Spray the racks/pan with oil to prevent sticking. Heat oven to 350° F. For two pans, place meatballs in oven on bottom rack and rack placed two rungs up. Bake for 15 minutes; switch position of pans on racks to assure even baking. Bake additional 15–20 minutes until meatballs are brown but juicy.

New Swedish Meatballs

The traditional Swedish meatball is made of beef seasoned with salt pork; the finished sauce calls for heavy cream. These New Swedish Meatballs use beef and lamb combined. They can just as easily be made of all beef if you like. They are a natural made with ground turkey.

Instead of cream, a delectable broth is made by using stock and adding goat's milk or soy milk. These are savory meatballs that continue to develop a delicate spiced taste when refrigerated. Excellent for brunches and buffets or served over Spelt noodles. Ask butcher to coarse grind the lamb when you buy it. While they are baking, the fragrance wafts about the room and makes the mouth water.

Blood Type: Not rated • Prep time: 20 minutes • Cook/bake time: 75 min • Yield: 5 dozen meatballs

Ingredients

1   pound 80% lean beef, coarse ground
1   pound boneless leg lamb (case lamb), coarse ground
2   cups fresh, fine Spelt bread crumbs (A Beginning Loaf is excellent for this)
1   egg, lightly beaten
2   tsp brown sugar
2   tsp allspice
2   tsp nutmeg, freshly ground
1   tsp salt
1   tsp pepper, freshly ground
¼   cup vegetable oil for browning in large skillet
3   cups low-sodium beef broth (or turkey, chicken or vegetable broth)
1   cup goat's milk or soy milk

1. Using food processor or stand mixer with grinding attachment:

    Combine the meats and breadcrumbs in a bowl. Fine grind the mixture. Repeat the process so the meats/crumbs are blended and finely ground together.

2. Add the beaten egg, brown sugar, spices, salt and pepper; mix so all ingredients are thoroughly incorporated.

3. Form into 1-inch balls. These develop an even more wonderful flavor if placed, covered, in the refrigerator for several hours prior to cooking. For immediate cooking, place ¼ cup vegetable oil in a large skillet and set on medium heat.

4. Brown the meatballs on all sides. Heat oven to 325° F. Place meatballs in a roasting pan and pour the broth over the meatballs. Cover with foil. Bake for 45 minutes.

5. Remove the foil. Add the goat's milk or soy milk. Bake uncovered for an additional 15 minutes.

Serve warm over Spelt noodles or as an appetizer or side dish. Roll meatballs ahead of time and freeze. Simply thaw in the refrigerator, brown and bake according to instructions. The baked meatballs keep well in freezer. Simply cool and place flat in freezer bag.

Sopa de Albondigas
(Meatball Soup)

This popular favorite in Mexican restaurants now comes to your table made with Spelt. Without the meatballs, you might recognize it as Tortilla Soup, which you can also make from this recipe by leaving out the meatballs and sprinkling baked Spelt Tortilla strips over the spicy broth.

The broth is delicate and can be dressed up or down—thin almost clear broth with no spice in the meatballs to a dark, rich broth with flavorful meatballs. It is the second version offered here. We grind our own meat for the meatballs—the finer the better. We roll them ahead of time and let them season in the refrigerator. This soup is a simple delight. Use beef or turkey.

Blood Type: Not rated • Prep time: 15 minutes • Cook time: browning 20 min, cooking 20 min • Yield: 8 servings

Ingredients

3   cloves garlic, minced
1½ cups (about 1 large) sweet brown onion, finely chopped
1   Tbsp fresh cilantro, finely chopped (optional)
2   Tbsp fresh green chile, chopped (optional) or canned
4   Tbsp Olive oil
1½ pounds ground beef or turkey (the more finely ground the better)
¾   cup dry, fine Spelt bread crumbs (mixture of White/Whole Grain)
2   large eggs, room temp, lightly beaten
1   tsp ground cumin
½   tsp Mexican oregano, crushed
1   tsp ground, mild red New Mexico Chili powder
dash of cayenne pepper (optional)
½   tsp salt
½   tsp black pepper or pepper medley, freshly ground
4   cups beef stock or broth
4   cups water
¼   cup red wine
2   scallions, white and green portions, chopped

1. Place large skillet with 2 Tbsp of oil in it over medium heat. Sauté the onion and garlic until soft. Stir in the green chile and chopped cilantro (optional). Remove skillet from heat.

2. Combine the ground meat, breadcrumbs, herbs, chili powder, cayenne (optional), salt and pepper in a large mixing bowl. Add the sautéed vegetables to the ground meat and mix thoroughly so all ingredients are thoroughly incorporated; roll into one-inch balls. Place skillet back on medium heat, adding additional oil.

3. Brown the meatballs, turning often to brown all sides.

4. Place a Dutch oven or stockpot over medium heat. Pour the water and beef broth into pot. As the liquid warms, add the wine and the chopped green onions. Bring to a boil.

5. Turn the heat to medium and simmer the liquid. Add the cooked meatballs. Cover; cook for 30 minutes. Serve hot with Spelt Tortilla Cheese Crisps (see Spelt Tortillas under *Many Small Things*).

Sopa de Albondigas con Camarones
(Shrimp Meatball Soup)

A very delicate and delicious soup for lunch or a light dinner. This recipe is also delicious made with fresh white fish and minced jalapeños—it's a lovely variation.

Blood Type: Not rated • Prep time: 15 min • Cook time: About 30 min • Yield: 4 servings

Ingredients

2 Tbsp Olive oil or other vegetable oil for browning
¼ cup celery, finely chopped
3 cloves garlic, minced
¾ cup Mayan sweet onions, finely chopped
1 tsp fresh cilantro, chopped (optional)
10–12 ounces cocktail-size frozen shrimp, thawed, finely chopped
2 eggs, room temperature, lightly beaten
1¼ cups fine, dried White Spelt breadcrumbs
1 tsp vegetable oil
¼ tsp ground celery seed
1 tsp salt (or dulse granules)
½ tsp white pepper OR
½ tsp lemon pepper
4 cups turkey, chicken or vegetable stock
1 cup water
a hint of Marsala or dry white wine
3 scallions, green and white portions, chopped
1 Tbsp lemon juice

1. Place large skillet over medium heat and add 2 Tbsp oil. Place celery, garlic and onions in skillet; sauté until soft. Remove from heat.

2. Place shrimp into large bowl. Combine with the sautéed vegetables, cilantro (optional), breadcrumbs, oil, celery seed, salt and pepper and the lightly beaten eggs. Mix until all ingredients are moist.

3. Turn the skillet to moderately high heat adding more oil if necessary for browning. Form the mixture into balls (about 1" diameter) and brown them lightly on *all* sides, turning them very gently.

4. While shrimp balls are browning, heat the broth and water in a Dutch oven or soup pot. Add the lemon juice and just a hint of wine. Add the chopped green onions. Bring to a boil; turn down to simmer as you finish browning the shrimp balls.

5. Transfer the browned shrimp balls to the broth and simmer very gently (covered) for 15 minutes. Serve immediately.

HOMEMADE HERITAGE SOUP OF THE DAY OR NIGHT

**Collard Greens and Turkey Ham Soup
with Spelt Dumplings**

Onion Soup

Ancient Soups for Modern Times—

**Minestrone di Farro
(Minestrone Soup Made of Spelt
or Other Farro)**

**Zuppa di Farro e Cannellini
(Tuscan Farro and Cannellini Bean Soup)**

Collard Greens and Turkey Ham Soup
with Spelt Dumplings

A traditional southern favorite, this is a one-pot down-home meal made with Turkey Ham and Spelt Dumplings. Make with either collard greens *or* chard, which is now available in many frozen food cases at grocery stores. Make this meal with your feet up. It is wonderful for a chilly rainy day.

Blood Type: Not rated • Prep time: 15 min • Cook time: 50 min • Yield: 8 servings (2.5 oz meat)

Ingredients for Soup

1¼ pounds (20 oz) Turkey Ham, cubed
    1" x 1½"
1   bunch collard greens or ¾ pounds frozen, chopped chard (thawed)
1   large sweet onion
10 cups water or low sodium turkey or chicken broth
pinch of sea salt
2   tsp vegetable oil

Ingredients for Dumplings

½ cup Whole Grain Spelt flour
½ cup White Spelt flour
2   tsp baking powder
½ tsp salt
1   egg, room temperature, well beaten
½ cup milk, room temperature
1   tsp rosemary, dried and crushed or other herb/seasoning (optional)

Soup:

1. Place stockpot with tight-fitting lid over medium high heat. Add water and pinch of salt. There needs to be enough room between water and lid for dumplings to steam so allow 3 inches in your choice-of-pot calculations.

2. Place skillet over medium high heat with oil in it and heat. Fry cubed turkey ham in skillet with vegetable oil. Cook till lightly brown on all sides. Set aside.

3. Wash collard greens. Trim leaves from stock. Tear into small to medium-sized pieces. Place in soup pot. Or add chopped chard that has been allowed to thaw.

4. Cut onion into 6–8 sections. Place in pot.

5. Add the turkey ham to the pot; cover and simmer for 20 minutes. Reduce the heat to low.

6. Prepare the dumplings (next page)

Spelt Dumplings

7. In mixing bowl, whisk together the Whole Grain and White Spelt flours, baking powder and salt.

8. To the mixing bowl, add ¼ cup of the milk and stir. Add the beaten egg; and mix rapidly. Add the remaining ¼ cup of milk mixing just long enough to blend.

9. Drop the batter by tablespoonfuls into the pot. Do not crowd. If the dough gets too sticky to drop, dunk the spoon into the soup; continue. After all the dumplings have been dropped into soup, sprinkle rosemary or other seasoning that pleases you over top of the dumplings.

10. Put cover on pot and let cook on low heat for 20 minutes *without* lifting the lid. (Resist the urge to look; heat and steam will escape which affects how the dumplings cook. They should be puffy and tasty not gummy.) At the end of 20 minutes, lift the lid and test if dumplings are ready by inserting a toothpick into the near center of one. If it comes out clean, the dumplings are done. Serve hot.

... From a Bygone Era ...
A Major Joe Tilden, bohemian and epicure, 1907 Recipe
Onion Soup

Place six ounces of butter in a large saucepan over the fire, and stir into it four large white onions cut up, not sliced. Stew this very slowly for one hour, stirring frequently to prevent scorching. Add salt, pepper, cayenne to taste, and about one quart of stock, and cook one hour longer. Then stir into the mixture one and a half cups of milk and simmer for a few minutes. Have ready a soup tureen. In it beat the yolks of four eggs with two tablespoons of grated Parmesan cheese. Stir the hot soup into this, beating until it thickens a little. A slice of toasted French bread should be placed in each plate, and the soup poured over it.

Ancient Soups for Modern Times
Minestrone di Farro
(Minestrone Soup Made of Spelt or Other Farro)

This is the essence of soup and has a very long pedigree. I encourage you to read Part II, Chapter 3 on Farro to know something of its history, maybe read about it while the Minestrone is cooking. *Minestra* means soup in Italian and refers to a vegetable soup containing vermicelli or barley in a meat broth. The Farro replaces the vermicelli in this older version. The Farro refers to Spelt berries.

This soup is a joy to make. The complex, mouthwatering aromas pervade the kitchen and waft out-of-doors then come back in on the breeze. The flavor is exquisite and sends the message of fresh, wholesome hearth food straight to your blood, your heart, down to your bones. It's real.

Make the sponge for Medi Crostini Bread the night before at the same time you set out the Spelt berries to soak. Prepare the bread while you are making the soup, just as has been done through the ages. No fresh bread? Make large Spelt croutons from stale bread, mix with oil and herbs in a skillet and toast. Put on top of the soup and sprinkle with Pecorino or other hard grated cheese. This is a remarkably rewarding and soul-satisfying meal, but please read the recipe thoroughly before you begin. The key to it is fresh ingredients—the Roma tomatoes need to be juicy ripe.

Notes on the Recipe:

About the bacon: Turkey Bacon provides a remarkably good substitute for the pork bacon customarily used in this and other Italian recipes.

About the Farro: Please read the section on "Farro" because there is not just Spelt Farro, there is emmer and einkorn farro available, both imported and domestic. Each of them cooks a different amount of time and has different textures and flavors.

Blood Type: Not rated • Prep and cook time: 2 to 2½ hours • Yield: 6 servings

---

Ingredients

6 oz Spelt or other Farro berries (1 cup dry measurement)
4 fresh, plump, RIPE Roma Tomatoes (about 12 oz) OR
14.5 oz can Whole Peeled Roma Tomatoes, rinsed, the heavy tomato juice discarded
4 slices lean Turkey bacon (about 2 ounces), diced
2 cloves garlic
1 sweet onion (about 2 cups), finely chopped
fresh basil (divided 1/3 cup chopped, handful of leaves)
fresh thyme (leaves stripped from stems to provide about 1/4 to 1/3 cup fresh)
fresh flat-leaf (Italian) parsley (do not substitute curly parsley) (1/3 cup chopped)
2 cubes Vegetable Bouillon dissolved in
5 cups water
1 cup or more finely grated Pecorino Romano or other aged cheese for sprinkling over soup

In Advance. The night before, rinse the Spelt berries; place in large bowl with 4" cold water to cover. Soak for 12 hours prior to cooking. Rinse well in cold water; drain and set aside.

Preparation. Peel the fresh Roma tomatoes or rinse the canned peeled Roma tomatoes and discard the heavy tomato juice. Dice the bacon. Prepare the garlic. Finely chop the sweet onion. Wash and pat dry the fresh herbs. Chop the basil sufficient to provide 1/3 cup chopped leaves and set aside 3–4 whole basil leaves. Chop 1/3 cup flat-leaf parsley. Strip the thyme leaves from the stems sufficient to provide 1/4 to 1/3 cup leaves. Heat 5 cups water and dissolve the bouillon cubes in it. Have on hand a stockpot with lid.

1. Place a stockpot over medium high heat and add 2–3 Tbsp olive oil and heat until light haze forms over the oil. Add the diced bacon and cook, stirring frequently, for 5–6 minutes until the bacon just starts to crisp but is not brown. Reduce the heat and add the garlic and finely chopped onion; cook for several minutes then add 1/4 cup fresh chopped thyme leaves and 1/3 cup chopped fresh basil. Cook, continuing to stir, gently, until bacon starts to brown and onions are soft and translucent. Remove the garlic cloves from the pot.

2. To the pot, add the peeled tomatoes, the chopped parsley and 3–4 whole basil leaves and allow mixture to reduce for 6–8 minutes. Add 5 cups bouillon water; bring to a boil.

3. Add the soaked, softened Spelt berries. Reduce heat (moderate, sufficient for a very low simmer) and cover the pot. Cook 1 hour, stirring every 15 minutes or so to keep Spelt from sticking. Add 1/2 to 1 cup more plain water to broth if necessary. It should not be a thick soup but one in which the broth is a rather clear light brown. The herbs and tomatoes will also be distinct elements floating very prettily in the broth. Check the texture of the Spelt at the end of an hour or so. The berries should be soft yet somewhat resistant to the tooth as that is the nature of cooked Spelt berries.

4. Turn off the heat. Remove pot from heat source and allow it to sit, lightly covered, for an hour and serve when moderately warm. Ladle into bowls and sprinkle with finely grated Pecorino cheese. Serve with fresh Spelt bread such as Medi Crostini.

Zuppa di Farro e Cannellini
(Tuscan Farro and Cannellini Bean Soup)

This is not an old recipe; it is an ancient one, the combination of Spelt and beans in a soup. This is an authentic Italian soup still made in the region where Farro is grown, Garfagnana, known for its Farro and its truffles and its position along the Wine Road of Lucca. The addition of beans to soup is an ancient one; however, Cannellini beans came to Europe after Columbus like the tomato and were ultimately so adapted into local cooking that it is hard to imagine Italy without either.

Zuppa di Farro smells like a garden in bloom as it cooks. It is extremely filling, a meal in itself as many of these ancient soups were. It combines Spelt, beans and greens to create a high-protein meal without meat and can easily absorb far more fresh herbs than the guidelines given here. Another thing about Zuppa de Farro—it makes an excellent dip with crudités especially since it can be served at room temperature or even chilled for this purpose.

You may be interested to read Part II, Chapter 3 about Farro as there is Spelt Farro as well as Emmer Farro and Einkorn Farro. Each has different cooking properties.

Blood Type: A, B, AB, O • Prep/cook time: approximately 2½ to 3 hours • Makes: 10 very filling servings

Ingredients

1½ cups (8 oz) dried Cannellini beans (or substitute Great Northern beans)
1   cup (8 oz) Spelt berries
2   Tbsp Extra Virgin Olive oil
1   sweet onion (1 cup), chopped
1   large carrot (1 cup), diced
1   large stalk celery (1 cup), diced
6   cloves fresh garlic, minced
4–5 fresh ripe Roma tomatoes, peeled, seeded, diced OR
1   14½ oz can of peeled, diced Plum (Roma) tomatoes
4   cups vegetable or beef broth
½   cup fresh basil, chopped
3   sage leaves, dried
4   sprigs fresh rosemary (3–4 tsp crushed, dried)
1   tablespoon marjoram, ground
2   tsp sea salt (coarse)
2   tsp pepper, freshly ground

In Advance:

1. Rinse and sort through Cannellini beans, removing any pebbles or debris. Soak the beans overnight in pan with 2 inches unsalted cold water to cover.

2. Soak the Farro (Spelt berries) overnight in bowl sufficiently large to cover Spelt with 4 inches unsalted cold water to cover.

Soup:

3. Drain the Cannellini beans. Put beans in saucepan and cover with 2–3 inches cold, unsalted water. Bring beans to a boil over high heat and cook for 10 minutes. Reduce heat to low and simmer until beans are tender. Cooking time varies based on age and size of Cannellini beans, so allow 1–2 hours. When cooked, drain the beans but *reserve* the cooking water.

4. Place a stockpot over medium heat; add 2 Tbsp Extra Virgin olive oil, and heat until a haze forms over oil. Add onions, carrots, celery and minced garlic and cook until the vegetables are soft (10–15 minutes).

5. Drain the Farro (Spelt berries) while vegetables are cooking. Set Spelt aside.

6. Place the cooked beans (1½ cups) in processor/blender with 1½ cups of the reserved bean cooking liquid. Puree until smooth paste is formed. (If blender/processor will not accommodate that amount, it can be done in two steps using ¾ cup beans and ¾ cup liquid.) Add the bean puree to the soup pot and stir.

7. Add the broth (4 cups) and the Spelt berries. Bring the pot to the boil, then immediately reduce heat. Add the chopped tomatoes, basil, sage, marjoram, rosemary, salt and pepper to the soup. Add more herbs and spices to taste. Simmer, stirring occasionally, until the soup is thick (about 20–30 minutes).

Serve with a drizzle of extra virgin olive oil on top.

SAUCES

Aioli (Garlic Mayonnaise)

Aglio e Olio (Garlic and Oil Sauce)

White Sauce (Béchemel)

See Also

Sweet and Sour Salad
in *The Vegetable Stand*

Enchilada Sauce Sabrosa
and Tsatsiki Sauce
in *Many Small Things*

Aioli
(Garlic Mayonnaise)

The remarkable sauce of Provence, Aioli (ay-OH-lee) is a light garlic-flavored mayonnaise to accompany crostini, breadsticks or raw vegetables or to serve on top of fish or lightly cooked vegetables such as asparagus. Instead of typical mayonnaise, try Aioli as a thin spread on deli-style sandwiches made with homemade Spelt bread. It really is best when made the old-fashioned way with mortar and pestle; however, here is an alternative method for the food processor that makes a slightly thinner version.

Blood Type: A, B, AB, O (without Dijon mustard) • Prep time: 15 minutes • Cook time: NA • Yield: 1¼ cups

Ingredients

4   garlic cloves, peeled, minced
⅛   tsp sea salt
2   egg yolks, room temperature
1¼ cups Virgin Olive oil or other vegetable oil
1   Tbsp lemon juice, room temperature
dash of cayenne or white pepper (optional)
Boil a cup of water in microwave; have on hand

1. Place minced garlic cloves and salt in a small bowl. Make a rough mash by lightly crushing with spoon against side of bowl. Add the room temperature egg yolks and lightly whisk without incorporating too much air.

2. Add mixture to bowl of food processor. On Run, slowly add ½ cup oil drop by drop blending completely before adding more oil. Continue until mixture starts to thicken; add oil by the drop more continuously now until ¾ cup oil has been incorporated.

3. Add remaining oil in very thin but steady stream until mixture thickens and becomes creamy. Remove from processor bowl and whisk in lemon juice by hand, adding just a hint of cayenne or white pepper if desired.

4. Should the mixture begin to curdle at any step of the process, quickly beat in from one to two teaspoons of boiling water.

5. The mixture will be somewhat thinner than commercial mayonnaise yet will be of good spreading consistency. It will grow stronger as it sits. Refrigerate remaining sauce for several days.

Aglio e Olio
(Garlic and Oil Sauce)

Basic oil and garlic sauce that can be made more "green" by increasing the amount of spinach or Italian parsley or adding other herbs like basil. This is a fine alternative to tomato sauce over the thin pastas such as spaghetti, angel hair or linguini. It works very well on vegetables such as steamed asparagus and as a spread on pizza and other flatbreads.

Blood Type: A, B, AB, O • Prep time: 5 min • Cook time: 10 min
Yield: a little over a cup or 4–6 servings for 1 lb pound of pasta

---

Ingredients

1 cup Olive oil
4 cloves garlic, minced
¼ cup minced Italian parsley (flat leaf) OR baby spinach
¼ tsp crushed, dried oregano
½ tsp sea salt
Dash white pepper (optional)
Freshly grated Parmesan, Romano, Pecorino Romano or Asiago for garnish (optional)

1. Place skillet over low heat and add olive oil. Heat until oil begins to waft and is fragrant. Add the minced garlic and cook, stirring continuously, until garlic is light gold.

2. Add the Italian parsley or baby spinach, the oregano and the salt. Continuing to stir, cook one minute longer then remove from heat and serve over drained, hot pasta. Sprinkle with grated cheese (optional).

White Sauce (Béchamel)

A medium white sauce for vegetables and soups.

Blood Type: Not rated • Prep time/cook time: 15 min • Yield: 1 cup

Ingredients

2   Tbsp butter
2   Tbsp White Spelt flour
⅛   tsp salt
1   cup milk, warm
dash white pepper or freshly grated nutmeg
(optional)

1. Warm milk in microwave without letting it bubble. Set aside. Place saucepan over low heat. Add butter and heat until it melts.

2. Stir in flour and salt; blend. Pour in all of the warm milk and stir constantly until mixture thickens and starts to bubble. Do not boil. Add a dash of nutmeg or white pepper (optional). Remove from heat immediately and serve. Or, after cooling, may be refrigerated for several days.

Note: Whole Grain Spelt may also be used to make a very tasty sauce. Let it brown for several minutes, stirring constantly, prior to adding milk.

THE VEGETABLE STAND

Harmonies of Nature: Phytochemicals

Spelt Sprouts: Sweet Burst of Power

Spelt Grünkern ("Green Kernel")

※

Caesar Salad with Spelt Croutons

Panzanella Salad with Spelt Italian Bread

Spelt Rotini and Turmeric Salad

Singla Salad

Turkey Waldorf Salad with Spelt Sprouts

※

Asparagus al Limon

Creamy Artichokes Side Dish, Dip or Topping

Portabella Mushrooms New Orleans (Stuffed Mushrooms)

Spaghetti Squash with Herbed Breadcrumbs

Tunisian Rice with Spelt Sprouts

Sweet Potato Fritters

Sweet Potato Puffs

Shredded Sweet Potato: The Alternative to Coconut

Zucchini Fries

Zucchini Fritters

※

See also Roasted Garlic, Fried Rice and Yusef's Hummus in
Many Small Things section

Harmonies of Nature: Phytochemicals

PHYTO (from the Greek, meaning Plants) PHYTOCHEMICALS = PLANT CHEMIC-ALS
CHEMIC , archaic meaning alchemy; modern usage, chemistry
NUTRIENT, from *nourish*, to supply with matter necessary to life

These are the Good Guys and they come riding in, naturally, on Whole Foods.

Phytochemicals (Phytos) are a source of many of nature's original prescription drugs. Plants developed these compounds to protect themselves against viruses, bacteria and fungi. As humans learned about plants, like Spelt, we learned to reap their benefits. It was trial and error.

Our beautiful tall, spiked garden Foxglove can kill us; it can also start the heart (digitalis) during surgery. The bitter cassava or manioc is an ancient root crop of the Amazon. It contains prussic acid, a killer. Through trial and error, the Amerindians there learned to render the acid inert. Manioc became a staple food, and is the source of the tapioca (Brazilian arrowroot) for puddings and is a thickener in many other products.

That is the alchemy of Phytochemicals: the original lore and wisdom that came with eons of experimentation with the plants around us. Modern "chemical" science is attempting to explain why these natural compounds work to the end of applying that knowledge to the synthetic creation of refined compounds. They are finding amazing things.

Fight-O's

What Phytos *do* is *protect* the body *from,* and *fight off,* diseases. They are among the most powerful forces of the natural world and there are many of these chemical compounds. For example, sterols, isoflavones, lignans, coumestans, saponins, phytases and phytoestrogens (see also the section on Spelt Healthy Ingredients in the Part III, *Spelta's Place*). The world of plant nature is the original and ongoing chemical factory.

When we eat spinach or a sweet potato, we are not eating "food" we are taking in chemicals that extend and enrich our lives. These are not synthetically reproduced chemicals from a lab; in eating whole foods we are eating many at one time to give a synergistic affect. Cooperative, combined interaction occurs when they are eaten in their natural form. The more refined our foods, the fewer of these fighters there are to protect against disease. Fruit, vegetables and whole grains are loaded with them. Most are antioxidants that help reduce the risks of the diseases like cancer and diabetes, some, like garlic, fight bacterial infections.

At this stage of research, scientists are still labeling Phytos as "Non-Nutritive" because Phytos do not seem to build or regenerate the body in the way Essential and Non-Essential Amino Acids do (see also *Why Choose Spelt?*). Yet they *do* supply chemicals necessary to life. That is the definition of a nutrient hence the Phytonutrients Supplement labels you may see on products.

Parsley, Sage, Rosemary and Thyme

Is there a reason for Parsley, Sage, Rosemary and Thyme being combined in food and song? Far more than taste, they form a battery of powerful antioxidants. So does the flavonoid called Quercetin found in yellow onions, cherries, broccoli, apples, cereals, red grapes and red onions.

What's in a Spelt Sprout?

It is a nutrient dense powerhouse loaded with Phytochemical antioxidants along with essential amino acids.

Spelt Sprouts

Sweet Burst of Power!

There are two basic ways of making grain digestible for humans: *sprouting* the grain and eating it fresh or *cooking* the grain as in porridge or using it as flour. The sprout is a means of pre-digestion so our body does not have to work as hard to metabolize it.

Germination is Life

The process of sprouting is germination, the process of life. Place the seed in clean fresh water; the seed swells as it absorbs the water. A tiny root grows. The grain turns into a vegetable packed with enzymes (proteins responsible for catalyzing chemical reactions), which are the bases of carbon-based life. Everything that happens in our bodies relies upon the activities of proteins. The complex carbohydrates in the endosperm, the protein, minerals and vitamins in the germ, all the nutrients stored in the seed are producing enzymes during germination.

No Grass Growing Here

These are not "grassy" sprouts like the Alfalfa or the Mung Bean sprouts you may be accustomed to eating on sandwiches. Spelt sprouts are chewy little nuggets that grow a short whitish tail (root). Bite into these little darlings and what you will experience is a refined crunch and a burst of sweet liquid loaded with vitamins, minerals and phytochemicals. (Note: Spelt Grass is available. The recipes in *Spelt Healthy!* use the form described here that are sold as Spelt Sprouts. Please see *Resources* section for both kinds.)

Easy to Sprout

Spelt sprouts are the simplest of all things to prepare. They require no special equipment. Your sprout vender will give you instructions, but the process is basic. A sprouter is nice but not necessary. A bowl and a plastic colander, for example, will do. Take a small amount of Sprout seed like half a cup (that will yield well over a cup of sprouts). Soak the seeds in plenty of cool water for 6–12 hours. Drain off the water or use it in cooking. Rinse the sprouts in cool water; drain them. (I drain the sprouts and let them germinate in the same colander.) Sample a seed. Repeat the procedure according to instructions. It is as simple as that. In a day and a half or two or three, depending on how you like them, you have sprouts ready to eat. What you do not eat immediately or use in cooking pack loosely in a plastic bag or container and store it in your refrigerator's crisper section for a few days. It is so easy to grow them there really is not much need for storing them.

Easy to Use

You will find Spelt Sprouts used in a variety of recipes in *Spelt Healthy!* May I encourage you to try the Spelt Sproutcakes on the Morning Menu or sprinkle them in a salad (Waldorf Turkey Salad). You may be happily surprised at the fresh and flavorful burst of sweetness and sunshine that comes from a Spelt seed. They are nature's miniature candy bars that you can eat by the handful, and feel good for a long time after eating and know they are doing good things for you. That is a good exchange.

Spelt Grünkern

("Green Kernel")

Parching green (immature) grain to eat is an ancient tradition in the Middle East and North Africa where the roasted grain is *frikeh*. That tradition extended into Eastern Europe, the Ukraine and Germany where it is *Grünkern* made from Spelt.

This is a tradition that goes back thousands of years. Parched grain is mentioned in the Bible, for example, Joshua 5:11: *And they did eat of the produce of the land on the morrow after the Passover, unleavened cakes and parched grain, in the selfsame day.* In Syria and Tunisia, the practice of making Frikeh (with Durum wheat or barley) is still being carried out by traditional methods because of its continued popularity. In Germany and some regions of Switzerland, Spelt Grünkern is still being made and sold as a gourmet food for use in soup, bread and side dishes.

Spelt Grünkern is now here thanks to the efforts of micro-farming maestro, Anthony Boutard of Ayres Creek Farm in Gaston, Oregon

Mr. Boutard suggests parched green grain is more than a way of preserving crops. It may always have been a treat, a delicacy of ancient times much as it is today.

It is a bit nutty, chewy and sweet with a slightly dusky taste that imparts lingering, wispy flavor. It is highly nutritious to be certain for along with protein, Grünkern is high in fiber and vital minerals such as potassium.

Mr. Boutard follows age-old by-hand practices to produce Grünkern. The delectable taste comes from harvesting the Spelt while it is green (the milk stage). At Ayers Creek Farm they char the grain heads over a fire made from the Spelt straw. The charred Spelt heads are then threshed, sieved, winnowed and dried for a short time.

Grünkern is easy to prepare and has many cooking applications. Cook it as you would rice (see the Tunisian Rice recipe). It works well in combination with rice in other dishes or as a stuffing for squash. You might try it in an omelet.

Please see the *Resources* section for contact information or visit the Hillsdale Farmers' Market in Portland, Oregon and look for Ayers Creek Farm.

Caesar Salad with Spelt Croutons

The Caesar is still my favorite salad. I first learned to make it many moons ago in a beautiful old and seasoned Mexican wooden salad bowl. With the bowl came the wonderful southwest story that an Italian chef invented the Caesar on the spot at his restaurant in Tijuana, Mexico during the 1920s. It turned out to be true. Viva Caesar Cardini! Day old Spelt French Bread makes fine croutons for Caesar Salad and taste fabulous freshly prepared. With a little organization, in half an hour you will be making the king of salads fresh at your tableside just like the original.

Blood Type: All types leave out mustard, black pepper, Tabasco and Worchestershire or travel the moderate road and eat these condiments sparingly as in this recipe. Substitute Pecorino Romano and leave out the anchovies if they aren't for you. • **Prep time:** 30 min • **Cook time:** 1 minute 10 sec • **Yield:** 4 servings

Ingredients

1   large head romaine lettuce
2–2½ cups Spelt croutons
2   large garlic cloves, minced
dash of sea salt
3   Tbsp Olive oil (preferably Virgin)
1   2 oz tin anchovies in Olive oil, select 2 for bowl and 8 for salad (optional)
1   large clove garlic
2   eggs, room temperature
3   Tbsp fresh lemon juice
1   tsp dry mustard OR prepared such as Dijon
several dashes of Tabasco (optional)
1   tsp Worcestershire sauce (optional)
1   tsp freshly ground black pepper
1   tsp coarsely ground sea salt
1   tsp garlic powder
⅓   cup Olive oil (preferably Virgin)
½   cup finely grated Parmesan, Asiago or Pecorino Romano

1.   Trim any discolored leaves from romaine so all the lettuce is fresh and crisp. If making for two, discard some of the tougher outer leaves. Wash; pat dry. Cut leaves crosswise into strips of a good size for eating, snipping in two where necessary. Place romaine in refrigerator and chill for 30 minutes.

2.   Prepare the croutons with 2 cloves minced garlic and sea salt using skillet or oven method (See section *Croutons and Crumbs*). Set aside to cool.

3.   Prepare salad bowl (preferably wooden as it absorbs the flavors of garlic and anchovies). Peel a large juicy garlic clove and rub against side of bowl with back of a wooden spoon. Remove the garlic mash. Repeat procedure with 2 of the anchovies. Leave anchovy pieces in bowl. Mince the remaining anchovies and place in bowl or leave whole to top individual salads as desired.

4.   Place 2 eggs in boiling water to coddle them. Cook for 1 minute 10 seconds exactly. Remove to cool water immediately.

5. In small bowl, mix together fresh lemon juice, dry mustard or Dijon mustard, dashes of Tabasco and/or a tsp of Worcestershire, black pepper, sea salt and garlic powder. Crack the cooled eggs and add to the bowl. Whisk to blend. Drizzle olive oil into bowl, steadily but slowly, whisking all the while to create a smooth creamy dressing. Do not add oil all at once or dressing will separate.

6. Pour half the dressing into salad bowl. Add half the Romaine, half the cheese, half the croutons. Toss. Add remaining Romaine, cheese and croutons and toss again. Serve from bowl and place on chilled plates or in wooden salad bowls.

Panzanella Salad
with Spelt Italian Bread

Traditional recipe for making a garden fresh salad with sun-ripened tomatoes and day-old Italian or Roman Bread. The Roasted Garlic and Mozzarella Baguette is very good in Panzanella as well. Add fresh zucchini or summer squash to the recipe for full garden flavors. If the soaked bread is not to your taste, use large *toasted* and seasoned croutons made from one of the specialty breads like Brundisi Pesto.

Blood Type: Not rated • Prep time: 10 min • Cook time: None • Yield: 4 salads

Ingredients

10–12 oz day-old Spelt Italian or Roman Bread (4 cups)
OR use large toasted croutons made from same or other Spelt bread(s)
2–4 cloves garlic, minced (to taste)
1 Tbsp dried, crushed thyme OR 3 Tbsp fresh
1 tsp dried, crushed oregano
¼ cup red wine vinegar
¾ cup Olive oil (preferably Extra Virgin)
1 pound sun-ripened tomatoes
fresh basil to taste
¼ cup red onions
¼ cup soft goat cheese or soft mozzarella (cubed or sliced)
salt and pepper to taste

1. Soak slices of Italian bread in cold water; squeeze the excess moisture out of the bread. Place in a mixing bowl or, use large toasted Spelt Italian Bread, Medi Crostini or Brundisi Pesto Bread croutons (see section *Croutons and Crumbs*).

2. Sprinkle garlic, thyme and oregano over the bread. Salt and pepper to taste.

3. Chop ripe tomatoes into wedges and add to the bowl. Add the basil, red onions and cheese.

4. Combine the oil and vinegar and pour over the salad. Toss.

5. Set Panzanella aside at room temperature for several hours prior to serving.

Spelt Rotini and Turmeric Salad

Under 30 minute dish. VitaSpelt Spelt Rotini is available in the health-food section of many good grocery stores along with natural food stores. This is a good side dish for sandwiches or picnics or as part of a larger salad with fresh greens and lemon.

Blood Type: See recommendations below • Prep time/cook time: 30 minutes • Yield: 4 servings

Ingredients

8	oz (1 box) VitaSpelt Spelt Rotini Pasta
⅓	cup Olive oil (Extra Virgin, Golden or Light)
¼	tsp turmeric
½	tsp paprika
¼	tsp garlic powder
¼	tsp dried lemon peel
2–3	Tbsp fresh basil OR tarragon OR 1 tsp each, dried, crushed
¼	tsp dulse granules (optional) OR sea salt to taste (optional)
4	oz (¼ cup) pimentos, diced
½	cup Italian (flat-leaf) parsley, finely chopped
½	cup celery, diced
1	cup soft Mozzarella cheese, cubed
1	egg, boiled, diced

Optional ingredients according to blood type:

⅓	cup Green olives, chopped (Type A, AB, O) B omit
½	cup fresh bell pepper (yellow, green) chopped (Type B, O) A, AB, omit
½	cup roasted red peppers + 1 Tbsp pepper juice (optional Type B, O)

1. Follow cooking directions for Spelt Rotini on package. Cook minimum time. The rotini should be al dente.

2. As pasta cooks, chop the vegetables and cube the cheese. Measure dry ingredients.

3. Drain the pasta in colander. While warm, place in large bowl. Stir in the olive oil and the turmeric, paprika, garlic powder, lemon peel, fresh basil or tarragon. Add the olives and fresh or roasted peppers (optional ingredients). Stir. Mix in the pimentos, parsley, celery, cheese and diced egg. Stir and serve at room temperature or place, covered, in refrigerator to season.

Singla Salad

This zesty lime based salad is a wonderfully versatile meal that can be made with steak (as the version here) or with prawns, tuna steak, lamb, chicken or turkey. The Spelt croutons should be especially crisp and herbed. It's a mouth-watering adventure in many textures and tastes, wonderfully suited to Blood-type eating. Excellent for al fresco entertaining. This is a good salad for variety breads such as the Brundisi Pesto and Calabrese breads.

PLAN AHEAD MEAL. Assemble Singla Salad in stages: 1. Make the marinade/dressing. Marinate the meat ahead of time. 2. Make the Spelt croutons. 3. Broil meat and vegetables. 4. While broiling, make the green salad.

Blood Type: All (Meat and Pepper according to Type)
Prep time: 15 min (+ time for marinating) • Cook time: 15–20 min • Yield: 4 servings

Ingredients

1 pound lean steak, ¾" to 1" thick (sirloin, New York) or other meat/fish/fowl

Marinade/Dressing (makes about ½ cup)

3–4 large limes, freshly squeezed (about 4 Tbsp)

5 Tbsp garlic/shallot mixture (see *Topping and Fillings* under *Many Small Things*) OR 5 garlic cloves, minced and mixed w/5 Tbsp Olive oil

¼ tsp ground ginger

1 tsp fresh ground pepper (optional)

1 tsp coarse sea salt

½ tsp ground cumin

2 tsp red pepper flakes (optional)

OR 1 fresh jalapeño, finely diced (optional)

With Steak in Broiler

1 large red onion, quartered

1 medium zucchini, ¼" thick slices

For the Salad

½ cup soft goat cheese, crumbled

1 head Romaine lettuce or mixture of greens according to taste

Tomatoes or other vegetables such as steamed asparagus
Seasoned Spelt Croutons

1. **Marinade/Dressing.** In small bowl, combine the ingredients for marinade/dressing; separate into two equal portions. Set one portion aside in small covered container for dressing. Refrigerate. Smear the marinade portion onto both sides of the steak and place in plastic bag or shallow covered dish and refrigerate for a minimum of 3 hours. Best when marinated 24 hours.

2. **Steak.** When it is time to cook—remove marinated steak and the dressing from the refrigerator. Heat oven to Broil (500° F.) Arrange steak, onion and zucchini on broiler pan rack spooning leftover marinade from meat over onions and zucchini; broil 7–8 minutes. Turn; broil additional time according to cut of beef. Remove from oven and set the meat and vegetables aside to cool slightly.

3. **Salad.** Toss the salad greens and cold vegetables with the crumbled goat cheese and herbed Spelt croutons. Place on large serving platter or individual chilled plates. Arrange the grilled vegetables on top of the salad. Thinly slice the meat and place alongside the grilled vegetables. Drizzle the reserved dressing over all. Serve immediately.

Turkey Waldorf Salad
with Spelt Sprouts

Fresh, crisp, slightly sweet, the Turkey Waldorf is accented by the crunchiness of fresh Spelt Sprouts. This is a fine luncheon salad placed in a Spelt bread bowl or large spelt tart shells. Or serve on bed of greens with quick breads from the **Bread Basket section** such as Carrot Nut Bread or Cherried Plum Bread.

Blood Type: B, AB, O (mayo) • Prep time: 20 min • Cook time: 5 min for walnuts • Yield: 4 servings

Ingredients

1   cup walnut halves
2   cups (10 oz) cooked turkey, thinly sliced or cubed
3–4 Gala or other apples such as Red Delicious sufficient for 3 cups
1   cup (4 oz) diced celery
½   cup raisins (optional)
1   cup home-style mayonnaise or vanilla goat's milk or other flavored/unflavored yogurt
4   Tbsp fresh Spelt Sprouts
1   Tbsp fresh lemon juice
dash ground cardamom or cinnamon (optional)
fresh ground black pepper (optional)
salt to taste (optional)

Salad greens
Spelt bread bowls or serve in large tart shells (optional)

1. Preheat oven to 325° F. Spread walnuts on small rimmed pan and toast in preheated oven for about 5 minutes, just until they are lightly toasted. Let cool.

2. Core and dice the apples. In a large bowl, mix the mayonnaise (or yogurt) and lemon juice.

3. Stir in the cooled walnuts, turkey, apples, celery, raisins (optional) and Spelt Sprouts, toss well. Season with a dash of ground cardamom or cinnamon, a grinding of black pepper and a dash of salt (optional).

4. Place on bed of chilled salad greens or scoop into Spelt bread bowls or tart shells.

Sweet and Sour Salad

An alternative to the vinegar and sugar recipe often used for wilted lettuce and other salads, this is a simple and good dressing to serve warm over baby spinach or other small, mixed greens with crisp Spelt croutons. Use as a marinade by setting aside the roasted pine nuts and sprinkling the nuts over the food, such as white fish, after grilling.

Blood Type: All types use lemon juice in place of vinegar
Prep time: 10 min • Cook time: 4–5 min • Yield: ½ cup

Ingredients

¼   cup pine nuts, chopped
2   shallots (about 2 Tbsp) peeled, thinly sliced
2   tsp dried, crushed tarragon (or other herbs such as savory or a blend) OR
2   tablespoons fresh, minced tarragon leaves or other fresh herbs
6   Tbsp Olive oil (preferably Extra Virgin)
1½ Tbsp balsamic or red wine vinegar OR fresh lemon juice
1   tsp sugar
½   tsp sea salt
fresh baby spinach or other small, mixed greens
1   cup toasted Spelt croutons

1. Coarsely chop the pine nuts in processor fitted with metal blade. Set small sauté pan over medium heat; add nuts to pan and toast about 4 minutes until light brown. Stir occasionally. Remove from pan to cool. Wipe pan with paper towel.

2. Place pan back over medium heat adding 1 Tbsp of the olive oil. Add the shallots and sauté lightly, about 2 minutes. Remove from pan.

3. In a small bowl, blend the tarragon, remaining oil, vinegar, sugar and salt. Stir in the nuts and the shallots and toss with greens. Add croutons. Serve.

Asparagus al Limon

Steamed asparagus with fresh lemon, Spelt breadcrumbs and a sprinkling of cheese

Blood Type: A, B, AB, O (A, AB use oil)
Prep time: 10 min (allow cooking time for asparagus) • Cook time: 5 mins • Yield: 4 servings

Ingredients

12–16 ounces fresh asparagus spears, cooked
  OR
8   oz frozen asparagus spears (1 pkg), cooked
¼   cup Pecorino Romano, Greek Kasseri, Parmesan or other hard cheese, finely grated
2   Tbsp Olive oil or melted butter
½   cup dried, seasoned Spelt bread crumbs
juice of one fresh lemon (about 3 Tbsp)

1. Preheat oven to 400° F.

2. Drain the cooked asparagus. Place in a single layer on an ovenproof serving platter. Sprinkle with the finely grated cheese and breadcrumbs then drizzle with olive oil or melted butter. Spoon the fresh lemon juice over all. Place platter in oven on center rack and cook for 5 minutes. Serve warm.

Creamy Artichokes Side Dish, Dip or Topping

Exceptionally easy to make, this is a savory dish with a variety of applications. It is one of the first things to disappear from the buffet table and makes a tasty high-fiber side dish with roasts or steak dinners and with game hens or baked chicken.

Blood Type: Not rated • Prep time: 10 min • Cook time: 30 min • Yield: 12 servings

Ingredients

2   cans (13¾ oz/ 8½ oz drained) Quartered Artichoke Hearts

1½ cups semi-soft Mozzarella, grated (divided 1 cup, ½ cup)

1   cup mayonnaise

2   tsp fresh lemon juice

1   tsp celery seed

½   tsp powdered garlic

⅓   cup dried or toasted Spelt breadcrumbs, finely processed

1. Preheat oven to 375° F (350° F for glass).

2. Break apart or roughly chop the artichoke quarters into slightly smaller pieces. Add to large mixing bowl.

3. Stir in the mayonnaise, lemon, celery seed and garlic. Add 1 cup of the grated cheese and mix thoroughly with other ingredients.

4. Spread in 9" well-oiled baking pan or a casserole dish. Sprinkle with the Spelt crumbs and the remaining grated cheese.

5. Place on center rack of preheated oven and bake until top is crisp and golden brown and mixture is bubbling. Serve warm or at room temperature.

Portabella Mushrooms New Orleans
(Stuffed Mushrooms)

This is a variation on Oysters Rockefeller, which originated in New Orleans and my father always prepared on Christmas Eve. Minus the oysters and plus the mushrooms, this can be eaten by all blood types. The stuffing is wonderful on crostini or as a base for eggs or for stuffing fish. Excellent first course for gatherings or a light vegetarian meal.

Blood Type: A, B, AB, O • Prep time: 15–20 min • Cook time: 40–50 min • Yield: 4 servings

Ingredients

12 oz (4 large, 5") Portabella Mushroom caps
6 oz (1 cup) Baby Bella mushrooms
3–5 Tbsp Olive oil
3 cloves garlic, minced
¼ tsp dried crushed thyme
¼ tsp dried crushed marjoram
¼ tsp dried crushed oregano (optional)
⅛ tsp dried lemon peel (optional)
salt and pepper to taste
⅓ cup (1 stalk) celery, diced
½ cup sweet onion, finely chopped
1¼ cups toasted, seasoned Spelt bread cubes
2 cups fresh baby spinach, chopped
½ cup vegetable broth or from vegetable bouillon cubes
½ cup semi-soft mozzarella, grated

1. Gently wash the Portabella caps and pat dry. Set aside. Fine chop the Baby Bellas. Place in a mixing bowl; set aside.

2. Heat 2 Tbsp olive oil in skillet set on medium low heat. Add the 4 Portabella caps and sauté for 2 minutes; place, cap down, in a lightly greased casserole dish or on a baking sheet, using stem as a handle to coat cap with oil. Set aside.

3. Add another Tbsp olive oil to the pan. Add the garlic, dried herbs, celery, onion and chopped Baby Bella mushrooms. Sauté, stirring frequently, until the celery is tender and onions are transparent. Add the Spelt bread cubes, toss and stir until they brown and pick up oil from the pan. Transfer mixture to mixing bowl that contains the Baby Bella mushrooms.

4. Add 2 Tbsp olive oil to the warm skillet. Add the chopped spinach and sauté for 2 minutes; add the broth and cook for an additional minute.

5. Preheat oven to 350° F; set an oven rack in middle position. Spoon spinach and broth from skillet; mix with the vegetables, herbs and bread. With a tablespoon, mound equal portions of the mixture onto the bottoms ("spoke" side) of the Portabella caps. Sprinkle with grated cheese and drizzle lightly (1 tsp each) with olive oil. Bake for 40–50 minutes until the tops are golden brown and the Portabellas are tender, not dry. Serve warm.

Spaghetti Squash with Herbed Breadcrumbs

Instead of pasta, try Spaghetti Squash as a side dish for dinner. Try crumbs from one of the herbed bread recipes or create a new herb mixture with plain dried Spelt breadcrumbs.

Blood Type: A, B, AB, O • Prep time: 5 minutes • Cook time: 45 minutes • Yield: 4 servings

Ingredients

1   spaghetti squash
¼   cup dried Spelt breadcrumbs

Herbs for Seasoning … Use your favorite mixture or try mixing the fresh crumbs with:
½   tsp celery salt or Dash
1   tsp fresh lemon zest, grated
½   tsp dried, crushed basil
1   tsp Mexican safflower (optional)
1   Tbsp Olive oil + additional for drizzling (OR other vegetable oil)

1. Preheat oven to 350° F. Wash the squash. Trim the stem. Cut squash in half lengthwise. Cut in half again so there are four equal quarters.

2. Place the quarters upside down (peel up) in a casserole dish. Add water to ½" depth and bake, uncovered, for 30 minutes.

3. Prepare the fresh herbed breadcrumbs mixing with celery salt, fresh lemon zest, basil and Mexican safflower. Stir in 1 Tbsp oil and moisten all ingredients.

4. Remove squash from oven. Turn the quarters right side up. Drizzle each with olive oil and sprinkle with the herbed breadcrumbs.

5. Return squash to the oven on lowest rack and cook 15–20 minutes longer until the squash is tender and the crumbs are browned but not dark.

Tunisian Rice with Spelt Sprouts

A savory rice dish that stands on its own, but is also excellent stirred into a frittata or as a stuffing for squash or peppers.

Blood Type: A, B, AB, O • Prep time: 5 min • Cook time: 45 min • Yield: about 5 cups

Ingredients

2 cups short grain brown rice
2 cups beef broth or stock (or chicken, turkey or vegetable stock or broth)
1¾ cups water
1 vegetable bouillon cube
1 medium size sweet onion (about 1 cup), finely chopped
2 Tbsp Olive oil
4 oz diced pimentos
½ cup Spelt Sprouts

1. Place large saucepan with tight-fitting lid on medium high heat. Add olive oil and heat until haze forms over oil. Add the rice and bouillon cube and sauté, continually stirring, until crackling hot. Add 1¾ cups water and bring to full boil. Reduce heat to medium and boil for 5 minutes.

2. Reduce heat to low and stir in the onions, pimentos and sprouts. Cover tightly. Cook on low heat for one hour. Stir at 15, 30 and 45 minutes, keeping covered at all other times. Remove from heat, let stand covered, for 10 minutes. Stir. Serve warm or at room temperature. Refrigerate or freeze the leftovers for use in omelets, as stuffing or a quick side dish for a meal.

Sweet Potato Fritters

Courtesy of Dr. J. Peter D'Adamo; this recipe was adapted from the recipe in his 1998 book, *Cook Right for Your Type*. Sweet potatoes are a Vitamin A-packed treat in general and a good substitute for the white potato in particular. We use Sweet Potato Fritters instead of hash browns in the morning or potatoes at night. Serve as accompaniment to grilled meats and roasts or poultry and fish.

Blood Type: B, AB, O • Prep time: 10 min • Cook time: 15–20 min (two skillets) • Yield: 14 patties (3")

Ingredients

1   large sweet potato or 4 cups, peeled and grated
½   red onion or ½ cup, grated or fine chopped
2   eggs, lightly beaten
1   Tbsp Olive or other vegetable oil
⅓   cup Whole Grain Spelt flour
¼   tsp salt
¼   cup Olive or canola oil for cooking

1.   Set a large skillet over medium heat; add 2 Tbsp olive oil to the pan and let it heat.

2.   Wash the sweet potato; pat dry and peel. Grate with food processor or with box grater.

Add grated sweet potato and grated onion to a large mixing bowl. Combine with 1 Tbsp olive oil, the lightly beaten eggs, salt and the Whole Grain Spelt flour. Use large slotted spoon or your hands to incorporate all ingredients. Form patties. If the mixture is too loose, adjust by adding a bit more flour and remixing.

3.   Place patties in skillet being careful not to crowd because it makes turning difficult. Cook 4–5 minutes or until golden brown; turn, cook other side until golden brown. Place on paper towels to drain then transfer to plate and keep warm in 250° F oven until all are cooked. Serve warm.

weet Potato Puffs

These are soufflé sweet potatoes, sweet and delicate deep orange colored "flowers". The puffs are very easy to make and are a different, delightful accompaniment to seafood and poultry meals.

Blood Type: B, AB, O • Prep time: 5 min • Cook time: 20 min

Ingredients

1   Garnet sweet potato (about 1 pound), peeled and boiled
¼   cup Whole Grain Spelt flour
¼   cup White Spelt flour
½   tsp salt
2   Tbsp Olive or other vegetable oil
4   Tbsp warm water
1   egg white, beaten stiff
vegetable oil for frying

1. Heat thin layer of vegetable oil (⅛" inch) in large skillet set on moderately high heat for frying.

2. Mash the boiled sweet potato. Mix in the Spelt Flours, salt and olive oil. Mix. Add warm water and blend. Fold beaten egg white into batter.

3. Drop batter by mounded tablespoonfuls into hot oil, without crowding, and cook for 6–8 minutes until the bottoms begin to caramelize, the edges brown and tops are set. Drain on paper towels. Keep warm until serving.

Shredded Sweet Potato
The Alternative to Coconut

The process requires a little work but it is worth it. The sweet potato stays moist and works like coconut and adds natural sweetness and texture to cookie recipes, coffeecake topping and breads.

Blood Type: B, AB, O • Prep time: 5 min • Cook time: 70–75 min • Yield: 2 cups

Ingredients

1   large Garnet Sweet Potato (1 pound)
½   cup granulated sugar (optional)

1. Add 2 quarts water to a large saucepan; boil. Reduce to simmering boil.

2. Wash, peel and finely grate the sweet potato. If you have a box grater, use it instead of processor. It makes a better shred for this purpose. Place grated sweet potato in water; cook for 2–3 minutes until tender but not mushy.

3. Drain in colander; spread out on double layer of paper towels placed over wire racks. Heat the oven to 280° F. Cover a large rimmed baking sheet with parchment. Place grated sweet potato in large bowl and sprinkle with the sugar, toss. Spread evenly on baking pan in single layer.

4. Bake on middle rack for 15 minutes. Toss and stir. Continue this process of tossing and stirring, separating the pieces the best you can, every 15 minutes until the water droplets dry from the pan and the sweet potato bits are significantly drier but still moist and flexible (70–75 minutes). They will lose about half their volume during this process.

5. Remove from oven. Set pan on wire rack. Toss and stir. When cool, put in plastic storage bag and place in freezer. Bring to room temperature before adding to recipe. Use as you would coconut.

Zucchini Fries

These are a wonderful replacement for French fries and great for entertaining. You make the recipe in two stages much like frying chicken or fish. Flour the zucchini, roll fries in egg, coat them again with cheese/flour mixture, dry them then fry them.

Blood Type: A, B, AB, O (A, AB and O use Pecorino Romano cheese)
Prep time: 40 min (including drying time) • Cook time: about 30 min • Yield: 5–6 dozen

Ingredients

4   medium zucchini (7–8 inches long)
½   cup White Spelt flour
3   eggs, room temp
3¼ Tbsp water
2   cups White Spelt flour (divided 1½, ½)
1½ cups Parmesan cheese, finely grated OR Pecorino Romano
½   tsp garlic powder or other seasonings
vegetable oil for deep frying

1. Preparation: Place ½ cup flour on a plate. Set aside. Beat the eggs with 3¼ Tbsp water; set aside. Combine 1½ cups White Spelt flour, garlic powder or other seasonings with the finely grated cheese and place on rimmed cookie sheet. Place a double layer of paper towels on countertop or on wire racks.

2. Wash zucchini; pat dry. Slice off zucchini tips and cut zucchini in half. Cut into narrow strips like French fries. Sprinkle the fries with salt; roll each fry in the plain flour (the half cup on plate) so each strip has a light coating of flour. Shake so excess flour falls away. Add any remaining flour to the flour/cheese mixture on pan.

3. Dip 5–6 fries at a time in the egg; roll in seasoned flour/cheese mixture. Set on paper towels and allow them to dry for half an hour. Line another rimmed baking sheet with paper towels.

4. Place 2–3 inches of vegetable oil in a heavy saucepan and heat oil to 375° F. Preheat oven to 250° F.

5. Place 5–6 zucchini strips at a time in the hot oil and fry until coating is a light golden brown and crisp (about 3 minutes per batch). Remove fries with tongs or slotted spoon and drain fries on paper towels covering rimmed baking sheet. Place in oven to keep warm. Serve in paper cups lined with napkins or mounded in napkin-lined baskets.

Zucchini Fritters

Change the cheese, change the taste in this recipe. Greek Kasseri Sheep cheese or Greek dried goat cheese provide a saltier, dryer taste but expand the range of these terrific fritters. This is another of those wonderful handy recipes that make humdrum meals special. Zucchini is a fine, nutritious, full of fiber, substitute for potatoes.

Blood Type: B (any cheese below); A, AB, O (Mozzarella or Pecorino Romano) • Prep time: 10 minutes (allow half hour for zucchini to dry) • Cook time: 30 minutes (6 at a time) • Yield: 18 fritters

Ingredients

3   cups zucchini, unpeeled, shredded (about 1½ lb or 4 medium)
2   eggs, room temperature
½   cup Whole Grain Spelt flour
1   cup semi-soft Mozzarella, coarsely grated
or   ½ cup Parmesan, Asiago, Romano, Kasseri or Pecorino Romano cheese, grated
1   tsp celery salt or Dulse granules
ground pepper to taste (optional)
vegetable oil for frying

Prep time: 10 minutes (allow half hour for zucchini to dry) • Cook time: 30 minutes (6 at a time; 12" skillet 10 at a time) • Yield: 18 fritters

1. Grate the zucchini, sprinkle lightly with salt, spread out on several layers of paper towels. Set aside for half an hour so excess moisture is released from the fresh zucchini.

2. Beat two eggs in large mixing bowl. Add the Whole Spelt flour and the grated cheese. Mix.

3. Blot the zucchini with paper towels then add it to the egg, flour and cheese mixture. Add celery salt. Add ground pepper to taste.

4. Heat vegetable oil in skillet (very thin layer). Drop mounded tablespoons of batter into the skillet and flatten each mound with the back of the spoon. Do not crowd or they will be hard to turn. Brown on one side (about 5 minutes), turn and brown other side.

5. Set on paper towels to drain and keep warm (in oven at lowest setting) until serving. These make very good leftovers either cold or reheated and store very well in the refrigerator.

On the Run and Working Out: Food to Fuel Increased Mental and Physical Activity

"Food is the fuel that runs your body. For it to run most efficiently you need the best, most nutritionally complete, type of fuel. Spelt is an excellent energy source packed with vitamins, fiber, antioxidants and phytochemicals. Carrying a high amino acid content, Spelt is great for sparing lean body mass. It provides high quality intake in relation to total calories and carbohydrates."

Don Ray, Certified Personal Trainer & Nutrition Counselor

Hais ("Traveler's Food")

Evil Don's Energy Bar

Applesauce Pecan Muffins

Hais
"Traveler's Food"

Hais was an ancient life-sustaining travelers' whole food across Southwest Asia. The combination of ingredients is so basic it continues to this day in a variety of recipes from energy bars and granola to the Date Layer Bars in this book to popular cookies. Bikers, hikers, athletes and active others will find this little bar a long-burning energy booster that is easy to pack and carry.

Blood Type: A, B, AB, O • Prep time: 15–20 min • Cook time: None • Yield: 12 2 oz bars

Ingredients for 12 2 oz bars

1¾ cups dried, fine Whole/White or Mixed Spelt breadcrumbs, unseasoned

1 cup dates, pitted, chopped (refrigerator temperature)

½ cup Spring water

¾ cup dates, pitted, chopped (refrigerator temperature)

¾ cup walnuts

⅔ cup slivered almonds

¾ cup pecans

1 Tbsp + 1 tsp walnut oil or Light Olive oil

¼ cup Confectioners' sugar for rolling

1. Heat oven to 325° F. Place walnuts, almonds and pecans in metal pie pan or on small rimmed baking sheet. Toast nuts for 10 minutes, stirring twice, until the almonds just start to brown. Remove from oven and cool.

2. To bowl of food processor fitted with metal blade, add 1 cup pitted dates and ½ cup Spring water. Process into slurry. Remove dates from processor bowl and set aside.

3. Into processor bowl, place ¾ cup chopped dates and cooled nuts. With motor running, add the Spelt breadcrumbs and the oil until mixture begins to form dough. Add the date slurry and process until mixture coheres.

4. Remove from processor bowl. Oil your hands lightly and form into 12 cylinders 2½" long and 1" thick. Roll in Confectioners' sugar. (The reason for rolling the bars is to keep them from sticking to the wrapping and to prevent your fingers from getting sticky when you eat them, a problem with many biking or backpacking foods.) Wrap each bar individually in plastic wrap and store bars in an airtight container in the refrigerator. Take out a few when needed. Kept wrapped and sealed, they will keep for an extended period.

Evil Don's Energy Bar

The Story of Evil Don

Don Ray is such an exacting trainer and taskmaster that many of his clients refer to him, affectionately, as *Evil Don*. He is highly regarded as a professional who always delivers results if the client does his/her part. An advocate of Chris Carmichael's *Food for Fitness* method (see *Bibliography*), his work with a client begins with a real examination of "intake." He rates the Evil Don Energy Bar as "high quality fuel."

One of the goals in writing the *Spelt Healthy!* series is to make a variety of foods that provide even, long-lasting fuel for physical and mental stamina. A great benefit of Whole Food Cooking with Spelt is the diminution of the spikes that are so hard on the body—that cycle of hyper-drive, crankiness, crash and sleep. For example, by substituting nonfat dry milk for some of the sugar, empty calories go down and the calcium and protein content go up. Vary this Energy Bar to your own taste, Blood Type and energy requirements by adding different nuts and dried fruit.

Blood Type: Not rated • Prep time: 10 min • Cook time: 25–30 min
Yield: 24 2" x 2" bars (approx 1.25 oz each)

Ingredients

1 cup whole or coarse chopped, toasted walnuts or other nuts
¾ cup Rolled Spelt
¼ cup Light Olive oil or other vegetable oil to taste (walnut, flax, canola)
½ cup brown sugar, firmly packed
½ cup light molasses
1½ cups Whole Grain Spelt flour
¼ cup nonfat dry milk
1½ tsp baking powder
½ tsp soda
½ tsp salt
1 tsp ground ginger
1 cup milk or soymilk
1½ cups dried, reconstituted fruit bits such as pineapple, apricots, dates, tart cherries

1. In processor fitted with metal blade, finely chop ½ cup toasted walnuts with ¾ cup Rolled Spelt for 8–10 seconds. Set aside. Finely chop remaining ½ cup walnuts; set aside. Preheat oven to 350° F.

2. In large mixing bowl, cream the oil, brown sugar and molasses.

3. In medium bowl, combine 1 cup Whole Grain Spelt flour, nonfat dry milk, baking powder, soda, salt and ginger. Whisk. Add to the creamed mixture alternately with milk (or soymilk); blend.

4. Stir in the Rolled Spelt/nut mixture and the chopped mixed fruit. Spoon into lightly greased 13" x 9" x 2" baking pan and spread evenly with back of spoon. Sprinkle with remaining ½ cup finely chopped walnuts.

5. Place in preheated moderate oven (350° F) and bake for 25–30 minutes. Test by inserting wooden toothpick into center. If toothpick comes out clean and the sides have shrunk slightly from the edges of the pan, the bars are cooked. Remove from oven and place on wire rack to cool. Cut into 24 2" x 2" bars. Stored in an airtight container at room temperature, they will stay fresh for weeks. If frozen, allow them to thaw at room temperature for 20–30 minutes prior to eating or stick in your pack and go.

Applesauce Pecan Muffins

Luscious, moist and savory muffins with a delicate, textured taste and heavenly baking aroma. This is the perfect muffin for people on the go.

Blood Type: B (A, O, AB use soy milk) Soy milk works very well in this recipe and complements the taste.
Prep time: 5 min • Cook time: 20–25 min • Yield: 12 (2 oz)

Ingredients

2¼ cups + 3 Tbsp + 1 tsp White Spelt flour
1   tsp baking soda
½   tsp baking powder
¼   tsp salt
1   tsp ground cinnamon (or cardamom)
    (Type B use cardamom)
¼   tsp ground nutmeg (or mace)
¾   cup chopped nuts (pecans, walnuts or other)
1   cup unsweetened applesauce
¾   cup granulated sugar
⅓   cup vegetable oil
2   eggs, room temperature
3   Tbsp milk or soymilk
Dark brown sugar for sprinkling

1. Preheat oven to 350° F. Set paper baking cups in muffin pan(s) or lightly oil the pan wells even if non-stick variety.

2. In a large mixing bowl, combine the White Spelt flour, soda, baking powder, salt and spices. Whisk together. Add the applesauce, sugar, oil, eggs and milk and blend until all ingredients are thoroughly incorporated. Do not beat; mixture should be rough, not smooth. Stir in the chopped nuts.

3. Spoon batter into each of the 12 muffin cups so each is ⅔ full. Sprinkle tops of each with a teaspoon dark brown sugar.

4. Bake on middle rack of preheated moderate (350° F) oven for 20–25 minutes. Tops will be a shiny, deep golden brown. The taste will continue to develop—if they last that long. Stored in an airtight container, these muffins will remain fresh and moist for several days; if frozen, they will keep for weeks.

Afternoon Tea or Coffee Break

Lemon Shorties

Cherry Almond Biscotti

Honey Scones

Maple Scones

Cranberry and Rolled Spelt
(or Oat) Scones

Blueberry Lemon Scones

Paradell (Sweet Crepe with Apples)

Lemon Shorties

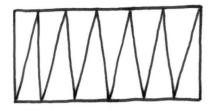

I wanted a Euro style biscuit that fits on a saucer and complements green tea so I created the Lemon Shorty. This is a tart, crunchy cross between shortbread and biscotti. Its triangle shape fits snugly on the saucer with cup and tastes great with many things besides tea. By using turbinado sugar, you get a crisp sweet tart taste fully developed with Spelt. Shorties are a breeze to make and require no leavening.

Blood Type: B, O • Prep time: 10 min (allow for toasting nuts) • Cook time: 25–30 min • Yield: 12 slices

Ingredients

¼ cup chopped, toasted pine nuts
½ cup turbinado sugar + additional for rolling
½ cup Whole Grain Spelt flour
1 cup Spelt Pastry flour
½ cup (1 stick) butter, softened
1 Tbsp fresh lemon zest, finely grated and/or ⅛ tsp food grade lemon oil (recommended)
egg white beaten with 1 Tbsp tepid water
turbinado sugar for rolling

1. **In Advance:** Toast chopped pine nuts by placing on rimmed baking sheet in preheated 350° F oven for 6–8 minutes. Leave oven on after taking nuts out to cool. Have the indispensable transparent plastic kitchen ruler handy to help with cutting the dough.

2. Combine ½ cup turbinado sugar with the butter in a large mixing bowl and cream.

3. Add the Whole and Pastry Spelt flours and the lemon zest and/or oil (stand mixer, low speed) to make a soft dough. Do not over-mix; this process takes a very short time.

4. Turn dough out on lightly floured surface. Pat into an oblong pan 8" long, 4" wide and about ½" high. With sharp knife, cut the dough into 12 elongated triangles. See picture above.

5. Brush the top of each slice with egg white/water. Sprinkle turbinado sugar onto top of each slice. Gently set pieces one inch apart on an oiled or parchment covered (preferable) rimmed cookie sheet. Bake 25 minutes or until tops start to turn golden brown. Remove from oven. Shift parchment with Shorties on it directly to wire rack or let them cool on pan for a minute and then shift them individually with a spatula. The Lemon Shorty is an item that seldom achieves leftover status. If it should happen, store them in glass with a loose fitting lid or in a tin lined with wax paper.

Cherry Almond Biscotti

One day when going through my father's old Italian cookbooks, I found a yellowed paper with a handwritten recipe for my Italian Aunt Annie's "Cherry Biscuit." It always wowed her friends and family—I hope you enjoy it too in this variation adapted to Spelt. This recipe uses almonds or pecans, both of which are neutral or beneficial for all Blood Types as are the cherries. It uses both Whole Grain and White Spelt flour for added sweet, nutty taste so characteristic of good biscotti. Because of its moisture-holding properties, you will find any biscotti made with Spelt stays fresh longer and are slightly softer for those growing long in the tooth and wanting to keep them.

Blood Type: A, B, AB, O (A, AB use Light Olive oil or canola oil instead of butter. Texture will change slightly but taste is excellent.) • Prep time: 20 min • Cook time: 25–30 min/10–15 min • Yield: 24 (2 lb biscotti)

Baking Tips: The biscotti is better when refrigerated 2–4 hours prior to forming and baking. This is optional but the dough performs better. The key to good biscotti, just like scones and pastry, is keeping mixing time down and handling the dough as little as possible. Also, have a plastic ruler at hand when forming and cutting. The ruler also helps to shape the sides.

Ingredients

⅔ cup slivered almonds or medium-chopped pecans
½ cup butter, room temperature
OR ¼ cup + 2 Tbsp Light Olive or other vegetable oil
1 cup light brown sugar, firmly packed
2 eggs, room temperature
½ tsp cherry flavoring
½ tsp almond flavoring
3 cups White Spelt flour (amount will vary with the type of White used)
¼ cups Whole Spelt flour
¼ tsp salt
1 tsp baking soda
¾ cup (4 oz) dried sweet or tart cherries, finely chopped

Chocolate Glaze (optional)

6 squares (6 oz) high quality dark or milk chocolate

1. **In Advance:** Place cherries in freezer for an hour so they will be easier to chop. Next, sprinkle cherries with 1 Tbsp of the White flour, shake to coat them then finely chop or snip the flour-coated cherries. Set cherries and excess flour in small bowl and set aside.

Heat oven to 350° F. Sprinkle nuts onto a rimmed baking sheet. Bake for 8–10 minutes until golden brown and aromatic. Remove from oven; let cool. If immediately baking the biscotti instead of refrigerating dough, reduce oven heat to 325° F and set oven rack to middle position.

2. In large mixer bowl, cream on medium mixer speed the butter and brown sugar. Add the room temperature eggs and flavorings; lightly beat.

3. Combine the White and Whole Spelt flours, salt and baking soda in a medium mixing bowl and whisk. Add the dry ingredients by the cupful to the butter/sugar/egg mixture and blend on low mixer speed until the ingredients are evenly incorporated. Do not over mix.

4. Scrape down bowl and turn dough out onto surface lightly floured with White Spelt. Sprinkle cherries and nuts over dough and knead dough gently 10 times to incorporate. If more flour is required, sprinkle it over dough and use pastry scraper to keep dough from sticking. (Optional: After kneading, refrigerate dough for 2–4 hours.)

5. This is sticky dough. Cover a cookie sheet or rimmed baking pan with parchment and sprinkle with flour. Or oil and dust pan with flour.

6. Divide dough in half. Pat each half into a 14" long log that is about 2" wide, and ½" high. Place the dough logs on the prepared baking sheet leaving 3" between each log and ample room on sides of pan. Bake at 325° F for 25–30 minutes until set.

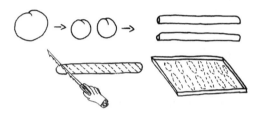

7. Remove from oven. Reduce heat to 300° F. Place biscotti on a wire rack and cool for 10 minutes. With a serrated knife, diagonally slice the log into ½" slices of length you desire. (5"–6" lengths work well for putting in glass quart jars for storage or as gifts.)

8. Gently place the biscotti cut side down on the baking sheet and return to oven to toast for an additional 10–15 minutes or longer depending on the consistency you want. The longer you bake them at this stage, the harder they become.

9. Remove from oven. Place pan on wire rack and prepare the Chocolate Glaze (optional). If not glazing, remove biscotti from pan to wire rack and cool before storing.

10. **Chocolate Glaze**. Place chocolate in microwave safe bowl and melt according to package instructions. Or melt chocolate in double boiler. Delicately spread chocolate over the tops of the biscotti using a thin spatula. Let biscotti cool and chocolate harden (about 2–3 hours) before storing. To store, place in a container with loose fitting lid. Glass bottles work very well. Airtight plastic containers make biscotti soft. Properly stored at room temperature, Spelt biscotti will keep for two weeks or so and still retain flavor without being hard as cement.

Honey Scones

This is a small, basic starter recipe for lean scones. Traditional scones use heavy cream and butter to make them rich and use dried fruit for most of the sweetening. This recipe calls for no cream; the milk is for brushing the tops.

Blood Type: B, O (O use soy milk for brushing tops); A, AB (use oil instead of butter)
Prep time: 10 min • Cook time: 12–15 min • Yield: 8 small scones

Baking Tip: Scones are at their best (most tender) when handled the least so work dough as little as possible.

Ingredients

1¼ cups White Spelt flour (reserve 2 Tbsp for shaping on floured surface) The amount will vary according to the flour used
2 tsp baking powder
3 Tbsp butter (or 2 Tbsp + 1½ tsp oil; oil will change texture slightly)
1 egg, room temperature, lightly beaten
3 Tbsp fluid honey
½ cup raisins, blueberries or softened dried fruit
egg white beaten with two Tbsp of milk (or soy milk)
granulated or turbinado sugar for sprinkling (optional)

1. **In Advance:** Soak the dried fruit in hot water with 2" water to cover; let stand 10 minutes to reconstitute. Drain and pat dry. Or use moisture-packed dried fruit which does not require reconstituting. Cover a cookie sheet with parchment (preferable) or lightly oil the pan.

2. Add flour and baking powder to large mixing bowl; whisk. Cut the butter (or oil) into the flour until the mixture is crumbly and the consistency of small peas.

3. In a small bowl, lightly beat the egg and blend honey with it; add to the flour/butter mixture. Mix briefly.

4. Turn out onto lightly floured surface; pat into thick small rectangle and sprinkle the fruit over dough. Knead briefly to mix in the dried fruit. Form dough into a ball by kneading briefly between the palms of your hands to form soft dough. Press into a circle ½" high. Place dough on prepared cookie sheet. With a pastry scraper or serrated knife, cut into 8 wedges. Slightly separate the wedges.

5. Gently brush the tops of the scones with egg white/milk (or soy milk). Sprinkle tops with sugar (optional).

6. Place on middle rack of preheated hot oven (425° F) for 12 minutes or until tops are golden brown. Remove from oven; let stand a couple of minutes at room temperature then re-cut the wedges. Enjoy them warm or transfer to wire racks to cool. To freeze, simply wrap scones individually in plastic and store in freezer bag. Take one out as desired.

Maple Scones

These are large, lovely scones: golden brown, flecked with pecans and maple sugar. I especially enjoy baking them around Thanksgiving and during the holiday season. There is that sharp morning chill in the air outside while the kitchen is warm and redolent with the aromas of baking and maple sugar.

Blood Type: A, B, AB, O (O use soy milk) • Prep time: 10 min • Cook time: 15–20 min • Yield: 16 (2½ oz each)

Ingredients

Scones
2½ cups White Spelt flour (reserve ¼ cup for kneading)
1½ cups Whole Grain Spelt flour
4 tsp baking powder
1 tsp salt
½ tsp cardamom (optional)
½ cup vegetable oil, especially Light Olive or canola
1 cup pecans, finely chopped
¾ cup milk or soy milk
½ cup maple syrup
1 tsp maple flavoring

Frosting (optional)
1 cup Confectioners' sugar
4 tsp milk or soy milk
¾ tsp maple flavoring
2 Tbsp maple sugar or turbinado sugar

1. Preheat oven to 425° F. Set one oven rack on bottom rung and the other two rungs up. Cover two cookie sheets with parchment (preferable) or spray with cooking oil.

2. Add the Spelt flours, baking powder, salt and cardamom to large mixing bowl. Whisk to combine. Add the oil; cut in until mixture becomes pebbly and size of small peas. Mix in the finely chopped pecans.

3. In small bowl, mix the milk, syrup and flavoring. Add to the flour/oil mixture and stir with fork to form dough. Turn dough out onto surface lightly floured with White Spelt. Knead very gently 6–8 times to incorporate more flour if necessary. Do not overwork dough. Divide into 2 equal portions.

4. Place the divided dough onto two pans. Pat each into a ¾" high round. Using pastry scraper or serrated knife, cut each round into 8 wedges. Very gently separate the wedges.

5. Place in preheated hot oven (425° F) and bake for 8 minutes. Shift scones to opposite rack turning each pan 180° to assure even baking. Bake scones an additional 8–10 minutes or until tops are golden brown and bottoms are lightly browned.

6. Remove from oven. Leave on pan to cool 10 minutes or shift parchment paper with scones to wire rack. Gently re-cut or pull the scones apart if required.

7. Prepare the frosting to desired consistency. Gently drizzle or spoon frosting over each scone. Let stand 10 or more minutes until frosting is set. To freeze, wrap each scone in plastic and place all in freezer bag. Take one out as desired.

Cranberry and Rolled Spelt (or Oat) Scones

Delectable, tender, large scones piquant with cranberry contrasted with the sweetness of orange and two variations of Spelt for texture and taste.

Blood Type: A, B, AB (A, AB use oil instead of butter)
Prep time: 15 min • Cook time: 18–20 min • Yield: 10 large (3 oz)

Ingredients

3 cups White Spelt flour (+ ¼ cup kneading)
1¼ cups Rolled Spelt or oats (uncooked)
4 tsp baking powder
½ tsp salt
½ cup granulated sugar
½ cup butter, room temperature
OR ¼ cup + 2 Tbsp vegetable oil
1 cup fresh cranberries (or thawed if frozen variety)
1 Tbsp orange zest
1 egg, room temperature
¾ cup goat's milk or other plain yogurt without additives
turbinado sugar for sprinkling

1. Place ¼ cup of the White Spelt flour in processor bowl fitted with metal blade. Add the Rolled Spelt or oats to the bowl. On run, process 10 seconds until Rolled Spelt is broken up; 6 seconds for rolled oats. Set aside. Place cranberries and orange zest in processor fitted with metal blade. On run, process 6–7 seconds to dice the berries. Place in colander and set aside.

2. Preheat oven to 425° F. Set one oven rack on bottom rung and the other two rungs up. Cover two cookie sheets with parchment (preferable) or spray with cooking oil.

3. In small bowl, combine yogurt and egg and beat. Set aside.

4. Place 2¾ cups White Spelt flour, baking powder, salt and sugar in large mixing bowl; whisk to combine. Add the Rolled Spelt/ flour mixture and mix. Cut in the butter or oil with fork or pastry blender until mixture is pebbly and the size of small peas.

5. Add the cranberries/orange zest; mix. Add the egg/yogurt and stir, adding flour if necessary to form soft dough. Turn dough out of bowl onto surface lightly floured with White Spelt and knead gently 4–5 times incorporating more flour if necessary to form soft, slightly tacky dough. Do not overwork the dough as scones lose their tenderness if handled too much.

6. Flour hands and pat dough into a circle ½" high. Cut into 10 3" rounds. Place 5 rounds each on prepared cookie sheets leaving 1½" between scones. Brush the tops with milk or soymilk and sprinkle the tops with turbinado sugar.

7. Place pans in preheated hot (425° F) oven. Bake for 10 minutes. Shift scones to opposite rack, turning each pan 180° to assure even baking. Bake scones an additional 8–10 minutes until tops are light golden brown.

8. Remove from oven. Shift parchment with scones on it directly to wire racks to cool or allow scones to sit 2 minutes on pan and transfer individually to wire racks. To freeze, wrap each scone in plastic and place all in freezer bag. Take one out as desired.

Blueberry Lemon Scones

Large, high rising scones with the fresh taste of blueberry combined with a hint of lemon and the natural sweetness of Spelt. Excellent for Blood Type eating because soymilk and oil can both be used instead of the traditional butter and cream. The texture changes slightly but the scones are still moist and tender and have excellent keeping properties unlike most scones that dry out the same day.

Blood Type: B, O (use soy milk), A, AB (use oil instead of butter)
Prep time: 15 min • Cook time: about 20 min • Yield: 8 large (4 oz) or 10 (3.5 oz)

Ingredients

2   cups White Spelt flour
1   cup Whole Grain Spelt flour
4   tsp baking powder
¼   tsp salt
⅓   cup granulated sugar
1   tsp cardamom (optional)
2   tsp fresh lemon zest, grated
½   cup butter (1 stick), room temperature
OR ¼ cup + 2 Tbsp vegetable oil, especially Light Olive or canola
½   cup milk or soy milk
½   cup fresh blueberries or frozen (partially thawed) set over colander

Confectioners' icing (see recipe under *Sweet Toppings*)

1. Preheat oven to 400° F. Place rack in center of oven. Cover a cookie sheet with parchment or spray with oil.

2. Add both Spelt flours, baking powder, salt, sugar, cardamom and lemon zest to large mixing bowl. Whisk to combine. Cut butter (or oil) into dry ingredients with pastry blender or fork until mixture is pebbly and the size of small peas. If mixture seems dry, wait to adjust liquid until the blueberries (next step) are added.

3. Add the milk and stir briefly. Add the blueberries, gently stirring until all ingredients are moist, adjusting with small amount of flour or milk if necessary to form a soft ball. Do not overwork the dough as scones lose their tenderness if handled too much.

4. Place the soft, smooth dough ball on the baking sheet and pat into a ½" high round. Using a pastry scraper or sharp knife, cut into 8 to 10 wedges. Slightly separate the wedges. Brush the tops with milk or soymilk.

5. Place in preheated hot (400° F) oven to bake for 10 minutes. Turn pan around 180° to assure even baking. Continue to bake an additional 8–13 minutes until top is light golden brown and toothpick inserted into top of scone comes out clean.

6. Remove scones from oven and lift parchment with scones on it to wire rack. Gently re-cut the wedges if required. For oiled pan, let scones stand 2 minutes on pan then re-cut wedges and shift each scone to wire rack to cool 10 minutes before eating. Prepare Confectioners' Icing (optional). Drizzle over tops of slightly warm scones. Let stand 10 or so minutes to harden a little before serving.

Paradell
(Sweet Crepe with Apples)

Of all the treats I make, this is my personal favorite. It is an anytime food, a delicate crepe, and is especially good with espresso or herbal tea in the afternoon or following a meal. It is light, subtly sweet, soulful and elegant.

Prep time: 5 min/1 hr • Cook time: 12–15 min • Yield: 9" Paradell (6 servings)

Ingredients

3½ Tbsp butter
2   eggs, room temperature
⅓   cup + 1 Tbsp milk or water
1   cup White Spelt flour
2   Granny Smith or other cooking apples (about 2 cups) or reconstituted dried apples
Confectioners' sugar for sprinkling

1. Melt 2 Tbsp of the butter. Let it cool. Lightly beat the eggs together with milk (or water), salt and the cooled butter. Gradually add the flour and beat until mixture is smooth (by hand, food processor or blender). Cover bowl and let mixture stand for 1 hour. It will become thicker and somewhat elastic.

2. Wash, peel, core and slice the apples and mix into the thickened batter.

3. In a skillet (preferably 9" non-stick) set over moderate heat, melt 1 Tbsp of the butter. Pour in the batter and, with spatula, spread it evenly in the pan. Cook for 5–7 minutes until edges start to dry and the bottom is golden brown and firm.

4. Slide it onto a plate or platter. Place ½ Tbsp of butter in skillet, and spread to coat bottom. Place the skillet face down over the Paradell and invert it. Cook 5 minutes until bottom is light golden brown. Slide onto plate and dust with Confectioners' sugar. Serve immediately.

MANY SMALL THINGS:
THE APPETIZING WORLD OF SPELT©

Call them tapas, small plates, dim sim, appetizers ...
they are all many small things from the heart.
The original in portion control food and the ultimate in
variety and lively taste sensations, these are the foods
we frequently eat away from home or order to-go.

Now you can eat them in ... fresh from your kitchen.

With gusto and verve come Many Small Things of Spelt.

Small Beginnings
Cheese Spuffs
Broiled Kasseri or Pecorino Cheese with Breadcrumbs
(The Original Mozzarella Stick)
Yogurt Cheese (Soft Cheese)
Roasted Garlic
Spinach Pesto

Pasta
Spelt Ricotta Gnocchi (Dumplings) Ancient Globi
Ready-made Spelt Pastas

✳

Flatbreads
Country Oven Focaccia (Country Oven Basic Flatbread Dough)
Country Oven Meatball Calzones
Country Oven Pizza

Pizza D'Adamo (Whole Grain Spelt Pizza Dough)

(continued)

Many Small Things (continued)

✳

Topping and Filling Many Small Things
Garlic and Shallots, Artichoke Hearts, California Pizza, Zucchini and Basil, Spinach and Ricotta, Roasted Peppers and Soft Goat Cheese, Garden Topping, Florentine, Greek, Turkey or Beef Meatballs with Marinara or Oil

✳

Going 'round the World
Spelt Flour Tortillas
Quesadillas, Cheese Crips, Tortilla Chips and Nachos

Empanadas Fritas de Chile Y Queso (Fried Turnovers with Chile and Cheese)
Empanadas Valencianas (Baked Meat Turnovers/Pasties)

Enchilada Sauce Sabrosa
Epic of Enchi-Mesh Sonoran Style Enchiladas

Pita Bread and Pita Wedges
Gyros (Doner Kebab)
Falafel with Tsatsiki Sauce
Yusef's Hummus

Tod Mun Pla (Thai Style Fish Cakes with Spicy Sauce)

Char Shiu Bao (Chinese Steamed Barbecue Buns
with Sweet, Cherried Filling)

Eggs Foo Young with Spelt Sprouts
Fried Rice with Spelt Sprouts

Small Beginnings
Cheese Spuffs

A substitute for a great-tasting addictive crispy American snack food that shall remain unnamed, this dainty spiced American traditional delicacy, is a delight in its own right. The Cheese Spelt Puff is a tiny soufflé to serve as an appetizer or as something different in the morning.

Blood Type: Not rated • Prep time: 15 min • Cook time: 10–12 min • Yield: 12 Spuffs

Ingredients

2 Tbsp butter
3½ Tbsp White Spelt flour
4 Tbsp finely shredded high quality White Cheddar cheese
¼ tsp salt
⅛ tsp cayenne
2 egg whites

1. Preheat oven to 350° F. Lightly spray a large cookie sheet or cover with parchment. Beat egg whites to stiff peaks.

2. In small saucepan over medium heat, melt the butter. Blend in the flour.

3. Remove pan from stovetop. Add the cheese, salt and cayenne. Stir.

4. With plastic spatula, carefully fold in the egg whites.

5. Drop the soon-to-be Spuffs by rounded tsp onto the lightly oiled cookie sheet. They spread so leave about 1½" between each Spuff and the edges of the pan. Bake on middle rack for 10–12 minutes until the edges are just slightly brown and the Spuffs are set. Remove from oven; serve immediately.

Broiled Kasseri or Pecorino Cheese
with Breadcrumbs

The Original Mozzarella Stick

Kasseri is a hard Greek cheese made with 80% sheep milk and 20% goat milk. Greeks use Kasseri in much the same way as semi-soft Mozzarella in Italy and the U.S. The Pecorinos are sheep cheeses from Italy, Sardinia and Sicily. These are not just grating cheeses. They are wonderful to eat alone with a fresh piece of Spelt Roman Bread and figs, as a hot appetizer, with salads or as Spelt Medi Crostini or pita toppings. Plain or herbed Spelt crumbs embellish the flavors of these distinctive imported hard regional cheeses. One thing about these cheeses: If the cheese says "Kasseri" and is made in the U.S., that cheese is probably made of cow's milk. Read the label closely before buying.

Blood Type: A, B, AB, O

Ingredients (typically sold in 5 to 8 oz packages):

Kasseri (imported Greek sheep's/goat's milk cheese)

Pecorino (imported sheep's milk cheese) such as Pecorino Romano, Pecorino Sardo, Pecorino Siciliano

Manchego (imported sheep's milk cheese)

Fresh Spelt Breadcrumbs either plain or mixed with crushed herbs such as thyme, French herbes

Olive oil

Cut cheese into ½" thick cubes. Coat very lightly with olive oil. Roll in fresh, fine plain or seasoned Spelt breadcrumbs. Cover broiler rack with sheet of foil or set cubes in a pie pan. Set oven to Broil and place rack on second to top rung. Set cheese cubes under broiler for 2 to 3 minutes until cheese has melted, starts to bubble and crumbs begin to brown. Serve immediately.

Yogurt Cheese
(Soft Cheese)

Soft Yogurt cheese is easy to make and *you* control the ingredients. Use plain as a spread, add herbs, mix in berries or use as a topping for many small things. I heartily recommend goat's milk yogurt for reasons stated elsewhere in *Spelt Healthy!*

People have made yogurt for millennia without benefit of refrigeration (they still do) so two methods are given here: Refrigerator (Method I) and the age-old Room Temperature (Method 2). The latter makes a tangier cheese. Salt is optional for either method as yogurt, like other dairy products, meat, poultry and fish naturally contains some natural sodium. The additional salt aids the draining process for a slightly firmer cheese.

Blood Type: A, B, AB • Prep time/cook time: Varies/no cook time • Yield: about 1½ cups soft cheese (12 oz)

Refrigerator (Method 1):

4 cups (32 oz) plain goat's milk or cow's milk yogurt

½ tsp salt (optional)

Arrange a double thickness of cheesecloth in a footed colander. (If using salt, whisk yogurt and salt together.) Pour in the yogurt. Tie the cheesecloth ends together or drape the ends over the yogurt so it is completely covered. Fit colander over a bowl to catch the liquid as it drips. Be certain bowl is deep enough to keep liquid from touching bottom of yogurt. Set in refrigerator and let drain overnight. Drain off the liquid in the morning. If you want a firmer cheese, repeat the process. Unwrap the cheese, scoop it into a bowl for immediate use or store in airtight container in refrigerator.

Room Temperature (Method 2):

4 cups (32 oz) plain goat's milk or cow's milk yogurt

¼ tsp salt (optional)

Prepare colander as above. Mix ¼ tsp salt into yogurt and whisk together thoroughly. Pour yogurt into colander with cheesecloth. Cover yogurt by folding excess cheesecloth over it. Set over bowl deep enough to catch liquid and keep liquid from touching bottom of yogurt. Set out at room temperature. Check bowl 2–3 times daily and drain. Let cheese form over period of 2–3 days. Scoop into a bowl for immediate use, or store in airtight container in refrigerator.

Some suggested additions: Pimentos with garlic powder and dash of paprika, fresh green chiles finely chopped and ground cumin to taste, fresh chopped dill or basil or mixture of other fresh garden herbs.

Serving suggestions: Spread over grilled meats or use as a marinade, spread on crostini, mix with fresh fruits in season and mix with honey.

Roasted Garlic

Garlic loses its pungency and takes on a deliciously different, sweeter taste when roasted. The mash created after roasting is perfect for topping pizzas or other flatbreads and toasts of various kinds. Spoon olive oil and roasted garlic over your homemade Spelt Italian bread and bake or broil.

Ingredients:

2 bulbs of garlic and 4 teaspoons Olive oil

1. Preheat oven to 375° F. Set out a small dish with a tight fitting lid for roasting.

2. Carefully remove as much of the garlic paper (skin) from each bulb as you can without breaking the bulb of garlic apart. Set the garlic head with its bulb side down in the dish. Drizzle 2 tsp of olive oil over each of the garlic heads such that it penetrates the openings between the cloves. Place ¼ cup of water in the dish, just enough so there is ¼" or slightly less of water in the bottom. Cover.

3. Roast the garlic for half an hour. Take out of oven and spoon the liquid from the dish over the garlic heads. Return to the oven to roast for an additional 20–30 minutes.

4. Remove from oven and let the garlic cool sufficiently to handle. Squeeze a garlic clove and press out the pulp. Repeat. The garlic mash is easy to spread on everything from steak to pizza. For you garlic lovers, it is delicious as is.

Spinach Pesto

Pesto is one of the most versatile of recipes. When made with spinach as an alternative to the traditional basil pesto it becomes ever more flexible. Serve with fresh pasta or use as a pasta stuffing. Make it as a vegetable dip. Use it as a topping for a pizza or Medi Crostini. Make the Brundisi Pesto Bread or Rolls. In our home we use Spinach Pesto as an alternative to mayonnaise on sandwiches. Change the taste by substituting spinach or basil with the flat leaf parsley (Italian Parsley). Complement other foods on your menu by adding fresh or dried herbs such as savory, tarragon or chervil. Substitute almonds, walnuts or pistachios for the pine nuts.

Blood Type: A, B, AB, O (A, AB, O use Pecorino Romano or Kasseri Greek cheeses)
Prep time: 10 min • Cook time: None • Yield: 1 cup

Ingredients

¼   cup pine nuts, toasted
2   cups (4–5 oz) fresh baby spinach, firmly packed
2   cloves garlic
½   cup Pecorino Romano or Kasseri Greek or Parmesan or Romano cheese, finely grated
1   Tbsp basil, dried or 3 Tbsp fresh, finely chopped or tarragon or savory or chervil or an herb blend
⅛   tsp freshly ground black pepper (optional)
½   cup Olive oil (preferably Virgin)

1. Place a sauté pan or small skillet over medium heat. Add pine nuts and lightly toast (5–7 minutes), stirring occasionally. Remove from pan. Set aside to cool.

2. Place the pine nuts, spinach and garlic in food processor bowl fitted with metal blade. Pulse 5–6 times. Add cheese; pulse several times until mixture is smooth yet still retains some texture. Add black pepper (optional).

3. With motor running, add oil in a steady, slow stream until mixture is blended. Place in container with tight lid and refrigerate. The pesto will stay fresh for several days to a week because the ingredients are coated with oil. Let Spinach Pesto stand 30 minutes to come to room temperature before use. Or freeze and use when needed by thawing at room temperature. If it becomes too thick, simply add oil and stir.

Pasta

Pasta is found around the world. It comes in a stupendous variety of forms and can be boiled, fried and baked—everything from the Chinese won-ton and noodles to luscious lasagna. The majority of people in the United States eat some kind of pasta once a week with spaghetti pasta being the favorite. Pasta is one of the original feel good foods because the starch takes time to digest. It not only tastes good, the starch actually increases the amount of serotonin in the bloodstream for that "Ah, that's good" feeling of satisfaction and contentment.

Drawing based on one of the earliest paintings depicting the pasta making process. This one is drying pasta (14th century). Pasta's origins are fascinating and somewhat of a mystery because exactly which grain was used for original pasta is unclear. Prior to semolina, now synonymous with durum (macaroni) wheat, fine flour was referred to as alica, which was Spelt in Roman times.

Spelt Ricotta Gnocchi (Dumplings)
Ancient Globi

"Gnocchi" are small Italian dumplings that come down to us from Roman times and perhaps before. These "little pillows" of flavorful dough are one of the easiest forms of pasta to create. Make them fresh and serve them straight from the pan, or make and freeze to serve another time. Either way you do it, they turn out moist, tender and delicious and are an alternative to other filled pastas. My father made them with semolina and made the characteristic gnocchi indentations with a flourish of his index finger, from tip to first joint, in one smooth movement. The same method works for Spelt. Serve Gnocchi with your favorite marinara or mix with fresh Spinach Pesto (see *Many Small Things: Small Beginnings*) or use the traditional Aglio e Olio Sauce (Garlic and Oil with Herbs) found under *Sauces.* Excellent side dish with steak, fish or fowl or on its own with a salad.

Blood Type: A, B, AB (Pecorino cheese recommended for A, AB)
Prep time: 15–20 min • Cook time: 10 min per batch • Yield: 1¾ lb

Ingredients

At refrigerator temperature:

2   cups (16 oz) Ricotta cheese, cold
2   eggs, cool
¼   cup finely grated Asiago, Romano or Pecorino cheese
2   cloves garlic, pressed
½   tsp garlic powder
1   tsp salt
1   cup Whole Grain Spelt flour
1   cup White Spelt flour

1.   In a large cool bowl, mix the Ricotta cheese, eggs and the finely grated cheese.

2.   Add the Whole and White Spelt flours. Mix until combined; turn out onto lightly floured work surface.

3.   Pluck a piece about the size of a ping-pong ball from the dough ball. Roll the piece between your palms so piece is dangling or shape on the floured surface to make a little rope about ¾" thick and round. With a pastry cutter or sharp knife, cut the rope into 1" pieces. Indent the center of each segment with your thumb or pinch it gently to make the traditional "pillow" shape. (See illustration above.)

4.   Set each Gnocchi on a floured baking sheet. If you are going to freeze them, dust with White Spelt flour, and place them flat in a large freezer bag (single layer) and freeze. The light dusting of flour and placing them in a single layer then squishing the air out of the bag, keeps them from sticking together and makes them very easy to use. (Note: Wax paper between layers has a tendency to stick even with being lightly floured, which is the reason for placing them in a single layer.)

5. To Cook: Heat water in a large wide saucepan with a drop of oil in it. Bring it to a boil.

6. Drop thirty or so Gnocchis in the boiling water. If some stick to the bottom, gently loosen. Cook for about 10 minutes. They should all be floating at the top. Remove them from the water with a slotted spoon, drain quickly over pan and transfer to a covered casserole dish while waiting for all the Gnocci to cook.

Serve hot dressed with garlic and olive oil sauce; with butter, olive oil and parmesan; with Spinach Pesto (see recipe) or your favorite marinara.

For frozen Gnocchi: Remove from freezer and drop into boiling water. Let them cook about 2 minutes longer than fresh Gnocchi. Continue as above.

Ready-Made Spelt Pastas

If you are a pasta lover like I am, and you want some already made, you are in luck because the world of organic Spelt Pasta and Italian foods is beginning to bloom. For example, Purity Foods/VitaSpelt produces the following pastas. You will find some of these products are already in your stores; if not, just ask and most venders will order them for you.

Organic Whole Grain Spelt Pastas: Spaghetti, Elbows, Rotini, Shells, Egg Noodles, Lasagna and Angel Hair.

Organic White Spelt Pastas: Spaghetti, Elbows, Rotini, Angel Hair, Lasagna and Penne.

And Pizzas

VitaSpelt garlic bread, either whole or white, is now available in the frozen food case of your local whole foods market. *Spelt French Bread Pizza* and the traditional round (vegetarian) are on the way and so are *Stuffed Hot Pockets*.

Check out www.spelthealthy.com for updates on pastas and pizzas and other ready-made Spelt products as we find them.

A dry pasta collage set on lasagna. From top to bottom some traditional and delightful forms: ravioli, spaghetti, penne (mostaccioli), seashells, cockscombs, rote, elbows, stellini, orzo and gemelli.

FLATBREADS
Country Oven Focaccia
(Country Oven Basic Flatbread Dough)

The Country Oven dough is the basis for many flatbreads. The recipe below is for traditional Focaccia rounds or oblong. Please read *Knead to Know* about working with Spelt dough for best results.

Blood Type: A, B, AB, O • Prep time: Varies (allow 1½ hrs) • Cook time: 30–35 min • Yield: 4 rounds

Ingredients

2 pkgs active dry yeast
½ cup warm water (110°–115° F)
1 cup lukewarm water (about 95° F)
2 Tbsp granulated sugar
1 tsp salt
¾ cup Olive oil
2 cups Whole Grain Spelt flour
3½ cups White Spelt flour (+ additional for kneading)

Topping

3 cloves garlic, crushed or minced
¼ cup Olive oil for topping
2 Tbsp dried crushed rosemary or fresh sprigs
1–2 Tbsp coarse sea or kosher salt
or other toppings to taste

1. **Ferment.** Place ½ cup warm water in small bowl. Add 2 Tbsp sugar to the bowl. Sprinkle 2 packages yeast over the water. Stir to dissolve. Let sit 10 minutes until creamy and foamy.

2. **Mix/Initial Knead.** Place 1 cup warm water in a large mixing bowl. Add the salt. Add the yeast/sugar mixture. Add the olive oil. Stir in the Whole Grain Spelt flour and 1 cup of the White Spelt flour.

Stand Mixer: Attach paddle and on speed 2/next to lowest speed, mix for 60 seconds or until rough dough forms. Add the remaining White Spelt flour by the ½ cup measure; mix 30 seconds and change to dough hook (lowest speed). Knead until soft dough forms and begins to clean sides of bowl (about 1 minute). Scrape down bowl and turn dough out onto surface lightly floured with White Spelt.

By Hand: Mix until rough dough forms; scrape down sides of bowl and add White Spelt flour by the ½ cup measure to form soft dough. Knead until dough starts to chase spoon/utensil around bowl. Turn out of bowl onto lightly floured surface.

3. **Knead/Rise.** Knead lightly, sprinkling additional flour over/under dough and using a pastry scraper to keep dough from sticking. Form soft, smooth dough into a round. Rub olive oil on hands and lightly rub exterior of dough. Place dough in clean bowl to rise in warm (80°–85° F), draft-free place until doubled in volume (30–40 minutes). This is fast dough so check at 30 minutes and 10 minute intervals thereafter by inserting fingertip into crown of dough. If impression remains when finger is removed, dough is ripe and ready for next step.

4. **Second Rise**. Depress dough by pressing it with lightly closed fist working around the bowl several times to deflate gently. Let dough rise in same place a second time, which will be shorter (check at 20 minutes and 5 minute intervals thereafter). Detach edges of dough from bowl with spatula, turning edges onto top of dough. Gently deflate dough. Turn dough out onto lightly floured board and cover. To make small rounds, divide into four portions and cover.

5. **Form Rounds (2–4).** Lightly oil 2–4 pie plates or two large rimmed baking pans (jelly roll pans). With fingertips flatten and dimple each portion into a ½" high round. The dimpling prevents them from rising too quickly and gives them the characteristic look of Focaccia. Place rounds on individual pie pans or on two large baking pans (allow for expansion during rising and baking). Cover each round with plastic wrap lightly sprayed with oil as you go. Let rounds rise in same draft-free place for 15–20 minutes. Do Fingertip Test to check for maximum rise.

   Form Oblong. Lightly oil a 15½" x 10½" rimmed baking pan (or 17½" x 10½" for thinner focaccia). With fingertips press the entire dough to fit pan. Cover with plastic wrap lightly sprayed with oil. Allow to rise in same draft-free place for 15–20 minutes until dough expands by about ¾ volume. Do Fingertip Test.

   Midway during rising of either Rounds or Oblong preheat oven to 375° F. If making 4 rounds, adjust racks so one is on bottom rung and other is two rungs up.

6. **Toppings.** Add the crushed or minced garlic to ¼ cup olive oil. Gently brush over the top of each round or across top of oblong. Focaccia is characterized by the liberal use of olive oil so brush dough well. It gives it flavor and moisture. Add Traditional Topping or make with a variety of Toppings (see *Topping and Filling Many Small Things*).

Traditional Toppings: Sprinkle the top of each round with coarse salt and dried crushed rosemary. OR sprinkle surface with salt and make tiny slits angled diagonally from surface not straight down and place fresh sprigs of rosemary under the slits and lightly press into dough OR top with sprinkling of salt and freshly chopped scallions.

7. **Bake.** Place pans in preheated hot (375° F) oven and bake for 15 minutes. Shift pans to opposite rack and turn each pan 180° to assure even baking. Bake an additional 10–15 minutes. Remove from oven and place on wire racks to cool. Serve warm or at room temperature. These freeze very well.

Country Oven Meatball Calzones

Perfect food for Friday night and excellent for leftovers because they freeze. These are about 4 oz for portion control. Experiment with using several fillings in a single recipe in addition to the Classic Meatball Calzone given here.

Blood Type: A, B, AB, O Dough: Fillings According to Type
Prep time: Varies (allow 1½ hrs) • Cook time: 15–20 min • Yield: 12 large (6") 4 oz

Ingredients

1   recipe of Country Oven Focaccia Dough
1   recipe Classic Meatballs or other filling (See *Topping and Filling Many Small Things*)
1½ cups semi-soft Mozzarella cheese, coarsely grated
3   cups prepared Marinara, warmed
Italian herbs, dried, crushed (optional)
Olive oil for brushing

1. Follow **Country Oven Focaccia** dough recipe through the first rise (Step 3). Depress the dough by detaching dough from edges of the bowl and laying over top of the dough then gently pressing down with loose fist working around the bowl to gently expel air. Turn dough out onto surface lightly floured with White Spelt.

2. Using pastry cutter or sharp knife, divide dough into 12 pieces (or 16 for smaller Calzones). Form each piece into a ball. Set balls 4" apart on floured surface or floured rimmed baking pan. Cover with oiled plastic wrap or damp tea towel and let rise in a warm (80°–85° F), draft-free place until not quite double in size (25–30 minutes). Preheat oven to 425° F. Oil two large baking sheets.

3. Pat and stretch, or roll, one of the pieces into a 6-inch round, ⅛" thick. Ladle 2 Tbsp of marinara over one half the round to within ½" of the edge. Place several sliced meatballs on the marinara and sprinkle with

2 Tbsp of cheese. Sprinkle with dried crushed Italian herbs if desired. Pour a little marinara over top of meatballs. Fold edge of dough over to make a half-moon and press the edges firmly together or crimp them with your fingers or the tines of a fork to seal.

4. Place each Calzone on an oiled baking sheet making sure Calzones are about 3" apart to allow for expansion during baking. Rub or gently brush each Calzone with olive oil. Make sure the Calzone is well sealed. Prick the dough in several places along the top with a fork or make several short clean cuts with a sharp knife for steam to escape during baking. While first batch is baking, make the second batch and place on oiled pan.

5. Place in preheated hot (425° F) oven for 15–20 minutes until deep golden brown. If they are browning unevenly, rotate pan 180°. Remove to wire rack to cool slightly before eating. Cool leftovers completely and freeze in heavy-duty freezer bags. These pack very well for lunch, picnics or road trips.

Country Oven Pizza

This dough has a remarkably fine taste and a crunchy crust without being dry. You can roll it so thin you can almost see through it yet it remains flexible. It stores well for that wonderful feast of leftover pizza the next day (it freezes well also.) Make a supply in advance so you can you pull one of your fantastic homemade pizzas out of the freezer for a Friday night. The dough is easy to make and if you follow the directions, it will not fail you.

Blood Type: See Focaccia; makes a minimum of four 12-inch pizzas; eight to ten individual pizzas (10" or less); or six to eight deep-dish individual pies.

Time for cooking varies with topping. Also, you may need to adjust racks as vegetable pizzas or those with few toppings or just oil instead of marinara cook faster and may need to be in center of oven instead of higher up.

Ingredients

1   recipe Country Oven Focaccia Dough
Olive oil and minced garlic
OR Shallot/Garlic mixture (see *Topping and Filling Many Small Things*)
Toppings to taste

1. Make **Country Oven Focaccia** dough and follow recipe instructions through first rise (Step 3). Depress the dough by detaching edges of dough from sides of bowl and turning them on to the top of the dough then gently working a loose fist around the bowl to gently expel gas. Turn dough out onto lightly floured surface.

2. With pastry scraper or sharp knife, cut into the number of pieces desired for pizzas. Form each piece into a ball. Set balls 4" apart on floured surface or on floured rimmed baking pan. Cover with plastic wrap or damp tea towel and let the dough rest for 15 minutes.

3. Depending on your oven, you can make 4 individual pizzas at a time or 2 12" pizzas. Set racks at bottom and two rungs up. Preheat oven to 475° F. If making individual pizzas, set the remaining balls on lightly

oiled pan and spray lightly with oil. Cover with plastic wrap or set pan in large plastic bag in refrigerator to retard dough while making/baking others.

4. Take a ball of dough and roll or pat/stretch it to size of pizza pan and crimp the edges over rim. If making pizzas flat on an oiled pan, turn up the dough edges just a little to make a slight rim.

5. Brush oil/garlic mixture on dough. If using tomato paste or marinara, spread desired amount over oiled crust. Sprinkle with herbs. Add toppings.

6. Place on bottom rack of preheated hot (475° F) oven and bake 15 minutes while making other pizza. Place first pan on upper rack and slide second pan onto lowest rack. Bake first pizza an additional 10–15 minutes depending upon toppings. Remove top pizza and slide second pizza onto top rack. Bake an additional 10–15 minutes. While making second pizza, remove remainder of dough from refrigerator. Repeat process.

Pizza D'Adamo
Whole Grain Spelt Pizza Dough

From Peter D'Adamo's 1998 book, *Cook Right for Your Type*, comes this Whole Grain recipe for pizza dough. "We wish that local pizzerias made spelt pizzas," he said. Until that time comes, enjoy making your own from this basic pizza dough and smorgasbord of toppings. This amended version is courtesy of Dr. D'Adamo. It is warm, fast dough designed to make thin pizzas but it also works deliciously well for focaccia and other foods such as light rolls.

Blood Type: A, B, AB, O • Prep time: about 90 min • Cook time: varies • Yield: 2 12" pies (3–4 individual pies)

Baking tip: If all you have on hand are packets of active dry yeast, use one entire package plus ¾ tsp of another package. Recipe works equally well using 1½ cups Whole Grain mixed with 1¾ cups White Spelt flour. If using all White Spelt flour you may need to adjust the amount upward by ¼ to ½ cup. It varies with the White Spelt flour.

Ingredients

1   Tbsp dry yeast
1   cup lukewarm water
3¼ to 3½ cups Whole Grain Spelt flour
     (+ additional for kneading)
2   Tbsp Olive oil
scant tsp salt
Olive oil for bowl

1. In a large mixing bowl, sprinkle the yeast over lukewarm water. Stir to dissolve. Add 1½ cups flour and mix well with a large spoon or with paddle of stand mixer (90 seconds). Add oil, salt and the rest of the flour in ½ cup increments (stand mixer, dough hook, lowest speed, 90 seconds) and work into manageable dough.

2. Turn onto a well-floured surface and knead briefly to form smooth dough, sprinkling additional flour over dough and using pastry scraper to keep dough from sticking. Form into a ball. Wash out the same bowl and grease with olive oil. Cover with plastic wrap or damp towel and let rise in warm place (80°–85° F), draft-free, until doubled in volume (30–45 minutes). Test by inserting a finger into crown of dough; if indentation remains when finger is removed, dough is ready.

3. Use rubber spatula to detach edges from sides of bowl and fold onto top of dough. Gently depress the dough with a loose fist working around the bowl several times. Turn out onto lightly floured surface and divide into 2 (or more) pieces. On a flat work area, gently form each piece into a ball and set aside to rest, covered, in a bowl or on a sheet pan for 15 minutes.

4. Preheat oven to 475° F and sprinkle a rectangular baking sheet or a classic round pizza pan with Whole Grain Spelt flour to keep the pizza from sticking. Take a ball of dough and press it out with your fingers, coaxing it to fit the pan. Brush with olive oil or the Garlic-Shallot Mixture that follows under *Topping and Filling Many Small Things*. Add toppings. Cooking time varies with toppings. See following pages.

Topping and Filling Many Small Things

Garlic-Shallot Mixture

Blood Type: A, B, AB, O

(**Garlic-Shallot Mixture** courtesy of Dr. Peter D'Adamo from *Cook Right for Your Type*)

The shallot is a much under-used vegetable in the United States yet it is one of the best of the onion/garlic family for cooking. I keep this mixture in my refrigerator all the time along with a mixture of garlic and sweet chopped onions. (Use a variety of onions to suit your tastes and blood type: scallions, leeks, sweet or purple onions). Having the mixture on hand reduces prep time and cook time for many dishes. After awhile you may discover these mixtures are almost indispensable. If you find garlic too strong, use its much larger cousin, Elephant Garlic, for a milder taste.

10 cloves garlic peeled
10 shallots, peeled
oil to cover

In a food processor or blender, combine garlic and shallots. Pulse on and off, scraping down sides of bowl as necessary, until finely chopped. When desired consistency is reached transfer to an airtight container and cover with oil. Refrigerate. It will keep for 10 days or longer.

Artichoke Hearts and Onions

For one 12" pizza / 2 calzones / 1 focaccia round • Blood Type: A, O

(Recipe courtesy of Dr. Peter D'Adamo from *Cook Right for Your Type*)

3 Tbsp Extra-Virgin Olive oil
1 medium sized onion, thinly sliced
4 artichoke hearts, thinly sliced
4 oz low-fat mozzarella, grated
2 oz goat cheese, crumbled
2 Tbsp chopped Italian parsley

Follow the general directions for pizza dough. In skillet, heat 2 Tbsp oil over medium heat. Preheat oven to 475° F. Add onion and sauté until it softens, about 5 minutes. Let cool slightly, then spread onion over dough. Place sliced artichoke hearts around the top and cover with mozzarella and crumbled goat cheese. Sprinkle with chopped parsley and drizzle with remaining oil. Bake 10–15 minutes. Serves 2 to 4.

California Pizza

For one 12" pizza / 2 to 3 calzones / 1 focaccia round • Blood Type: AB, O

(Recipe courtesy of Dr. Peter D'Adamo from *Cook Right for Your Type*)

3 Tbsp tomato sauce
½ pound mozzarella, sliced
2 tsp grated Romano
2 Tbsp goat cheese, crumbled
2 Tbsp chopped fresh basil
Olive oil

Follow the general directions for pizza dough. Preheat oven to 475° F. Spread dough with tomato sauce. Top with mozzarella, grated Romano and goat cheese. Sprinkle with basil and drizzle with olive oil. Bake in middle of preheated oven at least 10 minutes. Keep an eye on it. Let cool 5 to 8 minutes before serving. Serves 2 to 3.

Zucchini and Basil

For one 12" pizza or 3–4 individual pizzas / 3–4 calzones / 2–3 focaccia rounds • Blood Type: A, B, AB, O

(Recipe courtesy of Dr. Peter D'Adamo from *Cook Right for Your Type*)

2 medium-sized green zucchini
2 medium-sized yellow squash
½ tsp salt
2 Tbsp Garlic-Shallot Mixture
¼ tsp cup fresh basil, chopped
1 Tbsp Extra-Virgin Olive oil

Follow the general directions for pizza dough. Preheat oven to 475° F. Wash and dry all the squash. Slice on a long angle, about ¼ inch thick. Lay the zucchini out on paper towels and sprinkle with salt. Brush the dough with Garlic-Shallot Mixture. Blot moisture from basil and zucchini. Layer zucchini slices evenly around the top of the dough, alternating green with yellow, until the surface has been covered. Top with grated cheese and basil and drizzle with oil. Bake 15 to 20 minutes on the top rack of the oven until crust is browned and squash is cooked. Serves 2 to 4.

Spinach and Ricotta

For 1 12" pizza / 2–3 calzones / 2 focaccia rounds • Blood Type: A, B, AB

(Recipe courtesy of Dr. Peter D'Adamo from *Cook Right for Your Type*)

1   bunch fresh spinach, washed, dried and chopped
1   cup low-fat Ricotta cheese
2   Tbsp fresh garlic, put through a press
1   to 1½ tsp salt
2   Tbsp chopped fresh parsley or basil
⅓   cup grated Pecorino Romano cheese
1   cup grated Mozzarella cheese
1   Tbsp Olive oil

Follow the general directions for pizza dough. Preheat oven to 475° F. Carefully wash the fresh spinach to remove all grit and then lightly steam until wilted. Mix spinach with ricotta, garlic, salt and parsley or basil. Spread mixture evenly over dough. Top with grated cheeses and drizzle with olive oil. Bake on a lower rack 10 to 15 minutes or until golden brown. Serves 2 to 4.

Roasted Peppers and Soft Goat Cheese

For 1 12" pizza / 3 calzones / 2 focaccia rounds • Blood Type: B, O

3   Tbsp Garlic-Shallot or Garlic-Onion mixture
1   cup soft goat cheese
1   cup roasted peppers
4   Tbsp Pecorino Romano or Kasseri, finely grated
Olive oil

Preheat oven to 475° F. Paint crust with Garlic/Shallot or Garlic-Onion mixture. Place roasted pepper strips over dabs of goat cheese in a wheel design around crust. Sprinkle surface with grated cheese. Drizzle with olive oil. Bake 15 minutes on lower rack.

Garden Topping: Fresh Tomatoes, Basil and Mozzarella

For 2–3 individual pizzas / 2 focaccia rounds • Blood Type: AB

4   Tbsp Garlic-Shallot or Garlic-Onion mixture
2   large vine-ripened tomatoes or 6 vine-ripened Roma (Italian Plum) tomatoes
4   Tbsp chopped fresh basil
1   cup sliced soft mozzarella
Extra-Virgin Olive oil

Preheat oven to 475° F. Brush crust with garlic-shallot mixture. Place tomato slices over top. Sprinkle with fresh basil. Cover with thinly sliced soft mozzarella. Drizzle with olive oil. Bake 15 minutes on lower rack.

Florentine

For 1 12" pizza / 2–3 individual pizzas / 2 focaccia rounds / baguette sliced for crostini
Blood Type: A, B, AB, O (A and B use oil instead of marinara or puree)

1 bunch fresh spinach or 6 oz (1 bag) fresh baby spinach, washed, patted dry, chopped
4 Tbsp Garlic-Shallot mixture
1 cup red onions, coarsely chopped
½ cup pine nuts
1 cup Parmesan, Romano, Asiago or Pecorino Romano cheese, finely grated
Marinara OR tomato puree OR Olive oil
Cooked Chicken OR turkey in strips; Italian turkey sausage in chunks (optional)

Preheat oven to 475° F. Place sauté pan over medium heat; add 1 Tbsp of the garlic-shallot mixture to pan and let heat. Add the pine nuts and cook for 2 minutes; add the chopped spinach and cook 2–3 minutes. Remove from heat. Paint crust with garlic-shallot mixture or with tomato puree or marinara. Sprinkle with cooked chicken or sausage (optional). Sprinkle with the spinach, toasted nuts and onions. Sprinkle with finely grated cheese. Drizzle with olive oil. Bake 15 minutes on lower rack.

Turkey or Beef Meatballs n' Marinara or Oil

For 3–4 12" pizzas / 8 individual pizzas / 4 focaccia rounds / 6 large calzones
Blood Type: O (Beef), AB (Turkey)

½ cup Garlic-Shallot mixture
1 recipe **Classic Meatballs** (see recipe under *The Mighty Meatball* Section)
2 cups marinara
2 cups Mozzarella cheese
dried crushed Italian herbs such as marjoram, oregano, basil, rosemary
Olive oil

Preheat oven to 475° F. Paint pizza crust or top of focaccia or calzone with garlic-shallot mixture. Spread marinara with spatula or back of spoon. Sprinkle with dried, crushed Italian herbs. Dot with sliced meatballs. Cover with cheese. Drizzle lightly with olive oil. Bake on lowest rack for 10 minutes; switch to top rack and bake an additional 10–12 minutes.

See also Greek Topping (Spinach/Feta/Pine Nuts) under Bagels on the Morning Menu

Going Round the World (International)
Flour Tortillas

This is the recipe for the traditional Sonoran-style flour tortillas I grew up eating— handkerchief thin and pliable. However, oil and not the traditional lard is used to make them. The Spaniards introduced wheat to the New World. The northwest region of colonial New Spain, which once included Arizona, became the breadbasket of Mexico and flour tortillas are one of its most famous exports. When I did archaeology in Northwest Mexico, it was standard fare to heat fresh tortillas on a flat rock in the sun then make a burro of nopales (paddle cactus fruit) and frijoles (beans). No matter how you eat them—bean burros, quesadillas, seasoned chips, cheese crisps, roll-ups or with olive oil and grated cheese, or as *thin pizza crust*—they are wonderful and nutritious. They are also simple to make, quick to cook on griddle, in a skillet or on the grill.

Blood Type: A, B, AB, O • Prep time: 5 min (15 min dough rest)
Cook time: 25–30 min/dozen • Servings: 12 (1 lb dough)

White Flour Tortillas

2¼ cups White Spelt flour
1   tsp salt
3   Tbsp oil
½   cup + 1 Tbsp + 1 tsp warm water

1. Place flour and salt in mixing bowl; whisk. Add oil; cut in until mixture resembles coarse corn meal. Add warm water and mix to make soft dough, adding more water by the tsp if necessary. Knead in bowl or on a floured surface to form soft springy dough. Divide dough into 12 balls (6 balls will make large 8–9" tortillas). Cover and let rest 15 minutes.

2. Place an ungreased griddle or heavy skillet over medium high heat. Press out or roll tortilla until thinner than 1/16th". Place on griddle and cook 1–2 minutes until the characteristic brown patches show. Flip. Cook an additional 1–2 minutes. When bubbles form, press them down gently with the back of a spoon or a cloth. (Tip: Put a small skillet on the flipped side of the tortilla; it keeps bubbles down while you are rolling out the next tortilla.) When tortilla is cooked, place it in a folded tea towel to keep warm and moist. Keep adding tortillas to the pile, covering them as you go. Serve in tortilla basket or nested in a towel. If any tortillas remain, place them in a plastic bag and store in freezer.

Whole Grain Spelt Tortillas: Use 1 cup White Spelt flour and 1 cup Whole Grain Spelt flour in place of the 2¼ cups White Spelt flour called for in the master recipe. These are exceedingly tasty tortillas that hold together beautifully for all the variations below.

Quesadillas: Another form of turnover, the Quesadilla is a grilled/baked folded cheese crisp sprinkled inside with onions, peppers and some form of meat. Spray with oil or brush tortilla with oil or softened butter. Sprinkle grated cheese to cover half of the tortilla. Sprinkle morsels of spicy cooked chicken, turkey or shredded beef over the cheese then dot with tomatoes, fresh chopped onions and jalapeños or green chiles. Zucchini and crookneck squash mixed with sweet onions are also good on Quesadillas. Just slice into thin rounds, chop the onions. Place all in a warmed sauté pan with a little oil. Cook for 10 minutes. Dot the cheese with vegetables as above. ***Stovetop:*** Heat a griddle or skillet (medium high heat) with a small amount of oil/butter just enough to coat the bottom. Place the Quesadilla on griddle and cook until bottom is shiny golden brown and cheese is melting out of the tortilla. ***Oven:*** Preheat oven to 400° F. Place Quesadilla(s) on an ungreased baking sheet. Bake 5–7 minutes or until tortilla is turning crispy golden brown and cheese is bubbling out. They are also easy and delicious to throw on a grill either plain or wrapped in foil.

Cheese Crisps: My perennial favorite—it's a pizza by another name. Set tortilla on baking sheet, brush or spray with small amount of oil or spread with softened butter. Sprinkle tortilla with cheese(s). Add toppings such as grilled peppers, cooked shredded spicy beef, chicken or turkey. Place in preheated 400° F oven (middle rack) and bake for 5 minutes until cheese melts and tortilla edges are golden brown and edges start to crisp. Serve with salsa.

Tortilla Chips: Cut tortillas into small triangles. Brush or spray with small amount of oil. Can also be baked by just moistening with water. Place on baking sheet in preheated 350° F oven and cook about 8–10 minutes until they start to brown.

Nachos: Cut tortillas into small triangles. Spray with oil. Place on a sheet of foil on a large rimmed baking pan. Bake for 10 minutes at 350° F. Remove from oven and turn heat up to 475° F. Sprinkle chips with grated Monterey Jack, Colby-Jack or Mozzarella (for Blood Types A, O). Sprinkle with toppings such as diced tomatoes and green chiles or jalapeños and cooked shredded beef or chicken. Return to oven and bake 4–5 minutes until cheese melts and starts oozing off the chips.

Pizza: For the portion control or carb-conscious or thin-crust lover, use Spelt tortillas as a base for pizza and top as you would a regular pizza. See *Topping and Filling Many Small Things*.

Wraps: For wraps to really work, they must be moist *and* be able to hold moist foods. Spelt excels in both these categories. Use them as wraps for hot foods like broiled vegetables or for cold cuts, cheese and vegies. The wraps will stay fresh in a cooler for many days if wrapped well which makes them a wonderful travel and camping food.

Empanadas Fritas de Chile y Queso
Fried Turnovers with Chile and Cheese

I could not resist putting Empanadas Fritas in the book despite the fact they are deep-fried. It s a favorite recipe I have made for many years and now make, better, with Spelt. The variations are limited to your imagination: shredded beef, grated cheese, chiles; spinach and mozzarella; mashed sweet potatoes and raisins empanadas which I've eaten in Central America; shredded fish or shrimp with a bit of Farmers cheese, onion and chiles like you get in the beach towns of southern Mexico. These are foolproof and great for get-togethers. The recipe can be doubled with no problem.

Blood Type: Not rated • Prep time: 10–15 min • Cook time: 15–20 min • Yield: 6 Empanadas

Ingredients

½   cup Whole Grain Spelt flour
½   cup White Spelt flour
¼   tsp salt
1½ cups grated Mozzarella, Monterey Jack or Colby-Jack
½   cup (4 oz can) green chiles, roasted, peeled, chopped
¼   cup water, room temperature or broth, cooled
Vegetable oil for cooking

1. Heat oil (to a depth of ¼") in large skillet set on moderately high heat.

2. Mix the flour with salt, ½ cup of the shredded cheese and the water to form dough. Divide the dough into 6 balls. Lightly dust a small plate or saucer with flour.

3. Put a ball of dough on plate and flatten to 5" round. Place a rounded Tbsp of chopped green chiles and 2 Tbsp of shredded cheese on one side of the dough. Fold dough over and seal the edges to make a half moon. Crimp the edges with tines of a fork or by pressing between your index finger and thumb.

4. Put the turnover in the hot oil. Fry until golden brown (about 7–8 minutes). Turn. Fry other side, making sure you turn the empanada only once. Remove from pan and drain on paper towels. Serve hot. Any of the unfried turnovers can be frozen. Wrap in plastic; put into freezer bag. Let thaw for half an hour. Cook according to directions.

Empanadas Valencianas
Baked Turnovers

Empanadas are turnovers, a food deeply rooted in the past and still very much alive in the present. (See cover photograph.) They come by a different name in different places, for example, in Wales they are pasties. This particular recipe is very old, given to me by a Spanish friend who in turn learned it from her Andalusian grandmother (who did not have the benefit of a refrigerator for cold marination). Flour, olive oil, water and salt are the basic dough ingredients in this recipe and all over the Mediterranean and Near East. Traditional fillings include beef, lamb or fruit in season (see Empanadas de Fruta on the *Morning Menu*).

Blood Type: B and O make with Beef or Lamb; A and AB make with vegetable fillings, fish, turkey.
Prep time: 30 min • Cook time: 20–25 min • Yield: 10

Ingredients—Dough

1   Recipe White or Mixed Flour Double Pie Crust (see *Pastry/Pie Crust Chart* under *Pastries, Pies and Other Sweet Delights*)
1   Recipe Filling (next page)
1   egg, room temperature, beaten

1. Roll the dough into 10 balls. Cover the balls with plastic wrap or slightly damp towel. Set them aside to rest (at room temperature) while you prepare the filling (next page).

2. Preheat oven to 425° F. Roll or pat/stretch a ball to form a 6" circle. Using a ¼ cup dry measure as a guide, place filling slightly off center of one side of the circle as in illustration above. Spread to within a ½" of the edge. Fold the other half of the circle over the filling to make a half moon. Pinch edges to close in a fluted pattern or use tines of a fork to seal. Brush the Empanada with beaten egg. Prick top in several places with fork tines or make several slits with a sharp knife so steam can escape during baking.

3. Lightly oil a large baking sheet (15" x 10" jelly roll pan) or cover with parchment. Place each Empanada on baking sheet and set on middle rack of preheated hot (425° F) oven. Bake for 20–25 minutes or until golden brown and crisp and juices are bubbling. Serve warm or at room temperature. These freeze well. Place leftovers in a resealable freezer bag.

Empanada Fillings
for Baked Turnovers

Ingredients—Beef or Lamb Filling

1½ pounds beef or lamb, freshly chopped or ground
½ cup sweet onion, finely chopped
1 Tbsp garlic, minced
1 tsp salt (or Dulse granules)
¼ tsp freshly ground black pepper (optional)
2 Tbsp Olive oil
vegetable oil for browning

For additional flavor:

Beef: add ¼ cup fresh, chopped Serrano or Jalapeño chiles and ½ tsp cayenne
Lamb: add ½ tsp dried, crushed marjoram and 1½ tsp dried, crushed rosemary or a Tbsp or more of fresh

1. Combine the ingredients for beef or lamb filling. Add the olive oil and mix. If marinating, ahead of time, place ingredients in a resealable plastic bag or bowl with tight-fitting lid. Refrigerate a minimum of 4 hours; overnight is best.

2. Place large skillet containing 1 Tbsp of oil over medium high heat. Add the filling and brown (about 15–20 minutes). Remove from heat. Continue as directed for Empanadas.

Some Variations:

Shredded Beef With Green Chiles or Nopales with cooked/diced potatoes and onions. (The nopales are now found on grocery store shelves most everywhere.) Salt and pepper the beef and vegetables to taste. Add Mexican cheese such as Cotija or Farmers.

Fried or Baked Codfish with Buttered Potatoes and Onions. These are excellent and simple to make but are for eating warm, not to keep as leftovers. Chunk the fried or baked fish. Saute the sweet onions and diced, cooked potatoes in butter or light olive oil. Mix in the cooked fish. Add a grinding of fresh pepper and salt to taste or use lemon pepper. Sprinkle with fresh flat-leafed parsley (Italian Parsley). Spoon the ingredients over the Empanada dough. Seal and bake as above.

Enchilada Sauce Sabrosa

Sabrosa in Spanish means savory—rich, complex, aromatic, all of these things combined. This is a rich and flavorful, traditional sauce that can be used not just for enchiladas, but for baked chicken or turkey dishes, as the basis for a mole (chocolate/chili/peanut) sauce, and for those wonderful eggs, Huevos Rancheros, served on fresh Spelt flour tortillas and refried beans (see recipe under *Morning Menu*).

Blood Type: B, AB, O • Prep time: 5 min • Cook time: 15 min • Yield: about 1¼ cups

Ingredients

3   Tbsp Olive or other vegetable oil
3   Tbsp Whole Grain Spelt flour
2   cups warm water or warmed beef, chicken, turkey or vegetable stock
6   Tbsp mild New Mexico ground chili powder
1   Tbsp salt (optional)
½   tsp garlic powder
¼   tsp ground cumin

1. Place saucepan with oil over medium heat. Let oil warm. Add the flour and stir; brown the flour for several minutes.

2. Add the chili powder to the water or stock; stir to dissolve.

3. Add chili liquid to the flour, mixing well. Add the salt (optional), garlic power and cumin.

4. Continuing to stir, bring mixture to full bubbling boil. Reduce heat and simmer, covered, for 5 minutes. Serve warm. Cooled sauce may be refrigerated for several days.

Epic of Enchi-Mesh: Sonoran Style Enchiladas
(Chicken or Turkey)

There are few things as intensely satisfying as border-style enchiladas imbued with rich, deeply flavored chili sauce. *Spelt Healthy!* Enchiladas are the real thing— from sauce to tortillas to turkey filling. Not far from where I live in the Southwest U.S., archaeologists found the remains of ancient turkey pens attached to houses at an Anasazi site.

Blood Type: Unrated. These are World-Class enchiladas. Enough said.
Prep time: 20–30 min • Cook time: 10 min • Yield: 6 large and satisfying Enchiladas

Ingredients—In Advance

1 recipe Enchilada Sauce Sabrosa per 6 enchiladas (see preceding recipe)

1 recipe Spelt Flour Tortillas (6 6" to 7" tortillas) (see under *Many Small Things* section)

Enchiladas

1½ pounds turkey breast, cooked, shredded (about 2 cups, enough for ⅓ cup per enchilada

1 cup grated cheese such as Monterey Jack, Colby-Jack, Longhorn Cheddar, Mozzarella, Mexican Semi-Soft Farmers Cheese

1 cup Mayan onions, chopped

½ cup fresh jalapeños, finely diced (optional)

2 bunches fresh scallions (optional) for sprinkling

Olive or other vegetable oil for quick frying

¼ cup vegetable oil for dipping tortillas

Shredded lettuce, chopped olives or tomatoes for garnish (optional)

1. Place a large skillet over medium heat. Add sufficient oil to lightly cover bottom of pan and let oil heat. Add the chopped onions and fresh jalapeños (optional). Sauté for several minutes. Place saucepan with Enchilada Sauce in it over low heat, stirring occasionally. Warm the sauce but do not boil it.

2. Add the turkey to the skillet with onions/peppers adding additional oil if necessary to brown meat. Slightly increase heat. Stirring regularly, quickly brown and crisp the exterior while leaving the meat succulent on the inside. Remove from heat. Set aside.

3. Warm an 8" skillet with ¼ cup vegetable oil in it. The oil should be just warm enough to soften tortillas but not crisp them. (Skillet should be slightly larger than the size of a tortilla laid flat in it.)

4. Lightly oil an 8" x 12" or similar pan or baking dish that will accommodate the tortillas. Set aside. Preheat the oven to 350° F.

5. Dip a tortilla in oil; let excess oil drip off. Place tortilla on a plate. Fill it with ⅓ cup of the meat mixture. Sprinkle 1 Tbsp of cheese over the meat. Roll up the tortilla snugly. Set it in the baking pan. Repeat for remaining enchiladas. Sprinkle all with cheese. Sprinkle with scallions (optional). Pour the warmed sauce over the enchiladas.

6. Place pan on center rack of preheated 350° F oven. Let bake for 10 minutes until cheese melts and sauce bubbles. Garnish with finely shredded lettuce and chopped olives or tomatoes. Serve warm with traditional refried beans and Spanish rice.

Pita Bread

Ancient flatbread made from an ancient grain. Soft, pliable, cream-colored, lovely and smooth, this Pita Bread brings out the best in Spelt.

Blood Type: A, B, AB, O • Prep time: 10 min (+ rising time) • Cook time: 15–20 min • Yield: 12 4" or 8 large (4 oz)

Ingredients

1   pkg active dry yeast
1   Tbsp granulated sugar
½   cup warm water (110°–115° F)
1   cup warm water (110°–115° F)
2   tsp salt
1   cup Whole Grain Spelt flour
3   cups White Spelt flour
1   Tbsp Olive oil

1. In a large mixing bowl, place ½ cup warm water; add the sugar. Sprinkle the yeast over top. Stir to dissolve. Let stand 10 minutes until creamy and foamy.

2. Pour 1 cup warm water and salt into the bowl with yeast. Add the Spelt flours.

Stand Mixer (paddle, speed 2): Beat for a minute to form rough dough. Scrape down sides of bowl with spatula. Add the oil. Mix with paddle 30 seconds then change to dough hook. On lowest speed, knead for a minute to a minute and a half until soft dough forms, the oil is absorbed and dough cleans sides of bowl.

By Hand: Beat until rough dough forms. Add the oil and mix until dough absorbs the oil, forms soft dough that cleans sides of bowl (3–4 minutes).

3. Keep in same mixing bowl and cover with plastic wrap, plate or damp towel and place in a warm (80°–85° F), draft-free place. Let rise until dough doubles in volume. This is warm, fast-rise dough so check at 30 minutes and at 10 minute intervals thereafter.

4. Loosen dough from edges of bowl and lay them over top of dough ball. With loose fist, gently depress the dough by working loose fist around bowl.

Stand Mixer: Return bowl to stand. Knead with dough hook for 1½ to 2 minutes adding flour by the Tbsp if necessary to get smooth, elastic dough. Turn out onto lightly floured surface.

By Hand: Turn out onto lightly floured surface and knead lightly for several minutes to form soft, elastic smooth dough. Add flour if necessary by sprinkling it over dough in small amounts.

5. With pastry scraper or sharp knife, divide dough into the number of pieces desired (12 small 4" pitas, 10 5" pitas, 8 large 4 oz pitas). Cover the dough balls and let dough rest 10 minutes.

6. Preheat oven to 375° F and place one rack on bottom rung of oven. Lightly oil a cookie sheet. Gently roll or pat/stretch balls into a circle. Place 3 or 4 on the oiled cooking sheet, leaving 2 inches between each pita. Bake for 3–4 minutes. The edges will start turning dry. Turn with a metal spatula and bake 3–4 minutes more. They should be puffy, the edges dry, and pita pliable not stiff. Baking time will vary with the mix of flours and size of Pita. Bake an additional 2–3 minutes per side if necessary especially for the larger Pita. Do not overcook or they

crack and become hard. Undercooked, the pocket will not form and the interior will be gummy. As they are cooking, make the remainder of the pitas and cover with plastic wrap or damp cloth.

7. Remove the cooked pitas from oven and wrap in a cloth towel until all cooked. (Note: A good place to keep the bundle warm is inside the microwave.) Continue until all are baked. Serve fresh with your favorite fillings and sauces. (See following pages for recipes for Gyros, Falafel, and Tsatsiki Sauce.)

8. Store leftover pitas in a plastic bag and place in freezer. Use the leftovers for Pita Wedges (next page) or with soups and salads.

Pita Wedges

Flatbreads like Pita made from the ancient grains predate the first human writing as in the protocunieform pictured here showing grain and grain storage. Pita with goat/sheep cheese has been eaten for millenia.

Blood Type: A, B, AB, O • Prep time: 5 to 10 min • Cook time: 10–12 min • Yield: 24 wedges

Ingredients

4   Spelt pitas (4–5")

1. Preheat oven to 350° F. Cut each pita into 6 wedges. Set wedges on large, ungreased cookie sheet.

2. Make a **variety** (below) of pita wedges on the same pan to suit many tastes. Serve with salads or dips, as a snack or in a lunchbox.

Plain. Just cut and bake for 10–12 minutes.

Cheese Topping. Any of the drier, saltier cheeses work well on Spelt pita: Greek Kasseri Sheep Cheese ranks very high on my list of pita toppings as do Asiago, Pecorino, Parmesan and the drier form of Mozzarella. Finely grate the cheese (about 1 tsp per wedge). Sprinkle on a pita wedge or brush the wedge with a bit of olive oil and then add the cheese. Bake 10–12 minutes until cheese just starts to brown.

Olive Oil and Seasonings. Brush the wedges with olive oil and sprinkle with dried rosemary and sea salt or other fresh or dried herbs to taste. Bake 10–12 minutes.

Gyros (Doner Kabab)

What we in the U. S. call the Gyro (lamb slices in pita pocket with sauce and vegetables) has ancient origins in the Middle East. One version, *judhaba,* is lamb or goat meat slowly roasted in its juices; minced then scooped up or spread on flatbread. Another version of the Gyro is the Turkish *Doner Kebab:* meat slowly roasted and sliced. The modern version is lamb or lamb/beef composites cooked on a rotisserie grill and then thinly sliced for placing in pita bread.

Blood Type: B, AB, O • Prep/cook time varies • Yield: 2 lb Gyro meat

Lamb for Pita (Stovetop)

Two pounds of lamb shoulder. Wash and rinse then cut into small cubes or strips. Season 1 cup of White Spelt flour with salt, granulated garlic, pepper to taste and ground rosemary. Dredge meat in seasoned flour. Place a large (12") skillet over medium heat. Add 3 Tbsp olive oil. Warm the oil until a haze forms over it. Brown the lamb on all sides; reduce to moderate heat. Cook an additional 20–25 minutes or until tender. Place on fresh *Spelt Pita* or inside a Pita pocket, spoon on *Tsatsiki Sauce* and add fresh chopped lettuce, sliced tomatoes, cucumber or zucchini.

Lamb for Pita (Roasted)

Two pounds of lamb shoulder. Wash and rinse lamb; pat dry. Rub with olive oil. Place on rack in roasting pan. Sprinkle lightly with powdered garlic, salt and pepper if desired. Place in preheated slow (325° F) oven and allow to cook slowly for 1½ to 2 hours. Remove from oven and thinly slice off crisp but tender pieces from outside of the lamb roast. Place slices on or in fresh *Spelt Pitas,* spoon *Tsatsiki Sauce* over all, and serve with grilled vegetables such as roasted peppers, green onions or quartered brown onions. Return lamb to oven and repeat process as needed.

Falafel
with Tsatsiki Sauce

Traditional Middle Eastern recipe for Garbanzo (Chick Pea) Beans and Bulgur Wheat patties is translated *Spelt Healthy!* style to a piquant and fresh tasting vegetable delight with Whole Grain Spelt flour and crumbs. Serve in Pita Pockets with Tsatsiki Sauce (see next page) or as a side dish the way you would Hush Puppies. These are delicious and quick to make.

Blood type: O • Prep time: 10 min • Cook time: 15–20 min • Yield: 3 dozen (small)

Ingredients

1   15-oz can Garbanzo beans, rinsed and drained
½   cup cool water
½   cup Whole Grain Spelt flour
¾   cup dried Spelt crumbs (divided ¼ cup and ½ cup)
2   tsp Olive or canola oil
½   cup brown or sweet onion, coarsely chopped
¼   cup Italian parsley or baby spinach, chopped
3–4 cloves of fresh juicy garlic, minced
½   tsp ground cumin
1½   tsp dried, crushed marjoram OR oregano
¼   tsp ground coriander
½   tsp salt
dash of pepper or cayenne to taste (optional)
1   tsp fresh lemon juice
Olive or canola oil for frying

1. Rinse and drain the garbanzo beans. In food processor fitted with metal blade, process beans to a thick mash. Add the remaining ingredients, including ¼ cup dried Spelt breadcrumbs and pulse several times to blend, but not fine process, ingredients. The mix should be somewhat rough in texture.

2. Remove from processor and place in bowl. Cover and let stand, covered, for one hour.

3. Place large (12") frying pan over medium high heat with sufficient oil to lightly coat the bottom of pan. Let pan warm until haze forms over oil.

4. Form mixture into the traditional small balls the size of walnuts or into small patties. Roll in remaining Spelt crumbs.

5. Place in pan and cook about 4 minutes per side or until well browned. Turn; repeat until balls/patties are crisp adding oil as necessary. Allow to cool and set 5 minutes before placing in pita pockets with *Tsatsiki Sauce* spooned over top. Serve as a side dish to fish, poultry, or salads or using for dipping with Aioli (Garlic Mayonnaise under *Many Small Things—Small Beginnings).*

Tsatsiki Sauce

This traditional Middle Eastern sauce is usually made with cucumbers and onions. This version uses fresh zucchini, which can be eaten by almost anyone without suffering gastric distress. The same applies to using goat yogurt to impart the traditional and delicious taste to this sauce and make it easy for people to digest.

Blood Type: A, B, AB • Prep time: 10 min • Cook time: None • Yield: 2½ cups sauce

Ingredients (Makes 2½ cups sauce)

2   cups goat's milk yogurt
½   medium red onion (about ½ cup)
½   medium zucchini
¼   tsp salt (substitute Dulse granules if low-salt diet. Also, Dulse lends good color)
1   tsp garlic powder
1   tsp celery seed

1. Slice the zucchini lengthwise; process into thin slices.

2. Process the red onion into thin slices.

3. Using a glass or ceramic bowl, add all ingredients and stir together well.

4. Serve at room temperature.

Yusef's Hummus

Hummus is the classic Middle Eastern sauce to serve with Pita. It is a thick delicious mash of garbanzo beans and tahini (ground sesame seed). Spread on Pita bread or use as a dip to accompany not just Gyros but a variety of Middle Eastern and Mediterranean foods.

Blood Type: O • Prep time: 5 min • Cook time: None • Yield: 1¾ cups

Ingredients

1   15 oz can garbanzo beans (chick peas)
1   Tbsp Olive oil
½   tsp granulated garlic (or more to taste)
OR 1–2 cloves garlic, crushed
1   Tbsp lemon juice
2   Tbsp tahini
Dash of salt
Dash of Hungarian paprika (sweet or hot)
Olive oil for drizzling

1. Drain beans, preserving two Tbsp of liquid. Rinse; place in colander.

2. In processor or blender, add all ingredients and puree until desired dip texture is achieved. To thin, add some of the reserved bean liquid.

3. Pour into decorative serving dish (glass or ceramic). Lightly sprinkle with Hungarian paprika. Lightly drizzle olive oil over the surface. Let stand for a couple of hours at room temperature for flavor to fully develop.

4. Serve at room temperature. Spread on fresh Spelt Pita and sprinkle with Spelt Sprouts or as dip for crudités such as cherry tomatoes, zucchini sticks, bell peppers and toasted Pita.

Tod Mun Pla
Thai Style Fish Cakes with Spicy Sauce

This is a tingling, fresh Southwest version of Thai Style Fish Cakes with Spicy Sauce. It is a simple and delectable dish especially for light summer eating. The Tod Mun (fish cakes) are topped with a sweet/sour clear sauce made with fresh vegetables, more a salad than a sauce.

Blood Type: B, O (O use Apple Cider Vinegar)
Prep time: 10 min • Cook time: 25–30 min • Yield: 24 (3" patties)

Ingredients

1½ pounds codfish (24 oz) or other white fish to taste and Blood Type
1¼ cups fine, dried White Spelt crumbs
1 cup red onions, finely processed
1 Tbsp + 1 tsp Chinese Chili Sauce (Paste)
1 egg, room temperature, well beaten
vegetable oil for frying

1. Place a large (12") skillet over moderately high heat. Add 2 Tbsp vegetable oil.

2. In processor bowl fitted with metal blade, shred the codfish or chop the fish into fine pieces by hand.

3. Place fish in large mixing bowl; stir in the Chili Sauce and coat fish with it. Stir in the onions.

4. Add the beaten egg and the dried breadcrumbs. Stir until all ingredients are moist. If mixture is dry, simply add a drizzle of vegetable oil to the mixture.

5. Form the fish mixture into 3" patties; place patties in hot skillet without crowding them. Fry 3–4 minutes until browned. Gently turn patty over; repeat. Remove patties and set on paper towels to drain. Keep the fish patties warm until served. Serve with Tod Mun Pla Sauce.

Tod Mun Pla Sauce (Makes about 2 cups: varies with amount of vegetables used):

1 cup Rice Wine Vinegar or Apple Vinegar
½ cup (4 whole) fresh Serrano or Jalapeño Chilis, finely chopped
1 tsp red pepper flakes (optional)
1¼ cups red onions, chopped
½ cup zucchini or cucumber, chopped (or more to taste)
½ cup light brown sugar, tightly packed
½ cup cool water
Chopped, roasted peanuts for sprinkling (optional)

Pour vinegar, water and brown sugar in a large, glass mixing bowl; whisk. Stir in the chilis and pepper flakes (optional), red onions and zucchini or cucumber. Set aside at room temperature or, covered, in the refrigerator while fish patties are being cooked. Serve by spooning a little sauce over each warm patty. Sprinkle with the traditional chopped roasted peanuts.

Char Shiu Bao
Chinese Steamed Barbecue Buns
with Sweet, Cherried Beef Filling

Char Shiu Bao is the ultimate in Many Small Things, one of the dim sum delights of all time. We used to get a dozen in a pink box from a Chinatown bakery and take them on the road with us. They lasted for days. Now you can make them at home and enjoy them for a longer time.

We created this Spelt/Cherried Beef version of Char Shiu specifically for Whole Food, Diabetic and Blood Type eating. We replaced that special pink additive of Char Shiu Bao with a combination of Sweet Cherries, brown sugar and molasses. Beef replaces pork. The buns are a pure Spelt delight—they swell and shine and stay moist and inviting.

Cooking Tip: Char Shiu Bao takes time to make and the process seems a bit complicated at first. It just takes a little organization. If you get family and friends involved it goes very quickly. Please read the recipe carefully—twice before you begin. Lay out all of your utensils especially a steamer: a large double-decker works great for this recipe. If you do not have that large a steamer, simply retard the rise of the buns by placing them, covered with plastic, in the refrigerator as others are steaming. Bring them back out in time to rise (become springy again) before baking. The time will vary.

The Four Basic Steps: (1) *Making the filling.* It is best when allowed to marinate overnight. It also cuts down prep time on cooking day. But it can be made, and be good, the same day. (2) *Making the dough.* This is sweet, fast-rising yeast dough that takes 30–40 minutes to rise. (3) *Shaping, filling the dough and forming the Buns.* (4) *Steaming the buns.*

Blood Type: B, O • Prep time: 1½–2 hours (+ time for marinating and cooking meat ahead of time)
Cook time: 15–20 min/batch • Yield: 20 buns

Ingredients—Filling for 20 buns

1½ pounds beef (boneless chuck) cut into small cubes
¾ cup soy sauce
¾ cup cool water
¾ cup brown sugar
2   Tbsp Robust molasses (dark molasses)
2½ cups (about 18 ounces) frozen Sweet Cherries, thawed
⅓ cup water (or use part of the thawed Cherry water)
3   Tbsp granulated sugar

1. Combine the beef, soy sauce, ¾ cup cool water, brown sugar and the molasses and stir.

2. Place 3 cups thawed Sweet Cherries in food processor bowl fitted with metal blade. Add ⅓ cup water and the granulated sugar. Process on run, 8 seconds, to form a slurry. Stir into the meat mixture. Cover tightly. Marinate at least three hours but best if refrigerated overnight.

3. Bake in preheated slow (325° F) oven for two hours or until consistently but slowly bubbling. The low, slow bake thickens it and gives it flavor. When cooked, remove from oven and let cool on wire rack while preparing dough.

Note: The filling can also be made the fast way by mixing the ingredients and placing directly in 350° F oven for 35–40 minutes. Mixture will bubble and start to brown and form a crust. Let cool. The taste will be terrific but not quite as dark and sweet and thick as good barbecue should be.

Ingredients—Bun Dough

1¼ cups warm water (110°–115° F)
1   pkg active dry yeast
2   Tbsp vegetable oil
½   cup brown sugar, tightly packed or granulated sugar
1   cup Whole Grain Spelt Flour
4   to 4½ cups White Spelt Flour + additional for kneading
¾   tsp salt

4. Place 1¼ cups warm water in a large mixing bowl; add one Tbsp of the brown or granulated sugar. Sprinkle yeast over sugar water; stir until dissolved. Let stand 5 minutes until creamy and foamy. In a medium bowl, combine the Whole Grain Spelt flour and 2 cups of the White Spelt, salt and remaining sugar. Whisk.

5. Add oil to the yeast mixture. Gradually add the dry ingredients from the bowl and mix to form rough dough (about 1 minute). Slowly, add White Spelt by the ½ cup measure.

Stand Mixer (paddle, about 1 minute): Adjust consistency by adding water by the tsp or flour by the Tbsp. Change to dough hook and knead on lowest speed about 1½ minutes until the dough becomes smooth and begins to clean sides of bowl. Turn soft slightly sticky dough out onto lightly floured board and let rest 10 minutes, covered. Lightly knead to form smooth, elastic dough.

By Hand: Beat to form rough dough. Add water by the tsp or flour by Tbsp to adjust dough consistency to form smooth slightly sticky dough. When dough becomes too heavy to mix, turn out onto lightly floured board. Let rest, covered, for 10 minutes. Gently knead into smooth, elastic dough (even by hand this should take only a few minutes).

6. Place dough in a well-oiled bowl, turning to coat all surfaces with oil. Let rise in a warm (85° F), draft-free place until dough doubles in volume (30–40 minutes). Check by inserting a moistened or floured fingertip into crown of dough. If impression remains, the dough is ready for the next step.

Shaping and Filling:

7. Gently deflate dough by detaching edges of dough with spatula from sides of bowl and placing them over top. Gently press with loose fist working around bowl. Turn out onto lightly floured surface. Form into a long cylinder. Place ruler beside dough for best results. With pastry scraper or sharp knife, divide dough into 20 pieces. Place several inches apart on floured surface, cover with plastic wrap sprayed with oil and allow to rest 10 minutes.

8. Cut 20 3" rounds from parchment paper or foil. Put water in steamer and place over medium heat; have steamer trays and a rimmed baking pan(s) ready for setting the formed *Bao* on.

9. Roll or pat/stretch a ball of dough into a 4" circle (a large tuna can is a good model).

   a. Fill the dough circle with a Tbsp of the meat mixture. If there is excess liquid, drain off most. The Spelt will absorb the rest.

   b. Form a little pouch.

   c. Bring the edges together by pleating them and then twisting to seal (think of the twisty top of soft ice cream from a machine).

d. Place twisted side up or down on the paper/foil round (if foil, remember to lightly oil each round). The effect is more decorative and the bun higher if pleated side remains up. Just be certain to seal the bun well and have fun. Do it both ways. Experiment. Like bagels, no two *Bao* are alike.

11. Place remainder of formed buns on rimmed baking sheet(s). Cover buns with plastic wrap sprayed with oil or place in a large (tented) plastic bag and tuck ends under. Retard their rise by placing in refrigerator. Bring them out as others are steaming and let rise in the warm kitchen.

10. Set buns directly in steamer trays leaving 2"–3" between buns to allow for expansion during steaming and allow steam to circulate. (The buns will expand by $\frac{1}{3}$ to $\frac{1}{2}$ during steaming.) Let rise, covered, on steamer trays set on countertop (setting inside a large plastic bag works very well for this) until buns increase in volume by 75%. This will take 12–20 minutes. The time varies according to warmth of kitchen. Check dough ripeness by doing Finger Test. As they are rising, increase the heat under the steamer and bring the water to a simmering boil.

12. When first batch of buns is ready for steaming, stack the steamer racks containing the buns over the steamer. Close lid and steam 15–20 minutes or until dough is cooked. The buns should be shiny and puffy with an occasional oozing of sweet juices bursting from them.

13. Gently remove steamed buns from trays and place on wire racks covered with paper or light tea towels. Add the other buns to the steamer trays. Steam as above.

Eat Char Shiu Bao warm or at room temperature. These freeze exceedingly well. Let them cool completely and place in resealable freezer bags. They will keep for more than a month if frozen properly.

Eggs Foo Young with Spelt Sprouts

Easy to prepare Chinese egg pancakes accompanied by a delicate sweet/sour brown sauce. Excellent all vegetable meal or make with shrimp, chicken or turkey. Serve with a side of Fried Rice with Spelt Sprouts (see following recipe) or include day-old fried rice and other vegetables in the eggs. Like crepes, egg pancakes are a great way to use leftovers or a variety of vegetables in season.

**Blood Type: A (chicken), B (avoid because of soy in sauce), AB (turkey),
O (sub apple cider vinegar and make with all scallions)**

Note: Begin by making the sauce and keeping it on low burner until serving the egg pancakes.

Prep time: 15 min • Cook time: 30 min • Yield: 12 (¼ cup each)

Eggs Foo Young Sauce Ingredients (makes about 1¼ cups sauce)

4   Tbsp soy sauce
2   Tbsp Whole Grain Spelt flour
2   tsp brown sugar
1   tsp rice or apple cider vinegar
1   tsp salt
½   cup leeks OR scallions, white and pale green portion
1   cup cold water

1. Wash leeks thoroughly to get rid of any remaining grit. Pat dry. Cut into finely sliced rounds and set aside.

2. Combine the soy sauce and Spelt flour in a saucepan. Stir together.

3. Add brown sugar, vinegar, salt and stir.

4. Add the leeks and slowly add 1 cup cold water, stirring continually until sauce begins to thicken. Set on low temperature and stir occasionally thereafter. If it becomes too thick, simply add 1 tsp or 2 of water and stir.

Eggs Foo Young Ingredients

6   large eggs, room temperature
½   cup Spelt sprouts
1   cup scallions, thinly sliced (white part up through about half the deep green)
6–8 oz of frozen 91/110 shrimp, cooked tail off, coarsely chopped
OR 6–8 oz finely diced or shredded chicken OR turkey (cooked)
OR other vegetables
1–2 Tbsp vegetable oil

1. Heat oil in a skillet set over medium heat.

2. Combine the Spelt sprouts, scallions, shrimp (or alternative meat or vegetables) in a mixing bowl.

3. In a small bowl, lightly beat the eggs then add to the sprout/scallion mixture and stir.

4. Using a ¼ cup measure, pour mixture into skillet then fry until golden brown on one side, then turn once and fry other side until brown.

5. Place on platter and keep warm. Spoon warm sauce over each pancake and serve.

Fried Rice with Spelt Sprouts

Chinese-style fried rice. Use diced meat, poultry or fish in combination with vegetables such as Spelt Sprouts, peas and onions. The Spelt Sprouts add a sweet crunch to the dish and are used in addition to or as a substitute for vegetables such as water chestnuts.

Blood Type: A (chicken), B and AB (turkey), O (shrimp, chicken, turkey)
Prep time: 5 min (precook the rice) • Cook time: 15 min • Yield: 2 cups (varies with the vegetables)

Ingredients

2   eggs, room temperature
1   cup cooked rice
4   oz fresh or frozen shrimp, coarsely chopped
OR 4 oz cooked, diced meat (turkey or turkey ham, chicken, rabbit)
1   cup frozen green peas, thawed or 8–12 sugar snap peas and other vegetables as desired such as ½ cup brown or sweet onions
½   cup Spelt Sprouts (3 day germination preferable)
½   cup chopped scallions
1–2 tsp soy sauce or alternative
2–3 Tbsp canola or soy oil
salt to taste

1. To wok or large skillet, add 2 tsp of oil and heat on high. Add the eggs and stir about quickly then chop egg into pieces. Remove from wok and set aside in a mixing bowl.

2. Add a bit more oil as needed to the wok/skillet, heat the oil, then add the shrimp or other meat and stir-fry until shrimp is hot. Sprinkle 1 tsp of soy sauce over the shrimp, allow the shrimp to sizzle, then remove shrimp from wok and add to eggs in bowl without mixing.

3. Add a bit of oil to the wok/skillet and let it heat. Add the peas and the other vegetables but not the rice. Stir-fry the vegetables. Remove and add to the egg and shrimp in the bowl.

4. If using brown onions, follow same procedure and cook until they are translucent but not browned. Remove brown onions and add to egg/shrimp/pea mixture in bowl.

5. Add the cooked rice and the Spelt Sprouts to wok/skillet then add the diced meat, stir-frying the rice and meat until the ingredients are hot. Return all the ingredients to the mixing bowl (the eggs/shrimp/peas or other vegetables) and add to the wok/skillet. If using green onions, add them now and stir in. Sprinkle the whole mixture with soy sauce and mix until all ingredients are evenly distributed. Serve warm or at room temperature. Refrigerate leftovers and incorporate in an omelet or Eggs Foo Young (see previous page).

MAIN DISH (ENTRÉE)

Macao Pepper Steak

Meatloaf with Self-Gravy

Moussaka (Beef or Lamb)

Stuffed Pasilla Peppers

Lamb Tagine Maghrib

Lemon Chicken (or other Meat/Fish)

Asian Sunrise Chicken (or Rabbit)

Turkey (Chicken) Toscano

Skillet Variation Chicken/Turkey Toscano

Coated Pan Fried Fish Fillets

Oven Baked Fish Fillets with
Crunchy Lemon Herb Topping

Macao Pepper Steak

Savory and spicy yet delicate pepper steak.

Blood Type: O • Prep time: 10 min* • Cook time: 25–30 min • Yield: 4 servings (4 oz each)

*If serving over rice, allow 45–60 minutes for brown rice to cook (see Tunisian Brown Rice with Spelt Sprouts on the *Many Small Things Menu*).

Ingredients

2   Tbsp Olive or other vegetable oil
1   pound round steak, cut into strips
1   Tbsp Olive or other vegetable oil
1   large sweet onion (about 1 cup), sliced
4   garlic cloves, sliced
2   large jalapeños, cleaned of seeds and pulp, sliced lengthwise
OR 1 bell pepper, sliced lengthwise
½   cup beef broth or stock, low sodium
1   Tbsp sherry
1   tsp brown sugar
½   tsp salt
1½ tsp ginger root, grated
1   tsp red pepper flakes
4   scallions, white and green portions, chopped
¼   cup soy sauce
3   Tbsp White Spelt flour
⅓   cup tepid water

1. In large skillet set over medium high heat, sear the meat, stirring to cook all sides (about 4 minutes). Remove meat from skillet; set meat aside. Lower heat; add oil if needed. Add the onion, garlic and jalapeño (green pepper) and sauté (about 7 minutes).

2. Return the beef to the skillet and add beef broth, sherry, brown sugar, salt, ginger root, green onion and pepper flakes. Cook for 15 minutes on moderate heat, stirring occasionally.

3. Blend soy sauce, White Spelt flour and water until the mixture is smooth. Slowly add to the beef/broth mixture, stirring until the sauce thickens and texture is creamy. Ladle over brown rice.

Meatloaf with Self-Gravy

As a main course or for meatloaf sandwiches on fresh Spelt bread. This is a moist and tasty meatloaf not at all like the stiff dry cardboard covered in gooey gravy or the one slathered in catsup or sweet tomato sauce that pass for meatloaf nowadays.

Blood Type: O • Prep time: 10 min • Cook time: 90 min • Yield: 2 (1 lb loaves)

Ingredients for two one-pound loaves of meatloaf; one for dinner, freeze another for sandwiches

2   pounds 80–90% lean ground beef
1   Tbsp Olive oil
2   tsp garlic powder
1   tsp each crushed thyme, oregano, marjoram, basil
salt and pepper to taste
dash of cayenne (optional)
1   egg
1   14 oz can (1¼ cups) crushed Plum (Roma) tomatoes (divided ¼ cup, 1 cup)
1   cup seasoned, dried Spelt breadcrumbs
½   cup onion, chopped
4   oz soft mozzarella, sliced
oil for drizzling

1. Preheat oven to 350° F. With stand mixer or in food processor, mix meat, oil, garlic, herbs, breadcrumbs and ¼ cup of the crushed tomatoes until combined. Divide into two equal portions and form each into a rectangular loaf. Place in lightly greased 9" x 5" loaf pans so that loaf does not touch sides of pan (leave about ¾" all sides).

2. Sprinkle ¼ cup chopped onions over each loaf. Place mozzarella slices along top of each loaf. Ladle ½ cup crushed tomatoes over the cheese. Lightly drizzle with oil. Place in preheated moderate oven (350° F) and bake for 45 minutes. Juice will form in the pans. Ladle accumulated juices over top of each loaf. Bake additional 35–45 minutes or until done.

3. Remove from oven. Ladle juice out of the pans and into bowl to serve over meatloaf. Serve warm. Let one loaf completely cool, spooning out excess juices. Cut into slices; wrap in plastic and place in tightly covered plastic container and place in freezer. Allow to defrost before use in sandwiches.

For Meatloaf Sandwiches: Simply heat a slice of meatloaf in microwave safe dish (40–60 seconds). Serve on fresh bread or grill, topping with cheese.

Dinner Loaf Variation: Add ½ cup frozen baby peas (thawed), ½ cup sweet onions and ½ cup tomato sauce to the meat before forming into loaves. Reduce herbs to ½ tsp each. Eliminate the crushed tomatoes and cheese. Bake as directed spooning accumulated juices over each loaf as it cooks. Use juice as sauce or incorporate juices into brown gravy.

Moussaka (Beef or Lamb)

The hearty traditional Greek casserole but made with zucchini instead of eggplant and using Spelt crumbs for texture and taste. Make with beef or a mixture of beef and lamb to taste.

Blood Type: Not rated • Prep time: 50 min • Cook time: 45–60 min • Yield: 8 servings

Ingredients

2 pounds zucchini (5 zucchini 6"–7" inch)
¼ cup White Spelt flour
6 Tbsp Olive oil + additional drizzling
2–3 cloves minced garlic
1½ cups chopped onions
1½ pounds 80% lean ground beef
1 pounds ground lamb (or additional ground beef instead of lamb)
⅔ cup tomato puree
1½ cups beef OR vegetable broth (low sodium) OR water
3 Tbsp Italian parsley (flat-leaf parsley), chopped
¼ tsp cinnamon (optional)
1 bay leaf, crumbled
1 tsp coriander OR oregano, dried and crushed
3 eggs, room temperature
2½ cups goat's milk yogurt OR other plain yogurt without additives
1 cup Pecorino Romano or Parmesan cheese, coarse grated (divided ¾, ¼)
1 cup dried, coarse Spelt breadcrumbs
salt and freshly ground pepper to taste (optional)

1. Wash the zucchini; pat dry. Cut off stems. Cut into ¼" rounds. Shake rounds in a bag with ¼ cup White Spelt flour to lightly coat. Place large skillet with 3 Tbsp olive oil in it over medium heat. Lightly brown the zucchini. Remove from skillet; set on paper towels to drain.

2. To the warm skillet, add 3 Tbsp olive oil, minced garlic and chopped onions. Cook until tender. Gradually add the ground meat(s) and cook, stirring frequently, until meat begins to brown. Add the tomato puree, broth (or water), the chopped parsley, cinnamon, crumbled bay leaf, coriander or oregano. Stir in and lower heat to moderate. Stirring frequently, allow sauce to reduce (25–30 minutes) allowing some liquid to remain in pan to prevent Moussaka from being too dry. As it is simmering, make the sauce.

3. **Sauce:** Beat the eggs until foamy. Gradually stir in the yogurt, ½ cup at a time. Add ¾ cup cheese.

4. Preheat oven to 350° F. Grease a 2-quart casserole or shallow oven dish. Over the bottom of the dish, arrange a layer of zucchini. Sprinkle with half the Spelt breadcrumbs, salt and pepper to taste. Cover with meat sauce and the remaining zucchini. Spread the yogurt topping over the ingredients. Sprinkle with the remainder of the crumbs and remaining ¼ cup cheese. Drizzle with olive oil.

5. Bake in preheated moderate (350° F) oven for 45–60 minutes until top is golden brown. Remove from oven; let stand 10–15 minutes before serving. Cut into squares as you would lasagna.

Stuffed Pasilla Peppers

Gourmet Pasilla pepper stuffed with Tunisian Rice mixed with shrimp, beef, chicken, turkey or lamb to create complex layers of flavor.

The Pasilla. Larger than most of the mild Bell peppers, many grocery stores carry the Pasilla next to the hotter peppers such as serranos and jalapeños. The Pasilla should be waxy, lustrous and deep green without bruises or mold. Occasionally you will find the elegant purple Pasilla. These are not hot chiles; warm, yes, but exquisitely full of flavor. To further enhance this recipe, buy the dried variety of pasillas in the Mexican food section of the store. Grind (with mortar and pestle if you can) and season the dish with the dried pasillas to get full flavor. This recipe calls for elephant garlic, used widely in Mexican cooking. It is milder and much larger than its smaller garlic cousin.

Blood Type: Not rated • Prep/cook time: 30 min (cook rice in advance) • Yield: 4 servings

---

Ingredients

3 cups cooked Tunisian Rice (see recipe under *Vegetable Stand*)

1¼ pounds coarsely ground beef OR chopped shrimp or other meat, fish, fowl

1–2 cloves (3 Tbsp) elephant garlic, finely chopped

1 fresh plump jalapeño, minced

¼ tsp red pepper or ground pasilla flakes

½ tsp ground cumin

1 cup *fresh* (not dried) Spelt breadcrumbs, coarse

4 large, fresh Pasilla chiles

Olive oil for cooking

1. Place large skillet with 1 Tbsp oil in it over medium heat. As oil warms, add the ground or chopped meat or poultry and brown quickly, draining any excess liquid. Place meat in small bowl; set aside. Shrimp: place chopped shrimp in skillet, tossing and turning, cooking for 2 minutes. Remove. Set aside.

2. Reduce skillet heat to medium low and add a Tbsp olive oil. Add the elephant garlic and minced jalapeño and cook, stirring occasionally, for 3–4 minutes. Stir in red pepper or pasilla flakes and cumin. Remove from pan; set aside. Add 2 tsp olive oil to the pan. Add 1 cup fresh coarse Spelt breadcrumbs to the oil and any remaining pan juices. Toast for 8 minutes, stirring occasionally. Turn to low heat. Stir in 3 cups Tunisian rice. Add the meat (or shrimp) and the garlic/jalapeños. Stir all together. Cover; keep warm on stove.

3. Turn oven to Broil placing rack on second set of slots down below broiler heat. Grease a rimmed baking pan. Wash and pat dry the fresh Pasilla chiles. Place on pan in oven, turning often as skin chars and blisters and begins to peel. Place the pasillas in plastic bags to steam (15 minutes). Remove from bags; pull gently on stem to remove pulp along with stem.

4. Mound ¼ cup rice on individual plates. Place chiles on rice mound and stuff chiles with the rice/meat mixture. Serve warm or at room temperature. This is excellent served with basic Tsatsiki Sauce (see recipe under *Many Small Things* section).

Lamb Tagine Maghrib

Whole Grain Spelt flour lends its own slightly nutty taste to the rich flavor of Tagine. The Spelt Sprouts add crunch to the varied texture of this traditional North African dish. It is excellent alone or served with a side of Tunisian Rice (under *The Vegetable Stand*).

Blood Type: B, AB, O • Prep/Cook Time: about 2½ hours • Yield: 6 servings

Ingredients

- ½ cup dried Turkish apricots, soaked in 1½ cups hot water
- 3 Tbsp Olive oil
- 1½ pounds boneless lamb shoulder, cut into ¾ inch chunks
- ½ cup Whole Grain Spelt flour
- ½ tsp ground turmeric
- 1 tsp ground coriander
- ¼ cup warm water
- 4 cloves garlic, minced
- 1 cup brown onion, finely chopped
- ½ tsp ground cumin
- 1 tsp Hungarian hot paprika
- ¼ tsp ground allspice
- 1 cup water, room temperature
- ½ cup Spelt Sprouts (optional)

1. Place the apricots in a small bowl with 1½ cups hot water. Set aside.

2. Heat olive oil in a Dutch oven set over medium heat. Add the turmeric and coriander, stir in, and let the spices warm with the pan and the fragrance waft up from the pot.

3. Dredge lamb chunks in flour OR place flour in bag, add lamb and shake to lightly coat. Add the meat to the warm oil and spices, turning, until meat is lightly brown, about 8 minutes adding more oil to the pan if necessary.

4. Add ¼ cup warm water to the pan to loosen the crusting and infuse the flavors. Add the garlic and onion; stir in; reduce heat to low. Cover; let the mixture cook for 10 minutes.

5. Add the cumin, paprika, and allspice; stir. Add 1 cup of the apricot water and bring the mixture to a boil, stirring frequently. Immediately turn down the heat, cover; simmer for one hour.

6. Add the drained apricots and Spelt Sprouts (optional). Salt to taste. Cook an additional 30–40 minutes until the meat and apricots are tender and gravy forms. Serve warm.

Lemon Chicken (or other Meat/Fish)

Delectable lemon velvet sauce complements chicken, fish, turkey or rabbit. This is not the heavily glazed version of lemon chicken found in many Chinese restaurants. Lemon, ginger, roasted nuts and a sprinkling of green onions top chicken coated with seasoned White Spelt flour.

Blood Type: Not rated • Prep time: 15 min • Cook time: 35 min • Yield: 4 servings

Ingredients

3   Tbsp vegetable oil
½   cup chopped nuts (almonds, pine nuts, cashews, pistachios) according to Blood Type
3   garlic cloves, sliced
4   chicken breast fillets, skinless, thinly sliced (1 pound) OR other meat/fish
2   eggs, room temperature
1   Tbsp brown sugar
½   tsp salt
dash of pepper (OR substitute Lemon Pepper for salt/pepper)
¼   cup White Spelt flour
1   lemon, thinly sliced
2   scallions, thinly sliced (white and green portions)

Smooth Lemon Sauce

½   cup brown sugar
2   cups chicken OR turkey broth (14.5 oz)
¼   cup cool water
3   Tbsp White Spelt Flour
4   Tbsp lemon juice
¼   cup marsala or water
1½   tsp ground ginger
2   Tbsp soy sauce

1. Place large skillet over medium heat and add 1 Tbsp oil. Let warm. Add chopped nuts and sliced garlic to skillet; sauté for 5–6 minutes. Discard the garlic. Place nuts in small bowl; set aside to cool. Reduce skillet heat to moderate; add 2 Tbsp oil.

2. Rinse the chicken; pat dry. In a medium bowl, beat eggs with brown sugar. Set aside. Whisk the salt/pepper/flour together; place on small plate. Dip each piece of chicken in the egg/sugar mixture then dredge each piece of chicken in flour, lightly coating both sides. Place in skillet and lightly brown both sides (about 5 to 7 minutes).

3. Remove chicken from skillet; place in lightly oiled baking pan (13" x 9"). Set aside. Heat oven to 350° F.

4. Sauce: Place saucepan over medium heat. Blend the brown sugar, broth, cool water and White Spelt flour until smooth. Add the lemon juice, marsala (or water), ginger and soy sauce. Briefly blend.

5. Pour sauce into the still-warm skillet and stir, deglazing the skillet as you go. Bring sauce to a boil. Ladle the sauce over the browned chicken. Place in preheated moderate (350° F) oven and bake for 30 minutes. Remove from oven. Place lemon slices around each piece of chicken; sprinkle each piece with sliced scallion; top with toasted nuts. Return to oven and cook for 5 minutes. Remove from oven and place on warmed serving platter. Serve hot.

Asian Sunrise Chicken (or Rabbit)

Wake up the slumbering soul of your taste buds and make ordinary food more appealing with the vibrant colors and tastes of spices.

Cooking Note: This recipe is easily adapted to rabbit, which usually comes frozen, cut-up, in three pound packages. Use 4 Tbsp seasoning mix, 1 cup Whole Grain Spelt flour and one cup of broth. Let rabbit cook covered for 45 minutes after frying. It is delicious.

Blood Type: B, O without the black pepper; AB without the black or red pepper
Prep time: 5 min • Cook time: 50–55 • Yield: 4 servings

Ingredients

2   Tbsp Asian Sunrise Seasoning Mix (below)
1   pound chicken thigh fillets, boneless skinless
½   cup chicken (Type O) OR vegetable broth (Type B, AB)
½   cup Whole Grain Spelt flour
vegetable oil for frying (canola, soy)

1. Preheat large skillet over medium high heat with ¼ cup oil in pan. Rinse and pat dry chicken with paper towels. Mix flour and seasoning mix in a bag. Shake up to blend.

2. Place chicken, a piece at a time, into bag and shake until coated. Reserve the flour/seasoning mix.

3. Place pieces in hot skillet. Fry chicken until crisp on one side (about 10 minutes); turn and crisp on other side (about 10 minutes). Turn chicken again. Reduce to moderate heat; cover skillet. Cook until chicken is tender (about 30 minutes).

4. Remove chicken from skillet; set on warmed platter; keep warm.

5. To the pan drippings, stir in 2 tsp of flour/seasoning mixture; let brown for 2 minutes. Slowly add ½ cup of chicken stock or vegetable stock and stir, deglazing the skillet as you stir until the sauce thickens slightly. Pour over warm chicken. Serve immediately.

Asian Sunrise Seasoning Mix

2 Tbsp turmeric
2 tsp dried lemon peel
1 tsp powdered fenugreek
2¼ tsp celery salt
1 Tbsp ground coriander
1 Tbsp Whole Spelt flour
1 Tbsp dried, crushed cilantro leaves
pinch of cayenne and white pepper

Measure ingredients carefully and blend. Using a funnel, place in container with tightly fitting lid. Shake well. Use immediately or freeze. Whole Spelt is alive; also, spices age and lose their vibrant qualities.

Turkey (Chicken) Toscano

Turkey or chicken cutlets on bed of spinach and onion mixed with pine nuts and Spelt croutons with cheese and marinara sauce. Pleases the eye and the palate.

Blood Type: Not rated • Prep Time/Cook Time: 40 min • Yield: 6 servings

Ingredients

6   turkey OR chicken cutlets (approx 4 oz each)
½   cup Olive or other vegetable oil
1   Tbsp garlic, minced
½   tsp celery seed, freshly ground
1   tsp marjoram, dried, crushed
2   to 2¼ cups marinara sauce
¼   cup pine nuts
4–6 Tbsp Olive or other vegetable oil for cooking
½   cup onions, chopped
6   cups chopped fresh baby spinach
2   cups herbed, toasted Spelt bread cubes (¼") (see recipe under *Croutons and Crumbs*)
6   Tbsp grated Parmesan, Romano or Asiago cheese, finely grated
½   cup grated semi-soft Mozzarella

1. Marinate the turkey (or chicken) in ½ cup olive oil, minced garlic, celery seed and marjoram for 30 minutes as other ingredients are cooked. Leave in refrigerator. Reserve this marinade for later use in this recipe. Warm the marinara in small saucepan.

2. Place large skillet over medium heat. Add pine nuts to skillet and toast, stirring occasionally, until light brown (5 minutes). Remove from pan and place in small bowl.

3. Turn skillet down to moderate heat; add 2 Tbsp oil and sauté the onions until translucent. Add the pine nuts and the chopped spinach to the onions; cook spinach until slightly wilted. Add 2 Tbsp olive oil to pan. Add the bread cubes and stir to incorporate oil then add the grated cheese. Stir in. Divide the mixture into 6 mounds. Prepare broiler pan by spraying/wiping with oil. Place the individual mounds on the broiler pan, spaced 2–3 inches apart. Set aside.

4. Wipe the skillet with paper towels and place skillet over medium high heat, adding just enough olive oil to cover bottom of pan. Add cutlets without crowding and brown them on both sides (about 4 minutes per side). Heat oven to 500° F.

5. Place a cutlet on each mound of the spinach mixture. Ladle ¼ cup (or more to taste) of marinara over each cutlet. Sprinkle with mozzarella. Drizzle two tsp of the reserved marinade (remaining from cutlets) over the mozzarella. Place in oven and cook for 7–9 minutes or until cheese starts to brown. Serve immediately.

Skillet Variation Chicken/Turkey Toscano

Pan sautéed split chicken or turkey breast (or rabbit) coated with Spinach Pesto, rolled in fresh Spelt crumbs and covered with melted mozzarella. Marinara sauce optional. Serve with Caesar Salad (see recipe under *The Vegetable Stand*) and Toasted Spelt Croutons (see recipe under *Croutons and Crumbs* section).

Blood Type: A (Chicken and Pesto), O (Chicken or Turkey with Pesto and Marinara), B (Turkey or Rabbit with Pesto) AB (Turkey or Rabbit with Pesto and Marinara) Mozzarella okay for all.
Prep/Cook time: 20 minutes • Servings: 4

Ingredients

1   recipe Spinach Pesto, room temperature (see recipe under *Many Small Things*)
1½ pounds chicken OR turkey breasts OR cut-up rabbit
1½ cups herbed Spelt crumbs
Olive oil for cooking
2   cups Marinara (optional) Types AB and O

1. Split the chicken OR turkey breasts then split again for four portions. Brush with pesto, reserving remaining Spinach Pesto. Roll the split breasts in herbed Spelt crumbs.

2. Place large skillet over medium heat. Add the chicken and cook 5–7 minutes until browned on one side; turn and brown the other side. Turn pan to moderate temperature. Top each fillet with a slice of mozzarella. Top each with 1 Tbsp Spinach Pesto. Let cheese melt down sides and into pan to brown and crisp. Remove from skillet to platter or individual plates. Spoon remaining pesto from pan and spoon marinara (optional) over the chicken. Serve warm.

Coated Pan Fried Fish Fillets

Skinless white fish fillets coated with herbed breadcrumbs and nuts on a bed of seasoned Spelt croutons mixed with spinach and onions. The bedding is also a good stuffing for trout or other whole fish.

Blood Type: A, B, AB, O (all types Cod, Orange Roughy and avoid pepper in recipe. A and AB use all oil instead of oil and butter) • Prep Time: 20 min • Cooking time: 6–8 min • Yield: 4 servings

Ingredients

4–5 Tbsp vegetable oil for cooking
½   cup sweet onions, diced
1½ cups fresh baby spinach leaves
1   tsp fresh lemon zest, grated
1   cup Spelt croutons (see recipe under *Croutons and Crumbs* section)
1   pound Cod OR other whitefish fillets, skinned (cut into 4 half fillets)
2   tsp Lemon Pepper seasoning salt OR herbs (see below)
1   Tbsp butter
1   tsp *each* of crushed, dried thyme and savory or your favorite blend
1   cup Spelt breadcrumbs
½   cup pine nuts (4 oz) or other nuts such as walnuts
1   large egg, beaten

Crouton-Spinach-Onion Bedding Yield: two
½ cup servings or 4 ¼ cup servings.

1.   Place 10" skillet over medium heat; add 1 Tbsp oil to the pan. Let heat then add onions and sauté until soft and translucent. Add the spinach and cook for two minutes until tender.

2.   Add additional Tbsp or two of oil to the skillet. Add the croutons and mix with the onions/spinach. Stir in fresh lemon zest. Remove from heat source; set aside.

Breaded Fish Fillets

3.   Rinse the fillets and pat them dry. Sprinkle with Lemon Pepper seasoning salt or a mixture of dried lemon zest, dash of paprika, ground celery seed, cracked pepper and sea salt. Set aside.

4.   Place a 12" skillet over medium heat and add 2 Tbsp oil and 1 Tbsp butter. As pan heats place 1 cup Spelt breadcrumbs and ½ cup nuts in bowl of food processor. Add herbs. Pulse 8 or so times to achieve fine crumb consistency. Place mixture on a large plate.

5.   Dip each fillet in the beaten egg then roll each fillet in breadcrumb mixture to coat. Place fillets in skillet without crowding. Cook for 3–4 minutes per side or until coating is light brown and fish is flaky. Mound spinach bedding on individual plates and top with fish. Serve warm.

Oven Baked Fish Fillets
with Crunchy Lemon Herb Topping

This is a superb one-dish meal—layered and aromatic with complex textures and flavors—that accommodates all Blood Types. The bed of greens makes it seem as if the fish is cooked in leaves or thatch. The lemon, leeks and herbs give a tang, the breadcrumbs a crunch along with the al dente zucchini.

Blood Type: A, B, AB, O (The lovely Orange Roughy is neutral to all blood types; Cod beneficial to all. Types B and O try this sometime with Sole; it is delightful.)
Prep time: 20 minutes • Cook time: 30–40 minutes • Yield: 2 servings

Ingredients

2 fish fillets (about 1 lb) fresh or thawed (Orange Roughy, Cod or other)
1 large whole leek or 3 bunches fresh large scallions
½ pound zucchini (two small)
ground pepper to taste (optional)
3 Tbsp Olive oil
1 cup pale and light green portions of leek or scallions
2 cloves garlic, minced
¼ cup pine nuts (or other)
1 cup dried, fine Spelt breadcrumbs (see *Croutons and Crumbs* section)
1 tsp kosher or fine sea salt
1 Tbsp fresh, chopped basil
OR 1 tsp dried, crushed basil
1 tsp dried, crushed chervil (and/or others such as thyme or savory)
2 Tbsp fresh lemon zest, grated
2 Tbsp fresh lemon juice mixed with ¼ cup water

1. Lightly oil a shallow casserole that has a tight-fitting lid. Preheat oven to 350° F. Wash leek or scallions well to completely rid the greens of grit and dirt; pat dry. Thinly slice the white and pale green portions of the leek/scallions and reserve the long green portions. Wash the zucchini, pat dry and slice into thin rounds.

2. Place the dark green portion of leek/scallions in a single layer in casserole dish. Place the zucchini rounds in a single layer on top of the leek/scallions and sprinkle with freshly ground pepper (optional) and a very light sprinkling of water. Rinse the fillets and place lengthwise over the leek/zucchini so the greens and fish run in the same direction. Spoon half the lemon juice/water over the fillets.

3. Heat 2 Tbsp oil in sauté pan set over medium heat. Add the sliced leek/scallions, garlic and pine nuts; sauté for 8–10 minutes. Spoon/sprinkle evenly over fillets.

4. Add 1 Tbsp olive oil to the warm skillet. Add the breadcrumbs, salt, and dried, crushed herb(s). Stir to combine. Stir in the fresh basil (optional), grated lemon zest and the remainder of the lemon juice/water. Spoon/sprinkle the contents of skillet evenly over the fish fillets.

5. Place, covered, in moderate preheated oven (350° F) for 20 minutes. Remove lid during the last 10 minutes and continue baking until mixture is steaming, zucchini is al dente, fish is flaky and crumbs are golden brown. Remove from oven. Using spatula, serve fish on bed of greens. Serve immediately.

Cookie Tray

Lemon Blossom Cookies
Almond Cookies (Basic Sugar Cookie)

Good Day Cookie
Back to Basics Zucchini Spice Variety Cookie

Cacao Cashews
Chocolate Dipped Peanut Butter Cookies
Choco Spiced Dainties
Chocolate Chip Florentines
Black Forest Cookies

Date Layer Bars

Chocolate Transgression Spelt Brownies with
Fudge Crunch Topping
Flash Brownies

Ginger Medley:
Ginger Crisps
Gingersnaps
Ginger Daddies

Ice Cream Sandwiches:
Gingerfellas Ice Cream Sandwiches
Brownie Ice Cream Sandwich

Lemon Blossom Cookies

An attractive and delectable, light and subtly spiced little cookie.

Blood Type: A, B, AB (A, AB use oil) • Prep time: 15 min
Cook time (per batch): 10–12 minutes • Yield: 4 dozen (2")

Ingredients

½ cup butter (1 stick), softened
OR ¼ cup + 2 Tbsp oil (Oil will change texture. Cookie will be more friable)
½ cup light brown sugar, tightly packed
¼ cup granulated sugar
3 tsp lemon zest, finely shredded
½ tsp baking powder
½ tsp baking soda
⅛ tsp salt
½ tsp ground cardamom
1 egg, room temperature
½ cup sour cream OR goat's milk OR other plain yogurt (any without additives)
¼ cup lemon juice
1 cup + 2 Tbsp White Spelt flour
1 cup Whole Spelt flour
½ cup pine nuts, toasted

1. Preheat oven to 375° F. Place soft butter in large mixing bowl and whip for 30 seconds. Add brown sugar, granulated sugar, lemon peel, baking powder, soda, salt and cardamom. (If using oil, add directly to the brown sugar and other ingredients.) Cream.

2. Add the egg, sour cream (or yogurt), and lemon juice and beat until blended. In ½ cup increments, beat in the flours on low speed.

3. Drop batter by rounded Tbsp onto ungreased cookie sheet leaving 3" between cookies and side of pan. Press 5 pine nuts in a circular pattern on top of the cookie to form a blossom. Bake in preheated (375° F) oven for 8–9 minutes until cookies are set and edges are slightly browned. Remove from oven and transfer immediately to wire rack. Use an airtight container to store cookies, using wax paper to separate layers. These freeze well, retaining their taste and consistency for a couple of months.

Almond Cookies
(Basic Sugar Cookie)

Very easy to make—a good cooking with kids recipe. The cookie requires no rolling. It is a basic sugar cookie recipe substituting oil for butter. You can substitute other flavors such as vanilla or cherry and add a tsp of finely grated lemon peel or ¼ tsp lemon oil to get the traditional sugar cookie taste.

Blood Type: A, B, AB, O • Prep time: 15 min • Cook time: 8–10 min • Yield: 36 3" cookies

Ingredients

2	eggs, room temperature
⅔	cup vegetable oil
2	tsp almond flavoring
½	cup granulated sugar
3	Tbsp turbinado sugar
2	cups White Spelt flour
½	cup Whole Grain Spelt flour
2	tsp baking powder
½	tsp salt
¼	cup (1 ounce) slivered almonds

additional sugar for pressing

1. Preheat oven to 400° F. In a large mixing bowl, beat the eggs. Add the oil and almond flavoring. Blend in the sugars.

2. Whisk the Spelt flours, baking powder and salt together and add to egg/sugar mixture. Stir just until blended. The batter should be smooth and "slow".

3. Drop by tsp onto ungreased cookie sheet leaving 2" between cookies.

4. Take a kitchen glass that has a smooth base and coat the bottom lightly with oil. Mix 3 Tbsp granulated sugar and 2 Tbsp turbinado sugar in a small bowl. Dip the bottom of the glass into the sugar and stamp each cookie. Lightly press 3 almond slivers into each cookie to form petals. Repeat.

5. Bake in preheated hot (400° F) oven for 8–10 minutes until cookies are just starting to turn golden brown around the edges. Remove from oven and immediately place cookies on wire rack to cool. Stir batter once or twice between batches if baking only one pan at a time. Stored in an airtight container, these cookies will stay fresh and tasty for 4–5 days.

Good Day Cookie

Thin wins. These are not dry mounds of Chocolate Chip or Raisins and Oatmeal. The versatile **Good Day Cookie** is moist, chewy and crunchy with a hint of lemon, the sweet earthiness of chocolate and nuts all laced together with Rolled Spelt or oatmeal. This is also a basic recipe for **oatmeal/raisin** cookies. These are fantastic made with other combinations like cranberry or blueberry/oatmeal or dried cherry/chocolate chips.

Blood Type: B, O (use soy milk), A, AB (use oil and 2% milk or goat's milk or soy milk)
Prep time: 15 min • Cook time: 12–14 min/batch • Yield: 4 dozen 3" (1 oz) cookies

Ingredients

2½ cups Rolled Spelt or uncooked Rolled Oats
1 cup walnut halves or coarsely chopped walnuts
1 cup butter (2 sticks), softened
OR 1 cup vegetable oil such as Light Olive or canola
¾ cup dark brown sugar, firmly packed
½ cup granulated sugar
2 eggs, room temperature
2 Tbsp milk OR soy milk
½ tsp vanilla
1 tsp freshly grated lemon zest
1¼ cups White Spelt flour
½ cup Whole Grain Spelt flour
1 tsp soda
½ tsp salt
½ tsp cinnamon (Type B sub cardamom)
1 tsp nutmeg, freshly ground (Type O sub mace)
2 cups chocolate chips (12 oz or 1 package) OR raisins OR other dried fruit (soaked in hot water, drained)

1. Preheat oven to 350° F. Cover cookie sheets with parchment (preferable) or lightly oil large cookie sheet(s). In processor fitted with blade, combine the Rolled Spelt or oats with the walnuts and process for 12–15 seconds. Set aside.

2. In medium sized bowl, combine the White Spelt flour, Whole Spelt flour, soda, salt, cinnamon and nutmeg. Whisk. Set aside.

3. In large mixing bowl, cream the softened butter (or oil) with the brown and granulated sugars. Add the eggs and milk; beat just until blended. Add the vanilla and stir in the grated lemon zest.

4. Add the dry ingredients to the creamed mixture; mix until combined. Stir in chocolate chips alternately with the Rolled Spelt/walnut mixture. Mix just enough to incorporate all ingredients.

5. Drop by tsp onto prepared baking sheet, leaving 1½" between cookies. Place in preheated moderate (350° F) oven. Bake for 10–12 minutes. Remove from oven and let cookies cool for a minute on cookie sheet. With spatula, transfer them to wire rack covered with paper towels. Store in an airtight container or freeze. These stay fresh for many days and freeze exceptionally well.

Back To Basics Zucchini Spice Variety Cookie

This is my mother's recipe, adapted to Spelt, for one of the best cookies ever. The Back to Basics Cookie is not too sweet, is moist and soft. Vary ingredients to create different tastes and textures in a single, nutritious cookie. The version here uses zucchini, raisins, nuts and a lovely alternative to coconut—Shredded Dried Sweet Potato (see recipe under *The Vegetable Stand*). Try minced dried apricots, cranberries or dried pineapple bits or rolled Spelt or oats.

Blood Type: B, O; A, AB use oil (A, B, AB use goat's milk; O use soy milk)
Prep time: 15 min • Cook time: 12–16 min/batch • Yield: 48 (1 oz)

Ingredients

¾   cup butter, softened
OR ½ cup + 1 Tbsp vegetable oil
1   cup dark brown sugar
1   egg, room temperature
1   tsp vanilla
2½ tsp grated lemon zest
1½ cups Whole Grain Spelt flour (divided 1¼ cups, ¼ cup)
1½ cups White Spelt flour
1½ tsp baking powder
½   tsp cream of tartar
¾   tsp salt
1¼ tsp nutmeg (Type O sub mace)
1   tsp ginger
1½ tsp cinnamon (Type B leave out)
⅛   tsp ground cloves
½   cup + 2 tsp goat's milk OR cow's milk OR soy milk
1   cup zucchini, unpeeled, grated (1 6"–7" zucchini)
½   cup raisins OR finely chopped dried apricots (optional)
½   cup dried, grated sweet potato OR ¼ cup rolled Spelt OR rolled oats
1 cup walnuts (OR pecans), finely chopped

1. **Preparation.** Grate the zucchini; squeeze with paper towels to remove as much moisture as possible. Lay out on paper towels set on wire racks. Soak the raisins (or other dried fruit such as cranberries or finely chopped dried apricots) in hot water to cover for 10 minutes. Drain. In a small bowl, combine the raisins or other dried fruit with ¼ cup Whole Grain Spelt flour and stir until coated. Set aside.

2. In large mixing bowl, blend the butter (or oil) and brown sugar. Add the egg and continue mixing until combined but not frothy. Add vanilla and lemon zest.

3. In separate bowl, combine 1½ cups White Spelt flour, 1¼ cups Whole Grain Spelt flour, baking powder, cream of tartar, salt, nutmeg, ginger, cinnamon and cloves. Slowly add to the butter and sugar mixture alternately with the milk or soy milk.

4. Add the grated zucchini, the dried fruit, the dried sweet potato or rolled Spelt/oats, and the nuts. Mix until incorporated.

5. Drop by mounded tsp onto a parchment covered (preferable) or lightly greased cookie sheet. Bake in preheated hot (375° F) oven for 12–16 minutes until edges are golden brown. If using two pans, switch racks at 8 minutes. Remove from pan and cool on wire racks. Store in airtight container. These cookies stay moist and fresh at room temperature for several days; if refrigerated, a week. Frozen they will keep for months.

Cacao Cashews

Milk chocolate and toasted cashew cookies that are wafer thin with a honeycomb texture.

Blood Type: Unrated • Prep time: 15 min • Cook time: 15 min • Yield: 3 dozen (2") cookies

Ingredients

½   cup cashew nuts, coarsely chopped and toasted or roasted, salted (2 oz)
2   squares (2 oz) milk chocolate
½   cup butter, softened
¼   tsp salt
¾   cup granulated sugar
¼   cup turbinado sugar
1   egg, room temperature
1   tsp vanilla flavoring
¾   cup + 2 Tbsp Whole Grain Spelt flour

1. In sauté pan set over medium heat, toast the coarsely chopped cashews (5–7 minutes) and add a dash of salt. Or use cashews that are already roasted and salted. Set aside.

2. In small (microwave safe) bowl, melt the chocolate in microwave (1½–2 minutes). Or melt on stovetop using double boiler.

3. Preheat oven to 325° F. Cover two large cookie sheets with parchment paper (preferable) or grease cookie sheets well.

4. In mixing bowl, cream softened butter with salt. Slowly add the sugars. Beat in the egg. Blend in the vanilla and melted chocolate. Stir in the Whole Grain Spelt flour and then the nuts; blend.

5. Drop by rounded tsp onto cookie sheet, leaving 2½" between cookies. Lightly oil a flat-bottomed glass or custard dish and stamp each cookie. Bake cookies in slow oven (325° F) for 15 minutes or until cookies are set. If using two pans at once, bake one on lowest rack the other two rungs up. Switch racks midway through baking. Remove from oven; let cookies sit on pan for a minute before transferring to wire rack to cool completely.

Chocolate Dipped Peanut Butter Cookies

Spelt and peanut butter are natural partners, each accentuating the best in the other. This moist, scrumptious peanut butter cookie stands on its own if you have no wish to dip it.

Blood Type: A, AB • Prep time: 10 min • Cook time: 10–12 min • Yield: 28 2" cookies

Ingredients

4	oz (¾ cup) unsalted peanuts, crushed or lightly salted, roasted
1	cup White Spelt flour
¼	cup Whole Grain Spelt flour
½	tsp salt
½	tsp baking soda
3	Tbsp Olive OR other vegetable oil
½	cup chunky peanut butter
½	cup granulated sugar
¾	cup dark brown sugar, tightly packed
1	egg, room temperature
½	tsp vanilla
4	oz dark chocolate

1. Preheat oven to 350° F. Cover two cookie sheets with parchment (preferable) or lightly grease the cookie sheets. Place peanuts in processor fitted with metal blade and pulse to finely chop and crush the peanuts. If not using lightly salted, roasted peanuts then place peanuts in small skillet over medium heat and toast crushed peanuts, stirring occasionally (5–7 minutes). Add a dash of salt (optional). Set aside to cool.

2. In a small bowl, combine the Spelt flours, salt and baking soda. Whisk. Set aside.

3. In a large mixing bowl, combine oil and peanut butter, cream together. Add the sugars and continue beating. Add the egg and vanilla. Stir in the dry ingredients and mix until thoroughly combined.

4. Roll into 1" round balls and place each ball on cookie sheet leaving 1½" between each cookie. Lightly oil the base of a glass with 2" flat bottom; press the cookies into 2" rounds.

Bake in preheated 350° F oven for 8 minutes or until cookies are set, are slightly brown on edges and top has a crackle finish. Let cool on baking sheet for a minute before placing on wire racks to cool.

5. Melt chocolate in heavy saucepan placed over low heat. Or place chocolate in microwave safe bowl and microwave on high for 1 minute. Stir, then heat additional ½ minute. Remove from microwave and stir until chocolate completely melts.

6. Dip tip of cooled cookie into melted chocolate. Lightly dip into crushed toasted peanuts with a scooping motion. Shake off excess nuts. Set cookie on parchment or wax paper until chocolate hardens. Place cookies in airtight container using wax paper or parchment between layers. They keep moist and flavorful for up to a week.

Choco Spiced Dainties

In Choco Spiced Dainties, nuts and breadcrumbs take the place of the usual flour found in modern cookie recipes. This is a "haystack" cookie: much crunch yet soft and full of delicate spices that linger on the tongue. It is a cookie to savor. What a delicate delight this dainty is, especially if using cardamom seed freshly roasted in a dry pan and then ground along with using freshly ground nutmeg. This is an excellent cookie for gift giving or on the cookie tray for entertaining.

Blood Type: A, B, AB, O • Prep time: 30 min • Cook time: 15–20 min/batch • Yield: 4 dozen

Ingredients

3   squares (3 ounces) unsweetened chocolate, grated
2   cups walnuts OR pecans, coarsely chopped
1   cup turbinado sugar
⅛   teaspoon salt
2   large eggs, room temperature, lightly beaten
¼   cup very fine dry Spelt breadcrumbs
2   Tbsp Whole Grain Spelt flour
1   tsp ground cinnamon
½   tsp freshly ground nutmeg (Type O avoid)
½   tsp ground cardamom
vegetable oil for rolling

1. Have all ingredients out at room temperature. Prepare 2 large cookie sheets by lining with parchment paper (preferable) or spraying with sheen of oil. Preheat oven to 325° F.

2. Grate the chocolate and set aside. Finely grate the nutmeg. Set aside.

3. In food processor bowl fitted with metal blade, pulse the walnuts or pecans with ½ tsp of the Whole Spelt flour until fine chopped (6–8 times). Set aside.

4. In large mixing bowl, beat the eggs. To the beaten eggs, add the sugar a ¼ cup at a time. Stir in the grated chocolate; stir in the chopped nuts.

5. Add the Spelt breadcrumbs, the Whole Grain Spelt flour, the cinnamon, nutmeg, and cardamom and thoroughly mix.

6. The dough will be sticky so lightly oil your hands and form 1" balls or use light latex gloves and wipe lightly with oil. Place each cookie on parchment covered cookie sheet (or greased cookie sheet) leaving 1" between cookies.

7. Bake in preheated slow (325° F) oven for 15–20 minutes or until the tops of the cookies are crackled in appearance. If baking with two pans at a time, set one rack on lowest rung and the other rack two rungs up. Switch pans, very gently, at 10 minutes. (Note: this recipe works best if cookies are baked one pan at a time on middle rack of oven. Bake one batch while rolling cookies for the other large pan.)

8. Shift the cookies on parchment sheet directly to wire rack or let the cookies cool 2 minutes on greased cookie sheet then remove to wire racks to cool completely. Stored in an airtight container and kept in a cool, dark area of room, these cookies will keep for 10 days to 2 weeks. To freeze: set cookies in airtight container and cover each layer with wax paper. Defrost at room temperature (60 minutes) prior to serving to attain best flavor.

Chocolate Chip Florentines

As one of our tasters said, "Thin wins!" These are not the thick and floury chip-studded mounds that get hard by the end of the day. Spelt Florentines are thin cookies, crisp on the outside, chewy within, interspersed with chocolate chips and toasted nuts. These stay pliable and delicious for days.

Blood Type: B, O • Prep time: 15 min • Cook: 8–10 min/batch • Yield: 6 dozen (2½") cookies

Ingredients

1   cup finely chopped walnuts (OR pine nuts)
2¼ cups + 2 Tbsp Whole Grain Spelt flour
1   tsp baking soda
1   tsp salt
1   cup butter, softened
1½ cups brown sugar, packed
1   tsp vanilla
2   eggs, room temperature
2   cups (12 oz) chocolate chips or chunks

1. Preheat oven to 375° F. Place sauté pan over medium heat and toast the finely chopped nuts. Remove from heat. Stir in 2 tsp of the Whole Grain Spelt flour. Set aside.

2. Combine Spelt flour (less 2 tsp), baking soda and salt in a small bowl; whisk. Set aside.

3. In large mixing bowl, cream the softened butter and brown sugar (3 minutes, medium speed on mixer). Add the vanilla. Blend. Add eggs one at a time, beating briefly after each addition.

4. By ½ cup measure, gradually add the flour, soda, salt mixture. Mix on low speed until blended.

5. On slow speed, add the chocolate chips and the toasted nuts/flour.

6. Drop by measuring tsp onto a parchment covered or ungreased cookie sheet leaving 1½" inches on all sides for cookies to spread. Bake in preheated hot (375° F) oven for 8 minutes until they are set and the edges turn slightly brown. If baking more than one pan at a time, bake one sheet on lowest rack, the other two rungs up. Shift racks midway in baking (4 minutes) and allow 9–10 minutes if baking two pans at a time. Do not over bake.

7. Remove from oven and let cookies cool for a minute on the pan then transfer to wire racks covered with paper towels or parchment. These cookies remain moist and pliable for several days if kept in a plastic airtight container. Freeze unused dough; thaw at room temperature until soft enough to form into cookies.

Black Forest Cookies

Courtesy of Ocean Spray Cranberries, Inc. This is a winner recipe adapted to Spelt: deep, sweet and tart and exceptionally easy to make. If you are new to Spelt, this is a terrific first recipe to make.

Blood Type: B, O • Prep time: 15 min • Cook time: 12–14 min • Yield: About 2½ dozen

Ingredients

1   11.5–12 oz package milk chocolate morsels (divided 1¼, ¾)
½   cup brown sugar
¼   cup butter, softened
2   eggs, lightly beaten
1   tsp vanilla extract
¾   cup Whole Grain Spelt flour
¼   tsp baking powder
1   6 oz package Ocean Spray Craisins® Cherry Flavor Sweetened Dried Cranberries
1   cup pecans OR walnuts, coarsely chopped

1. Preheat oven to 350° F. Lightly grease cookie sheets or cover baking sheets with parchment. Pour 1¼ cup morsels into an uncovered large microwave safe bowl. Set remaining morsels aside.

2. Microwave morsels for 2 minutes on high. Stir until chocolate is smooth. Stir in brown sugar, butter, eggs and vanilla. Add Whole Spelt flour and baking powder, mixing thoroughly until combined.

3. Stir in remaining ¾ cup morsels, the Cherry Flavor Sweetened Dried Cranberries and the nuts.

4. Drop by Tbsp onto cookie sheet. Bake for 12–14 minutes or until cookies puff and set to the touch. If using 2 cookie sheets, switch racks at 6 minutes. Remove from oven. Cool on cookie sheet for 2 minutes. Transfer to a wire rack and cool completely.

Date Layer Bars

Ancient recipe for ancient Spelt flour, these Date Layer Bars leave the popular fig and shortbread cookies at the supermarket in the dust because that is what they taste like in comparison.

Blood Type: A, B, AB, O • Prep time: 15 min • Cook time: 30–35 min • Yield: 32 small bars

Ingredients

Layer

1½ cups Whole Spelt flour
½   tsp soda
1   tsp salt
¼   cup + 3 Tbsp light Olive or other vegetable oil
1   cup brown sugar
1½ cups Rolled Spelt or Rolled oats
2   Tbsp cool water

Date Filling

2   cups pitted, chopped dates
½   cup raisins
1½ cups water

Layer:

1. Preheat oven to 350° F. In small bowl, combine the Whole Grain Spelt flour, soda and salt. Whisk. Set aside.

2. In large mixing bowl, blend the oil and brown sugar. Stir in the dry ingredients then add the Rolled Spelt and 2 Tbsp cool water. Using your fingers or slotted spoon, mix all ingredients until lightly moistened and crumbly. Press half of the mixture firmly into a 13" x 9" pan. Set aside.

Filling:

3. Place a saucepan over moderately high heat. Add the chopped dates, raisins and 1½ cups water to the pan and cover. Cook, stirring frequently, about 8 minutes or until the filling thickens and comes to a jam-like consistency.

4. Remove from heat and spread the date filling evenly over the prepared layer. Sprinkle the remaining half of the layer mix over the filling. With the back of a spoon or with your fingers, press gently until layer is smooth.

5. Bake the bars in moderate preheated (350° F) oven for 35 minutes or until juices start to bubble a little and topping starts to brown lightly. Remove from oven and place on wire rack to cool completely before cutting. Lightly cover and store at room temperature.

Chocolate Transgression
Spelt Brownies with Fudge Crunch Topping

This is a moist, rich cake-like and oh so delectable brownie. Eat plain or with a sprinkling of Confectioners' sugar. Or make with Fudge Crunch Topping—and freeze. Why freeze? The brownie becomes a dense moist confection with candy bar topping that is out of this world, another dessert altogether.

Blood Type: Not rated • Prep time: 15 min • Cook time: 30–35 min • Yield: 18 (3" x 2" inch brownies)

Ingredients

1   cup Whole Grain Spelt flour
1½ cups White Spelt flour
2   cups brown sugar, tightly packed
1   tsp baking soda
¼   tsp salt
¾   cup water
1   cup butter (2 sticks), softened
⅓   cup cocoa powder (unsweetened)
2   large eggs, room temperature
½   cup plain goat's milk yogurt OR other plain unflavored yogurt without sugar additives
1½ tsp vanilla

1. Preheat oven to 350° F. Lightly grease a 13" x 9" x 2" baking pan. Combine the two Spelt flours, brown sugar, baking soda and salt in a large mixing bowl. Whisk. Set aside.

2. Place butter, cocoa and water in a medium saucepan. Stirring constantly, heat the mixture to point where it just begins to boil and immediately remove from heat.

3. Add the butter/chocolate mixture to the dry ingredients; beat to combine.

4. Add the eggs, yogurt and vanilla and beat until combined (mixer on medium speed, about 1 minute) to make a thin batter. Pour into prepared pan and bake in preheated moderate (350° F) oven for 30–35 minutes. Test by inserting wooden toothpick or skewer into the center. If it comes out clean, remove brownies from oven. Do not over bake.

5. Place pan on wire rack and let cool. Prepare Fudge Crunch Topping (optional) on following page.

Fudge Crunch Topping

Fudge Crunch topping is like a candy bar or fudge on top of brownies—yet Spelt flour replaces half the sugar. Drizzle Fudge Crunch Topping over tarts, cannoli, cupcakes or cookies. The topping is at its best when allowed to cool completely before serving. It freezes exceptionally well.

Blood Type: Not rated • Prep/cook time: 10 min • Yield: About 1½ cups

Ingredients

½ cup + 3 Tbsp White Spelt flour
OR ½ cup + 1 Tbsp Whole Grain Spelt flour
½ cup toasted or roasted nuts (macadamias, cashews, walnuts, pecans, pistachios)
4 squares unsweetened chocolate
1 cup butter, softened
1 cup brown sugar, firmly packed
¼ cup turbinado sugar

1. Add Spelt flour and roasted nuts to bowl of processor fitted with metal blade. Pulse 6–8 times to finely dice the nuts. Set aside.

2. Melt chocolate and butter in large microwave safe bowl in microwave or melt using double boiler. Remove from heat.

3. Add brown sugar; stir until smooth and shiny. Add the turbinado sugar. Stir.

4. While mixture is still warm, add the flour/nut mixture; stir to blend. The mixture will become thicker as it sits but still be of spreading consistency. Add additional 1 to 2 Tbsp flour if you want it even thicker or thin with 1 to 2 tsp of warm water. Allow the brownies to cool (about 30 minutes).

5. Spread the topping over the brownies. Set the pan in a cool place (not the refrigerator) for a couple of hours so the topping stiffens. Cut and serve. Brownies with this topping freeze exceptionally well. Simply wrap individual brownies loosely in plastic and place within an airtight container. Allow to defrost 30–45 minutes before serving.

Flash Brownies

These quick as a flash brownies are very thin yet moist and delicious. They do not dry out like microwave brownies. Give these a try next time you have the munchies or you want a fast, good dessert for the kids.

Blood Type: B, O (A, AB use oil) • Prep time: 5 min • Cook time: 20 min • Yield: 18 brownies

Ingredients

½   cup butter, softened (OR ¼ cup + 2 Tbsp + 2 tsp oil)
1   cup brown sugar tightly packed
2   eggs, room temperature
1   cup Whole Grain Spelt flour
½   tsp baking powder
¼   tsp salt
½   cup powdered unsweetened cocoa
1   tsp vanilla
½   cup nuts, coarsely chopped nuts (optional)

1. Preheat oven to 350° F. Lightly grease a 13" x 9" x 2" baking pan. Melt butter with sugar in a saucepan. Remove from stovetop. (If using oil, eliminate step 1 melting.)

2. Blend in the eggs. Stir in the flour, baking powder and salt. Stir in the cocoa. Add the vanilla; stir until the mixture shines. Stir in the nuts. Spoon mixture into pan.

3. Place in preheated oven (350° F) and bake for 18–20 minutes. Place pan on wire rack, cool for 10 minutes before cutting.

Flash Brownie Ice Cream Sandwich (see *Ice Cream Sandwiches* in this section)

Ginger Medley
❀ Ginger Crisps

These are the first of the Ginger Medley, going from small to large … Ginger Crisps are zingy, crisp cookies that melt in the mouth. They are dainty delights to set on the cookie tray with Choco Spice Cookies and are excellent with Chinese or Indian foods.

Blood Type: B, O; A, AB (use oil) • Prep time: 15 min • Cook time: 10–12 min • Yield: about 3 dozen

Ingredients

¾ cup brown sugar, tightly packed
¼ cup butter, melted OR 3 Tbsp vegetable oil (texture will change slightly with oil; cookie will be more friable)
1 egg, room temperature
1 cup Whole Grain or White Spelt flour
1 tsp baking powder
¼ tsp salt
½ tsp ground ginger
4–6 pieces candied ginger, finely snipped

1. Preheat oven to 325° F. Cover cookie sheets with parchment or lightly grease the pans. In large mixing bowl, combine the brown sugar and melted butter. Add the egg; beat until mixture is creamy (about 10 seconds).

2. Blend in the Spelt flour, baking powder, salt and ground ginger.

3. Using an oiled teaspoon, drop the cookies onto cookie sheet, leaving 2" between the cookies. Sprinkle a couple of the snipped ginger pieces onto the top of each cookie.

4. Bake in preheated slow oven (325° F) for 10 to 12 minutes. Let the cookies cool on the cookie sheet for about 30 seconds, then immediately transfer them to a wire rack. If the cookies should stick to the sheet, simply return to the oven briefly.

Ginger Medley

Gingersnaps

Sweet, spicy, snappy traditional favorite.

Blood Type: A, B, AB, O • Prep time: 10 min • Cook time: 10–12 min • Yield: About 60

Ingredients

½   cup Light Olive oil OR canola oil
1   cup dark brown sugar, firmly packed
¼   cup molasses
1   egg, room temperature
2   cups Whole Grain Spelt flour
2   tsp soda
½   tsp salt
1   tsp ground ginger
1   tsp ground cinnamon (Type B leave out)
½   tsp ground cloves
turbinado sugar for rolling

1. Preheat oven to 375° F. Cover cookie sheet(s) with parchment or lightly oil them. In large mixing bowl, cream the oil with the brown sugar, molasses and egg.

2. In separate bowl, whisk together the Whole Spelt flour, soda, salt, ginger, cinnamon and cloves. Add to the creamed mixture; mix.

3. Lightly oil hands and shape dough into ¾" balls. Roll the balls in turbinado sugar. Set the balls 1½" apart on prepared cookie sheet(s).

4. Bake in preheated moderately hot (375° F) oven for 10–12 minutes. If using two cookie sheets, switch at five minutes. When done, leave cookies on pan briefly then remove to wire racks for further cooling. Store in airtight container or freeze.

Ginger Medley
Ginger Daddies

It's a big one! Almost four inches of spicy cookie that is crunchy on the outside, moist on the inside, with lots of pizzazz. Superb keeping qualities make it an excellent lunch box cookie. Double the recipe and freeze the remainder of the dough until you get the yen for more of these big guys.

Blood Type: A, B, AB, O • Prep time: 20 min • Cook time: 12–14 min/batch • Yield: 24 cookies (1½ oz each)

Ingredients

1¾ cups White Spelt flour
½   cup Whole Grain Spelt flour
1   tsp baking soda
⅛   tsp salt
1   tsp ginger
¾   tsp ground cinnamon (Type B leave out)
¼   tsp ground cloves
½   tsp ground cardamom
⅔   cup Olive OR other vegetable oil
1   cup dark brown sugar, tightly packed
1   large egg, lightly beaten
¼   cup Robust molasses
⅓   cup turbinado sugar for rolling

1. Preheat oven to 350° F. In medium bowl, combine the White and Whole Spelt flours, baking soda, salt and spices. Whisk. Set aside. Place turbinado sugar in a small bowl; set aside.

2. In large mixing bowl, combine the oil with brown sugar; blend. Add the egg and molasses and briefly blend. Add the dry ingredients and mix until ingredients are moist and thoroughly incorporated.

3. These are very sticky so lightly coat your hands with oil then roll dough into 1½" balls. Roll the balls in turbinado sugar to coat. Place cookies 2½" apart on a parchment covered or ungreased cookie sheet. They will spread into circles of 3½" or more so give them lots of room.

4. Bake in a preheated moderate (350° F) oven for 12–14 minutes or until cookies are puffed and edges are lightly browned. If using two pans, set one oven rack on lowest rung and other rack two rungs up. Switch cookies to opposite rack at 6 minutes. Do not over bake. Let cool for 30 seconds on cookie sheet then transfer to wire racks. Stored in an airtight container, these cookies will remain fresh and zesty for more than a week. Freeze by wrapping 4–6 together in plastic wrap then place in heavy duty freezer bag. They will keep for months, as will the dough.

Ice Cream Sandwiches

Gingerfellas

Ginger Daddies (cookies) form the wafers for this munchy ice cream sandwich treat that makes the store-bought ice cream sandwich a thing of the past. Our tasters rated the Gingerfella as best ice cream sandwich ever. You be the judge.

Blood Type: A, B, AB, O • Prep time: 15 min • Yield: 6 large ice cream sandwiches

Ingredients

½   recipe (12 cookies) Ginger Daddies, cooled

1   container French Vanilla Soy Ice Cream

1.   Remove soy ice cream from freezer and allow top 2" to 3" to soften (about 10 minutes) at room temperature. (The remainder will soften as you go, especially soy, which melts quickly.)

2.   Place a plastic container without lid in freezer where it is easy to reach. Set the 12 cookies out in pairs on paper towels. Place a large scoop of softened soy ice cream on the bottom half of a cookie. Gently place the top cookie onto the ice cream and press lightly so the ice cream spreads to the edge of the cookies and top cookie is level. If the edges are uneven or there is excess ice cream, deftly work around the edge of the sandwich with a cold knife to smooth the edges.

3.   Place sandwich in plastic container in freezer. Go on to the next sandwich until all are completed. Take container with sandwiches out of freezer and quickly wrap each sandwich in plastic wrap then place all of them in freezer storage bag or container with lid. These will remain fresh and tasty for more than 2 weeks and the wafer will still be both chewy and crunchy.

Brownie Ice Cream Sandwich

The Flash Brownie (see recipe this section) makes terrific chocolate ice cream sandwich wafers. All you have to do is make the following changes in the Flash Brownie recipe:

* Instead of using a 13" x 9" x 2" pan, use two large cookie sheets and set parchment on them or lightly oil the pans.

* Make the recipe of Flash brownies as directed but instead of spooning into pan, make 12 rounds. Do this by mounding 2 Tbsp of batter for each wafer onto the cookie sheet, leaving 2" between each wafer.

* Slightly flatten each mound with the back of an oiled spoon. The dough mounds will expand into 12 uniform 3½" rounds.

* Bake for 14 minutes on center rack of oven. If using 2 pans, switch pans at 7 minutes and turn them 180° for even baking. Do not over bake. Test by inserting wooden toothpick into top. If it comes out clean, they are ready to take out of oven. Remove from pans and shift to wire racks to cool completely. Follow instructions on previous page for turning them into ice cream sandwiches.

See also Chocolate Walnut Waffles Ice Cream Sandwich under *Morning Menu Waffles*

PASTRIES, PIES AND OTHER SWEET DELIGHTS

Pastry and Pie Crust Chart

Some Spelt Pastry Guidelines

✳

American Apple Pie

Pinyon Pie (or Pecan Pie)

Crostate di Fichi (Fig Tarts with Dried Plums and Raisins)

Cannoli (Cream-Filled Italian Pastry)

Pineapple Cheese Pie

Old Times Pumpkin or Sweet Potato Pie

Pineapple-Blueberry Upside Down Cake

Spelt Pound Cake

Raspberry Valentine Cake

Pastry and Pie Crust Chart

It is easy and quick to make Spelt pastry with oil. You will find it is flaky, tasty, more nutritious and easier to digest than the pastry and crusts you may be accustomed to eating made from butter or shortening. (Nutritional information is in Appendix 1.)

The Pastry/Pie Crust Chart offers guidelines, not absolutes. The mixed flour versions are the foundation for recipes like empanadas and meat pies. The white flour versions call for White Spelt. As mentioned in KNEAD TO KNOW (Chapter 4), White Spelt flours vary, some are more finely sifted than others so you will need to take this into account and adjust accordingly. You can mix and match your flours depending on the taste and texture you want to make excellent pastries and crusts.

Again, these are guidelines, not absolutes. Besides the excellent taste and nutritional benefits, another thing about using Spelt in your pastries and pies is that it excels in keeping quality both at room temperature and frozen because of its ability to hold moisture.

7"–8" SINGLE CRUST

Mixed Flour

¾ cup White Spelt flour

¼ cup Whole Grain Spelt flour

¼ tsp salt

3 Tbsp vegetable oil

2 Tbsp + 1–2 tsp cool water

All White

1 cup + 2 Tbsp White Spelt flour

¼ tsp salt

3 Tbsp vegetable oil

2 Tbsp cool water

The 7"–8" recipe easily fits the common aluminum 8" pie pan or 7" spring-form tart pans. It can be rolled thin to fit the standard 8¾ x 1⁵⁄₃₂" low-rim aluminum (almost 9") pan but without the 1½"–2" overlap generally needed for pie crusts.

7"–8" DOUBLE CRUST

Mixed Flour

1¼ cup White Spelt flour

½ cup Whole Grain Spelt flour

½ tsp salt

¼ cup + 2 Tbsp vegetable oil

4 Tbsp + 2–3 tsp cool water

All White

1¾ cup + 3 Tbsp White Spelt flour

½ tsp salt

¼ cup + 2 Tbsp vegetable oil

4 Tbsp + 2–3 tsp cool water

8"–9" SINGLE CRUST

Mixed Flour

1 cup White Spelt flour

¼ cup Whole Grain Spelt flour

¼ tsp salt

3 Tbsp vegetable oil

2–3 Tbsp cool water

All White

1¼ cup + 1 tsp White Spelt flour

¼ tsp salt

3 Tbsp vegetable oil

2 Tbsp + 2 tsp cool water

This recipe makes 6 4" tarts; four 5" tarts; 3 6" tarts.

8"–9" DOUBLE CRUST

Mixed Flour

1¾ cups White Spelt flour

½ cup Whole Grain Spelt flour

½ tsp salt

⅓ cup + 1 Tbsp + 1 tsp vegetable oil

5 Tbsp + 2–3 tsp cool water

All White

2¼ cups + 3 Tbsp White Spelt flour

½ tsp salt

⅓ cup vegetable oil

5 Tbsp + 2–3 tsp cool water

This recipe makes 12–14 4" tarts; 10 5" tarts; 6 6" tarts.

9"–10" SINGLE CRUST

Mixed Flour

1¼ cups White Spelt flour

¼ cup Whole Grain Spelt flour

¼ tsp salt

¼ cup + 1–2 Tbsp vegetable oil

3 Tbsp cool water

All White

1½ cups + 3 Tbsp White Spelt flour

¼ tsp salt

¼ cup + 1 Tbsp vegetable oil

3 Tbsp cool water

This recipe makes 8 4" tarts; 5–6 5" tarts; 4 6" tarts. Both the single and double 9"–10" recipes are generous crusts.

9"–10" DOUBLE CRUST

Mixed Flour

2 cups White Spelt flour

1 cup Whole Grain Spelt flour

½ tsp salt

½ cup + 2 Tbsp vegetable oil

¼ cup + 2 Tbsp cool water

All White

3 cups White Spelt flour

½ tsp salt

½ cup + 1 Tbsp + 1 tsp vegetable oil

¼ cup + 1 Tbsp + 1 tsp cool water

SWEET CRUSTS: For single pastry, add 2 Tbsp firmly packed brown sugar or granulated sugar to recipe. Add 4–5 Tbsp for double crust. These pastry/pie crust recipes allow for use of coarser sugars such as maple or turbinado sugars for different textures and tastes. If desired, brush with egg white/1 Tbsp cool water for a shiny crust.

ROLLED SPELT OR OATS SWEET PASTRY CRUST: 1 cup Rolled Spelt or Rolled Oats, uncooked, ⅓ cup light or dark brown sugar, firmly packed; ⅓ cup finely chopped nuts (pecans, walnuts, pistachios, hazelnuts, pine nuts or other); 3 Tbsp Olive or other vegetable oil OR 4 Tbsp butter, softened; 1 tsp cinnamon, ½ tsp nutmeg, ½ tsp allspice (optional).

Preheat oven to 375° F (350° F for glass plate). Lightly spray or oil pie plate. In mixing bowl, combine all ingredients and mix until thoroughly incorporated. Press the dough into the bottom of the plate and work dough up the sides of the pie plate. Bake on center rack of preheated oven for 8–10 minutes. Remove when the crust is toasted golden brown. Place on wire rack to cool. Use cooled or chilled according to recipe you are using for cream pie, cheesecake or other. To freeze, leave in pan and carefully wrap in plastic; set on level surface. Will stay fresh for several weeks to a month if packaged securely.

Some Spelt Pastry Guidelines

Basic Directions for Making Pastry/Crust:

By hand: Whisk together the flour(s), salt (and sugar if using). Pour in the oil, using a pastry blender or your fingers gently work in the oil until mixture resembles coarse cornmeal. It is all right to have some loose flour in the bowl. Gently stir in the water (or soy milk, fruit juice or other liquid) with a fork until soft dough forms. After you become accustomed to working with Spelt pastry, you will find it is easy just to place the oil and liquid in a measuring cup (without stirring) and add both at the same time. With your hands, gently form into a ball. Roll on pastry cloth, marble, or between two pieces of wax paper or simply on lightly floured board. Roll or press to desired dimension. Wrap around rolling pin and place in pie pan, lift on pastry cloth or piece of wax paper and set in pan, or gently fold and place in pan.

Whole Grain Spelt has a rougher texture than dough you may be used to using. If the dough tears, simply press it back into shape without adding more liquid or dip your fingertips lightly in oil and press it in. It also has a tendency to create an uneven edge. When you have rolled or pressed out the dough, simply create an even edge by cutting with a sharp knife or smoothing it with your fingers while you are crimping the crust.

Note: I do not recommend using the Food Processor for Spelt pastry dough. It over mixes it and can add too much heat in the process. If using, chill the dough before rolling. The stand mixer, low speed, makes excellent dough (lowest speed). Even then, be careful not to over mix.

Baking Tips:

If using glass or ceramic wares, bake at 25° F less than stated in recipe. If using the thin aluminum pans commonly found in supermarkets, check your pastry/pie before the end of the specified recipe cooking time.

Baked Single Crust/Shell: Prick bottom and sides in many places. Set in preheated hot oven (400° F) and bake until bottom starts to brown (17–21 minutes, less for glass/ceramic and lightweight aluminum pans). Let cool before filling. Partially baked shells: 8–12 minutes; tart shells 8–10 minutes (less for glass/ceramic and lightweight aluminum pans). If pastry starts to puff and swell during baking, gently push the swelling back down with back of spoon or clean cloth and continue baking. For meat pies or heavier pies, brush bottom of crust with egg white mixed with 1 Tbsp water before filling.

Unbaked Single Crust/Shell: Follow directions for filling. Bake in preheated oven on lowest rack.

Two-Crust Pie: Follow directions for 1 crust pie. Form into 2 balls. Roll or press one ball into the pie pan/plate leaving 1"–2" beyond the edge. Refrigerate for half an hour while assembling other pie ingredients and rolling out top crust. Fill according to directions. Fit top crust over pie. Crimp/flute the crust and cut several vents in top or prick all over with a fork making a design. Brush with egg white mixed with 1 Tbsp water or soymilk for a shinier crust. Bake pie on lowest rack in preheated oven.

Making Pastry Ahead of Time:

Refrigerator: Make the dough ahead of time. Wrap the dough balls securely in plastic and place in resealable plastic bag to keep from drying out in the refrigerator. The dough will keep for 2–3 days. Set out at room temperature for 10–15 minutes before handling dough.

Freezer:

Single crust: Roll out and place in pan/plate. Crimp edges. Prick bottom and sides. Wrap securely in plastic. Freeze flat. Multiple shells: nest the shells and wrap the whole package in foil. Take one out as needed.

Pastry scraps: Press leftover dough into 4" tart pans; wrap with plastic and freeze. Nest in freezer until you accumulate 4 to 6 and use for many small things such as fruit tarts or quiche or Lively Vegetable and Goat Cheese Scramble.

American Apple Pie

The first time I was involved in apple pie making I was about 6. We were at my uncle's ranch where there was an old orchard near the house. The apples were small, green and tart. My sister and I shinnied up some apple trees and picked a bunch. Mom cut up the apples while my aunt made the pastry then cooked the pies in a wood burning stove. Our little kid contributions were the apples and the kindling and I would like to think some really big smiles which never hurt any kind of baking. I have never forgotten the spicy taste or that smell that seemed to waft along in sunlight.

This makes the large classic apple pie that goes in the 9½" glass pie plate with 1½" rim or the basic 9"–10" pan with flared rim.

Blood Type: Not rated • Prep time: 20 min • Cook time: 50–60 min • Yield: 10 servings

Ingredients

1 recipe unbaked 9"–10" White Spelt Double Crust (see *Pastry and Pie Crust Chart*)

5–6 Granny Smith or other large baking apples for cooking (dehydrated, reconstituted apples work perfectly well as do other kinds of apples that are not quite as tart as the Grannies)

1 tsp lemon juice

1 Tbsp tepid water

1 cup light or dark brown sugar, firmly packed

½ tsp salt

1½ tsp cinnamon

1 tsp freshly ground nutmeg

OR 3 tsp apple pie spice instead of cinnamon and nutmeg

2 Tbsp White Spelt flour

3 Tbsp butter

1 egg beaten with 1 Tbsp tepid water (optional)

In advance: Prepare recipe of 9"–10" double crust pastry. Roll bottom crust ⅛" thick. Place in pie plate or pan and trim pastry to about ½" from edge of the pie plate. Pierce sides and bottom in 5–6 places each with tines of fork. Cover with plastic; set aside. Wrap unrolled top crust in plastic.

1. In large bowl, combine and whisk together the dry ingredients (sugar, salt, spices and flour).

2. Wash the apples and pat dry. Pare, core and thinly slice into uniform pieces. Place in separate bowl and sprinkle with lemon and 1 Tbsp tepid water; toss. Combine with dry ingredients and toss until evenly coated. Preheat oven to 425° F (400° F for glass pie plate).

3. Heap the apples in unbaked bottom crust and distribute evenly. Dot the apples with butter.

4. Roll out top crust; drape over pie. Seal and flute the edges. Cut 3–4 vents in the top crust or pierce in 5–6 places with tines of a fork. Brush crust with egg beaten with water (optional).

5. Place on lowest rack and bake in preheated hot oven (425° F; 400° F for glass pie plate) for 10 minutes. Reduce heat to 350° F (325° F for glass) and bake for 40–45 minutes until crust is lightly browned (if brushed it will be brown and shiny), juice starts to bubble through vent(s) and apples are tender when pierced (use a cocktail fork or skewer inserted through vent to test for doneness. Remove from oven and set on wire rack to cool 15 minutes before serving. Traditionally served with vanilla ice cream or a slice of cheddar cheese; try serving with French Vanilla Soy Ice Cream or Frozen Yogurt. Stored loosely covered in cool dry place, the leftover pie will keep for a couple of days without the crust becoming soggy.

Pinyon Pie
(or Pecan Pie)

This is a basic luscious recipe for Pecan Pie adapted to Spelt and pine nuts. I grew up in the Southwest where the Pinyon Pine grows. Here as in Italy, Greece and elsewhere around the Mediterranean, people have used pine nuts (pignolas) in cooking since ancient times. I remember well both Navajo and Apache Indians collecting the nuts in quiet groups in the mountains of Arizona, and I still see them collecting the nuts occasionally as I did just a few months ago. As children, we would buy the roasted nuts from a Navajo family and eat them on the way to school.

Blood Type: O • Prep time: 10 min • Cook time: 40 min • Yield: 8 servings

Ingredients

1   recipe unbaked White Spelt single pie shell 8"–9" (see *Pastry and Pie Crust Chart*)

½   cup fluid honey, light to medium grades

½   cup light or dark brown sugar, firmly packed

¼   cup butter

3   eggs, lightly beaten

¾   cup (4 oz) pine nut kernels

OR 1 cup pecan halves

1. Preheat oven to 400° F and set out an 8¾"–9" pie pan. Place a heavy saucepan over medium heat. Add honey and sugar; blend. Cook slowly, stirring frequently, to make a smooth syrup (about 5–8 minutes).

2. Reduce heat; add butter and stir. Remove pan from heat and gently stir in beaten eggs and the pine nuts (or pecans).

3. Prick bottom and sides of unbaked pie shell 5–6 times each with tines of fork. Pour mixture into pie shell.

4. Place in preheated hot (400° F) oven and bake for 10 minutes. Reduce the heat to 350° F and bake for an additional 30 minutes. (If using glass pie plate, bake at 375° F then reduce heat to 325° F). Test for doneness by inserting skewer or knife into center. If it comes out with no sticky residue on it, the pie is cooked. Remove from oven and cool completely on wire rack before serving.

Crostate di Fichi
(Fig Tarts with Dried Plums and Raisins)

The classic Italian recipe made anew with White Spelt flour is a joy to make and eat. These Fig Tarts are made with the succulent honey-flavored Calimyrna Fig that exquisitely complements the flavors of Spelt, nuts and wildflower honey in particular.

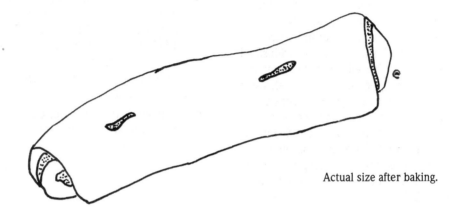

Actual size after baking.

Blood Type: Not rated • Prep time: 15 min/30 min • Cook time: 14–15 min • Yield: 60 1 oz tarts

Ingredients

Filling
1   cup Calimyrna figs
1   cup pitted dried plums packaged to retain moisture
OR other dried plums low in moisture soaked in hot water (15 minutes), drained, patted dry
1   cup raisins, soaked in hot water (15 minutes), drained, patted dry
1   cup walnuts, finely chopped
½   cup fluid honey

Pastry for Tarts
1   pkg active dry yeast
⅔   cup milk

½   cup light brown sugar
½   tsp salt
¼   cup + 2 Tbsp Olive or other vegetable oil
4 to 4½ cups White Spelt flour (the finer the sift the better for this recipe)
1   Tbsp tepid water
Confectioners' sugar for dusting

Filling
1.   Remove any stems from the figs. Place in food processor bowl fitted with metal blade and chop. Empty the figs into a medium size bowl. Chop the plums and raisins in food processor. Add to bowl with figs. To the bowl, add the chopped nuts and honey. Stir to combine all ingredients. Set aside.

Pastry

1. Sprinkle 1 package yeast over 2 Tbsp warm water (110°–115° F). Stir to dissolve. Let stand until creamy and foamy (10 minutes).

2. Heat milk until it bubbles but does not boil and cool to lukewarm (about 95° F). Stir in the sugar, salt and oil. Preheat oven to 350° F.

3. In large mixing bowl, add the yeast and the milk mixture. Add 2½ cups White Spelt flour. Mix to combine. Add 1 Tbsp tepid water and remaining flour in ½ cup increments. Knead by hand or with stand mixer (lowest speed, paddle) to form soft, heavy dough. Do not over mix—this should be a very tender dough. Turn out onto lightly floured surface and knead briefly until the dough is smooth. Divide into two equal portions. Cover one portion with bowl or plastic wrap or damp towel so it will not dry out while working with the other half.

4. Roll one portion of the dough into an 18" x 14" rectangle. Cut it into 30 2½" x 3" rectangles. Drop a generous tablespoon of filling onto each rectangle. Roll into shape of a finger (about size of an adult's index finger). The rolling will seal the dough and spread the filling. Make two small slits on top of each tart. Dust the bottoms lightly with flour.

5. Set ¾" apart on parchment paper (preferable) or a lightly oiled large baking sheet (jelly roll pan). Bake in moderate oven (350° F) for 14–15 minutes or until the crust just begins to brown—just a tinge. As first half of recipe is baking, repeat the process with the remainder of the dough.

6. Remove from oven; place on wire racks to cool. Dust with Confectioners' sugar. Store in airtight container.

Cannoli
(Cream-Filled Italian Pastry)

These are pastry shells formed around a tube and fried then filled with luscious whipped ricotta mixed with liqueur and chocolate bits, the traditional citron or candied orange peel. My father made them in the shape of cornucopia and used homemade dowels for the forms. The red wine version creates plum-colored dough that holds the taste of the wine. White wine or flavored water create a fragrant dough that turns traditional golden brown and is slightly crisper. Please read recipe thoroughly before beginning as this recipe can be made over a couple of days. Have 4–8 Cannoli tubes on hand.

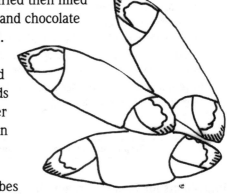

Blood Type: Unrated • Shells Prep time: 5–10 min/1 hour to cool • Cook time: 30–40 min • Yield: 24 shells

---

Ingredients for 24 Cannoli Shells

3   cups White Spelt flour
3   Tbsp melted butter
⅛   tsp salt
1   Tbsp granulated sugar
about ⅔ cup white wine OR water flavored with vanilla or almond, red wine
1   egg yolk, slightly beaten
oil for deep frying (sufficient for 3" oil)

1.   In large mixing bowl, combine the flour, melted butter, salt and sugar, mix, adding just enough liquid (water or wine) to make a sticky rough dough.

Stand Mixer: Once rough dough forms, scrape down sides of bowl. Attach dough hook and knead on lowest speed for about 2 minutes, adding a Tbsp or more of flour if necessary to make soft, smooth dough or adjusting the liquid by the tsp if necessary if dough is crumbly. The amount of flour will vary according to the White Spelt used. Turn out onto lightly floured surface and lightly knead to form soft, very smooth dough.

By Hand: Once rough dough forms, beat to form soft sticky dough, continually scraping down sides of bowl and adding sprinklings of White Spelt flour to adjust consistency. As dough becomes smooth, it will start to chase spoon around bowl and become too heavy to mix. Turn out onto lightly floured surface and knead lightly to form soft, smooth dough, sprinkling additional flour over dough to form soft, very smooth dough.

2.   Form into ball, set in a clean bowl and cover tightly with plastic wrap or lid. Refrigerate for one hour.

3.   Begin heating the oil for deep frying (about 365° F). Divide the dough into two pieces. Keep one piece covered while rolling the other into paper-thin sheets (less than ¼"). Cut into 12 4" squares or circles depending on the form desired. Dust the squares/circles with a sprinkling of flour and stack them so each piece is offset or layer with wax paper to make peeling them apart easier. Repeat with other piece of dough.

4. For squares, place the cannoli tube diagonally across dough. Wrap one corner around the tube; fold the other corner over it, sealing the corners with the beaten egg yolk. Press together to seal.

5. Fry cannoli, two at a time, without allowing them to settle on bottom. Use a slotted spoon or tongs to lift and turn so all sides brown evenly (under a minute and a half). Remove with tongs or slotted spoon and gently place on several layers of paper towels; let cool for a few seconds; slip the cannoli from the tube. Repeat.

6. Cool the shells completely. Once cooled, fill them immediately before serving so they remain crisp. Or store them in a tin or a paper bag in a cool, dry place and fill them later. They will remain fairly crisp for a couple of days should you desire to make them well in advance of serving.

Tip: Once they have cooled, brush lips of Cannoli with melted high quality dark chocolate. Let chocolate cool and harden and then fill immediately with cream and dip in nuts (see below). OR drizzle Fudge Crunch Topping over the Cannoli (see recipe under *Cookie Tray*).

Prep time: 15 min • Cook time: None/Chill at least 4 hours; best if overnight

---

Ingredients for Cannoli Cream Filling

3 pounds whole milk Ricotta cheese, drained
1½ cups Confectioners' sugar
¼ cup sweet liqueur (Amaretto, Cointreau, Crème de Cacao or other)
OR 2 tsp vanilla extract
3 Tbsp grated high quality dark chocolate
3 Tbsp high quality dark chocolate, chopped (optional)
3 Tbsp candied orange peel and/or citron
½ cup roasted, chopped pistachios (optional)

1. Blend the drained Ricotta cheese until smooth. Add the sugar; blend. Add the liqueur or vanilla and blend several minutes until smooth. Stir in the grated dark chocolate, the chopped chocolate (optional), and the candied orange peel and/or citron.

2. Place in airtight container and chill a minimum of four hours. It is best if refrigerated overnight. It will last for several days so it can be made well ahead of time just like the shells.

3. Use a pastry tube or spoon to fill shells. Place roasted pistachios in small bowl; dip the ends of the stuffed Cannoli into pistachios. Serve immediately or freeze.

Pineapple Cheese Pie

An exquisite, delicate cheesecake that has a lengthy pedigree. This is a form of the Roman *Libum* or cheese pie. White Spelt flour replaces cornstarch as a thickener.

Blood Type: Not rated • Prep time: 20 min • Cook time: 50–60 min • Yield: 8 servings

Ingredients

1   recipe unbaked 9"–10" White Spelt pie shell (see *Pastry and Pie Crust Chart*)
1   cup fresh, crushed, drained pineapple
OR 2 8 oz cans chunk pineapple, drained and crushed
OR 1 9 oz can crushed pineapple, drained
⅓   cup honey
2   Tbsp White Spelt flour
1   8 oz package cream cheese, softened (room temperature)
½   tsp salt
⅓   cup granulated sugar
2   eggs, room temperature
½   cup milk, room temperature
1   tsp vanilla
½   cup diced walnuts
OR ¼ cup minced pine nuts

1. In advance prepare a 9"–10" single crust White Spelt pie shell. Prick sides and bottom with tines of fork in 5–6 places each. Cover with plastic. Set aside. Preheat oven to 400° F.

2. Set a 2-quart saucepan over medium heat. Add the crushed pineapple, honey and White Spelt flour. Cook, stirring constantly, until mixture bubbles and thickens. Remove from heat and let cool. Heat oven to 400° F. Place rack on middle shelf.

3. In large mixing bowl, blend the softened cream cheese, salt and granulated sugar. Add eggs one at a time, being careful not to over beat. Add the milk and vanilla; blend.

4. Spread the pineapple mixture evenly into the unbaked shell; pour the cheese filling over the pineapple. Sprinkle evenly with nuts.

5. Place pie in preheated hot (400° F) oven and bake for 10 minutes. Reduce heat to 325° F and bake 40–50 minutes until the filling is firm and skewer or knife gently inserted into center comes out clean. Do not over bake or filling will be dry. Remove from oven and place on wire rack to cool. Serve plain or with a berry sauce (see *Sweet Toppings* section).

Old Times Pumpkin or Sweet Potato Pie

This is a simple, old-fashioned pumpkin pie—made without the milk. The texture is dense, much like a pecan pie, with deep undertones of sweet, nutty squash, Spelt and spices. Use the equivalent amount of mashed sweet potatoes to make a Sweet Potato Pie.

Blood types: A, AB, O (O use mace instead of nutmeg; AB eliminate the allspice)
Prep time: 10 min • Cook time: 40–50 min • Yield: 2 8" pies

Ingredients

2   8-inch unbaked White or Mixed Spelt pastry shells (see *Pastry and Pie Crust Chart*)
3   eggs, room temperature
3   cups plain, canned mashed pumpkin (1 lb 13 oz can)
1½ cups dark brown sugar, firmly packed
2   tsp cinnamon OR cardamom
1   tsp ginger
½   tsp freshly ground nutmeg
¼   tsp allspice
¼   tsp salt
pecan OR walnut halves (optional)

1. Prick the edges and bottom of the unbaked pie shells. Set aside. Preheat oven to 350° F.

2. In large mixing bowl, beat the eggs until light but not frothy.

3. Add the pumpkin, brown sugar, spices and salt; mix until thoroughly combined.

4. Pour mixture into pastry shells. Decorate top with pecan or walnut halves (optional). Place pies on lowest rack in preheated moderate oven (350° F); bake for 40–50 minutes until knife or skewer inserted in center comes out clean. Remove from oven and cool before serving for best flavor. Cut into small wedges. Does not require refrigeration and saves at room temperature for a couple of days without developing a soggy crust.

Pineapple-Blueberry Upside Down Cake

Tasters rated the Spelt Pineapple-Blueberry Upside Down Cake very high particularly because of the unusually delicious combination of fruits. Besides being more nutritious than a frosted cake, upside-downers can be made with many combinations of fleshy fruits and berries besides the one offered here. Take advantage of fruits in season such as peaches or use those wonderful organic dehydrated fruits such as blueberries, cherries and apples.

Blood Type: B, O (O use mace not nutmeg); A, AB (use oil instead of butter)
Prep time: 30–35 min • Cook time: 35–40 min • Yield: 8 servings

Ingredients

2 eggs, room temperature
⅔ cup Whole Spelt flour
⅔ cup White Spelt flour
2 tsp baking powder
1 tsp finely grated lemon zest
½ tsp coriander OR mace
¼ tsp nutmeg, freshly ground
4 Tbsp brown sugar, tightly packed
2 Tbsp butter, melted
OR 1½ Tbsp Light Olive or other vegetable oil (does not caramelize same way as butter)
1 Tbsp water
OR pineapple juice
2 cups crushed pineapple, drained (use the juice for the 1 Tbsp water)
½ cup fresh blueberries
OR reconstituted berries
½ cup turbinado sugar (divided ¼, ¼)
¼ cup butter, softened
1 tsp vanilla
⅔ cup plain soy milk

1. Preheat oven to 350° F; oil a 9" x 1½" round baking pan. For a more caramelized topping, use a heavy skillet of similar proportions for making the butter version. Separate the eggs; leave whites in small bowl for beating later.

2. In small bowl, combine Whole Grain and White Spelt flours, baking powder, lemon zest and spices. Whisk. Set aside.

3. In small bowl, combine 4 Tbsp brown sugar, 2 Tbsp melted butter or 1½ Tbsp oil and water or pineapple juice. Spread on bottom of the oiled pan/skillet. Sprinkle the pineapple over the sugar/butter then sprinkle the blueberries over all. Set aside.

4. Beat the egg whites to form soft peaks. Gradually add ¼ cup turbinado sugar to whites and beat to stiff peaks. Set aside.

5. Using stand mixer with paddle or electric hand mixer, add the ¼ cup softened butter to a large mixing bowl and cream (30 seconds, speed 3 to 4); beat in the remaining ¼ cup turbinado sugar.

6. Add the flour mixture and soymilk alternately to the butter/sugar mixture, beating on low speed just until all ingredients are moist and thoroughly incorporated. By hand, gently fold the beaten egg whites into batter.

7. Gently spoon the batter onto the fruit in the pan/skillet. Place on middle rack and bake in preheated moderate (350° F) oven for 35–40 minutes.

8. Cool the cake in the pan/skillet on a wire rack for 5 minutes. Go around the edges of the pan with a knife or spatula to loosen edges then invert the cake onto a platter. Slice and serve warm.

pelt Pound Cake

Light golden brown with cream colored interior, this is a dense, fine-grained cake made with yogurt, honey and butter or oil. This is the traditional base for many desserts. Let Spelt Pound Cake be the base for serving fresh fruit in season or fruit puree, or with chocolate sauce and Batangas Bananas (see in *Sweet Toppings*).

Blood Type: A, B, AB (A, AB use oil. Texture will be slightly grainier.)
Prep time: 15 min • Cook time: 50–55 min • Yield: 9" x 5" loaf

Ingredients

2¾ cups White Spelt flour
1½ tsp baking powder
½   tsp baking soda
¼   tsp salt
⅔   cup fluid honey
½   cup butter, softened
OR ¼ cup + 2 Tbsp vegetable oil
1   tsp vanilla
2   eggs, room temperature, separated
1   cup plain goat's milk OR other plain yogurt without additives

1. Preheat oven to 350° F. Lightly spray loaf pan with oil even if non-stick variety. Separate the eggs. Lightly beat the yolks and set aside. Beat the whites until they form stiff peaks. Set aside.

2. In a medium bowl, combine the flour, baking powder, baking soda and salt. Set aside.

3. In a large mixing bowl, cream the honey and butter (or oil) with electric or stand mixer (medium speed). Add the vanilla. Add the egg yolks to the creamed honey mixture and blend briefly.

4. Alternately and gradually (lower speed) add the yogurt and the dry ingredients to the creamed honey/egg mixture; mix until blended. By hand, gently fold in the egg whites with spoon or rubber spatula and blend.

5. Turn batter into an oiled 9" x 5" loaf pan. Bake on middle rack of preheated moderate (350° F) oven for 50–55 minutes until cake is a light golden brown and cake has shrunk slightly from edges of pan. Test by inserting a wooden toothpick or skewer into center. If it comes out clean the cake is done. Remove from oven and place on wire rack to cool for 10 minutes. Tip out of pan to cool completely before serving.

Raspberry Valentine Cake

Creamy white and bright tasting, this small, light Spelt cake is made with raspberries and topped with raspberry puree.

Blood Type: A, B, AB, O • Prep time: 10 min • Cook time: 25–30 min • Yield: 8" x 8" cake

Ingredients

¼ cup Extra Light Olive oil or other vegetable oil
1 large egg, room temperature, lightly beaten
½ cup plain soymilk
1 cup White Spelt Flour
¾ cup Whole Grain Spelt flour
¾ cup brown sugar, tightly packed
2 tsp baking powder
½ tsp salt
1 cup fresh raspberries OR frozen raspberries, thawed over colander
turbinado sugar for sprinkling
1 cup fresh or frozen (thawed) raspberry puree (optional) (see under *Sweet Toppings*)

1. Preheat oven to 350° F. Lightly spray or oil an 8" x 8" cake pan or a 9" round layer cake pan or mold of similar size.

2. In medium mixing bowl, combine the Spelt flours, sugar, baking powder and salt. Whisk. Set aside.

3. In large mixing bowl, combine the oil, lightly beaten egg and soymilk; blend. Gradually add the dry ingredients to the oil/egg/milk mixture and blend. Do not over beat.

4. Fold in the raspberries and stir just enough to incorporate into the batter. Spoon into prepared pan. Sprinkle with turbinado sugar.

5. Place on middle rack of preheated moderate (350° F) oven and bake for 25–30 minutes or until cake is done and top is golden brown. Test by inserting toothpick or skewer into center. If it comes out clean, remove cake from oven and place on wire rack to cool. Prepare Raspberry Puree (optional). Cut cooled cake into squares and spoon the Raspberry Puree over each square.

SWEET TOPPINGS

Crumble (Streusel) Topping

Honey Butter-Nut (Caramel) Topping

**Fudge Crunch Topping (see Chocolate
Transgression Brownies)**

Basic Confectioners' Sugar Icing

✳

Fruit Toppings, Purees, Sauces

Batangas Bananas (Caramelized Bananas)

Fruit Purees

Fruit Sauces

Sweet Toppings

CRUMBLE (STREUSEL) TOPPING Makes
2 cups

¼   cup butter, softened OR 3 Tbsp vegetable
    oil such as Light Olive oil or canola
½   cup light brown sugar, firmly packed
¾   cup finely chopped nuts (walnuts,
    pecans, peanuts, pine nuts, pistachios,
    other)
¼   cup White Spelt flour
¼   cup Whole Grain Spelt flour
OR ⅓ cup Rolled Spelt or Rolled Oats
½   tsp salt
½   tsp each of cinnamon, cardamom, mace
    OR freshly grated nutmeg, other

Work butter or oil into the dry ingredients with
pastry blender, two forks or your fingers until the
texture is crumbly. Sprinkle over cakes, fruit
bars, crisps, cereal or other foods and bake. Use
what you need and freeze the rest.

HONEY BUTTER-NUT (CARAMEL)
TOPPING Makes about ¾ cup of toffee-like
topping

¼   cup butter, softened
⅓   cup dark brown sugar, tightly packed
¼   cup fluid honey
½   cup walnuts or pecans, finely chopped

Whip the butter, brown sugar and honey to a
fluffy, light consistency. Add a few drops of
warm (105° F+) water if mixture is too thick.
Spread evenly over the dough and sprinkle with
the chopped nuts. Bake as recipe directs. Use
over Spelt quick breads, coffeecakes, muffins or
cupcakes.

FUDGE CRUNCH TOPPING (See Chocolate
Transgression Brownies in *Cookie Tray*
section)

BASIC CONFECTIONERS' SUGAR ICING
Makes about 1 cup

¼   cup milk
1   cup Confectioners' sugar
½   tsp vanilla OR other flavoring such as
    almond or lemon juice or cooking grade
    oils such as spearmint or peppermint

Pour milk into a small bowl. Stir in the sugar and
the flavoring. Adjust according to consistency
desired such as glaze (thin) over rolls or cakes
or as icing (thicker) for cupcakes and cookies.
Chocolate Glaze: Add 2 Tbsp cocoa.

Fruit Toppings, Purees, Sauces

BATANGAS BANANAS
(Caramelized Bananas)

2   Tbsp butter OR 1½ Tbsp Light Olive or other vegetable oil
2   large bananas
1   Tbsp light brown sugar
½   tsp lemon juice

Place a skillet over medium heat. Add butter or oil and heat. Slice bananas lengthwise and place, cut side up in skillet. Cook for 3 minutes until brown. Sprinkle the tops with brown sugar and drizzle with lemon juice. Turn the bananas and cook for 5 or so minutes to glaze. Serve hot over Pao Doce, Pound Cake, Shortcake, Brownies.

FRUIT PUREES

Fresh, delicious alternative to traditional sauces such as butterscotch or chocolate. Spoon over Athena Crepes, Spelt Pancakes and Waffles, Pao Doce or Pound Cake or Raspberry Valentine Cake. Blend with yogurt or blend into Soft Yogurt Cheese and spread on Spelt Bagels, Spelt breads such as Spelt Honey Wheat Berry, on Scones, over Pineapple Cheese Pie. Use as a dip for Ebelskivers.

Strawberry Puree: 2 cups fresh strawberries, washed and drained, topped and sliced in half. Place in blender; puree. Stir in 2 tsp granulated sugar.

Blackberry or Raspberry Puree: 1 cup fresh blackberries or raspberries, washed and drained. Place in blender; puree. If desired, strain to remove seeds. Stir in ½ tsp fresh lemon juice and 2 tsp granulated sugar.

FRUIT SAUCES
From DRIED FRUITS. Try different combinations of dried fruits and liquids to achieve amazing and delicious flavors.

Begin with 1 cup dried fruit (cranberries, raisins, sour cherries, sweet cherries, dried apricots, mangos, blueberries, apricots, varieties of apples, plums). Finely chop the dried fruit (Tip: if placed in freezer an hour before use they will chop easier.) Add ½ cup water with 2 Tbsp granulated sugar OR ½ cup liqueur or brandy such as Kirsch, red or white wine to small saucepan and place on moderate heat. Add cup of fruit. Cover and gently cook, without boiling, until fruit is tender and absorbs most of the liquid. Let stand until serving. Serve over cold or hot cereals or waffles and pancakes.

SAUCE FROM FRESH or FROZEN FRUITS AND/OR BERRIES.
Make with raspberries, blueberries, marionberries, mangos, peaches, pineapple, plums, other. Sauce can be made with a single fruit or, as above, with a combination of fruits and berries. Use as preserves to serve on Scones. Spread Medi Crostini with smooth goat cheese or cream cheese and top with fruit sauce.

½   cup granulated sugar
2   Tbsp + 3–4 tsp White Spelt flour
½   cup water or water from thawed fruit
2   cups fresh or frozen fruits or berries (thawed over colander; reserve juice)

For mangos, pineapples or other such fruit, chop into smaller pieces or chunks. Halve or quarter the plums. Place saucepan over high heat; add sugar, water and flour and bring to a boil. Add 1 cup of fresh fruit and bring to a boil again. As soon as mixture bubbles, remove it from the heat and add the remaining fruit. Stir. Let stand until serving.

Ancient Offerings
Page from the Past

Should auld acquaintance be forgot,
And never brought to mind?
Should auld acquaintance be forgot,
And days of auld lang syne.

And ther's a hand, my trusty friend,
And gie's a hand o'thine;
We'll tak' a cup o' kindness yet,
For auld lang syne.

From a Traditional Folk Song,
Written down by Robert Burns

Food is life. Throughout human time, the search for food was paramount. The hearth was the focus of life because that is where the food was prepared and communally eaten. In recipes for food—oral or written—the story of humankind unfolds. Foods, and the recipes for preparing them, cross all borders and time.

We forget that until recently we all beseeched the gods and goddesses for their help and their blessings on the harvest and the lambs in Spring. Should they become vengeful, fickle or mischievous, we propitiated them and fed them, as if they were we, through offerings. Some foods, the ancient grains, had religious significance they were so important to human life. Spelt is one of those. The épi loaf, lean French bread cut to resemble ears of wheat, is a living example of this tradition. So is cheese pie. So is leaving a plate of good cookies and milk for Santa Claus.

Those frosted holiday cookies in shapes of trees and animals, angels and gingerbread men, oh what a long tradition, one most of us do not think about when—or if—we make those once-a-year cookies. The tradition is so deeply rooted in the past we have forgotten they were once ancient offerings to remember the gods, ancestors, friends and remarkable events like comets and super-novae.

All over the world we find evidence food and drink were buried with the dead to help them on their journey. We bring flowers and foods to graves or set foods on household shrines to worship or remember our ancestors or people important to our lives or the life of our particular nation (Memorial Day). We make Festival breads and "celebrate" everything from birth to death and things beyond with food. Food is more than sustenance; it is our social cement.

I think it fitting to end the book where *it* begins—with an ancient grain and an ancient way of paying tribute to the powers-that-be by making special bread.

Auld Lang Syne (Remembrance) Bread is wonderful bread that has many uses, like simple raisin toast in the morning. It makes lovely plump rolls and good loaves. The full sweet taste and character of Spelt that I have spoken to you about throughout this book are in it. It is also the bread of the New Year, a time of looking back and looking forward, and being present in the right here and right now.

The making of this bread is a way of passing on tradition to your children and your grandchildren or starting your own tradition—just you in the kitchen with whimsy and spirit setting out to create something anew. Hang the forms from your tree or from a cactus, hang them from the rafters if that is your inclination.

It is dough for making forms of beings and things that we remember in humility, grace, wonder and thankfulness for our lives and our daily bread.

Auld Lang Syne Bread
(Remembrance Bread)

This bread is a treasure: for its taste, its forgiving nature, its simplicity and the variety of recipes you can make with this basic dough. It is a joy to make in all its forms: loaves for toast, rolls, coiled figurines, braided or coiled breads. The basic Andean quinoa recipe appears in the wonderful book *Body, Mind & Spirit: Native Cooking of the Americas* (2004) by Beverly Cox & Martin Jacobs. The amended Spelt version appears here courtesy of *Native Peoples* magazine. In the original recipe, the Andeans color the faces or forms with annatto seeds (natural food coloring) mixed with lard.

Blood Type: A, B, AB, O • Prep time: about 2–2½ hours including making dough, proofing, shaping forms
Cook time: Varies 20 min/batch for figurines • Yield: 6–8 figurines (depending upon the forms)
or 1 loaf (9" x 5"), 2 loaves (8" x 4"), two braids or coiled forms

Ingredients

1   pkg active dry yeast
1   Tbsp sugar divided (1 tsp, 2 tsp)
¾   cup tepid water, flavored or plain (add flavorings to suit your fancy: almond, vanilla, spearmint, cherry, lemon, other)
2½ to 3 cups White Spelt flour (divided 1, 1½)
1   cup Whole Grain Spelt flour
1   tsp salt
1   egg, room temperature, beaten
¼   cup vegetable oil (particularly Light Olive and canola)
1   egg yolk beaten with 2 Tbsp water (or 1 teaspoon flavoring + 1 Tbsp + 2 tsp water)
Confectioners' Icing and Food Colorings (optional)
Dried fruit, nuts, candies for decorating (optional)

1. **Ferment/Sponge.** In large mixing bowl, place ¾ cup tepid water. Sprinkle yeast and 1 tsp sugar over the water; stir to dissolve. Let stand 10 minutes until creamy and foamy.

2. To the yeast mixture, add 1 cup Whole Grain and 1 cup White Spelt flour ½ cup at a time and mix until well combined. Scrape down sides of bowl. Cover the bowl with plastic wrap, damp tea towel or plate and set in draft-free place at room temperature or warmer (75° F–85° F) until sponge doubles in volume (30–40 minutes). The sponge will be tacky and have air bubbles.

3. **Dough Mix/Knead.** Gently deflate the sponge dough and add the remaining 2 tsp sugar, salt, beaten egg and oil. Add 1 cup of the remaining White Spelt.

Stand Mixer: Paddle, speed 1/lowest speed, mix to form rough dough (1 minute). Change to dough hook and add remaining ½ cup White Spelt. Knead for 60 seconds adjusting flour by the Tbsp or water by the tsp if necessary to form smooth, moist dough that begins to clean sides of bowl.

By Hand: Gradually add the remaining ½ cup of White Spelt to form smooth, moist dough.

4. **Dough Rise.** Turn dough out onto lightly floured surface and sprinkle with White Spelt. Knead very lightly to form soft, smooth ball. Place in an oiled bowl, turning dough so all surfaces are lightly oiled. Let rise in same place (25–35 minutes). Dough is vigorous—do not let it rise too long or it will become flaccid. Do Fingertip Test to check at 25 minutes and 5 minute intervals thereafter.

5. **Degas/Divide/Form.** Detach dough from sides of bowl and turn onto top of dough. Gently deflate dough. Turn out onto lightly floured board.

Coiled Figurines: Prepare one or two large rimmed baking pans by covering with parchment or oiling/greasing the pans. Preheat oven to 400° F. If using two pans, adjust one rack to lowest position and the other two rungs up.

With pastry scraper or sharp knife, divide the dough into 6–8 pieces, depending on the size of the figures desired. Cover the rest of the dough. Working on prepared baking sheet or on floured surface, roll dough with fingertips into coil(s). Shape the coil(s) into figurines and place on pan. Use currents or raisins for eyes, sliced almonds for mouths or bits of dried fruit for decorations or wait to decorate with Confectioners' icing (see *Sweet Toppings*) and bits of fruit, nuts or candies after baking.

Set baking sheet in large plastic bag or cover with lightly oiled plastic wrap. Let figurines rise 15–20 minutes until almost doubled in size. Gently brush with egg wash.

Place in preheated (400° F) oven and bake for 10 minutes. Shift pans to opposite rack and turn each pan 180° to assure even baking. Bake an additional 10 minutes. Figurines will expand in

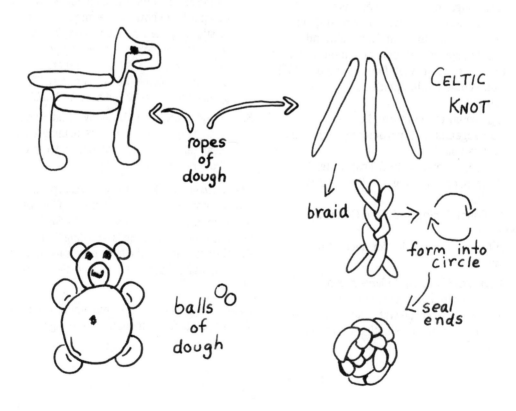

oven and become golden brown. Remove pans from oven and shift figurines on parchment to wire racks to cool prior to icing and decorating.

Loaf: Preheat oven to 400° F. Turn deflated dough out onto a lightly floured board. Let dough rest, covered, 10 minutes. Shape into a 9" long cylinder and place in oiled 9" x 5" loaf pan so dough touches ends of pan. Or divide into 2 equal portions, let rest 10 minutes, covered, and then work into 8" cylinders and place in oiled/greased 8" x 4" pans for smaller loaves.

Cover loosely with plastic wrap sprayed with oil or oil surface of dough lightly and place in large plastic bag to rise by ¾ volume. Place on center rack of preheated hot (400° F) oven and bake 35–40 minutes (30–35 for smaller loaves) and rich golden brown. Remove from oven. Tip out of pan(s) and place on wire rack. Thump bottoms and sides. If they sound hollow versus reverberating with a dull thud, the bread is baked. Let cool completely before slicing.

Braided/Coiled Bread: Preheat oven to 400° F. Adjust racks: one on lowest rung, the other two rungs up. Divide dough into two equal portions. Cover one portion with plastic wrap or bowl. Cover large rimmed baking pans with parchment or oil the pans. Dust with White Spelt flour.

Divide one portion of dough into three equal strands. Place strands on baking sheet. Sprinkle strands liberally with Whole Grain Spelt Flour to prevent them from bleeding together after forming. Braid (to refresh yourself, see instructions under *Knead to Know©*). Form braid into a circle, seal edges and tuck underneath. Or seal ends by pressing together and tucking under the end of the braid. Lightly spray a piece of plastic wrap and place loosely over bread or lightly spray surface with oil and place in large plastic bag to rise (20–25 minutes). Repeat with other half of dough.

Prior to baking, gently brush the braids with egg wash. Place in preheated hot (400° F) oven and bake 15 minutes; change to opposite rack and rotate pans 180° to assure even baking. Continue baking additional 20–25 minutes or until light golden brown. Remove from oven and slide onto wire racks. Let braids cool. If not baked on parchment, place paper towels, wax paper or parchment under wire racks for icing. Paint the bread with plain or colored, flavored or unflavored, Confectioners' icing (see under *Sweet Toppings*). Decorate the braid with bits of dried fruit or candies.

For Kids: Divide the dough into balls and coils and form into teddy bears or gorillas or any forms the bright eyes of their imagination can see. Follow directions above for baking.

AFTERWORD

A TOAST TO TODAY

Not to the Future, nor to the Past

No drink of Joy or Sorrow

We drink alone to what will last—

Memories on the Morrow

Let us live as Old Time passes

To the Present let us bow

Let us raise on high our glasses

To Eternity—

The ever-living Now.

Toast from the 1914 Art of Dining
Bohemian Restaurants Cookbook
San Francisco, California

Glossary

Bake: Cook by dry heat in an oven. Includes method of using cloche or cover for trapping steam during baking.

Batter: A mixture of flour, liquid and other ingredients with liquid consistency sufficient for pouring or ladling.

Beat: Mix by stirring repeatedly and somewhat rapidly.

Beat with a spoon: Using a spoon, lift mixture quickly in an over and under manner so underneath portion is brought to the surface and all ingredients are evenly mixed.

Blend: Combining two or more ingredients until each loses its individual texture or appearance; to thoroughly mix.

Boil: Cook in liquid heated at sea level to 212° F. Bubbles constantly come to surface and break as they pass from liquid to vapor.

Coat: To cover (shake in a bag, roll) with layer of flour, sugar, etc.

Combine: Bring individual ingredients or sets of ingredients together.

Cook: (Noun) The person who prepares the food. (Verb) Preparing food for eating.

Cream: (Noun) The part of milk that rises to the top and is oily in texture and yellowish-white in color. (Adjective) Custard-like, smooth, creamy consistency. (Verb) With paddle on mixer or by hand with spoon, working butter or shortening and sugar against the side of the bowl until mixture has a creamy consistency.

Crouton: Air dried (stale) or toasted bread made crisp by toasting, baking or frying in oil and/or butter. Croutons are cut into squares that are generally cubed ($\frac{1}{2}$") or larger (1" or more). Served with soups, salads and appetizers.

Cube: Cut into square pieces about $\frac{1}{2}$" on a side.

Cut in: Working butter or shortening into flour or a flour mixture to achieve flour coating of fat particles. The end of the process optimally results in particles that are typically described as pea sized or texture of coarse corn meal. Process is accomplished by using 2 knives, a fork or a pastry blender (hand methods) or with food processor fitted with metal blade.

Dice: Make cubes by cutting into small square pieces $\frac{1}{4}$" or less on a side.

Dough: a mix of flour, liquid and other ingredients worked into a soft, thick mass for baking, frying, boiling, etc.

Dredge: Sprinkle or coat lightly with flour, sugar, etc.

Egg Terms: Slightly/lightly beaten is just enough so yolk and whites are blended. Well beaten is to beat until frothy and light. The purpose is to incorporate air and increase the volume. Egg whites beaten stiff to the point where they form peaks; surface is glossy and moist and peaks droop just a bit. Egg whites beaten very stiff. The surface will be dry looking and the peaks will be upright.

Fold in: (Such as beaten egg whites) Put on top of a mixture such as a batter, gently bring a spoon, spatula or whip down through that mixture and across the bottom drawing the mixture up until it is now on top. Gently repeat the process until the egg whites are combined with the batter. Folding leaves some of the air in beaten egg whites thus creating a lighter texture.

Garlic clove/bulb: The individual crescent-shaped portions covered in thin papery skin that form the bulb from which the garlic plant grows.

Knead: Process of working dough that develops the gluten matrix for bread to expand during baking. (See Part IV *Knead to Know.*)

Marinate: To steep or soak in a mixture for a specified time.

Melt chocolate: (Microwave) Place in microwavable bowl and cook on HIGH for 1 minute. Stir. Cook another 30–60 seconds. Remove from microwave. To melt the chocolate completely, stir until the block loses form. (Saucepan) Place chocolate in heavy saucepan; set on very low heat; stir continuously until melted. (Double boiler) Fill bottom of a saucepan with about 2" water; heat until water is barely simmering. Put chocolate in a bowl/pan that fits loosely over the saucepan. Melt the chocolate stirring continuously.

Mince: Chop into very fine squares usually about ⅛".

Mix: Putting ingredients together to unite into a compound such as batter.

Pan-Fry: Food cooked on stovetop in skillet with small amount oil/fat.

Peel: Take off outer covering of fruit and vegetables. See also **Zest**.

Puree: (Verb) Prepare food by straining the pulp through a sieve as with blackberries.

Sauté: Fry quickly in a skillet with a small amount of fat or oil stirring frequently.

Scald: Heat milk to just below boiling point; heat until tiny bubbles appear around edge.

Scallions: Variously called green onion, spring onion or chives depending on the type, are all related to garlic (*Allium* species). The whole plant, green and white is edible. The hollow, cylindrical green portion, whole or chopped is "chives".

Simmer: To cook gently just below the boiling point (185° F sea level simmer).

Stock/Broth: Is the liquid that results from simmering meat, fish, poultry, vegetables, etc. in water, usually containing aromatic herbs, for an extended period.

Toast: (Verb) To brown bread in oven, toaster, broiler or on grill or coals.

Zest: (Noun) Peel of lemon, lime, orange. Used for flavoring. The peel (excluding the white portion below peel) is grated or cut into fine strips used whole or minced.

APPENDIX 1:

NUTRITION INFORMATION FOR THE RECIPES

MORNING MENU

BINGEN SPELT PORRIDGE (WHOLE SPELT BERRIES) makes about **17** servings per 28 oz/bag. **Amount per serving:** ¼ cup (46g raw). **Calories:** 130 **Calories from Fat:** 10 / %=Daily Values based on a 2,000 calorie diet. Your daily values may differ. **Total Fat** 1g (2%), **Saturated Fat** 0g (0%), **Trans Fat** 0g (0%), **Cholesterol** 0mg (0%), **Sodium** 0mg (0%), **Total Carbohydrates** 32g (11%), **Dietary Fiber** 8g (33%), **Sugars** 0g, **Protein** 7g. Vitamin A 0%, Vitamin C 0%, Calcium 0%, Iron 8%.

ROLLED SPELT HOT BREAKFAST CEREAL makes **12** servings per 18 oz bag. **Amount per serving:** ½ cup dry (40g). **Calories:** 130 **Calories from Fat:** 10 / %=Daily Values based on a 2,000 calorie diet. Your daily values may differ. **Total Fat** 1.5g (2%), **Saturated Fat** 0g (0%), **Cholesterol** 0mg (0%), **Sodium** 0 mg (0%), **Total Carbohydrates** 28g (9%), **Dietary Fiber** 3g (12%), **Sugars** 0g, **Protein** 5g. Vitamin A 0%, Vitamin C 0%, Calcium 0%, Iron 8%.

ATHENA CREPES makes **4** servings. **Amount per serving: Calories:** 232 **Calories from Fat:** 98 / %=Daily Values based on a 2,000 calorie diet. Your daily values may differ. **Total Fat** 10.9g (17%), **Saturated Fat** 3.8g (19%), **Cholesterol** 68mg (23%), **Sodium** 529mg (22%), **Total Carbohydrates** 25.2g (8%), **Dietary Fiber** 2.7g (11%), **Protein** 8.3g. Additional information: 42.2% of calories from Fat; 43.4% from Carbohydrates; 14.3% from Protein.

SPELT SPROUTCAKES makes **16** servings. **Amount per serving: Calories:** 47 **Calories from Fat:** 3 / %=Daily Values based on a 2,000 calorie diet. Your daily values may differ. **Total Fat** 0.3g, **Saturated Fat:** 0.1g (1%), **Cholesterol** 4mg (1%), **Sodium** 80mg (3%), **Total Carbohydrates** 9.4g (3%), **Dietary Fiber** 1.2g (5%), **Protein** 1.7g. Additional information: 6.3% of calories from Fat; 79.3% from Carbohydrates; 14.3% from Protein.

SPUKWHEAT PANCAKES makes **5** servings. **Amount per serving: Calories:** 397 **Calories from Fat:** 173 / %=Daily Values based on a 2,000 calorie diet. Your daily values may differ. **Total Fat** 19.2g (30%), **Saturated Fat** 3.7g (19%), **Cholesterol** 50mg (17%), **Sodium** 825mg (34%), **Total Carbohydrates** 44.6g (15%), **Dietary Fiber** 4.1g (16%), **Protein** 11.3g. Additional information: 43.6% of calories from Fat; 45% from Carbohydrates; 11.4% from Protein. Recipe based on 2% milk.

EBLESKIVERS makes **36** servings. **Amount per serving: Calories:** 58 **Calories from Fat:** 19 / %=Daily Values based on a 2,000 calorie diet. Your daily values may differ. **Total Fat** 2g (3%), **Saturated Fat** 0.3g (2%), **Cholesterol** 18mg (6%), **Sodium** 41mg (2%), **Total Carbohydrates** 8.4g (3%), **Dietary Fiber** 0.6g (2%), **Protein** 1.3g. Additional information: 32.9% of calories from Fat; 58.1% from Carbohydrates; 9% from Protein.

BASIC TASTY WAFFLES makes **16** servings. **Amount per serving: Calories:** 81 **Calories from Fat:** 31 /%=Daily Values based on a 2,000 calorie diet. Your daily values may differ. **Total Fat** 3.3g (5%), **Saturated Fat** 0.6g (3%), **Cholesterol** 28mg (9%), **Sodium** 82mg (3%), **Total Carbohydrates** 9.8g (3%), **Dietary Fiber** 0.7g (3%), **Protein** 2.7g. Additional information: 38.3% of calories from Fat; 48.4% from Carbohydrates; 13.3 % from Protein.

WHOLE GRAIN WAFFLES WITH SPELT SPROUTS AND FRUIT BITS makes **18** servings. **Amount per serving: Calories:** 124 **Calories from Fat:** 49 / %=Daily Values based on a 2,000 calorie diet. Your daily values may differ. **Total Fat** 5.4g (8%), **Saturated Fat** 0.9g (4%), **Cholesterol** 25mg (8%), **Sodium** 73mg (3%), **Total Carbohydrates** 16.2g (5%), **Dietary Fiber** 1.5g (6%), **Protein** 2.6g. Additional information: 39.5 % of calories from Fat; 52.2% from Carbohydrates; 8.4% from Protein.

CHOCOLATE WALNUT WAFFLES makes **9** servings. **Amount per serving: Calories:** 334 **Calories from Fat:** 161 /%=Daily Values based on a 2,000 calorie diet. Your daily values may differ. **Total Fat** 17.9g (28%), **Saturated Fat** 4.1g (20%), **Cholesterol** 49mg (16%), **Sodium** 409mg (17%), **Total Carbohydrates** 35.3g (12%), **Dietary Fiber** 3.2g (13%), **Protein** 7.9g. Additional information: 48.2% of calories from Fat; 42.3% from Carbohydrates; 9.5% from Protein.

BASIC BAKING POWDER BISCUITS makes **12** servings. **Amount per serving: Calories:** 149 **Calories from Fat:** 43 / %=Daily Values based on a 2,000 calorie diet. Your daily values may differ. **Total Fat** 4.8g (7%), **Saturated Fat** 0.8g (4%), **Cholesterol** 1mg (0%), **Sodium** 228mg (10%), **Total Carbohydrates** 22g(7%), **Dietary Fiber** 1.5g (6%) **Protein** 4.4g. Additional information: 28.9% of calories from Fat; 59.2% from Carbohydrates; 11.8% from Protein. Recipe based on 2% milk.

BREAKFAST BISCUITS TO GO makes **4** servings. **Amount per serving: Calories:** 457 **Calories from Fat:** 229 / %=Daily Values based on a 2,000 calorie diet. Your daily values may differ. **Total Fat** 25.5g (39%), **Saturated Fat** 8.5g (42%), **Cholesterol** 276mg (92%), **Sodium** 865 (36%), **Total Carbohydrates** 24.7g (8%), **Dietary Fiber** 1.5g (6%), **Protein** 32.4g. Additional information: 50.1% of calories from Fat; 21.6% from Carbohydrates; 28.3% from Protein. Recipe based on part-skim Mozzarella cheese and 2% milk in the biscuits.

LIVELY VEGETABLE AND GOAT CHEESE SCRAMBLE IN TART SHELL makes **4** servings. **Amount per serving: Calories:** 257 **Calories from Fat:** 185 / %=Daily Values based on a 2,000 calorie diet. Your daily values may differ. **Total Fat:** 20.6g (32%), **Saturated Fat:** 6.7g (33%), **Cholesterol** 236 mg (79%), **Sodium** 380mg (16%), **Total Carbohydrates** 6.6g (2%), **Dietary Fiber** 1.4g (6%), **Protein** 11.5g. Additional information: 71.9% of calories from Fat; 10.3% from Carbohydrates; 17.9% from Protein.

QUICHE makes **8** servings. **Amount per serving: Calories:** 136 **Calories from Fat:** 79 / %=Daily Values based on a 2,000 calorie diet. Your daily values may differ. **Total Fat:** 8.9g (14%), **Saturated Fat:** 2.3g (11%), **Cholesterol** 92mg (31%), **Sodium** 283mg (12%), **Total Carbohydrates** 5.6 (2%), **Dietary Fiber** 0.8g (3%), **Protein** 8.6g. Additional information: 58.2% of calories from Fat; 16.5% from Carbohydrates; 25.3% from Protein.

FRITTATA WITH RICOTTA AND HERBED SPELT CRUMBS makes **8** servings. **Amount per serving: Calories:** 323 **Calories from Fat:** 182 / %=Daily Values based on a 2,000 calorie diet. Your daily values may differ. **Total Fat** 20.3g (31%), **Saturated Fat** 7.9g (40%), **Cholesterol** 191mg (64%), **Sodium** 273mg (11%), **Total Carbohydrates** 20.5g (7%), **Dietary Fiber** 2.8g (11%), **Protein** 14.7g. Additional information: 56.4% of calories from Fat; 25.4% from Carbohydrates; 18.2% from Protein.

BREAKFAST BURRITOS makes **2** servings. **Amount per serving: Calories:** 254 **Calories from Fat:** 120 / %=Daily Values based on a 2,000 calorie diet. Your daily values may differ. **Total Fat** 13.3g (20%), **Saturated Fat** 3.6g (18 %), **Cholesterol** 237mg (79%), **Sodium** 506mg (21%), **Total Carbohydrates** 17.6g (6%), **Dietary Fiber** 0.8g (3%), **Protein** 15.8g. Additional information: 47.3% of calories from Fat; 27.8% from Carbohydrates; 24.9% from Protein.

CHILES RELLENOS makes **18** servings. **Amount per serving: Calories:** 146 **Calories from Fat:** 74 / %=Daily Values based on a 2,000 calorie diet. Your daily values may differ. **Total Fat** 8.2 g(13%), **Saturated Fat** 4.5g (22%), **Cholesterol** 115mg (38%), **Sodium** 274mg (11%), **Total Carbohydrates** 5.7g (2%), **Dietary Fiber** 1.1g (4%), **Protein** 12.4g. Additional information: 50.5% of calories from Fat; 15.6% from Carbohydrates; 33.9% from Protein.

HUEVOS RANCHEROS makes **4** servings. **Amount per serving: Calories:** 309 **Calories from Fat:** 153 / %=Daily Values based on a 2,000 calorie diet. Your daily values may differ. **Total Fat** 16.9 g (26%), **Saturated Fat** 4.5g (22%), **Cholesterol** 436mg (145%), **Sodium** 435mg (18%), **Total Carbohydrates** 17.8g (6%), **Dietary Fiber** 0.8g (3%), **Protein** 21.3g. Additional information: 49.5% of calories from Fat; 23% from Carbohydrates; 27.5% from Protein.

EMPANADAS DE FRUTA makes **16** servings. **Amount per serving: Calories:** 213 **Calories from Fat:** 91 / %=Daily Values based on a 2,000 calorie diet. Your daily values may differ. **Total Fat** 10.1 g (16%), **Saturated Fat** 1.3g (6%), **Cholesterol** 13mg (4%), **Sodium** 80mg (3%), **Total Carbohydrates** 26.8g (9%), **Dietary Fiber** 2.2g (9%), **Protein** 3.6g. Additional information: 42.8% of calories from Fat; 50.4% from Carbohydrates; 6.8% from Protein. Nutrition information is based on Empanadas de Manzana (Apple Turnovers).

NEW BRAUNFELS, TEXAS CUSTARD TOAST makes **4** servings. **Amount per serving: 4 oz. Calories:** 192 **Calories from Fat:** 56 / %=Daily Values based on a 2,000 calorie diet. Your daily values may differ. **Total Fat** 6.3g (10%), **Saturated Fat** 2.7g (14%), **Cholesterol** 166mg (55%), **Sodium** 227mg (9%), **Total Carbohydrates** 23.6g (8%), **Dietary Fiber** 1.1g (4%), **Protein** 10.3g. Additional information: 29.2% of calories from Fat; 49.3% from Carbohydrates; 21.5 % from Protein.

CHEESE AND PINEAPPLE DANISH MODERN makes **16** servings. **Amount per serving: Calories:** 284 **Calories from Fat:** 123 / %=Daily Values based on a 2,000 calorie diet. Your daily values may differ. **Total Fat** 13.7g (21%), **Saturated Fat** 7.4g (37%), **Cholesterol** 70mg (23%), **Sodium** 236mg (10%), **Total Carbohydrates** 33.7g (11%), **Dietary Fiber** 1.8g (7%), **Protein** 6.5g. Additional information: 43.3% of calories from Fat; 47.5 % from Carbohydrates; 9.2% from Protein.

BEIGNES makes **36** servings. **Amount per serving: Calories:** 61 **Calories from Fat:** 9 / %=Daily Values based on a 2,000 calorie diet. Your daily values may differ. **Total Fat** 1g (2%), **Saturated Fat** 0.2g (1%), **Cholesterol** 6mg (2%), **Sodium** 54mg (2%), **Total Carbohydrates** 10.9g (4%), **Dietary Fiber** 0.4g (2%), **Protein** 2.2g. Additional information: 14.7% of calories from Fat; 71% from Carbohydrates; 14.3% from Protein.

BAGELS (WATER BAGELS) makes **12** servings. **Amount per serving: Calories:** 177 **Calories from Fat:** 5 / %=Daily Values based on a 2,000 calorie diet. Your daily values may differ. **Total Fat** 0.5g (1%), **Saturated Fat** 0.1g (1%), **Cholesterol** 18mg (6%), **Sodium** 202mg (8%), **Total Carbohydrates** 36.3g (12%), **Dietary Fiber** 2.6g (10%), **Protein** 6.8g. Additional information: 2.8% of calories from Fat; 81.8% from Carbohydrates; 15.3% from Protein.

CARNS ENGLISH MUFFINS makes **8** servings. **Amount per serving: Calories:** 251 **Calories from Fat:** 21 / %=Daily Values based on a 2,000 calorie diet. Your daily values may differ. **Total Fat** 2.3g (4%), **Saturated Fat** 0.4g (2%), **Cholesterol** 2mg (1%), **Sodium** 304mg (13%), **Total Carbohydrates** 48.7g (16%), **Dietary Fiber** 5.2g (21%), **Protein** 8.9g. Additional information: 8.4% of calories from Fat; 77.5% from Carbohydrates; 14.2% from Protein.

SWEET MUFFINS WITH CRUMBLE TOPPING makes **12** servings. **Amount per serving: Calories:** 253 **Calories from Fat:** 126 / %=Daily Values based on a 2,000 calorie diet. Your daily values may differ. **Total Fat** 13.9g (21%), **Saturated Fat** 2.8g (14%), **Cholesterol** 25mg (8%), **Sodium** 209mg (9%), **Total Carbohydrates** 26.1g (9%), **Dietary Fiber** 2.1g (8%), **Protein** 5.7g. Additional information: 49.8% of calories from Fat; 41.2% from Carbohydrates; 9% from Protein.

SPELTA'S CINNAMON ROLLS makes **24** servings. **Amount per serving: 3 oz. Calories:** 276 **Calories from Fat:** 117 / %=Daily Values based on a 2,000 calorie diet. Your daily values may differ. **Total Fat** 12.7g (20%), **Saturated Fat** 4.6g (23%), **Cholesterol** 43mg (14%), **Sodium** 141mg (6%), **Total Carbohydrates** 33g (11%), **Dietary Fiber** 2.4g (10%), **Protein** 6.7g. Additional information: 42.4% of calories from Fat; 47.9% from Carbohydrates; 9.7% from Protein.

PISTACHIO STICKY BUNS makes **18** servings. **Amount per serving: 4 oz. Calories:** 463 **Calories from Fat:** 134 / %=Daily Values based on a 2,000 calorie diet. Your daily values may differ. **Total Fat** 14.8g (23%), **Saturated Fat** 7.3g (37%), **Cholesterol** 64mg (21%), **Sodium** 197mg (8%), **Total Carbohydrates** 73.2g (24%), **Dietary Fiber** 3.6g (14%), **Protein** 9g. Additional information: 29% of calories from Fat; 63.3% from Carbohydrates; 7.8% from Protein.

THE BAKERY

A BEGINNING LOAF makes **12** servings. **Amount per serving: Calories:** 108 **Calories from Fat:** 23 / %=Daily Values based on a 2,000 calorie diet. Your daily values may differ. **Total Fat** 2.6g (4%), **Saturated Fat** 0.3g (2%), **Cholesterol** 0mg (0%), **Sodium** 27mg (1%), **Total Carbohydrates** 18g (6%), **Dietary Fiber** 2.9g (12%), **Protein** 3.2g. Additional information: 21.3% of calories from Fat; 66.8% from Carbohydrates; 11.9% from Protein.

SPELTESSENCE BREAD makes **16** servings. **Amount per serving: Calories:** 120 **Calories from Fat:** 24 / %=Daily Values based on a 2,000 calorie diet. Your daily values may differ. **Total Fat** 2.6g (4%), **Saturated Fat** 0.3g (2%), **Cholesterol** 0mg (0%), **Sodium** 1mg (0%), **Total Carbohydrates** 20.8g (7%), **Dietary Fiber** 2.3g (9%), **Protein** 3.2g. Additional information: 20% of calories from Fat; 69.3% from Carbohydrates; 10.7% from Protein.

MOLASSES AND SPELT NO-KNEAD BREAD makes **16** servings. **Amount per serving: Calories:** 160 **Calories from Fat:** 6 / %=Daily Values based on a 2,000 calorie diet. Your daily values may differ. **Total Fat** 0.6g (1%), **Saturated Fat** 0.3g (2%), **Cholesterol** 2mg (1%), **Sodium** 18mg (1%), **Total Carbohydrates** 32.9g (11%), **Dietary Fiber** 3.1g (12%), **Protein** 5.7g. Additional information: 3.7% of calories from Fat; 82% from Carbohydrates; 14.2% from Protein.

CLASSIC WHITE SPELT BREAD makes **32** servings. **Amount per serving: Calories:** 105 **Calories from Fat:** 11 / %=Daily Values based on a 2,000 calorie diet. Your daily values may differ. **Total Fat** 1.3g (2%), **Saturated Fat** 0.8g (4%), **Cholesterol** 3mg (1%), **Sodium** 150mg (6%), **Total**

Carbohydrates 19.8g (7%), **Dietary Fiber** 0.9g (4%), **Protein** 3.6g. Additional information: 10.5% of calories from Fat; 75.7% from Carbohydrates; 13.8% from Protein.

TRADITIONAL FEAST ROLLS makes **48** servings. **Amount per serving: Calories:** 92 **Calories from Fat:** 19 / %=Daily Values based on a 2,000 calorie diet. Your daily values may differ. **Total Fat** 2.1g (3%), **Saturated Fat** 0.4g (2%), **Cholesterol** 10mg (3%), **Sodium** 106mg (4%), **Total Carbohydrates** 15.3g (5%), **Dietary Fiber** 1g (4%), **Protein** 2.9g. Additional information: 20.7% of calories from Fat; 66.7% from Carbohydrates; 12.6% from Protein.

BRUNDISI PESTO BREAD makes **36** servings. **Amount per serving: Calories:** 97 **Calories from Fat:** 27 / %=Daily Values based on a 2,000 calorie diet. Your daily values may differ. **Total Fat** 3g (5%), **Saturated Fat** 0.9g (4%), **Cholesterol** 9mg (3%), **Sodium** 162mg (7%), **Total Carbohydrates** 13.9g (5%), **Dietary Fiber** 1g (4%), **Protein** 3.5g. Additional information: 28% of calories from Fat; 57.6% from Carbohydrates; 14.5% from Protein.

BRUNDISI PESTO ROLLS makes **12 large** rolls. **Amount per serving:** about 4 oz each. **Calories: 315 Calories from Fat:** 96 / %=Daily Values based on a 2,000 calorie diet. Your daily values may differ. **Total Fat** 10.5g (16%), **Saturated Fat** 3.7g (19%), **Cholesterol** 30mg (10%), **Sodium** 539mg (22%), **Total Carbohydrates** 42.3g (14%), **Dietary Fiber** 3.1g (12%), **Protein** 12.5g. Additional information: 30.5% of calories from Fat; 53.7% from Carbohydrates; 15.9% from Protein.

FRENCH BREAD makes **28** servings. **Amount per serving: Calories:** 98 **Calories from Fat:** 0 / %=Daily Values based on a 2,000 calorie diet. Your daily values may differ. **Total Fat** 0g (0%), **Saturated Fat** 0g (0%), **Cholesterol** 0mg (0%), **Sodium** 170mg (7%), **Total Carbohydrates** 20.6g (7%), **Dietary Fiber** 1.5g (6%), **Protein** 3.9 g. Additional information: 0% of calories from Fat; 84.1% from Carbohydrates; 15.9% from Protein.

FRENCH ROLLS makes **16** servings. **Amount per serving: Calories:** 173 **Calories from Fat:** 1 / %=Daily Values based on a 2,000 calorie diet. Your daily values may differ. **Total Fat** 0.1g (0%), **Saturated Fat** 0g (0%), **Cholesterol** 0mg (0%), **Sodium** 298mg (12%), **Total Carbohydrates** 36.1g (12%), **Dietary Fiber** 2.5g (10%), **Protein** 6.8g. Additional information: 0.6% of calories from Fat; 83.7% from Carbohydrates; 15.8% from Protein.

FRENCH BREADSTICKS see **FRENCH BREAD** above.

CHALLAH makes **32** servings. **Amount per serving: Calories:** 88 **Calories from Fat:** 21 / %=Daily Values based on a 2,000 calorie diet. Your daily values may differ. **Total Fat** 2.3g (4%), **Saturated Fat** 0.4g (2%), **Cholesterol** 27mg (9%), **Sodium** 82mg (3%), **Total Carbohydrates** 13.8g (5%), **Dietary Fiber** 1.3g (5%), **Protein** 3g. Additional information: 23.8% of calories from Fat; 62.6% from Carbohydrates; 13.6% from Protein.

CARDAMOM GOLD PUMPKIN BREAD makes **32** servings. **Amount per serving: Calories:** 81 **Calories from Fat:** 12 / %=Daily Values based on a 2,000 calorie diet. Your daily values may differ. **Total Fat** 1.3g (2%), **Saturated Fat** 0.2g (1%), **Cholesterol** 13mg (4%), **Sodium** 80mg (3%), **Total Carbohydrates** 14.8g (5%), **Dietary Fiber** 1.1g (4%), **Protein** 2.5g. Additional information: 14.8% of calories from Fat; 72.9% from Carbohydrates; 12.3% from Protein.

DARK RYE BREAD makes **32** servings. **Amount per serving: Calories:** 96 **Calories from Fat:** 10 / %=Daily Values based on a 2,000 calorie diet. Your daily values may differ. **Total Fat** 1.2g (2%), **Saturated Fat** 0.5g (2%), **Cholesterol** 10mg (3%), **Sodium** 302 mg (13%), **Total Carbohydrates** 18.3g (6%), **Dietary Fiber** 2.1g (8%), **Protein** 3.2g. Additional information: 10.4% of calories from Fat; 76.2% from Carbohydrates; 13.3% from Protein.

BRIOCHE (SPELT SWEET DOUGH) BASIC RECIPE makes **32** servings. **Amount per serving: Calories:** 207 **Calories from Fat:** 87 / %=Daily Values based on a 2,000 calorie diet. Your daily values may differ. **Total Fat** 9.7g (15%), **Saturated Fat** 3.2g (16%), **Cholesterol** 33mg (11%), **Sodium** 105mg (4%), **Total Carbohydrates** 24.9g (8%), **Dietary Fiber** 1.8g (7%), **Protein** 5.1g. Additional information: 42% of calories from Fat; 48.1% from Carbohydrates; 9.9% from Protein.

BRIOCHES WITH HINT OF LEMON makes **18** servings. **Amount per serving:** 2 oz. **Calories:** 369 **Calories from Fat:** 156 / %=Daily Values based on a 2,000 calorie diet. Your daily values may differ. **Total Fat** 17.3g (27%), **Saturated Fat** 6.2g (31%), **Cholesterol** 57mg (19%), **Sodium** 187mg (8%), **Total Carbohydrates** 44.1g (15%), **Dietary Fiber** 3.1g (12%), **Protein** 9.1g. Additional information: 42.3% of calories from Fat; 47.8% from Carbohydrates; 9.9% from Protein.

PAO DOCE (PORTUGUESE SPELT SWEET BREAD) makes **36** servings. **Amount per serving: Calories:** 135 **Calories from Fat:** 35 / %=Daily Values based on a 2,000 calorie diet. Your daily values may differ. **Total Fat** 3.8g (6%), **Saturated Fat** 2.2g (11%), **Cholesterol** 33mg (11%), **Sodium** 76mg (3%), **Total Carbohydrates** 21.3g (7%), **Dietary Fiber** 0.7g (%), **Protein** 3.8g. Additional information: 25.8% of calories from Fat; 62.9% from Carbohydrates; 11.2% from Protein.

SPELT WHEAT BERRY AND HONEY BREAD makes **32** servings. **Amount per serving: Calories:** 126 **Calories from Fat:** 16 / %=Daily Values based on a 2,000 calorie diet. Your daily values may differ. **Total Fat** 1.8g (3%), **Saturated Fat** 0.2g (1%), **Cholesterol** 0mg (0%), **Sodium** 111mg (5%), **Total Carbohydrates** 23.7g (8%), **Dietary Fiber** 2.7g (11%), **Protein** 3.8g. Additional information: 12.7% of calories from Fat; 75.2% from Carbohydrates; 12.1% from Protein.

LIGHT RYE BREAD makes **36** servings. **Amount per serving: Calories:** 115 **Calories from Fat:** 7 / %=Daily Values based on a 2,000 calorie diet. Your daily values may differ. **Total Fat** 0.8g (1%), **Saturated Fat** 0.4g (2%), **Cholesterol** 2mg (1%), **Sodium** 133mg (6%), **Total Carbohydrates** 23.8g (8%), **Dietary Fiber** 2g (8%), **Protein** 3.1g. Additional information: 6.1% of calories from Fat; 83.1% from Carbohydrates; 10.8% from Protein.

ROMAN BREAD makes **32** servings. **Amount per serving: Calories:** 74 **Calories from Fat:** 4 / %=Daily Values based on a 2,000 calorie diet. Your daily values may differ. **Total Fat** 0.4g (1%), **Saturated Fat** 0.1g (1%), **Cholesterol** 0mg (0%), **Sodium** 147mg (6%), **Total Carbohydrates** 15.1g (5%), **Dietary Fiber** 1.5g (6%), **Protein** 2.5g. Additional information: 5.4% of calories from Fat; 81.2% from Carbohydrates; 13.4% from Protein.

CALABRESE BREAD makes **36** servings. **Amount per serving: Calories:** 107 **Calories from Fat:** 5 / %=Daily Values based on a 2,000 calorie diet. Your daily values may differ. **Total Fat** 0.5g (1%), **Saturated Fat** 0.5g (2%), **Cholesterol** 2mg (1%), **Sodium** 169mg (7%), **Total Carbohydrates** 21.3g (7%), **Dietary Fiber** 2.5g (10%), **Protein** 4.1g. Additional information: 4.7% of calories from Fat; 79.9% from Carbohydrates; 15.4% from Protein.

CALABRESE BREAD BOWLS OR PETIT BOULES see **CALABRESE BREAD**.

CAMPOCOSENZA (COUNTRY WHEEL FOR PANINI/BRUSCHETTA) makes **36** servings. **Amount per serving: Calories:** 95 **Calories from Fat:** 0 / %=Daily Values based on a 2,000 calorie diet. Your daily values may differ. **Total Fat** 0g (0%), **Saturated Fat** 0g (0%), **Cholesterol** 0mg (0%), **Sodium** 131mg (5%), **Total Carbohydrates** 20.2g (7%), **Dietary Fiber** 2g (8%), **Protein** 3.5g. Additional information: 0% of calories from Fat; 85.2% from Carbohydrates; 14.8% from Protein.

ALL-PURPOSE ITALIAN BIGA/DOUGH makes **36** servings. **Amount per serving: Calories:** 79 **Calories from Fat:** 0 / %=Daily Values based on a 2,000 calorie diet. Your daily values may differ. **Total Fat** 0g (0%), **Saturated Fat** 0g (0%), **Cholesterol** 0mg (0%), **Sodium** 131mg (5%), **Total Carbohydrates** 16.8g (6%), **Dietary Fiber** 1.4g (6%), **Protein** 3g. Additional information: 0% of calories from Fat; 84.8% from Carbohydrates; 15.2% from Protein.

ALL-PURPOSE ITALIAN SUBMARINE ROLLS makes 8–10; **FOCACCIA**, makes 2; **PIZZA** 8 individual 10" or 3 medium size; **CALZONES** makes 12–18; **BREAD ROUNDS** makes 4–6; **LOAVES** makes 2–3; **WHEEL** makes 1; **BREADBOWLS** makes 8. See above for nutrition information.

ROASTED GARLIC AND MOZZARELLA BAGUETTES makes **36** servings. **Amount per serving: Calories:** 96 **Calories from Fat:** 14 / %=Daily Values based on a 2,000 calorie diet. Your daily values may differ. **Total Fat** 1.5g (2%), **Saturated Fat** 0.2g (1%), **Cholesterol** 0mg (0%), **Sodium** 133mg (6%), **Total Carbohydrates** 17.5g (6%), **Dietary Fiber** 1.5g (6%), **Protein** 3.1g. Additional information: 14.5% of calories from Fat; 72.6% from Carbohydrates; 12.9% from Protein.

MEDI CROSTINI LOAVES makes **32** servings. **Amount per serving: Calories:** 97 **Calories from Fat:** 0 / %=Daily Values based on a 2,000 calorie diet. Your daily values may differ. **Total Fat** 0g (0%), **Saturated Fat** 0g (0%), **Cholesterol** 0mg (0%), **Sodium** 222mg (9%), **Total Carbohydrates** 20.5g (7%), **Dietary Fiber** 1.5g (6%), **Protein** 3.8 g. Additional information: 0% of calories from Fat; 84.4% from Carbohydrates; 15.6% from Protein.

PAN ANDREA FESTIVAL AND WEDDING BREAD makes **54** servings. **Amount per serving: Calories:** 93 **Calories from Fat:** 12 / %=Daily Values based on a 2,000 calorie diet. Your daily values may differ. **Total Fat** 1.3g (2%), **Saturated Fat** 0.1g (1%), **Cholesterol** 0mg (0%), **Sodium** 87mg (4%), **Total Carbohydrates** 17.8g (6%), **Dietary Fiber** 1.3g (5%), **Protein** 2.5g. Additional information: 12.9% of calories from Fat; 76.4% from Carbohydrates; 10.7% from Protein.

BREAD MACHINE

SPELTESSENCE BREAD see under **Bakery** above.

ROSEMARY CHEESE BREAD makes **16** servings. **Amount per serving: Calories:** 129 **Calories from Fat:** 27 / %=Daily Values based on a 2,000 calorie diet. Your daily values may differ. **Total Fat** 3g (5%), **Saturated Fat** 1g (5%), **Cholesterol** 17mg (6%), **Sodium** 199mg (8%), **Total Carbohydrates** 19.9g (7%), **Dietary Fiber** 1.7g (7%), **Protein** 5g. Additional information: 21% of calories from Fat; 61/9% from Carbohydrates; 17.1% from Protein.

SEATTLE SUPREME SANDWICH LOAF makes **16** servings. **Amount per serving: Calories:** 132 **Calories from Fat:** 16/ %=Daily Values based on a 2,000 calorie diet. Your daily values may differ. **Total Fat** 1.8g (3%), **Saturated Fat** 0.3g (2%), **Cholesterol** 1mg (0%), **Sodium** 151mg (6%), **Total Carbohydrates** 25.2g (8%), **Dietary Fiber** 1.5g (6%), **Protein** 3.9g. Additional information: 12.1% of calories from Fat; 76.1% from Carbohydrates; 11.8% from Protein.

CROUTONS AND CRUMBS see individual breads.

DRESSING

DRESSING / STUFFING makes **8** servings. **Amount per serving: Calories:** 222 **Calories from Fat:** 123 / %=Daily Values based on a 2,000 calorie diet. Your daily values may differ. **Total Fat** 13.6g (21%), **Saturated Fat** 7.7g (38%), **Cholesterol** 58mg (19%), **Sodium** 1033mg (43%), **Total Carbohydrates** 20.6g (7%), **Dietary Fiber** 2.4g (10%), **Protein** 4.2g. Additional information: 55.4% of calories from Fat; 37.1% from Carbohydrates; 7.6% from Protein.

DRESSING STICKS makes **8** servings. **Amount per serving:** 2 oz. **Calories:** 320 **Calories from Fat:** 87 / %=Daily Values based on a 2,000 calorie diet. Your daily values may differ. **Total Fat** 9.6g (15%), **Saturated Fat** 1.3g (6%), **Cholesterol** 27mg (9%), **Sodium** 604mg (25%), **Total Carbohydrates** 49.5g (16%), **Dietary Fiber** 7.4g (30%), **Protein** 8.7g. Additional information: 27.2% of calories from Fat; 61.9% from Carbohydrates; 10.9% from Protein.

BREAD BASKET (QUICK BREADS / BATTER BREADS)

BLUEBERRY WHOLE SPELT COFFEECAKE WITH CRUMBLE TOPPING makes **10** servings. **Amount per serving:** 2.5 oz. **Calories:** 387 **Calories from Fat:** 147 / %=Daily Values based on a 2,000 calorie diet. Your daily values may differ. **Total Fat** 16.2g (25%), **Saturated Fat** 4.1g (20%), **Cholesterol** 33mg (11%), **Sodium** 328mg (14%), **Total Carbohydrates** 52.9g (18%), **Dietary Fiber** 4.4g (18%), **Protein** 7g. Additional information: 38% of calories from Fat; 54.7% from Carbohydrates; 7.2% from Protein.

DOVE'S FARM SODA BREAD makes **12** servings. **Amount per serving: Calories:** 109 **Calories from Fat:** 5 / %=Daily Values based on a 2,000 calorie diet. Your daily values may differ. **Total Fat** 0.5g (1%), **Saturated Fat** 0.2g (1%), **Cholesterol** 2mg (1%), **Sodium** 508mg (21%), **Total Carbohydrates** 22.1g (7%), **Dietary Fiber** 3.3g (13%), **Protein** 4g. Additional information: 4.6% of calories from Fat; 80.8% from Carbohydrates; 14.6% from Protein.

CHERRIED PLUM BREAD makes **24** servings. **Amount per serving: Calories:** 125 **Calories from Fat:** 8 / %=Daily Values based on a 2,000 calorie diet. Your daily values may differ. **Total Fat** 0.9g (1%), **Saturated Fat** 0.6g (3%), **Cholesterol** 11mg (4%), **Sodium** 120mg (5%), **Total Carbohydrates** 26.3g (9%), **Dietary Fiber** 1.7g (7%), **Protein** 2.9g. Additional information: 6.4% of calories from Fat; 84.3% from Carbohydrates; 9.3% from Protein.

CARROT NUT BREAD makes **12** servings. **Amount per serving: Calories:** 249 **Calories from Fat:** 72 / %=Daily Values based on a 2,000 calorie diet. Your daily values may differ. **Total Fat** 7.9g (12%), **Saturated Fat** 0.9g (4%), **Cholesterol** 35mg (12%), **Sodium** 399mg (17%), **Total Carbohydrates**

37.6g (13%), **Dietary Fiber** 2.5g (10%), **Protein** 6.6g. Additional information: 28.9% of calories from Fat; 60.5% from Carbohydrates; 10.6% from Protein.

GINGERBREAD makes **16** servings. **Amount per serving: Calories: 226 Calories from Fat:** 32 / %=Daily Values based on a 2,000 calorie diet. Your daily values may differ. **Total Fat** 3.5g (5%), **Saturated Fat** 2.1g (10%), **Cholesterol** 22mg (7%), **Sodium** 179mg (7%), **Total Carbohydrates** 44.6g (15%), **Dietary Fiber** 1.5g (6%), **Protein** 4g. Additional information: 14.1% of calories from Fat; 78.8% from Carbohydrates; 7.1% from Protein.

CHOCOLATE VARIETY BREAD makes **32** servings. **Amount per serving: Calories:** 182 **Calories from Fat:** 72 / %=Daily Values based on a 2,000 calorie diet. Your daily values may differ. **Total Fat** 8g (12%), **Saturated Fat** 1g (5%), **Cholesterol** 20mg (7%), **Sodium** 165mg (7%), **Total Carbohydrates** 23.7g (8%), **Dietary Fiber** 1.5g (6%), **Protein** 3.8g. Additional information: 39.6% of calories from Fat; 52.1% from Carbohydrates; 8.4% from Protein. Based on zucchini.

ZUCCHINI BREAD makes **32** servings. **Amount per serving: Calories:** 213 **Calories from Fat:** 87 / %=Daily Values based on a 2,000 calorie diet. Your daily values may differ. **Total Fat** 9.6g (15%), **Saturated Fat** 1.2g (6%), **Cholesterol** 27mg (9%), **Sodium** 134mg (6%), **Total Carbohydrates** 27.5g (9%), **Dietary Fiber** 1.4g (6%), **Protein** 3.9g. Additional information: 40.9% of calories from Fat; 51.7% from Carbohydrates; 7.3% from Protein.

THE MIGHTY MEATBALL

CLASSIC MEATBALL makes **72** servings. **Amount per serving: Calories:** 12 **Calories from Fat:** 6 / %=Daily Values based on a 2,000 calorie diet. Your daily values may differ. **Total Fat** 0.6g (1%), **Saturated Fat** 0.2g (1%), **Cholesterol** 5mg (2%), **Sodium** 45mg (2%), **Total Carbohydrates** 0.4g (0%), **Dietary Fiber** 0g (0%), **Protein** 1.2g. Additional information: 48.4% of calories from Fat; 12.9% from Carbohydrates; 38.7% from Protein. Based on Turkey.

NEW SWEDISH MEATBALLS makes **60** servings. **Amount per serving: Calories:** 68 **Calories from Fat:** 40 / %=Daily Values based on a 2,000 calorie diet. Your daily values may differ. **Total Fat** 4.4g (7%), **Saturated Fat** 1.5g (8%), **Cholesterol** 15mg (5%), **Sodium** 71mg (3%), **Total Carbohydrates** 3.6g (1%), **Dietary Fiber** 0.5g (2%), **Protein** 3.5g. Additional information: 58.5% of calories from Fat; 21.1% from Carbohydrates; 20.5% from Protein.

SOPA DE ALBONDIGAS (MEATBALL SOUP) makes **8** servings. **Amount per serving: Calories:** 206 **Calories from Fat:** 77 / %=Daily Values based on a 2,000 calorie diet. Your daily values may differ. **Total Fat** 8.6g (13%), **Saturated Fat** 2.3g (11%), **Cholesterol** 120mg (40%), **Sodium** 308mg (13%), **Total Carbohydrates** 13.4g (4%), **Dietary Fiber**1.9g (8%), **Protein** 18.9g. Additional information: 37.3% of calories from Fat; 26% from Carbohydrates; 36.7% from Protein.

SOPA DE ALBONDIGAS CON CAMARONES (SHRIMP MEATBALL SOUP) makes **4** servings. **Amount per serving: Calories:** 413 **Calories from Fat:** 130 / %=Daily Values based on a 2,000 calorie diet. Your daily values may differ. **Total Fat** 14.5g (22%), **Saturated Fat** 2.9g (15%), **Cholesterol** 237mg (79%), **Sodium** 1950mg (81%), **Total Carbohydrates** 33.7g (11%), **Dietary Fiber** 3.4g (14%), **Protein** 37g. Additional information: 31.5% of calories from Fat; 32.7% from Carbohydrates; 35.9% from Protein.

HOMEMADE HERITAGE SOUP OF THE DAY (OR NIGHT)

COLLARD GREENS AND TURKEY HAM SOUP WITH DUMPLINGS makes **8** servings.
Amount per serving: Calories: 197 **Calories from Fat:** 55 / %=Daily Values based on a 2,000 calorie diet. Your daily values may differ. **Total Fat** 6.1g (9%), **Saturated Fat** 1.9g (9%), **Cholesterol** 79mg (26%), **Sodium** 1027mg (43%), **Total Carbohydrates** 18.8g (6%), **Dietary Fiber** 2.8g (11%), **Protein** 16.6g. Additional information: 28% of calories from Fat; 38.3% from Carbohydrates; 33.8% from Protein.

MINESTRONE DE FARRO makes **6** servings. **Amount per serving: Calories:** 209 **Calories from Fat:** 49 / %=Daily Values based on a 2,000 calorie diet. Your daily values may differ. **Total Fat** 5.4g (8%), **Saturated Fat** 2.8g (14%), **Cholesterol** 18mg (6%), **Sodium** 643mg (27%), **Total Carbohydrates** 30.1g (10%), **Dietary Fiber** 7.4g (30%), **Protein** 9.9g. Additional information: 23.4% of calories from Fat; 57.6% from Carbohydrates; 18.9% from Protein.

ZUPPA DE FARRO E CANNELLINI (TUSCAN FARRO AND CANNELLINI BEAN SOUP) makes **12** servings. **Amount per serving: Calories:** 178 **Calories from Fat:** 25 / %=Daily Values based on a 2,000 calorie diet. Your daily values may differ. **Total Fat** 2.9g (4%), **Saturated Fat** 0.4g (2%), **Cholesterol** 0mg (0%), **Sodium** 394mg (16%), **Total Carbohydrates** 30.2g (10%), **Dietary Fiber** 8.4g (34%), **Protein** 8.1g. Additional information: 14% of calories from Fat; 67.8% from Carbohydrates; 18.2% from Protein.

SAUCES

AIOLI (GARLIC MAYONNAISE) makes **20** servings. **Amount per serving: Calories:** 123 **Calories from Fat:** 122 / %=Daily Values based on a 2,000 calorie diet. Your daily values may differ. **Total Fat** 13.5g (21%), **Saturated Fat** 1.8g (9%), **Cholesterol** 1mg (0%), **Sodium** 15mg (1%), **Total Carbohydrates** 0.3g (0%), **Dietary Fiber** 0g (0%), **Protein** 0g. Additional information: 99% of calories from Fat; 1% from Carbohydrates; 0% from Protein.

AGLIO E OLIO (GARLIC AND OIL FOR PASTA AND DIPPING) makes **6** servings. **Amount per serving: Calories:** 327 **Calories from Fat:** 324 / %=Daily Values based on a 2,000 calorie diet. Your daily values may differ. **Total Fat** 36g (55%), **Saturated Fat** 4.9g (25%), **Cholesterol** 0mg (0%), **Sodium** 198mg (8%), **Total Carbohydrates** 0.7g (0%), **Dietary Fiber** 0g (0%), **Protein** 0g. Additional information: 99.1% of calories from Fat; 0.9% from Carbohydrates; 0% from Protein.

WHITE SAUCE (BÉCHAMEL) makes **1** servings. **Amount per serving: 1 cup Calories:** 379 **Calories from Fat:** 249 / %=Daily Values based on a 2,000 calorie diet. Your daily values may differ. **Total Fat** 27.7g (43%), **Saturated Fat** 17.2g (86%), **Cholesterol** 80mg (27%), **Sodium** 420mg (18%), **Total Carbohydrates** 22.2g (7%), **Dietary Fiber** 0.5g (2%), **Protein** 10.3g. Additional information: 65.7% of calories from Fat; 23.4% from Carbohydrates; 10.9% from Protein.

THE VEGETABLE STAND

CAESAR SALAD WITH SPELT CROUTONS makes **4** servings. **Amount per serving: Calories:** 830 **Calories from Fat:** 391 / %=Daily Values based on a 2,000 calorie diet. Your daily values may differ. **Total Fat** 43.3g (67%), **Saturated Fat** 8.4g (42%), **Cholesterol** 106mg (%), **Sodium** 1412mg (59%), **Total Carbohydrates** 88.2g (29%), **Dietary Fiber** 7.2g (29%), **Protein** 21.5g. Additional information: 47.1% of calories from Fat; 42.5% from Carbohydrates; 10.4% from Protein.

PANZANELLA SALAD makes **8** servings. **Amount per serving: Calories:** 315 **Calories from Fat:** 197 / %=Daily Values based on a 2,000 calorie diet. Your daily values may differ. **Total Fat** 21.9g (34%), **Saturated Fat** 3.7g (19%), **Cholesterol** 3mg (1%), **Sodium** 162mg (7%), **Total Carbohydrates** 24.2g (8%), **Dietary Fiber** 3g (12%), **Protein** 5.4g. Additional information: 62.5% of calories from Fat; 30.7% from Carbohydrates; 6.8% from Protein.

SPELT ROTINI AND TURMERIC SALAD makes **8** servings. **Amount per serving: Calories:** 163 **Calories from Fat:** 33 / %=Daily Values based on a 2,000 calorie diet. Your daily values may differ. **Total Fat** 3.6g (6%), **Saturated Fat** 2.1g (10%), **Cholesterol** 12mg (4%), **Sodium** 109mg (5%), **Total Carbohydrates** 22.8g (8%), **Dietary Fiber** 1.2g (5%), **Protein** 9.8g. Additional information: 20.2% of calories from Fat; 55.8% from Carbohydrates; 24% from Protein.

SINGLA SALAD makes **4** servings. **Amount per serving: Calories:** 295 **Calories from Fat:** 197 / %=Daily Values based on a 2,000 calorie diet. Your daily values may differ. **Total Fat** 21.8g (34%), **Saturated Fat** 6.1g (30%), **Cholesterol** 13mg (4%), **Sodium** 710mg (30%), **Total Carbohydrates** 15.6g (5%), **Dietary Fiber** 3.5g (14%), **Protein** 8.8g. Additional information: 66.9% of calories from Fat; 21.2% from Carbohydrates; 11.9% from Protein.

TURKEY WALDORF SALAD makes **4** servings. **Amount per serving: Calories:** 498 **Calories from Fat:** 200 / %=Daily Values based on a 2,000 calorie diet. Your daily values may differ. **Total Fat** 22.3g (34%), **Saturated Fat** 3.1g (15%), **Cholesterol** 38mg (13%), **Sodium** 339mg (14%), **Total Carbohydrates** 46.3g (15%), **Dietary Fiber** 7.4g (30%), **Protein** 28.1g. Additional information: 40.2% of calories from Fat; 37.2% from Carbohydrates; 22.6% from Protein.

SWEET AND SOUR SALAD OR MARINADE makes **1** servings. **Amount per serving:** 2 Tbsp **Calories:** 1487 **Calories from Fat:** 886 / %=Daily Values based on a 2,000 calorie diet. Your daily values may differ. **Total Fat** 98.4g (151%), **Saturated Fat** 13.7g (68%), **Cholesterol** 0mg (0%), **Sodium** 2091mg (87%), **Total Carbohydrates** 120.5g (40%), **Dietary Fiber** 9.7g (39%), **Protein** 29.7g. Additional information: 59.6% of calories from Fat; 32.4% from Carbohydrates; 8% from Protein.

ASPARAGUS AL LIMON makes **4** servings. **Amount per serving: Calories:** 166 **Calories from Fat:** 72 / %=Daily Values based on a 2,000 calorie diet. Your daily values may differ. **Total Fat** 8g (12%), **Saturated Fat** 2.2g (11%), **Cholesterol** 0mg (0%), **Sodium** 126mg (5%), **Total Carbohydrates** 18.2g (6%), **Dietary Fiber** 4.2g (17%), **Protein** 5.2g. Additional information: 43.5% of calories from Fat; 44% from Carbohydrates; 12.6% from Protein.

CREAMY ARTICHOKE SIDE DISH, DIP OR TOPPING makes **12** servings. **Amount per serving: Calories:** 196 **Calories from Fat:** 152 / %=Daily Values based on a 2,000 calorie diet. Your daily values may differ. **Total Fat** 16.9g (26%), **Saturated Fat** 2.9g (15%), **Cholesterol** 19mg (6%), **Sodium** 405mg (17%), **Total Carbohydrates** 6.8g (2%), **Dietary Fiber** 2.4g (10%), **Protein** 4.2g. Additional information: 77.6% of calories from Fat; 13.9% from Carbohydrates; 8.6% from Protein.

PORTABELLA MUSHROOMS NEW ORLEANS (STUFFED MUSHROOMS) makes **4** servings. **Amount per serving: Calories:** 333 **Calories from Fat:** 141 / %=Daily Values based on a 2,000 calorie diet. Your daily values may differ. **Total Fat** 15.7g (24%), **Saturated Fat** 3.1g (15%), **Cholesterol** 8mg (3%), **Sodium** 503mg (21%), **Total Carbohydrates** 38.3g (13%), **Dietary Fiber** 3.5g (14%), **Protein** 9.8g. Additional information: 42.3% of calories from Fat; 46% from Carbohydrates; 11.8% from Protein.

SPAGHETTI SQUASH WITH HERBED BREAD CUBES makes **4** servings. **Amount per serving: Calories:** 110 **Calories from Fat:** 38 / %=Daily Values based on a 2,000 calorie diet. Your daily values may differ. **Total Fat** 4.3g (7%), **Saturated Fat** 0.7g (3%), **Cholesterol** 0mg (0%), **Sodium** 431mg (18%), **Total Carbohydrates** 16g (5%), **Dietary Fiber** 3.1g (12%), **Protein** 1.9g. Additional information: 34.7% of calories from Fat; 58.4% from Carbohydrates; 6.9% from Protein.

TUNISIAN RICE WITH SPELT SPROUTS makes **1** servings. **Amount per serving:** 5 cups **Calories:** 1614 **Calories from Fat:** 216 / %=Daily Values based on a 2,000 calorie diet. Your daily values may differ. **Total Fat** 24g (37%), **Saturated Fat** 3.8g (19%), **Cholesterol** 0mg (0%), **Sodium** 1027mg (43%), **Total Carbohydrates** 316.8g (106%), **Dietary Fiber** 15.8g (63%), **Protein** 32.7 g. Additional information: 13.4% of calories from Fat; 78.5% from Carbohydrates; 8.1% from Protein.

SWEET POTATO FRITTERS makes **14** servings. **Amount per serving: Calories:** 73 **Calories from Fat:** 16 / %=Daily Values based on a 2,000 calorie diet. Your daily values may differ. **Total Fat** 1.8g (3%), **Saturated Fat** 0.3g (2%), **Cholesterol** 30mg (10%), **Sodium** 56mg (2%), **Total Carbohydrates** 12.2g (4%), **Dietary Fiber** 1.6g (6%), **Protein** 2g. Additional information: 22% of calories from Fat; 67% from Carbohydrates; 2% from Protein.

SWEET POTATO PUFFS makes **18** servings. **Amount per serving: Calories:** 53 **Calories from Fat:** 15 / %=Daily Values based on a 2,000 calorie diet. Your daily values may differ. **Total Fat** 1.6g (2%), **Saturated Fat** 0.2g (1%), **Cholesterol** 0mg (0%), **Sodium** 68mg (3%), **Total Carbohydrates** 8.7g (3%), **Dietary Fiber** 0.8g (3%), **Protein** 0.8g. Additional information: 28.3% of calories from Fat; 65.7% from Carbohydrates; 6% from Protein.

SHREDDED SWEET POTATO makes **1** servings. **Amount per serving:** 2 cups. **Calories:** 358 **Calories from Fat:** 4 / %=Daily Values based on a 2,000 calorie diet. Your daily values may differ. **Total Fat** 0.4g (1%), **Saturated Fat** 0.1g (1%), **Cholesterol** 0mg (0%), **Sodium** 28mg (1%), **Total Carbohydrates** 82.4g (27%), **Dietary Fiber** 6.3g (25%), **Protein** 6g. Additional information: 1.1 % of calories from Fat; 92.2% from Carbohydrates; 6.7% from Protein.

ZUCCHINI FRIES makes **72** servings. **Amount per serving: Calories:** 28 **Calories from Fat:** 8 / %=Daily Values based on a 2,000 calorie diet. Your daily values may differ. **Total Fat** 0.8g (1%), **Saturated Fat** 0.5g (2%), **Cholesterol** 11mg (4%), **Sodium** 42mg (2%), **Total Carbohydrates** 3.2g

(1%), **Dietary Fiber** 0.2g (1%), **Protein** 1.8g. Additional information: 28.6% of calories from Fat; 45.7% from Carbohydrates; 25.7% from Protein.

ZUCCHINI FRITTERS makes **18** servings. **Amount per serving: Calories:** 39 **Calories from Fat:** 13 / %=Daily Values based on a 2,000 calorie diet. Your daily values may differ. **Total Fat** 1.5g (2%), **Saturated Fat** 0.8g (4%), **Cholesterol** 27mg (9%), **Sodium** 129mg (5%), **Total Carbohydrates** 4g (1%), **Dietary Fiber** 0.7g (3%), **Protein** 2.6g. Additional information: 33% of calories from Fat; 40.6% from Carbohydrates; 26.4% from Protein.

ON THE RUN AND WORKING OUT

HAIS makes **12** servings. **Amount per serving: Calories:** 333 **Calories from Fat:** 143 / %=Daily Values based on a 2,000 calorie diet. Your daily values may differ. **Total Fat** 16g (25%), **Saturated Fat** 1.3g (6%), **Cholesterol** 0mg (0%), **Sodium** 87mg (4%), **Total Carbohydrates** 41.7g (14%), **Dietary Fiber** 6.4g (26%), **Protein** 5.8g. Additional information: 42.9% of calories from Fat; 50.1% from Carbohydrates; 7% from Protein.

EVIL DON'S ENERGY BAR makes **24** servings. **Amount per serving: Calories:** 176 **Calories from Fat:** 51 / %=Daily Values based on a 2,000 calorie diet. Your daily values may differ. **Total Fat** 5.5g (8%), **Saturated Fat** 0.6g (3%), **Cholesterol** 1mg (0%), **Sodium** 116mg (5%), **Total Carbohydrates** 27.5g (9%), **Dietary Fiber** 2g (8%), **Protein** 3.7g. Additional information: 29% of calories from Fat; 62% from Carbohydrates; 8.4% from Protein.

APPLESAUCE PECAN MUFFINS makes **12** servings. **Amount per serving: Calories:** 262 **Calories from Fat:** 104 / %=Daily Values based on a 2,000 calorie diet. Your daily values may differ. **Total Fat** 11.4g (18%), **Saturated Fat** 1g (5%), **Cholesterol** 35mg (12%), **Sodium** 75mg (3%), **Total Carbohydrates** 33.3g (11%), **Dietary Fiber** 1.7g (7%), **Protein** 6.2g. Additional information: 39.7% of calories from Fat; 50.8% from Carbohydrates; 9.5% from Protein.

AFTERNOON TEA AND COFFEE BREAK

LEMON SHORTIES makes **12** servings. **Amount per serving: Calories:** 272 **Calories from Fat:** 70 / %=Daily Values based on a 2,000 calorie diet. Your daily values may differ. **Total Fat** 7.8g (12%), **Saturated Fat** 5.1g (25%), **Cholesterol** 21mg (7%), **Sodium** 1mg (0%), **Total Carbohydrates** 48.1g (16%), **Dietary Fiber** 1.4g (6%), **Protein** 2.4g. Additional information: 25.7% of calories from Fat; 70.7% from Carbohydrates; 3.5% from Protein.

CHERRY ALMOND BISCOTTI makes **24** servings. **Amount per serving: Calories:** 168 **Calories from Fat:** 52 / %=Daily Values based on a 2,000 calorie diet. Your daily values may differ. **Total Fat** 5.7g (9%), **Saturated Fat** 0.8g (4%), **Cholesterol** 18mg (6%), **Sodium** 87mg (4%), **Total Carbohydrates** 25.5g (8%), **Dietary Fiber** 1.5g (6%), **Protein** 3.4g. Additional information: 31% of calories from Fat; 60.9% from Carbohydrates; 8.1% from Protein.

HONEY SCONES makes **8** servings. **Amount per serving: Calories:** 176 **Calories from Fat:** 46 / %=Daily Values based on a 2,000 calorie diet. Your daily values may differ. **Total Fat** 5g (8%), **Saturated Fat** 2.9g (15%), **Cholesterol** 39mg (13%), **Sodium** 283mg (12%), **Total Carbohydrates**

28.8g (10%), **Dietary Fiber** 1.1g (4%), **Protein** 3.7g. Additional information: 26.1% of calories from Fat; 65.5% from Carbohydrates; 8.4% from Protein.

MAPLE SCONES makes **16** servings. **Amount per serving:** 2½ oz. **Calories:** 299 **Calories from Fat:** 145 / %=Daily Values based on a 2,000 calorie diet. Your daily values may differ. **Total Fat** 16.2g (25%), **Saturated Fat** 1.7g (9%), **Cholesterol** 1mg (0%), **Sodium** 246mg (10%), **Total Carbohydrates** 33.1g (11%), **Dietary Fiber** 3.4g (14%), **Protein** 5.5g. Additional information: 48.4% of calories from Fat; 44.2% from Carbohydrates; 7.3% from Protein.

CRANBERRY AND ROLLED SPELT (OR OAT) SCONES makes **16** servings. **Amount per serving:** 2 oz. **Calories:** 245 **Calories from Fat:** 107 / %=Daily Values based on a 2,000 calorie diet. Your daily values may differ. **Total Fat** 11.9g (18%), **Saturated Fat** 4.3g (22%), **Cholesterol** 30mg (10%), **Sodium** 177mg (7%), **Total Carbohydrates** 29.5g (10%), **Dietary Fiber** 1.6g (6%), **Protein** 4.9g. Additional information: 43.7 % of calories from Fat; 48.2% from Carbohydrates; 8% from Protein.

BLUEBERRY LEMON SCONES makes **8** servings. **Amount per serving:** 4 oz. **Calories:** 313 **Calories from Fat:** 109 / %=Daily Values based on a 2,000 calorie diet. Your daily values may differ. **Total Fat** 12g (18%), **Saturated Fat** 7.4g (37%), **Cholesterol** 32mg (11%), **Sodium** 268mg (11%), **Total Carbohydrates** 44.4g (15%), **Dietary Fiber** 3.2g (13%), **Protein** 6.7g. Additional information: 34.8% of calories from Fat; 56.7% from Carbohydrates; 8.6% from Protein.

PARADELL makes **6** servings. **Amount per serving: Calories:** 192 **Calories from Fat:** 78 / %=Daily Values based on a 2,000 calorie diet. Your daily values may differ. **Total Fat** 8.8g (14%), **Saturated Fat** 4.9g (25%), **Cholesterol** 90mg (30%), **Sodium** 31mg (1%), **Total Carbohydrates** 22.9g (8%), **Dietary Fiber** 1.4g (6%), **Protein** 5.6g. Additional information: 40.6% of calories from Fat; 47.7% from Carbohydrates; 11.7% from Protein.

MANY SMALL THINGS

CHEESE SPUFFS makes **12** servings. **Amount per serving: Calories:** 37 **Calories from Fat:** 25 / %=Daily Values based on a 2,000 calorie diet. Your daily values may differ. **Total Fat** 2.8g (4%), **Saturated Fat** 1.8g (9%), **Cholesterol** 8mg (3%), **Sodium** 74mg (3%), **Total Carbohydrates** 1.5g (0%), **Dietary Fiber** 0.1g (0%), **Protein** 1.5g. Additional information: 67.6% of calories from Fat; 16.2% from Carbohydrates; 16.2% from Protein.

BROILED KASSERI OR PECORINO CHEESE WITH BREADCRUMBS makes **16** servings. **Amount per serving: Calories:** 81 **Calories from Fat:** 52 / %=Daily Values based on a 2,000 calorie diet. Your daily values may differ. **Total Fat** 5.8g (9%), **Saturated Fat** 2.9g (15%), **Cholesterol** 14mg (5%), **Sodium** 262mg (11%), **Total Carbohydrates** 3.1g (1%), **Dietary Fiber** 0.2g (1%), **Protein** 4.1g. Additional information: 64.4% of calories from Fat; 15.3% from Carbohydrates; 20.3% from Protein.

YOGURT CHEESE SPREAD makes **1** servings. **Amount per serving:** 12 oz. **Calories:** 488 **Calories from Fat:** 200 / %=Daily Values based on a 2,000 calorie diet. Your daily values may differ. **Total Fat** 22.2g (34%), **Saturated Fat** 20g (100%), **Cholesterol** 120mg (40%), **Sodium** 1069mg (45%), **Total Carbohydrates** 40g (13%), **Dietary Fiber** 0g (0%), **Protein** 32g. Additional information: 41% of calories from Fat; 32.8% from Carbohydrates; 26.2% from Protein.

ROASTED GARLIC makes **1** servings. **Amount per serving:** ⅔ cup. **Calories:** 309 **Calories from Fat:** 166 / %=Daily Values based on a 2,000 calorie diet. Your daily values may differ. **Total Fat** 18.5g (28%), **Saturated Fat** 2.5g (12%), **Cholesterol** 0mg (0%), **Sodium** 15mg (1%), **Total Carbohydrates** 30g (10%), **Dietary Fiber** 1.9g (8%), **Protein** 5.8g. Additional information: 53.7% of calories from Fat; 38.8% from Carbohydrates; 7.5% from Protein.

SPINACH PESTO makes **1** servings. **Amount per serving:** 1 cup. **Calories:** 1305 **Calories from Fat:** 1126 / %=Daily Values based on a 2,000 calorie diet. Your daily values may differ. **Total Fat** 125.1g (192%), **Saturated Fat** 28.1g (141%), **Cholesterol** 40mg (13%), **Sodium** 982mg (41%), **Total Carbohydrates** 17.7g (6%), **Dietary Fiber** 7.4g (30%), **Protein** 27.1g. Additional information: 86.3% of calories from Fat; 5.4% from Carbohydrates; 8.3% from Protein.

SPELT RICOTTA GNOCCHI (DUMPLINGS) makes **8** servings. **Amount per serving: Calories:** 238 **Calories from Fat:** 73 / %=Daily Values based on a 2,000 calorie diet. Your daily values may differ. **Total Fat** 8.2g (13%), **Saturated Fat** 4.7g (23%), **Cholesterol** 78mg (26%), **Sodium** 473mg (20%), **Total Carbohydrates** 26.8g (9%), **Dietary Fiber** 2.5g (10%), **Protein** 14.4g. Additional information: 30.7% of calories from Fat; 45.1% from Carbohydrates; 24.2% from Protein.

COUNTRY OVEN FOCACCIA makes **32** servings. **Amount per serving: Calories:** 122 **Calories from Fat:** 46 / %=Daily Values based on a 2,000 calorie diet. Your daily values may differ. **Total Fat** 5.1g (8%), **Saturated Fat** 0.7g (3%), **Cholesterol** 0mg (0%), **Sodium** 74mg (3%), **Total Carbohydrates** 16.3g (5%), **Dietary Fiber** 1.4g (6%), **Protein** 2.8g. Additional information: 37.6% of calories from Fat; 53.3% from Carbohydrates; 9.2% from Protein.

COUNTRY OVEN CALZONES see **COUNTRY OVEN FOCACCIA** for dough nutrition. See **CLASSIC MEATBALLS** for filling nutrition. Other fillings vary.

COUNTRY OVEN PIZZA see **COUNTRY OVEN FOCACCIA** for dough nutrition. Toppings vary.

PIZZA D'ADAMO WHOLE GRAIN SPELT PIZZA DOUGH makes **16** servings. **Amount per serving: Calories:** 113 **Calories from Fat:** 16 / %=Daily Values based on a 2,000 calorie diet. Your daily values may differ. **Total Fat** 1.8g (3%), **Saturated Fat** 0.2g (1%), **Cholesterol** 0mg (0%), **Sodium** 147mg (6%), **Total Carbohydrates** 20.6g (7%), **Dietary Fiber** 3.5g (14%), **Protein** 3.6g. Additional information: 14.2% of calories from Fat; 73% from Carbohydrates; 12.8% from Protein.

FLOUR TORTILLAS (WHOLE GRAIN OR WHITE SPELT) makes **12** servings. **Amount per serving: Calories:** 105 **Calories from Fat:** 30 / %=Daily Values based on a 2,000 calorie diet. Your daily values may differ. **Total Fat** 3.4g (5%), **Saturated Fat** 0.5g (2%), **Cholesterol** 0mg (0%), **Sodium** 197mg (8%), **Total Carbohydrates** 15.8g (5%), **Dietary Fiber** 0.8g (3%), **Protein** 3g. Additional information: 28.5% of calories from Fat; 60.1% from Carbohydrates; 11.4% from Protein.

EMPANADAS FRITAS DE CHILE Y QUESO makes **6** servings. **Amount per serving: Calories:** 134 **Calories from Fat:** 38 / %=Daily Values based on a 2,000 calorie diet. Your daily values may differ. **Total Fat** 4.2g (6%), **Saturated Fat** 2.6g (13%), **Cholesterol** 15mg (5%), **Sodium** 248mg (10%), **Total Carbohydrates** 16.1g (5%), **Dietary Fiber** 0.6g (2%), **Protein** 7.9g. Additional information: 28.4% of calories from Fat; 48.1% from Carbohydrates; 23.6% from Protein.

EMPANADAS VALENCIANAS makes **10** servings. **Amount per serving: Calories:** 471 **Calories from Fat:** 295 / %=Daily Values based on a 2,000 calorie diet. Your daily values may differ. **Total Fat**

32.8g (50%), **Saturated Fat** 8.5g (42%), **Cholesterol** 71mg (24%), **Sodium** 401mg (17%), **Total Carbohydrates** 27.2g (9%), **Dietary Fiber** 2.4g (10%), **Protein** 16.8g. Additional information: 62.6% of calories from Fat; 23.1% from Carbohydrates; 14.3% from Protein.

ENCHILADA SAUCE SABROSA makes **1** serving. **Amount per serving:** 1¼ cups. **Calories:** 561 **Calories from Fat:** 365 / %=Daily Values based on a 2,000 calorie diet. Your daily values may differ. **Total Fat** 40.6g (62%), **Saturated Fat** 5.5g (28%), **Cholesterol** 0mg (0%), **Sodium** 615mg (26%), **Total Carbohydrates** 41.1g (14%), **Dietary Fiber** 8.7g (35%), **Protein** 8g. Additional information: 65% of calories from Fat; 29.3% from Carbohydrates; 5.7% from Protein.

EPIC/SONORAN STYLE ENCHILADAS makes **6** servings. **Amount per serving: Calories:** 412 **Calories from Fat:** 188 / %=Daily Values based on a 2,000 calorie diet. Your daily values may differ. **Total Fat** 20.9g (32%), **Saturated Fat** 5.4g (27%), **Cholesterol** 84mg (28%), **Sodium** 365mg (15%), **Total Carbohydrates** 23.6g (8%), **Dietary Fiber** 2.5g (10%), **Protein** 32.4g. Additional information: 45.6% of calories from Fat; 22.9% from Carbohydrates; 31.5% from Protein.

PITA BREAD makes **12** servings. **Amount per serving: Calories:** 153 **Calories from Fat:** 11 / %=Daily Values based on a 2,000 calorie diet. Your daily values may differ. **Total Fat** 1.2g (2%), **Saturated Fat** 0.2g (1%), **Cholesterol** 0mg (0%), **Sodium** 394mg (16%), **Total Carbohydrates** 30.3g (10%), **Dietary Fiber** 2.3g (9%), **Protein** 5.3g. Additional information: 7.2% of calories from Fat; 79% from Carbohydrates; 13.8% from Protein.

PITA WEDGES makes **24** servings. **Amount per serving: Calories:** 26 **Calories from Fat:** 2 / %=Daily Values based on a 2,000 calorie diet. Your daily values may differ. **Total Fat** 0.2g (0%), **Saturated Fat** 0g (0%), **Cholesterol** 0mg (0%), **Sodium** 66mg (3%), **Total Carbohydrates** 5g (2%), **Dietary Fiber** 0.4g (2%), **Protein** 0.9g. Additional information: 7.8% of calories from Fat; 78.1% from Carbohydrates; 14.1% from Protein.

DONER KEBAB (GYROS) makes **16** servings. **Amount per serving: Calories:** 103 **Calories from Fat:** 34 / %=Daily Values based on a 2,000 calorie diet. Your daily values may differ. **Total Fat** 3.8g (6%), **Saturated Fat** 1.4g (7%), **Cholesterol** 38mg (13%), **Sodium** 40mg (2%), **Total Carbohydrates** 5.2g (2%), **Dietary Fiber** 0.2g (1%), **Protein** 12.1g. Additional information: 32.9% of calories from Fat; 20.2% from Carbohydrates; 46.9% from Protein.

FALAFEL WITH TSATSIKI SAUCE makes **36** servings. **Amount per serving: Calories:** 34 **Calories from Fat:** 4 / %=Daily Values based on a 2,000 calorie diet. Your daily values may differ. **Total Fat** 0.5g (1%), **Saturated Fat** 0g (0%), **Cholesterol** 0mg (0%), **Sodium** 47mg (2%), **Total Carbohydrates** 6.4g (2%), **Dietary Fiber** 1g (4%), **Protein** 1.1g. Additional information: 11.8% of calories from Fat; 75.3% from Carbohydrates; 12.9% from Protein.

TSATSIKI SAUCE makes **20** servings. **Amount per serving: Calories:** 14 **Calories from Fat:** 5 / %=Daily Values based on a 2,000 calorie diet. Your daily values may differ. **Total Fat** 0.6g (1%), **Saturated Fat** 0.5g (2%), **Cholesterol** 3mg (1%), **Sodium** 41mg (2%), **Total Carbohydrates** 1.5g (0%), **Dietary Fiber** 0.1g (0%), **Protein** 0.8g. Additional information: 35.2% of calories from Fat; 42.3% from Carbohydrates; 22.5% from Protein.

YUSEF'S HUMMUS makes **1** servings. **Amount per serving:** 1¾ cup. **Calories:** 848 **Calories from Fat:** 313 / %=Daily Values based on a 2,000 calorie diet. Your daily values may differ. **Total Fat**

34.6g (53%), **Saturated Fat** 4.6g (23%), **Cholesterol** 0mg (0%), **Sodium** 1275mg (53%), **Total Carbohydrates** 106.6g (36%), **Dietary Fiber** 20.7g (83%), **Protein** 27.1g. Additional information: 36.9% of calories from Fat; 50.3% from Carbohydrates; 12.8% from Protein.

TOD MUN PLA (THAI FISH CAKES) makes **24** servings. **Amount per serving: Calories:** 50 **Calories from Fat:** 5 / %=Daily Values based on a 2,000 calorie diet. Your daily values may differ. **Total Fat** 0.5g (1%), **Saturated Fat** 0.1g (1%), **Cholesterol** 21mg (7%), **Sodium** 65mg (3%), **Total Carbohydrates** 5g (2%), **Dietary Fiber** 0.5g (2%), **Protein** 6.2g. Additional information: 10% of calories from Fat; 40.2% from Carbohydrates; 49.8% from Protein.

CHAR SIU BAO (CHINESE STEAMED BBQ BUNS) makes **20** servings. **Amount per serving: Calories:** 230 **Calories from Fat:** 36 / %=Daily Values based on a 2,000 calorie diet. Your daily values may differ. **Total Fat** 4g (6%), **Saturated Fat** 1g (5%), **Cholesterol** 22mg (7%), **Sodium** 725mg (30%), **Total Carbohydrates** 37.1g (12%), **Dietary Fiber** 1.8g (7%), **Protein** 11.5g. Additional information: 15.6% of calories from Fat; 64.4% from Carbohydrates; 20% from Protein.

EGGS FOO YOUNG WITH SPELT SPROUTS makes **12** servings. **Amount per serving: Calories:** 127 **Calories from Fat:** 51 / %=Daily Values based on a 2,000 calorie diet. Your daily values may differ. **Total Fat** 5.6g (9%), **Saturated Fat** 1.2g (5%), **Cholesterol** 142mg (47%), **Sodium** 330mg (14%), **Total Carbohydrates** 6.4g (2%), **Dietary Fiber** 1.5g (6%), **Protein** 12.6g. Additional information: 40.2% of calories from Fat; 20.2% from Carbohydrates; 39.7% from Protein.

FRIED RICE WITH SPELT SPROUTS makes **8** servings. **Amount per serving: Calories:** 150 **Calories from Fat:** 50 / %=Daily Values based on a 2,000 calorie diet. Your daily values may differ. **Total Fat** 5.5g (8%), **Saturated Fat** 0.6g (3%), **Cholesterol** 74mg (25%), **Sodium** 82mg (3%), **Total Carbohydrates** 17g (6%), **Dietary Fiber** 3.4g (14%), **Protein** 8g. Additional information: 33.3% of calories from Fat; 45.3% from Carbohydrates; 21.3% from Protein.

MAIN DISH (ENTRÉE)

MACAO PEPPER STEAK makes **4** servings. **Amount per serving: Calories:** 168 **Calories from Fat:** 99 / %=Daily Values based on a 2,000 calorie diet. Your daily values may differ. **Total Fat** 11.1g (17%), **Saturated Fat** 1.7g (9%), **Cholesterol** 4mg (1%), **Sodium** 1344mg (56%), **Total Carbohydrates** 12g (4%), **Dietary Fiber** 1.5g (6%), **Protein** 5.2g. Additional information: 59% of calories from Fat; 28.6% from Carbohydrates; 12.4% from Protein.

MEATLOAF WITH SELF-GRAVY makes **16** servings. **Amount per serving: Calories:** 208 **Calories from Fat:** 118 / %=Daily Values based on a 2,000 calorie diet. Your daily values may differ. **Total Fat** 13.1g (20%), **Saturated Fat** 5g (25%), **Cholesterol** 57mg (19%), **Sodium** 307mg (13%), **Total Carbohydrates** 8.2g (3%), **Dietary Fiber** 0.9g (4%), **Protein** 14.4g. Additional information: 56.6% of calories from Fat; 15.7% from Carbohydrates; 27.6% from Protein.

MOUSSAKA (BEEF/LAMB) makes **8** servings. **Amount per serving: Calories:** 618 **Calories from Fat:** 377 / %=Daily Values based on a 2,000 calorie diet. Your daily values may differ. **Total Fat** 41.8g (64%), **Saturated Fat** 17.4g (87%), **Cholesterol** 191mg (64%), **Sodium** 420mg (18%), **Total Carbohydrates** 23.9g (8%), **Dietary Fiber** 2.9g (12%), **Protein** 36.3g. Additional information: 61% of calories from Fat; 15.5% from Carbohydrates; 23.5% from Protein.

STUFFED PASILLA PEPPERS makes **4** servings. **Amount per serving: Calories:** 989 **Calories from Fat:** 385 / %=Daily Values based on a 2,000 calorie diet. Your daily values may differ. **Total Fat** 42.8g (66%), **Saturated Fat** 12.5g (62%), **Cholesterol** 105mg (35%), **Sodium** 511mg (21%), **Total Carbohydrates** 109.1g (36%), **Dietary Fiber** 23.3g (93%), **Protein** 42g. Additional information: 38.9% of calories from Fat; 44.1% from Carbohydrates; 17% from Protein.

LAMB TAGINE MAGHRIB makes **6** servings. **Amount per serving: Calories:** 355 **Calories from Fat:** 156 / %=Daily Values based on a 2,000 calorie diet. Your daily values may differ. **Total Fat** 17.3g (27%), **Saturated Fat** 5g (25%), **Cholesterol** 98mg (33%), **Sodium** 79mg (3%), **Total Carbohydrates** 18.7g (6%), **Dietary Fiber** 3.1g (12%), **Protein** 31g. Additional information: 44% of calories from Fat; 21.1% from Carbohydrates; 34.9% from Protein.

LEMON CHICKEN makes **4** servings. **Amount per serving: Calories:** 408 **Calories from Fat:** 207 / %=Daily Values based on a 2,000 calorie diet. Your daily values may differ. **Total Fat** 22.8g (35%), **Saturated Fat** 3.2g (16%), **Cholesterol** 171mg (57%), **Sodium** 405mg (17%), **Total Carbohydrates** 15.5g (5%), **Dietary Fiber** 2.6g (10%), **Protein** 34.8g. Additional information: 50.7% of calories from Fat; 15.2% from Carbohydrates; 34.1% from Protein.

ASIAN SUNRISE CHICKEN (OR RABBIT) makes **4** servings. **Amount per serving: Calories:** 383 **Calories from Fat:** 227 / %=Daily Values based on a 2,000 calorie diet. Your daily values may differ. **Total Fat** 25.1g (39%), **Saturated Fat** 2.7g (14%), **Cholesterol** 95mg (32%), **Sodium** 518mg (22%), **Total Carbohydrates** 14.4g (5%), **Dietary Fiber** 2.5g (10%), **Protein** 24.7g. Additional information: 59.2% of calories from Fat; 15% from Carbohydrates; 25.8% from Protein.

TURKEY OR CHICKEN TOSCANO makes **6** servings. **Amount per serving: Calories:** 662 **Calories from Fat:** 290 / %=Daily Values based on a 2,000 calorie diet. Your daily values may differ. **Total Fat** 32.3g (50%), **Saturated Fat** 5.2g (26%), **Cholesterol** 5mg (2%), **Sodium** 717mg (30%), **Total Carbohydrates** 50.4g (17%), **Dietary Fiber** 4.8g (19%), **Protein** 42.5g. Additional information: 43.8% of calories from Fat; 30.5% from Carbohydrates; 25.7% from Protein.

SKILLET VARIATION TURKEY OR CHICKEN TOSCANO makes **4** servings. **Amount per serving: Calories:** 699 **Calories from Fat:** 301 / %=Daily Values based on a 2,000 calorie diet. Your daily values may differ. **Total Fat** 33.4g (51%), **Saturated Fat** 7.6g (38%), **Cholesterol** 108mg (36%), **Sodium** 697mg (29%), **Total Carbohydrates** 45.6g (15%), **Dietary Fiber** 4.9g (20%), **Protein** 53.9g. Additional information: 43.1% of calories from Fat; 26.1% from Carbohydrates; 30.8% from Protein.

COATED PAN FRIED FISH FILLETS makes **4** servings. **Amount per serving: Calories:** 512 **Calories from Fat:** 156 / %=Daily Values based on a 2,000 calorie diet. Your daily values may differ. **Total Fat** 17.4g (27%), **Saturated Fat** 5.5g (28%), **Cholesterol** 118mg (39%), **Sodium** 746mg (31%), **Total Carbohydrates** 53.2g (18%), **Dietary Fiber** 5.8g (23%), **Protein** 35.7g. Additional information: 30.5% of calories from Fat; 41.6% from Carbohydrates; 27.9% from Protein.

OVEN BAKED FISH FILLETS WITH CRUNCHY LEMON HERB TOPPING makes **2** servings. **Amount per serving: Calories:** 724 **Calories from Fat:** 277 / %=Daily Values based on a 2,000 calorie diet. Your daily values may differ. **Total Fat** 30.9g (48%), **Saturated Fat** 30.9g (48%), **Cholesterol** 45mg (15%), **Sodium** 1686mg (70%), **Total Carbohydrates** 63.5g (21%), **Dietary Fiber** 8.7g (35%), **Protein** 48.2g. Additional information: 38.3% of calories from Fat; 35.1% from Carbohydrates; 26.6% from Protein.

COOKIE TRAY

LEMON BLOSSOM COOKIES makes **48** servings. **Amount per serving: Calories:** 60 **Calories from Fat:** 25 / %=Daily Values based on a 2,000 calorie diet. Your daily values may differ. **Total Fat** 2.8g (4%), **Saturated Fat** 1.4g (7%), **Cholesterol** 9mg (3%), **Sodium** 13mg (1%), **Total Carbohydrates** 7.7g (3%), **Dietary Fiber** 0.5g (2%), **Protein** 1.1g. Additional information: 41.5% of calories from Fat; 51.2% from Carbohydrates; 7.3% from Protein.

ALMOND COOKIES makes **36** servings. **Amount per serving: Calories:** 98 **Calories from Fat:** 43 / %=Daily Values based on a 2,000 calorie diet. Your daily values may differ. **Total Fat** 4.8g (7%), **Saturated Fat** 0.4g (2%), **Cholesterol** 12mg (4%), **Sodium** 56mg (2%), **Total Carbohydrates** 12.2g (4%), **Dietary Fiber** 0.5g (2%), **Protein** 1.6g. Additional information: 43.8% of calories from Fat; 49.7% from Carbohydrates; 6.5% from Protein.

GOOD DAY COOKIE makes **48** servings. **Amount per serving: Calories:** 134 **Calories from Fat:** 56 / %=Daily Values based on a 2,000 calorie diet. Your daily values may differ. **Total Fat** 6.3g (10%), **Saturated Fat** 0.8g (4%), **Cholesterol** 9mg (3%), **Sodium** 56mg (2%), **Total Carbohydrates** 17.2g (6%), **Dietary Fiber** 1g (4%), **Protein** 2.2g. Additional information: 41.9% of calories from Fat; 51.5% from Carbohydrates; 6.6% from Protein.

BACK TO BASICS VARIETY COOKIE makes **48** servings. **Amount per serving: Calories:** 95 **Calories from Fat:** 37 / %=Daily Values based on a 2,000 calorie diet. Your daily values may differ. **Total Fat** 4.2g (6%), **Saturated Fat** 0.3g (2%), **Cholesterol** 4mg (1%), **Sodium** 51mg (2%), **Total Carbohydrates** 12.5g (4%), **Dietary Fiber** 0.8g (3%), **Protein** 2g. Additional information: 38.9% of calories from Fat; 52.6% from Carbohydrates; 8.4% from Protein.

CACAO CASHEWS makes **36** servings. **Amount per serving: Calories:** 82 **Calories from Fat:** 33 / %=Daily Values based on a 2,000 calorie diet. Your daily values may differ. **Total Fat** 3.7g (6%), **Saturated Fat** 1.9g (9%), **Cholesterol** 13mg (4%), **Sodium** 30mg (1%), **Total Carbohydrates** 11.4g (4%), **Dietary Fiber** 0.5g (2%), **Protein** 0.9g. Additional information: 40.1% of calories from Fat; 55.5% from Carbohydrates; 4.4% from Protein.

CHOCOLATE DIPPED PEANUT BUTTER COOKIES makes **28** servings. **Amount per serving: Calories:** 149 **Calories from Fat:** 66 / %=Daily Values based on a 2,000 calorie diet. Your daily values may differ. **Total Fat** 7.2g (11%), **Saturated Fat** 1.8g (9%), **Cholesterol** 8mg (3%), **Sodium** 102mg (4%), **Total Carbohydrates** 17.6g (6%), **Dietary Fiber** 1g (4%), **Protein** 3.2g. Additional information: 44.2% of calories from Fat; 47.2% from Carbohydrates; 8.6% from Protein.

CHOCO SPICED DAINTIES makes **48** servings. **Amount per serving: Calories:** 101 **Calories from Fat:** 38 / %=Daily Values based on a 2,000 calorie diet. Your daily values may differ. **Total Fat** 4.1g (6%), **Saturated Fat** 0.9g (4%), **Cholesterol** 9mg (3%), **Sodium** 12mg (0%), **Total Carbohydrates** 13.9g (5%), **Dietary Fiber** 0.7g (3%), **Protein** 1.9g. Additional information: 37.5% of calories from Fat; 54.9% from Carbohydrates; 7.5% from Protein.

CHOCOLATE CHIP FLORENTINES makes **72** servings. **Amount per serving: Calories:** 93 **Calories from Fat:** 43 / %=Daily Values based on a 2,000 calorie diet. Your daily values may differ. **Total Fat** 4.8g (7%), **Saturated Fat** 2.4g (12%), **Cholesterol** 14mg (5%), **Sodium** 57mg (2%), **Total Carbohydrates** 11.2g (4%), **Dietary Fiber** 0.7g (3%), **Protein** 1.3g. Additional information: 46.2% of calories from Fat; 48.2% from Carbohydrates; 5.6% from Protein.

BLACK FOREST COOKIES makes **32** servings. **Amount per serving: Calories:** 139 **Calories from Fat:** 61 / %=Daily Values based on a 2,000 calorie diet. Your daily values may differ. **Total Fat** 6.7g (10%), **Saturated Fat** 2.7g (14%), **Cholesterol** 19mg (6%), **Sodium** 15mg (1%), **Total Carbohydrates** 18g (6%), **Dietary Fiber** 1.3g (5%), **Protein** 1.6g. Additional information: 43.8% of calories from Fat; 51.6% from Carbohydrates; 4.6% from Protein.

DATE LAYER BARS makes **32** servings. **Amount per serving: Calories:** 133 **Calories from Fat:** 27 / %=Daily Values based on a 2,000 calorie diet. Your daily values may differ. **Total Fat** 3.1g (5%), **Saturated Fat** 0.4g (2%), **Cholesterol** 0mg (0%), **Sodium** 97mg (4%), **Total Carbohydrates** 25g (8%), **Dietary Fiber** 2.2g (9%), **Protein** 1.4g. Additional information: 20.4% of calories from Fat; 75.4% from Carbohydrates; 4.2% from Protein.

CHOCOLATE TRANSGRESSION BROWNIES makes **18** servings. **Amount per serving: Calories:** 261 **Calories from Fat:** 100 / %=Daily Values based on a 2,000 calorie diet. Your daily values may differ. **Total Fat** 11.2g (17%), **Saturated Fat** 6.8g (34%), **Cholesterol** 53mg (18%), **Sodium** 124mg (5%), **Total Carbohydrates** 36.8g (12%), **Dietary Fiber** 1g (4%), **Protein** 3.5g. Additional information: 38.3% of calories from Fat; 56.4% from Carbohydrates; 5.4% from Protein.

CHOCOLATE FUDGE CRUNCH TOPPING makes **18** servings. **Amount per serving: Calories:** 211 **Calories from Fat:** 111 / %=Daily Values based on a 2,000 calorie diet. Your daily values may differ. **Total Fat** 12.3g (19%), **Saturated Fat** 6.5g (32%), **Cholesterol** 28mg (9%), **Sodium** 6mg (0%), **Total Carbohydrates** 23.5g (8%), **Dietary Fiber** 0.3g (1%), **Protein** 1.5g. Additional information: 52.6% of calories from Fat; 44.5% from Carbohydrates; 2.8% from Protein.

FLASH BROWNIES makes **18** servings. **Amount per serving: Calories:** 128 **Calories from Fat:** 51 / %=Daily Values based on a 2,000 calorie diet. Your daily values may differ. **Total Fat** 5.7g (9%), **Saturated Fat** 3.4g (17%), **Cholesterol** 38mg (13%), **Sodium** 23mg (1%), **Total Carbohydrates** 17.6g (6%), **Dietary Fiber** 0.9g (4%), **Protein** 1.7g. Additional information: 39.8% of calories from Fat; 54.9% from Carbohydrates; 5.3% from Protein.

GINGER CRISPS makes **36** servings. **Amount per serving: Calories:** 45 **Calories from Fat:** 13 / %=Daily Values based on a 2,000 calorie diet. Your daily values may differ. **Total Fat** 1.4g (2%), **Saturated Fat** 0.8g (4%), **Cholesterol** 9mg (3%), **Sodium** 30mg (1%), **Total Carbohydrates** 7.3g (2%), **Dietary Fiber** 0.4g (2%), **Protein** 0.6g. Additional information: 29.1% of calories from Fat; 65.5% from Carbohydrates; 5.4% from Protein.

GINGER SNAPS makes **60** servings. **Amount per serving: Calories:** 52 **Calories from Fat:** 18 / %=Daily Values based on a 2,000 calorie diet. Your daily values may differ. **Total Fat** 2g (3%), **Saturated Fat** 0.3g (2%), **Cholesterol** 7mg (2%), **Sodium** 66mg (3%), **Total Carbohydrates** 7.7g (3%), **Dietary Fiber** 0.5g (2%), **Protein** 0.7g. Additional information: 34.9% of calories from Fat; 59.7% from Carbohydrates; 5.4% from Protein.

GINGER DADDIES makes **24** servings. **Amount per serving: Calories:** 173 **Calories from Fat:** 56 / %=Daily Values based on a 2,000 calorie diet. Your daily values may differ. **Total Fat** 6.2g (10%), **Saturated Fat** 0.9g (4%), **Cholesterol** 9mg (3%), **Sodium** 73mg (3%), **Total Carbohydrates** 27.4g (9%), **Dietary Fiber** 0.6g (2%), **Protein** 1.8g. Additional information: 32.4% of calories from Fat; 63.4% from Carbohydrates; 4.2% from Protein.

GINGERFELLAS ICE CREAM SANDWICHES see the **GINGER DADDIES** and ice cream nutrition information.

BROWNIE ICE CREAM SANDWICH see the **FLASH BROWNIE** recipe and ice cream nutrition information.

PASTRIES, PIES AND OTHER SWEET DELIGHTS

PASTRY/PIE CRUST, SINGLE, MIXED SPELT FLOUR, 7"–8" makes **1** serving. **Amount per serving:** 1 crust. **Calories:** 787 **Calories from Fat:** 371 / %=Daily Values based on a 2,000 calorie diet. Your daily values may differ. **Total Fat** 41.2g (63%), **Saturated Fat** 2.9g (15%), **Cholesterol** 0mg (0%), **Sodium** 592mg (25%), **Total Carbohydrates** 88g (29%), **Dietary Fiber** 7g (28%), **Protein** 16g. Additional information: 47.1% of calories from Fat; 44.7% from Carbohydrates; 8.1% from Protein.

PASTRY/PIE CRUST, SINGLE, WHITE SPELT FLOUR, 7"–8" makes **1** serving. **Amount per serving:** 1 crust. **Calories:** 820 **Calories from Fat:** 370 / %=Daily Values based on a 2,000 calorie diet. Your daily values may differ. **Total Fat** 41.1g (63%), **Saturated Fat** 2.9g (15%), **Cholesterol** 0mg (0%), **Sodium** 4mg (0%), **Total Carbohydrates** 94.5g (32%), **Dietary Fiber** 4.5g (18%), **Protein** 18g. Additional information: 45.1% of calories from Fat; 46.1% from Carbohydrates; 8.8% from Protein.

PASTRY/PIE CRUST, SINGLE, MIXED SPELT FLOUR, 8"–9" makes **1** serving. **Amount per serving:** 1 crust. **Calories:** 887 **Calories from Fat:** 371 / %=Daily Values based on a 2,000 calorie diet. Your daily values may differ. **Total Fat** 41.2g (63%), **Saturated Fat** 2.9g (15%), **Cholesterol** 0mg (0%), **Sodium** 593mg (25%), **Total Carbohydrates** 109g (36%), **Dietary Fiber** 8g (32%), **Protein** 20g. Additional information: 41.8% of calories from Fat; 49.2% from Carbohydrates; 9% from Protein.

PASTRY/PIE CRUST, SINGLE WHITE SPELT FLOUR, 8"–9" makes **1** serving. **Amount per serving:** 1 crust. **Calories:** 871 **Calories from Fat:** 371 / %=Daily Values based on a 2,000 calorie diet. Your daily values may differ. **Total Fat** 41.2g (63%), **Saturated Fat** 2.9g (15%), **Cholesterol** 0mg (0%), **Sodium** 594mg (25%), **Total Carbohydrates** 105g (35%), **Dietary Fiber** 5g (20%), **Protein** 20g. Additional information: 42.6% of calories from Fat; 48.2% from Carbohydrates; 9% from Protein.

PASTRY/PIE CRUST, DOUBLE, MIXED SPELT FLOUR, 9"–10" makes **2** servings. **Amount per serving:** 2 crusts. **Calories:** 2498 **Calories from Fat:** 1234 / %=Daily Values based on a 2,000 calorie diet. Your daily values may differ. **Total Fat** 137.1g (211%), **Saturated Fat** 9.6g (48%), **Cholesterol** 0mg (0%), **Sodium** 1187mg (49%), **Total Carbohydrates** 268g (89%), **Dietary Fiber** 24g (96%), **Protein** 48g. Additional information: 49.4% of calories from Fat; 42.9% from Carbohydrates; 7.7% from Protein.

PASTRY/PIE CRUST, DOUBLE, WHITE SPELT FLOUR, 9"–10" makes **2** servings. **Amount per serving:** 2 crusts. **Calories:** 2351 **Calories from Fat:** 127.8 / %=Daily Values based on a 2,000 calorie diet. Your daily values may differ. **Total Fat** 127.8g (197%), **Saturated Fat** 9g (45%), **Cholesterol** 0mg (0%), **Sodium** 1191mg (50%), **Total Carbohydrates** 252g (84%), **Dietary Fiber** 12g (48%), **Protein** 48g. Additional information: 49% of calories from Fat; 42.9% from Carbohydrates; 8.2% from Protein.

AMERICAN APPLE PIE makes **10** servings. **Amount per serving: Calories:** 393 **Calories from Fat:** 148 / %=Daily Values based on a 2,000 calorie diet. Your daily values may differ. **Total Fat** 16.5g (25%), **Saturated Fat** 3g (15%), **Cholesterol** 9mg (3%), **Sodium** 246mg (10%), **Total Carbohydrates** 56.1g (19%), **Dietary Fiber** 2.5g (10%), **Protein** 5.1g. Additional information: 37.7% of calories from Fat; 57.1% from Carbohydrates; 5.2% from Protein.

PINYON PIE makes **8** servings. **Amount per serving: Calories:** 408 **Calories from Fat:** 193 / %=Daily Values based on a 2,000 calorie diet. Your daily values may differ. **Total Fat** 21.5g (33%), **Saturated Fat** 5.9g (30%), **Cholesterol** 96mg (32%), **Sodium** 114mg (5%), **Total Carbohydrates** 47.3g (16%), **Dietary Fiber** 2.5g (10%), **Protein** 6.5g. Additional information: 47.3% of calories from Fat; 46.3% from Carbohydrates; 6.4% from Protein.

CROSTATE DI FICHE (FIG TARTS) makes **60** servings. **Amount per serving: Calories:** 99 **Calories from Fat:** 23 / %=Daily Values based on a 2,000 calorie diet. Your daily values may differ. **Total Fat** 2.7g (4%), **Saturated Fat** 0.3g (2%), **Cholesterol** 0mg (0%), **Sodium** 22mg (1%), **Total Carbohydrates** 17g (6%), **Dietary Fiber** 1.1g (4%), **Protein** 2.1g. Additional information: 23.1% of calories from Fat; 68.4% from Carbohydrates; 8.5% from Protein.

CANNOLI SHELLS makes **24** servings. **Amount per serving: Calories:** 64 **Calories from Fat:** 13 / %=Daily Values based on a 2,000 calorie diet. Your daily values may differ. **Total Fat** 1.4g (2%), **Saturated Fat** 0.9g (4%), **Cholesterol** 5mg (2%), **Sodium** 12mg (0%), **Total Carbohydrates** 10.7g (4%), **Dietary Fiber** 0.5g (2%), **Protein** 2g. Additional information: 20.4% of calories from Fat; 67.1% from Carbohydrates; 12.5% from Protein.

CANNOLI CREAM FILLING makes **24** servings. **Amount per serving: Calories:** 135 **Calories from Fat:** 71 / %=Daily Values based on a 2,000 calorie diet. Your daily values may differ. **Total Fat** 8g (12%), **Saturated Fat** 0.9g (4%), **Cholesterol** 29mg (10%), **Sodium** 48mg (2%), **Total Carbohydrates** 9.5g (3%), **Dietary Fiber** 0.2g (1%), **Protein** 6.5g. Additional information: 52.6% of calories from Fat; 28.1% from Carbohydrates; 19.3% from Protein.

PINEAPPLE CHEESE PIE makes **8** servings. **Amount per serving: Calories:** 363 **Calories from Fat:** 153 / %=Daily Values based on a 2,000 calorie diet. Your daily values may differ. **Total Fat** 17.2g (26%), **Saturated Fat** 7.7g (38%), **Cholesterol** 86mg (29%), **Sodium** 329mg (14%), **Total Carbohydrates** 44.8g (15%), **Dietary Fiber** 2.3g (9%), **Protein** 7.7g. Additional information: 42.1% of calories from Fat; 49.4% from Carbohydrates; 8.5% from Protein.

OLD TIMES PUMPKIN / SWEET POTATO PIE makes **16** servings. **Amount per serving: Calories:** 213 **Calories from Fat:** 55 / %=Daily Values based on a 2,000 calorie diet. Your daily values may differ. **Total Fat** 6.2g (10%), **Saturated Fat** 0.7g (3%), **Cholesterol** 40mg (13%), **Sodium** 132mg (6%), **Total Carbohydrates** 35.5g (12%), **Dietary Fiber** 1.5g (6%), **Protein** 4g. Additional information: 25.8% of calories from Fat; 66.7% from Carbohydrates; 7.5% from Protein.

PINEAPPLE-BLUEBERRY UPSIDE DOWN CAKE makes **8** servings. **Amount per serving: Calories:** 399 **Calories from Fat:** 117 / %=Daily Values based on a 2,000 calorie diet. Your daily values may differ. **Total Fat** 13.1g (20%), **Saturated Fat** 6.1g (30%), **Cholesterol** 77mg (26%), **Sodium** 114mg (5%), **Total Carbohydrates** 65.2g (22%), **Dietary Fiber** 2.6g (10%), **Protein** 5.2g. Additional information: 29.4% of calories from Fat; 65.4% from Carbohydrates; 5.2% from Protein.

POUND CAKE makes **16** servings. **Amount per serving: Calories:** 185 **Calories from Fat:** 61 / %=Daily Values based on a 2,000 calorie diet. Your daily values may differ. **Total Fat** 6.7g (10%), **Saturated Fat** 4.1g (20%), **Cholesterol** 45mg (15%), **Sodium** 128mg (5%), **Total Carbohydrates** 26.8g (9%), **Dietary Fiber** 0.7g (3%), **Protein** 4.2g. Additional information: 33% of calories from Fat; 57.9% from Carbohydrates; 9.1% from Protein.

RASPBERRY VALENTINE CAKE makes **8** servings. **Amount per serving: Calories:** 341 **Calories from Fat:** 71 / %=Daily Values based on a 2,000 calorie diet. Your daily values may differ. **Total Fat** 7.8g (12%), **Saturated Fat** 1.1g (6%), **Cholesterol** 27mg (9%), **Sodium** 264mg (11%), **Total Carbohydrates** 62.6g (21%), **Dietary Fiber** 3.2g (13%), **Protein** 5g. Additional information: 20.8% of calories from Fat; 73.3% from Carbohydrates; 5.9% from Protein.

SWEET TOPPINGS

CRUMBLE (STREUSEL) TOPPING makes **1*** serving. **Amount per serving:** 1 cup. **Calories:** 842 **Calories from Fat:** 447 / %=Daily Values based on a 2,000 calorie diet. Your daily values may differ. **Total Fat** 49.6g (76%), **Saturated Fat** 16g (80%), **Cholesterol** 62mg (21%), **Sodium** 614mg (26%), **Total Carbohydrates** 83.1g (28%), **Dietary Fiber** 5.4g (22%), **Protein** 15.6g. Additional information: 53.1% of calories from Fat; 39.5% from Carbohydrates; 7.4% from Protein. *Recipe makes 2 cups. Nutrition information calculated on one cup Crumble Topping.

HONEY BUTTER-NUT CARAMEL TOPPING makes **1** serving. **Amount per serving:** ¾ cup. **Calories:** 1389 **Calories from Fat:** 732 / %=Daily Values based on a 2,000 calorie diet. Your daily values may differ. **Total Fat** 81.4g (125%), **Saturated Fat** 31g (155%), **Cholesterol** 124mg (41%), **Sodium** 36mg (2%), **Total Carbohydrates** 148.6g (50%), **Dietary Fiber** 3.1g (12%), **Protein** 15.7g. Additional information: 52.7% of calories from Fat; 42.8% from Carbohydrates; 4.5% from Protein.

CHOCOLATE FUDGE CRUNCH TOPPING see **CHOCOLATE TRANSGRESSION** under **COOKIE TRAY SECTION**.

BASIC CONFECTIONERS' SUGAR ICING makes **1** serving. **Amount per serving:** 1 cup. **Calories:** 510 **Calories from Fat:** 12 / %=Daily Values based on a 2,000 calorie diet. Your daily values may differ. **Total Fat** 1.3g (2%), **Saturated Fat** 0.7g (3%), **Cholesterol** 4mg (1%), **Sodium** 31mg (1%), **Total Carbohydrates** 122.6g (41%), **Dietary Fiber** 0g (0%), **Protein** 2g. Additional information: 2.4% of calories from Fat; 96.1% from Carbohydrates; 1.6% from Protein.

BATANGAS BANANAS makes **1** serving. **Amount per serving:** * **Calories:** 494 **Calories from Fat:** 217 / %=Daily Values based on a 2,000 calorie diet. Your daily values may differ. **Total Fat** 24.1g (37%), **Saturated Fat** 14.7g (73%), **Cholesterol** 62mg (21%), **Sodium** 10mg (0%), **Total Carbohydrates** 66.7g (22%), **Dietary Fiber** 5.4g (22%), **Protein** 2.5g. Additional information: 43.9% of calories from Fat; 54% from Carbohydrates; 2% from Protein. *Serving information is for two large bananas, which make 2–4 actual servings.

ANCIENT OFFERINGS

AULD LANG SYNE (REMEMBRANCE) BREAD makes **16** servings. **Amount per serving:** **Calories:** 130 **Calories from Fat:** 33 / %=Daily Values based on a 2,000 calorie diet. Your daily values may differ. **Total Fat** 3.7g (6%), **Saturated Fat** 0.9g (4%), **Cholesterol** 26mg (9%), **Sodium** 152mg (6%), **Total Carbohydrates** 20.1g (7%), **Dietary Fiber** 1.6g (6%), **Protein** 4.1g. Additional information: 25.4% of calories from Fat; 61.9% from Carbohydrates; 12.6% from Protein.

APPENDIX 2:

SHOPPING FOR SPELT—RESOURCES AND INFORMATION

Every day more Spelt products arrive on line and in gourmet, whole food/natural food stores and in the natural foods sections of major supermarkets. Here is a starter list of sources, selected from around the country, and internationally, to make Spelt shopping easier for you. Check www.spelthealthy.com for updates on resources.

STARTER LIST OF SOURCES OF PRODUCTS AND INFORMATION

purityfoods.com (517-351-9231, Okemos, Michigan)
Purity Foods is a major purveyor (wholesale) of organic, natural foods in the United States through its **Vita-Spelt** line of Spelt flours, pastas, granola, snack items like pretzels and sesame sticks and specialty freezer case items such as pizza, hot pockets and Spelt garlic breads. Products are Kosher. Web site contains much information including nutrition information for Spelt flour. Retail outlets/distributor links.

bobsredmill.com / Bob's Red Mill (800-349-2173, Milwaukie, Oregon)
Bob's Red Mill Natural Foods operates its own stone mill. Established internet presence; new Whole Grain Store and Visitors' Center just outside Oregon City, Oregon (800-553-2258) complete with baking classes. Bob's Red Mill sells a wide variety of Spelt products ground at their mill: Whole Grain Spelt, Light Spelt flours; rolled Spelt (Spelt flakes), Spelt berries. They offer baking aids such as non-aluminum baking powder and a variety of sugars: turbinado, maple, molasses crystals; active dry yeast.

shopnatural.com / Shop Natural (520-884-0745, Tucson, Arizona)
Established internet presence with storefront located at 350 South Toole Avenue, Tucson, Arizona. Large assortment of natural food products including plain canned pumpkin, Lundberg rice, organic baking cocoa and cacao powder, and Italian Chestnut Flour. Wide variety of Purity Foods (Vita-Spelt) products from Angel Hair pasta to White and Whole Grain flours, both small quantities and bulk. Spelt berries and kernels. Sprouted Spelt products include Cream of Sprouted Spelt Cereal and Sprouted Spelt flour. Click on Search for White Spelt flour.

kingarthurflour.com / King Arthur Flour Company (802-649-3881, Norwich, Vermont)
Historic flour company well known for providing fine flours to the trade and home gourmets. The Baker's Catalogue is now on-line for retail customers. This is a specialty baking site that sells Organic Whole Spelt and King Arthur Organic White Spelt Flour. Variety of ingredients and baking tools from the Nordic Ware Ebelskiver (Aebelskiver) pans to Scharffen Berger and Merckens chocolate.

speltlife.com / SpeltLife (517-663-4206, Eaton Rapids, Michigan)
Turbo Farms (SpeltLife) is a major Spelt producer. Midwestern internet source of White and Whole Grain Spelt flours and other Spelt products. Product line includes Spelt gourmet (handmade) pastas such as Lemon Pepper Flavored Fettucine.

amazon.com
Go to Gourmet Foods section and Search for Whole Grain or White Spelt flours and other Spelt products. Links with suppliers such as www.shopnatural.com and Barry Farms.

organickingdom.com / Organic Kingdom (866-436-1390, Orem, Utah)
Offers a wide variety of natural foods including Organic Whole Grain Spelt. Specialty products include Black and Pinto Bean flours. **Global shipping**.

sproutpeople.com / The Sprout People (877-777-6887, San Francisco, California)
Highly informative site, in fact, it is probably all you ever wanted to know about sprouts. The Sprout People stock a tremendous range of sprouting seeds including Spelt seeds (sprouts) and Spelt Grass Seed. They also carry hard to find seeds including Fenugreek and the Alliums for those of you who enjoy Ancient and Medieval Cooking.

indianharvest.com / Indian Harvest (800-294-2433, Bemidji, Minnesota)
Specialty foods for the home cook with emphasis on wild rice such as Giant Canadian Lake Wild Rice. Specialty grains/beans include Farro, Cranberry or Runner Cannellini Beans for Tuscan Farro Soup.

gourmetstore.com / The Gourmet Store (e-mail only, Gurnee, Illinois)
Internet store featuring gourmet and exotic specialty food items such as dried mushrooms, herbs, chilis, pine and other nuts. They sell Spelt Farro, White Spelt flour.

sourdo.com / Sourdoughs International (Ed Wood, Author) (208-382-4828, Cascade, Idaho)
Home of Tasmanian Devil Spelt Sourdough starter (White Spelt and unbleached bread flour). Ed Wood's book, *World Sourdoughs From Antiquity*, includes Spelt and description of ancient breadmaking from Egypt, the bread originally made from Emmer, one of Spelt's parents. Book available at bookstores or book sites but not at sourdo.com.

stillsitting.com / Still Sitting (206-463-1997 Vashon, Washington)
Only source in U.S. of Zafu meditation cushions stuffed with spelt hulls.

wholegrainscouncil.org (617-421-5500, Boston, MA)
Informational site of Whole Grains Council/Oldways Preservation Trust devoted to the Whole Grains (find a list there of Grains A-Z). Read more about the Whole Grain stamps now being used to identify products in the markets and how the products are graded. Nutritional information and links.

FRESH FROM FIELD TO YOU

lentzspelt.com / Lentz Spelt Farms (509-345-2483, Marlin, Washington)
These are the only private farms in the United States producing the Big 3 Ancient Grains: Spelt, Emmer and Einkorn. The Lentz folks offer an array of products you will not find on a regular basis elsewhere. Products you may order (by telephone) include Spelt berries, Organic Emmer-Farro Berries, Emmer-Farro flour, Spelt and Emmer Pancake mixes, Emmer and Spelt nuts, Rolled Spelt flakes and Bulk Spelt flour.

Their specialty products include large, good lathering Spelt Soaps in Sage and Lemongrass. Lentz sells health food products for animals: Cat Greens in a seed package; Spelt Dog Treats; Spelt Bird and Livestock Feed. This is a good way to put to the test the old German saying of give the chickens a mix of Spelt and other grains and see how they pick out the Spelt grains first.

OTHER SPECIALTY PRODUCTS FROM COMMUNITY GROWERS (Community Supported Agriculture and Cooperatives)

The shortest and freshest line from farm to you is often the community or farmer's markets around the country.

Ayers Creek Farm (503-985-0177, Gaston, Oregon)
See also "Grünkern" page in *The Vegetable Stand* section. Anthony Boutard makes Spelt Grünkern which is seasonally available. Check Ayers Creek Farm out at the Hillsdale Market in Portland or go to the website: hillsdalefarmersmarket.com.

esimplythebest.com (Seattle, Washington)
Five-farmer cooperative offering seasonal dried fruit products from Washington orchards including dried Gala apples, pears, Bing and Rainier dried cherries and now Spelt through their location at Seattle's Pike's Market. Look for the Rolled Spelt with Blueberries.

tpg-usa.com / Tart is Smart / TPG Enterprises (509-488-1049, Othello, Washington)
Tart is Smart is concentrated tart Cherry Juice fresh from the farms. Information on health benefits of tart cherries at site. Source of dried cherries, yogurt or chocolate-covered cherries and apples.

STORES AND MARKETS THAT CARRY SPELT PRODUCTS

Your local Natural Foods Stores stock and will generally special-order a variety of Spelt products for you.

Whole Foods Market, the world's largest retailer of organic/natural foods. Go to site for store nearest you via internet at wholefoodsmarket.com.

Wild Oats Natural Marketplace, sells natural and organic foods such as Spelt flour and other Spelt products. Go to website at wildoats.com for location near you.

Sprouts Farmers Market, an Arizona-based company currently in 3 states. Sprouts.com for locations.

Trader Joe's Specialty Grocery Store, home of exotic items, carries fresh Spelt breads in their bakery section (look for Pacific Bakery products). Go to traderjoes.com for locations.

Berlin Natural Bakery (speltbread.com, 800-686-5334, Berlin, Ohio)
All products are made from Spelt. Information on-site from sprouting to St. Hildegard and her teachings on Spelt. Call or click on search button at berlinnaturalbakery.com for store near you. They now ship product direct to consumer via UPS.

INTERNATIONAL

United Kingdom

dovesfarm-organic.co.uk / Dove's Farm Foods (UK 01488-684-880, supplier to British Isles) Spelt millers/Spelt products. Dove's Farm maintains a highly informative website about Spelt, including ancient to modern methods of milling and general information about the grain. Their foods are available at natural foods stores in UK including As Nature Intended, Fresh and Wild, and Planet Organic in the London area; Grassroots in Scotland.

Australia/New Zealand

Australia is a growing source of Spelt and exports flour to the United States. There is a well-established organic and whole food network with a presence on the web such as **Celtic Organic Wholefoods** (usenature.com/organic; Queensland, 07 5526 4844). They make Spelt sourdough breads and sell Spelt pies and rolls.

Bio-Oz (bio-oz.com.au, New South Wales, 61-2/6862 5954) grows Spelt, einkorn and emmer grains and sells Spelt flours. There is a growing number of artisan bakeries in Australia and New Zealand, just as in the United States that specialize in Spelt and other hulled grain and antique/heritage grain breads. For example, **Breadman** (breadman.co.nz, Christchurch, New Zealand, 03 365 0990) that uses overnight fermentation to make their Dinkel (Spelt) loaf.

Germany

abtei-st-hildegard de/English/monastic/spelt.htm is the website for the Abtei St. Hildegard, Benedictine Abbey inspired by Hildegard of Bingen now located at Rudesheim am Rhein, Germany. The sisters make Spelt products and liqueurs from Abbey-grown Spelt; available at the Abbey's shop.

See also Part II Speltoids: Chapter 3 under **Spelt and the Spirits** for information on Spelt Beers.

APPENDIX 3

BIBLIOGRAPHY

I INTRODUCTION

Abdel-Aal, Elsayed, *Specialty Grains for Food and Feed*, American Association of Cereal Chemists, 2005.

American Diabetes Association, "All About Diabetes," "Reading Food Labels," "Sweeteners and Desserts," and "What is a Healthy Diet?" at www.diabetes.org.

Bojnanska, T. and H. Francakova, "The Use of Spelt Wheat *(Triticum spelta L.)* for Baking Applications," in *Rostlinna Vyroba*, 48, 2002 (4):141–147.

Carmichael, Chris, *Food for Fitness: Eat Right to Train Right*, Berkley Books, 2004.

celiac.com, "Forbidden List—Foods and Ingredients Not Safe for a Gluten-Free Diet," at www.celiac.com.

Commonwealth Government/Grains Research and Development Corporation, "Nutrient Composition of Grains" at www.gograins.grdc.com.au/grains.

Cubadda, R. and E. Marconi, "Technological and Nutritional Aspects in Emmer and Spelt," pp. 203–211 in *Hulled Wheat: Proceedings of the First International Workshop on Hulled Wheats,* International Plant Genetic Resources Institute, 1996.

D'Adamo, Peter J. with C. Whitney, *Cook Right For Your Type: The Practical Kitchen Companion to Eat Right For Your Type*, G. P. Putnam's Sons, 1998.

D'Adamo, Peter J. with C. Whitney, *Eat Right For Your Type: Complete Blood Type Encyclopedia*, Riverhead Books, 2002.

D'Adamo, Peter J. with C. Whitney, *Eat Right For Your Type: The Individualized Diet Solution to Staying Healthy, Living Longer & Achieving Your Ideal Weight,* G. P. Putnam's Sons, 1996.

Food Allergy and Anaphylaxis Network, "Common Food Allergens" at www.foodallergy.org.

Harvard School of Public Health, "Carbohydrates: Going with the Whole Grain," "Fiber: Start Roughing It," and "Food Pyramids: What Should You Really Eat?" at www.hsph.harvard.edu/nutrition source.

health-heart.org, "Adult Diabetes, Nutrition and Heart Disease" at www.health-heart.org.

Lemonick, Michael D., "How We Grew So Big: Diet and Lack of Exercise Are Immediate Causes—But Our Problem Began in the Paleolithic Era," *Time,* June 7, 2004.

National Institute of Allergy and Infectious Diseases/NIH, "Report of the Expert Panel of Food Allergy Research," June 30 and July 1, 2003 at www.niaid.nih.gov/dait/pdf.

National Institute of Allergy and Infectious Diseases, *Food Allergy: An Overview,* NIH Publication No. 04–5518, July 2004 at www.niaid.nih.gov.

National Institute of Health, Food Allergy Research Consortium and Statistical Center, 24 August 2004, Department of Health and Human Services/NIH at grants2.nih.gov/grants/guide.

National Institute of Health, Risk Assessment: Third National Health and Nutrition Examination Survey and 2006 at www.nih.gov.

NutriBase, *Complete Book of Food Counts,* Avery Press, 2001.

Parker-Pope, Tara, "The Secrets of Successful Aging: What Science Tells Us About Growing Older— And Staying Healthy," Personal Health Section (R1) in *Wall Street Journal,* June 20, 2005.

Skrabanja, V. *et al,* "Effect of Spelt Wheat Flour and Kernel on Bread Composition and Nutritional Characteristics," pp. 497–500 in *Journal of Agricultural Food Chemistry,* 49(1), Jan 2001, and at www.nebi.nlm.nih.gov/entrez(PubMed).

Stallknecht, G. F. *et al.* "Alternative Wheat Cereals as Food Grains: Einkorn, Emmer, Spelt, Kamut and Triticale," pp. 156–170 in J. Janick (ed.), *Progress in New Crops,* ASHS Press, Alexandria, VA, 1996 and at www.hort.purdue.edu/newcrop/proceedings.

U.S. National Library of Medicine/NIH, "Food Allergy" at www.nlm.nih.gov/medlineplus.

USDA Nutrient Data Laboratory and USDA Food and Nutrition Information Center at www.usda.gov.

USDA 2005 Dietary Guidelines for Americans at www.mypramid.gov.

Westcott, Scott, "Keep Moving," *Delicious Living,* March, 2005.

Whole Grains Council/Oldways Preservation Trust, "Definition of Whole Grain," "What Are the Benefits of Whole Grains?," "Whole Grains and Health," and "Whole Grains A-Z," at www.wholegrainscouncil.org.

II SPELTOIDS: FACTS AND OTHER CURIOUS THINGS ABOUT SPELT AND HER CLOSEST RELATIVES

Alighieri, D., *The Divine Comedy,* Carlyle-Okey-Wicksteed translation, Vintage Books, New York, 1950.

Bober, P., *Art Culture & Cuisine: Ancient and Medieval Gastronomy,* University of Chicago Press, 1999.

Boland, M., "Spelt Industry Profile," in *AgMRC* (Agricultural Marketing Resource Center), Department of Agricultural Economics, Kansas State University, August 2003, and at www.purityfoods.com.

Cereal Breeding Research, Darzau (Germany), *Einkorn: Cosmic Light From Oldest Grain Einkorn,* 2004, darzau.de/en/projects/einkorn and www.einkorn.org.

Florio, I., *Queen Anna's New World of Words or Dictionarie of the Italian and English Tongue,* London, 1611 at www.pbm.com.

Gill, B. S. and B. Friebe, *Cytogenetics, Phylogeny and Evolution of Cultivated Wheats.* FAO.org Repository/DOCREP, nd.

Jaradat, A. *et al.,* "*Ex situ* Conservation of Hulled Wheats," pp. 120–127 in *Hulled Wheat: Proceedings of the First International Workshop on Hulled Wheats,* International Plant Genetic Resources Institute, 1996.

Kuster, H., "Northern Europe-Germany and Surrounding Regions," in *The Cambridge World History of Food,* (eds.) K. Kiple and K. Ornelas at www.us.cambridge.org/books nd.

Miller, J. *et al.,* "Unusual Food Plants from Oakbank Crannog, Loch Tay, Scottish Highlands: Cloudberry, Opium Poppy and Spelt Wheat," *Antiquity* 72(278), Dec 1998 and at www.purityfoods.com.

Mitrofanova, O. *et al.*, "Diversity in Vir Spelt Wheat Collection." N.I. Vavilov Institute of Plant Industry, St. Petersburg, Russia, nd.

Nesbitt, M. and D. Samuel, "From Staple Crop to Extinction? The Archaeology and History of the Hulled Wheats," pp. 40–99 in *Hulled Wheat: Proceedings of the First International Workshop on Hulled Wheats,* International Plant Genetic Resources Institute, 1996.

Oliveira, J., "North Spanish Emmer and Spelt Wheat Landraces: Agronomical and Grain Quality Characteristics Evaluation," pp. 16–20 in *PGR Newsletter* of FAO-IPGRI, No. 125 and at ipgri.cgiar.org.

Papa, C. "The Farre de Montelione," pp. 156–168 in *Hulled Wheat: Proceedings of the First International Workshop on Hulled Wheats,* International Plant Genetic Resources Institute, 1996.

Peña-Chocarro, L., "*In situ* Conservation of Hulled Wheat Species: The Case of Spain," pp. 128–146 in *Hulled Wheat: Proceedings of the First International Workshop on Hulled Wheats,* International Plant Genetic Resources Institute, 1996.

Perrino, P. *et al.*, "Ecogeographical Distribution of Hulled Wheat Species," pp. 100–118 in *Hulled Wheat: Proceedings of the First International Workshop on Hulled Wheats,* International Plant Genetic Resources Institute, 1996.

Pliny the Elder, *The Natural History*, (eds.) J. Bostock and F. Riley, London, 1855 at www.perseus.tufts.edu.

Seagan, F. *The Philosopher's Kitchen: Recipes from Ancient Greece and Rome for the Modern Cook,* Random House, 2004.

Spufford, Peter, *Power and Profit: The Merchant in Medieval Europe,* Thames & Hudson, 2002.

Stallknecht, G. F. *op cit.*

Szabo, A. and K. Hammer, "Notes on the Taxonomy of Farro: *Triticum monococcum, T. dicoccon* and *T. spelta*," pp. 2–39 in *Hulled Wheat: Proceedings of the First International Workshop on Hulled Wheats,* International Plant Genetic Resources Institute, 1996.

Tannahill, R., *Food in History*, Three Rivers Press, 1988.

USDA, United States Standards for Wheat, Subpart M: Terms Defined/Section 810.2201, Effective May 1993.

Vallega, V., "The Quality of *Triticum monococcum L.* in Perspective," pp. 212–220 in *Hulled Wheat: Proceedings of the First International Workshop on Hulled Wheats,* International Plant Genetic Resources Institute, 1996.

Victoria County, "A History of the County of Shropshire, Volume 4: Agriculture," 1989 at www.british-history.ac.uk/report.

Autumn Rose Press
Payson, Arizona

Look for upcoming volumes in the
Autumn Rose Press
Spelt Healthy! series

Spelt Healthy II! Many Small Things:
The Appetizing Word of Spelt©

Spelt Healthy III! Knead to Know:
Around the World of Spelt Baking©

www.spelthealthy.com

Autumn Rose Press, 2123 S. Priest Drive, Suite 215, Tempe, AZ 85282

About the Author
Marsha Cosentino, M.A.

Ms. Cosentino is a graduate of Arizona State University and the
University of Arizona. She has a wide range of experience as it applies to
food and culture. From excavating the ruins of ancient hearths to
working in the Scottsdale Resort industry, her knowledge of food and
culture is from the ground up. Field archaeologist, historian, geographer
and business executive, she was also a recipient of a Sustainable
Agriculture Grant and continues her vital interest in the preservation
and rescue of heirloom plants—Spelt is one—and rare breeds of
domestic livestock. As a scientist, she has observed first hand the effects
of nutrition on culture.

Cooking is not just science. It is alchemy and art, experimentation and
whimsy. Ms. Cosentino's passion for cooking began 45 years ago when
she was nose-high to a countertop. Her parents, wonderful whole food
cooks from two distinct traditions including Mediterranean, encouraged
art, experimentation and the coming together of people to share good
food and life. The illustrations in the book are her tribute to the lively
illuminated manuscript art form and artifacts that celebrated food and
life in centuries past and the recipes are a way of bringing Old World
and New World cooking traditions to new life using ancient Spelt.

With this book, she joins those on the leading edge of the
Whole Food nutrition and culinary Renaissance. This volume
is the first of four whole food cookbooks by Ms. Cosentino
in the Autumn Rose Press *Spelt Healthy!* series.

INDEX

QUALITY WHOLE FOOD COOKING AND BAKING WITH SPELT

SPELT HEALTHY!

MORE THAN 200 DELICIOUS & EASY TO FOLLOW RECIPES

BLOOD TYPE DIET NOTATIONS (A, B, AB, O)

Marsha Cosentino, M.A.

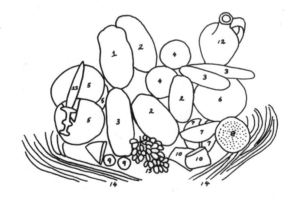

1. Pao Doce
2. Medi Crostini
3. All Purpose Italian Biga/Breads
4. Dark Rye
5. Roman Bread Rounds
6. Brundisi Pesto Bread
7. Empanadas Valencianas
8. Whole Grain Spelt Berries
9. Garlic
10. Aged Cheese
11. Roman Pugio (soldier's knife)
12. Greek Amphora (oil, wine, water)
13. Grapes
14. Spelt Spikes/Sheaves

Spelt Healthy! is a Forest Friendly book printed on 50% recycled paper.